Y0-AFU-585

The Economics of Trade Unions

The Economics of Trade Unions: New Directions

edited by

Jean-Jacques Rosa

Kluwer · Nijhoff Publishing
a member of the Kluwer Academic Publishers Group
Boston-The Hague-Dordrecht-Lancaster

Distributors for North America:
Kluwer Boston, Inc.
190 Old Derby Street
Hingham, MA 02043, U.S.A.

Distributors Outside North America:
Kluwer Academic Publishers Group
Distribution Centre
P.O. Box 322
3300AH Dordrecht, The Netherlands

Library of Congress Cataloging in Publication Data
Main entry under title:

The Economics of trade unions.

(Boston studies in applied economics. Series on labor and employment)
1. Trade-unions—Economic aspects—Addresses, essays, lectures. I. Rosa, Jean-Jacques. II. Title.
III. Series.
HD6483.E26 1983 331.88 83-6168
ISBN 0-89838-147-9

Printed in the United States of America

Contents

List of Tables

List of Figures

PREFACE

The crisis in trade unionism is now a prevailing concern in the United States, as well as in Europe. Its main symptom is, of course, the decrease in union membership. Still, other, less observable elements account for the concern, namely the obsolescence of discourse, the decrease of militant motivation, and the question of efficiency of strikes or collective bargaining. One must keep in mind, however, that trade unions will evolve differently from one country to another.

What we know about trade unions has changed over the years. We can now more accurately assess the effects of union action, especially with regard to labor market, wages, and productivity. This book adds to the assessment by integrating the new theories of organizations, contracts, and property rights. In doing so, we shift from a study of markets to one of hierarchies. Thus, the current literature comes back to its sources (but with improved analytical instruments) by returning to the Ross-Dunlop debate on the *nature* of the trade union. This more complex outlook of trade unions as an organization—not only as an abstract or bodyless supplier of monopolistic labor—allows one to understand better the apparent differences between unions (mainly American) whose action is oriented towards work relationships and labor contract management and unions (European or "Latin") who are closer to a pressure group wielding power on the political front.

This book is based on conferences held by the *Fondation Nationale d'Economie Politique* in Paris. The first part assembles empirical chapters dealing with the effects of unions on the labor market and the wage-strike-productivity nexus. The second part is more theoretical and, sometimes, even more speculative in character. It gathers several attempts at analysis of trade unions as organizations. Finally, the third part presents the prospects for research that stemmed from the conference work.

The ambition of this book, as well as the object of the conference at which it originated, was to investigate the present trends taken by the research into the economics of trade unions. Should the satisfaction of the readers equal the stimulation felt by the conference participants, our goals will have been surpassed.

I UNIONS, WAGES, STRIKES, AND PRODUCTIVITY

1 CHANGES OVER TIME IN THE UNION-NONUNION WAGE DIFFERENTIAL IN THE UNITED STATES

George E. Johnson

The increased interest among labor economists during the 1970s in trade unionism has yielded several estimates of the union-nonunion wage differential. This differential is defined as the percentage wage advantage of a worker represented by a union over a worker with comparable skills and nonpecuniary job attributes but not represented by a union. This question is an interesting and important one in the United States because, unlike most European countries, about a quarter of all workers and about half of production workers are represented by unions. Thus, a large union relative wage effect may cause significant distortions in both labor and product markets, especially if there is queue unemployment caused by the existence of the differential.[1]

My initial intention in writing this chapter was to explore some of the macroeconomic implications of the existence of unionism. For example, to what extent is unionism responsible for the rise of the natural rate of unemployment in the United States from 5.0 to 5.5 percent in 1970 to 6.0 to 7.0 percent (or higher) in 1980? Did unionism contribute to the decline in productivity (to virtually zero) experienced in the past seven years? Is unionism a partial explanation of the existence of business cycles?

Table 1-1. Percentage of Production Workers Organized and Percentage Wage Change, 1972-1979, for Selected Industries

Industry	*Percent Unionized*	*Percent wage change**
Basic steel	98	150
Major vehicles	98	115
Cigarettes	95	124
Railroads	99	130
Knitting mills	26	83
Clothing stores	11	75
Banks	8	62
Laundries	29	89

*1970–1979

Much of the substance of these questions rests on what happens to the union-nonunion wage differential over time. For example, unionism can cause an increase in the natural rate through its impact on queue unemployment only if the union-nonunion wage differential increases. An initial glance at the data for the 1970s, such as provided by table 1–1, suggests that there might have been a huge increase in the differential during this period.[2] For example, the ratio of wages of persons producing cigarettes, with 95 percent of production workers covered by collective bargaining agreements, to wages of production workers in banking, with unionization of only 8 percent, increased to (2.24/1.62) = 1.38 of its 1970 value. In other terms, the average per annum growth of wages of cigarette workers exceeded that of banking workers by 3.9 percent during the 1970s.

A necessary step to understanding the macroeconomic implications of unionism is an explanation of the large divergences in the movement of union and nonunion wages over time. On a more fundamental level are the questions of how general was the phenomenon observed in table 1–1 and whether it represents a change in the true (i.e., quality adjusted) differential. The purpose of this chapter is therefore addressed to the issue of the determinants of changes in the union-nonunion wage differential over time.

The recent work on the relative wage effects of unionism is, of course, inspired by the earlier work of H. G. Lewis (1963). Lewis's most important point, however, is that the union-nonunion wage differential has varied considerably over time. As seen in table 1–2 (taken from Lewis's tables 72 and 64), Lewis's estimated differential increased a great deal during the early part of the Great Depression and decreased almost to zero through World War II and the immediate postwar years. It then increased steadily through

Table 1-2. H. G. Lewis Estimates of the Union-Nonunion Differential, 1920-1958, and a Crude Extension to Later Periods

Period	*Estimated Differential**
1920–1924	.16
1925–1929	.23
1930–1934	.38
1935–1939	.20
1940–1944	.06
1945–1949	.02
1950–1954	.11
1955–1958	.15
1960–1964	.22
1965–1969	.17
1970–1974	.17
1975–1979	.26

*Logarithmic

the 1950s. In section two of this chapter, I present estimates of what has happened to the differential since the end of Lewis's period of estimation. These estimates, which are shown in table 1–2, assume that Lewis's .15 estimate for the 1955–1958 period is correct and extends what has happened to union versus nonunion wages since that time. Note that the method by which the extensions are made is both different from Lewis's and very crude. Indeed, most of the remainder of this paper is concerned with an investigation of the validity of this extension.

An Aggregate Union Relative Wage Effect Index

To explain the determinants of the union-nonunion wage differential over time, it is first necessary to construct an index of this differential over time. If workers represented by trade unions receive 100 $\lambda(t)$ percent more than nonunion workers with comparable skills in year t, then

$$\lambda(t) = \frac{W_u(t) - W_n(t)}{W_n(t)}, \qquad (1.1)$$

where $W_u(t)$ and $W_n(t)$ are, respectively, the union and nonunion wage rates in that year. One procedure of estimating λ over a long period of time notes that the average wage in industry i is a geometric weighted average of the union and nonunion wage rates, i.e.,

$$\log W_i(t) = U_i(t) \log W_u(t) + (1 - U_i(t)) \log W_n(t)$$
$$= \alpha(t) + \beta(t) U_i(t), \tag{1.2}$$

where $U_i(t)$ is the proportion of workers in the industry who are represented by trade unions. The slope coefficient in (1.2) is the logarithm of the union-nonunion relative wage, $\log (W_u(t)/W_n(t))$. Thus, the proportionate impact of unionism on relative wages is

$$\lambda(t) = \exp(\alpha(t)) - 1, \tag{1.3}$$

where $\alpha(t)$ is interpreted as the logarithm of the nonunion wage.

As an example of this procedure, I regressed the logarithm of the average hourly earnings of production workers in 20 two-digit manufacturing industries on the Douty estimates of the extent of collective bargaining in 1958 for each year from 1958 to 1970. The regressions were weighted by production worker employment by industry in 1960. The estimated coefficient in each year less its value in 1964 (times 100) is reported as $D1$ in table 1–3. For example, the value of $D1$ in 1968 is -10.5, which means that union wages in 1968 relative to nonunion wages were $\exp(-.105) = .900$ of their value in 1964. In other words, $\lambda(68)$ was, according to the $D1$ estimates, ten percentage points less than $\lambda(64)$; union wages increased by 2.6 percent less per year than did nonunion wages between 1964 and 1968.

The two other sets of estimated differentials in table 1–3 are based on similar regressions for 27 industries, the 20 two-digit manufacturing plus the seven private nonagricultural one-digit industries (mining, construction, transportation, and services). The unionism estimates are those by Freeman and Medoff (1979) from 1968–1972 EEC surveys. The regressions were weighted by the square root of industry production worker employment in 1970. The $D2$ estimates include all 27 industries, and the $D3$ estimates exclude the construction industry, which behaved quite differently from other industries during both the 1960s and 1970s.

There are several potential difficulties with this procedure. First, because U_i is observed in only one year for each of the indices, it is likely that the true values of $U_i(t)$ depart from the values used in the regressions as t gets further away from the year to which the unionization estimates refer. This implies that, assuming the deviations of $U_i(t)$ from estimated unionization rates in the base years are uncorrelated with $U_i(t)$, the estimates of $\beta(t)$ may have a

Table 1-3. Estimated Union-Nonunion Wage Differentials over Time, 1955-1979*

Year	D*1*	D2	D*3*
1955	−14.2		
1956	−14.3		
1957	−10.5		
1958	− 3.1		
1959	− 1.0		
1960	− 0.6		
1961	1.1		
1962	1.8		
1963	3.0		
1964	0	0	0
1965	− 1.3	−1.5	− 1.6
1966	− 2.9	−4.5	− 4.9
1967	− 8.4	−6.7	− 7.3
1968	−10.5	−7.1	− 8.0
1969	−10.4	−8.1	− 9.4
1970	−12.1	−9.6	−11.7
1971		−7.2	− 8.9
1972		−3.7	− 5.8
1973		−2.9	− 4.7
1974		−3.3	− 4.7
1975		−1.4	− 2.5
1976		1.2	0.6
1977		3.7	3.6
1978		4.1	4.3
1979		4.7	5.1

*1964 = 0

negative bias. If this were a serious problem, one would expect that the change from 1964 to 1970 in $D1$, based on the Douty unionism estimates for 1958, would be much more negative than the change in $D3$, based on the Freeman-Medoff (1979) unionism estimates for 1968–1972 (exclusive of construction). The fall in $D1$ during this period, however, was .121 compared to .117 for $D2$. Moreover, the large increases in $D2$ and $D3$ during the 1970s are larger only to the extent that the distribution of unionism changed during this period.

A second difficulty with the indices concerns the possibility that relative average quality of workers across the industries may change during the time span of estimation. The nonunion wage rate in industry i may be written as

$$\log W_{ni}(t) = \gamma(t) + \mu X_{ni}(t), \qquad (1.4)$$

where $X_{ni}(t)$ is a composite variable denoting the components of labor quality (education, experience, etc.) and the nonpecuniary job characteristics for nonunion workers. Since the union wage rate in industry i is $1 + \lambda(t)$ times what it would be if workers were not represented by a union, the average wage in the industry is

$$\begin{aligned} \log W_i(t) &= U_i(t) \log W_{ui}(t) + (1 - U_i(t)) \log W_{ni}(t) \\ &= \gamma(t) + (1 + \lambda(t))\, U_i(t) + \mu X_i(t), \qquad (1.5) \end{aligned}$$

where $X_i(t) = U_i(t)\, X_{ui}(t) + (1 - U_i(t))\, X_{in}(t)$ is the average value of the composite variable for the ith industry.

However, the indices are necessarily biased in (1.2) in which $X_i(t)$ is obviously omitted. This implies that, ignoring the problem of errors in the measurement of U_i, the estimated value of $\beta(t)$ in (1.2) is biased by $\mu b_{xu}(t)$, where $b_{xu}(t)$ is the slope coefficent in a regression of $X_i(t)$ on $U_i(t)$.

There is no question about the sign of $b_{xu}(t)$ in the United States; the average union production would earn a higher wage in the nonunion sector than does the average present nonunion worker.[3] What is relevant for the present purposes, however, is the question of the *stability* of $b_{xu}(t)$ over time. The indices are normalized to equal zero in an arbitrary year, so the bias in the value of the index in year t compared to year t-0 is

$$\mu[b_{xu}(t) - b_{xu}(t - 0)].$$

This means that the indices are subject to a systematic bias due to omitted variables only if there is a cyclical and/or secular pattern to the relationship between $X_i(t)$ and $U_i(t)$.

Of particular concern is the possibility that $b_{xu}(t)$ may depend systematically on the union-nonunion differential: $\lambda(t)$. For example, a strong intuitive case could be made for the proposition that during the 1970s, as the differential was increasing by fifteen percentage points, unionized firms raised their hiring standards relative to those of nonunion firms. Conversely, when the observed differential between union and nonunion wages was falling during the 1960s, the average quality of persons applying for nonunion jobs was presumably increasing relative to that of those persons applying for union jobs. This story implies that the magnitude of the two increases and the single increase in $\lambda(t)$ reported in table 1–1 may overstate the magnitude of the movement in the true differential.

On the other hand, it is not necessarily so that union firms will increase their hiring standards in response to an increase in the wage they must pay relative to nonunion firms. Suppose that the wage a firm must pay nonunion workers of a given quality level X is given by the labor supply condition $W_n = h(X)$, where $h > 0$. The flow of labor services is an efficiency parameter q times total persons hours H. The efficiency parameter presumably depends positively on X, say $q = q(X)$. Thus the cost of an efficiency unit of labor to a nonunion firm is given by

$$C_n = \frac{h(X)}{q(X)} . \tag{1.6}$$

This is minimized when $d(\log q)/dX = d(\log h)/dX$, i.e., when X is set such that the proportionate increase in labor efficiency with respect to X equals the proportionate increase in the wage with respect to X. This is represented in Figure 1-1 by the values X_n and W_n.

Now if this firm were organized and were forced to pay a wage of W_u rather than what it would choose to pay, or W_n, the previous argument is that the firm will attempt to minimize its losses by increasing its hiring standard to X_u. Over time, of course, the union-nonunion wage differential adjusted for quality and other differences would completely erode. If, on the other hand, the union responded by demanding a wage increase such that its members' wages were $1 + \lambda$ times what they would be in the nonunion sector, the firm would not increase X above X_n. In this case C_u is simply $1 + \lambda$ times C_n, and C_u and C_n are obviously minimized at the same value of X.

There is, however, evidence that the union-nonunion wage differential declines as X increases.[4] This means that the wage the unionized firm must pay is

$$W_u = (1 + \lambda(X))\frac{h(X)}{q(X)} , \tag{1.7}$$

which is minimized when

$$\frac{d(\log q)}{dX} = \frac{d(\log h)}{dX} + \frac{1}{1 + \lambda}\,\frac{d}{dX} . \tag{1.8}$$

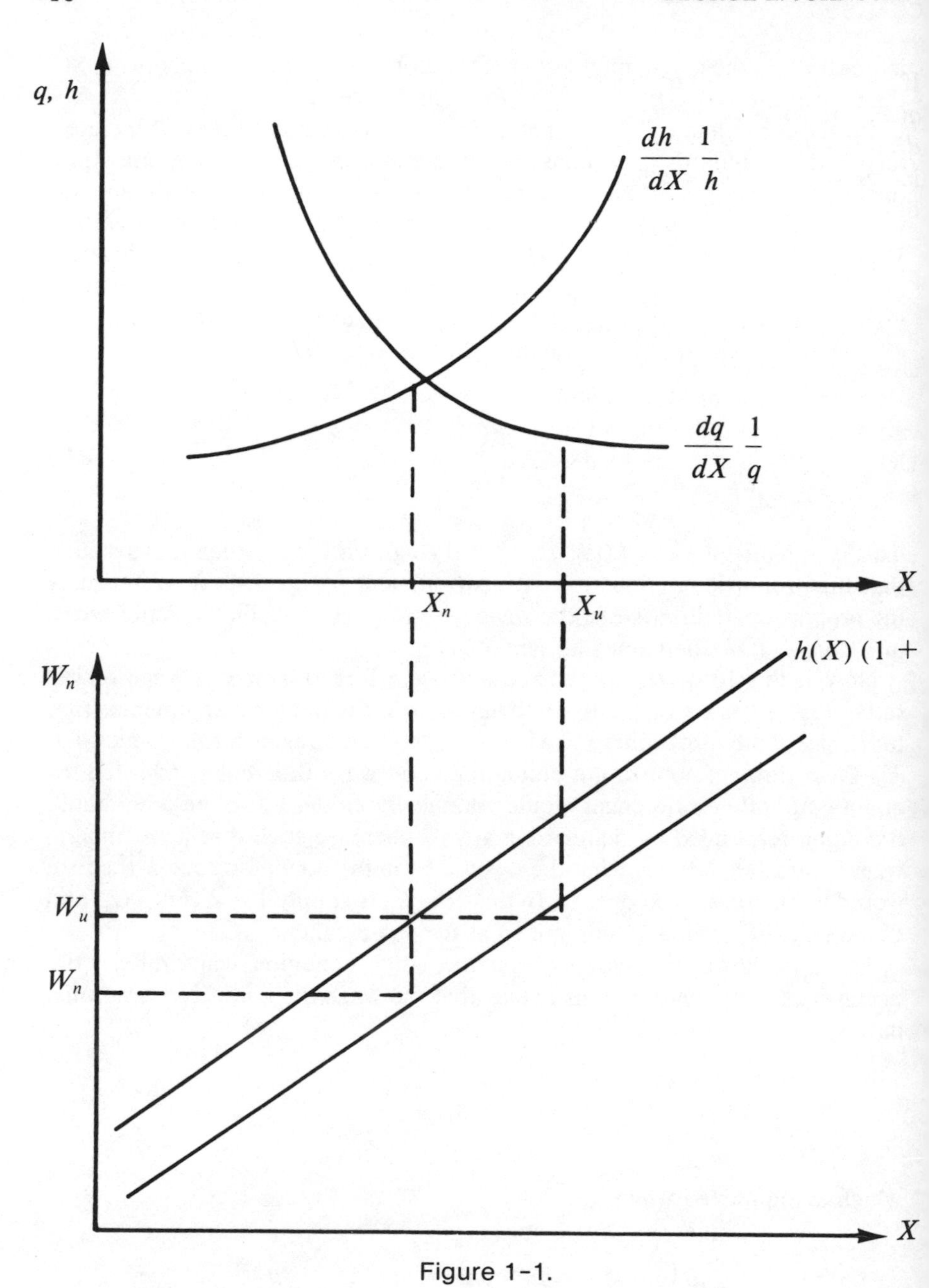

Figure 1-1.

If $d\lambda/dX < 0$, X will be higher in union than in nonunion firms with identical $q(X)$ functions. More important for purposes of this chapter is the fact that if $d\lambda/dX < 0$, the firm whose employees are represented by trade unions will increase its hiring requirements as the overall union-nonunion wage differential increases.

An attempted resolution of several of these issues with micro data is presented in the following section. As a preliminary test of the effect of omission of quality variables from the indices, I turn to more disaggregated aggregate data. Since 1972 the Bureau of Labor Statistics has collected wage and employment data for most three-digit industries. The bureau has also collected data on the most potent single variable in explaining industry wage variation: the proportion of total employees who are women WOM_i. Unionization data by three-digit SIC code for the 1968–1972 period are from the Freeman-Medoff study.

Table 1–4 reports the results of regressions (weighted by production worker employment in 1972) of the change in the logarithm of average hourly earnings from 1972 to 1979 on the unionization variable, U_i; a dummy variable for construction trades, CON_i; and the change in the fraction of total employment composed of women from 1972 to 1979, ΔWOM_i. The changes during this period in $D1$ and $D2$ are, respectively, 8.4 and 10.9, and the analogous results for the three-digit data are given by 100 times the coefficients on U_i in (1–4.1) and (1–4.2) in table 1–4: 11.3 and 11.9. Addition of the ΔWOM_i variable to each of these regressions lowers the estimated impact of unionism on the 1972 to 1979 wage change by 0.4 and 0.5 points. This confirms the expectation that the indices are biased in an

Table 1-4. Determinants of Wage Changes for 195 Three-Digit Industries, 1972-1979*

Equation	U_i	CON_i	ΔWOM_i	*Constant*	R^2
(1–4.1)	.113 (8.3)	—	—	.472	.283
(1–4.2)	.119	−0.32 (−3.5)	—	.472	.319
(1–4.3)	.109 (8.1)	—	−.252 (−3.3)	.477	.311
(1–4.4)	.114 (8.7)	−.031 (−3.5)	−.243 (−3.3)	.477	.347

**t*-statistics in parentheses.

Table 1-5. Effect of Union Membership on Logarithm of Wage Rate of Male and Female Family Heads, 1969 and 1977

	1969		*1977*	
	Unadjusted	*Adjusted*	*Unadjusted*	*Adjusted*
Males	.198	.157	.307	.268
	(10.1)	(8.8)	(13.0)	(11.8)
Females	.176	.185	.387	.366
	(2.2)	(2.5)	(5.9)	(5.9)

upward direction due to the omission of quality variables. However, the size of the bias, at least as far as this one "quality" variable is concerned, is not very large.

Testing the Validity of the Indices with Micro Data

One way to test the hypothesis that the indices in table 1–3 reflect a change in the true union effect rather than changes in worker quality across industries is to estimate earnings functions on comparable micro data sets for two different periods. If the change in the estimated union impact between the two time periods is much smaller than the equivalent change in the relevant index, we may conclude that unionized firms were able to raise their quality levels to minimize the damage of the higher λ. If, on the other hand, the micro and macro results are similar, one can be a trifle more confident in the latter.

In table 1–5 the estimated coefficients on a dummy variable for union membership in a standard earnings function are presented for male and female households in 1969 and 1977. The data are the national probability sample (i.e., excluding the oversample of poor persons) of the Michigan Income Dynamics study; there are 1,287 and 909 men in 1969 and 1977 and 198 and 190 women in the two years. The "unadjusted" estimates are simply a simple regression of the logarithm of the regular hourly wage on unionism; the "adjusted" estimates include education, potential experience and its square, race, three regional dummies, and rural residence.

As seen in table 1–5, all estimated coefficients increased markedly from

Table 1-6. Estimated Coefficients on Unionism and Its Interaction with Human Capital Variables for Male Household Heads, 1969 and 1977

	1969	*1977*
U	.521	.734
	(5.1)	(8.4)
$U \times$ ED	−0.22	−0.29
	(3.6)	(2.9)
$U \times X$	−0.11	−0.13
	(2.2)	(2.0)
$U \times X^2$	.00019	.00022
	(2.2)	(1.8)
F	16.8	8.9

1969 to 1977. For males the increase is .109 in the unadjusted estimate and .111 in the adjusted estimate, and for females the equivalent increases are .211 and .181. The index in table 1–3 equivalent to these results is $D2$, and this increased by 11.8 (divided by 100) over the period. This finding is quite consistent with the micro results; indeed, it is slightly smaller than a weighted average of the increases for men and women. Thus, I conclude that the huge increase in λ estimated from aggregate data has not been eroded by quality adjustments. It represents, instead, an increase in the monopoly point differential.

Another interesting fact about the increase in λ is that it has been much larger for low-skilled than for high-skilled union workers. This result was initially suggested by an analysis of changes from 1969 to 1978 in BLS indices of compensation for three skill groups in 52 cities. These results were that λ increased by 10 percent for clerical workers, essentially zero for skilled plant workers, and by a highly significant 26 percent for unskilled plant workers.

These results are consistent with those for males reported in tables 1–6 and 1–7. The union membership variable is interacted with education, experience, and experience squared, and the estimated effect of "human capital" on the wages is significantly smaller for union than for nonunion workers. Further, this effect became important between 1969 and 1977. The estimated value of log $(1 + \lambda)$ for a worker with eight years of schooling and five years of experience increases by .15; for a worker with 16 years of schooling and 25 years of experience, the increase was only .07.

Table 1-7. Estimated Impact of Unionism on Logarithm of Wage Rate of Male Family Heads by Years of Schooling and Experience, 1969 and 1977

	Years of Schooling					
	8		*12*		*16*	
Years of Experience	*1969*	*1977*	*1969*	*1977*	*1969*	*1977*
5	.29	.44	.21	.33	.12	.21
15	.22	.36	.13	.24	.05	.12
25	.19	.31	.10	.20	.01	.08
35	.19	.32	.10	.20	.02	.08
45	.23	.36	.15	.25	.06	.13

An Alternative Index

A third potential difficulty with the indices in table 1–3 is that the wage impact of unionism may vary systematically with the extent of unionism in the industry. First, nonunion firms in relatively heavily unionized industries may pay their workers a premium to forestall unionization, the so-called "threat effect." Second, unions in heavily unionized industries may push for higher wages than do unions in lightly organized industries because of a lower demand elasticity arising from competition with nonunion labor. A recent study by Freeman and Medoff (1978) concluded that for 1972–73 the threat effect (defined in this way) was of little quantitative significance, but the second effect, the impact of percent organized on the union wage advantage, was quite large. Indeed, the estimated value of λ for union members in manufacturing industries that were 80 percent unionized was about ten percentage points higher than for union members in industries that were only 20 percent organized.

This suggests in terms of the notation of this chapter that the union-nonunion wage differential in year t is:

$$\lambda(t) = \exp(\beta(t)) - 1,$$

where $\beta(t) = \beta_0(t) + \beta_1(t)\, U_i(t)$.

(Freeman and Medoff's estimate of α_1 for 1972–73 was .168.) If α_1 is not zero, $\lambda(t)$ does not have the same straightforward interpretation as was

Table 1-8. Nonlinear Effects of Unionism on Wage Changes, 1972-1979

Equation	U_i	U_i^2	CON_i	ΔWOM_i	*Constant*	R^2
(1–8.1)	.033	.093			.472	.291
	(0.7)	(1.8)				
(1–8.2)	.052	.077	−.031		.478	.324
	(1.1)	(1.5)	(−3.3)			
(1–8.3)	.029	.092		−.252	.485	.320
	(0.6)	(1.8)		(−3.3)		
(1–8.4)	.048	.076	−0.30	−.243	.483	.349
	(1.0)	(1.5)	(−3.3)	(−3.3)		

presented earlier. One must focus on a "heavily unionized–lightly unionized" ratio or on a similar concept.

In order to see whether *changes* in union wages depend on the extent of organization, a source of potential bias in the indices in table 1–3, I first examine the three-digit data on wage changes from 1972 to 1979.

Table 1–8 contains the same estimated equations as table 1–3 except that the quadratic term U_i^2 is added. The results show that the addition of U_i to the equation is not worth the loss of a degree of freedom. However, the estimated coefficient on U_i^2 is consistently larger than that on U_i. Moreover, the predicted difference between the change in the logarithm of wages in heavily unionized industries (80 percent) and lightly unionized industries (20 percent) is a full percentage point with construction included (.076 with an .066 without U_i^2) and 0.6 percentage point with construction excluded.

Given the nature of these results, it appears desirable to calculate a second set of indices of differentials. By regressing the logarithm of the wage in industry *i* on the appropriate estimate of collective bargaining coverage and its square, one can calculate the estimated differential between heavily unionized (U_i = 80 percent) and lightly unionized industries (U_i = 20 percent).

Index $D4$ in table 1–9 is based on the Douty unionization estimates and is analogous to $D1$ in table 1–3. Index $D5$ is based on the Freeman-Medoff estimates, and, like $D3$, it excludes construction. These indices are correlated with the relevant ones in table 1–3. The simple correlation coefficient between $D1$ and $D4$ is .79 and between $D3$ and $D5$ .96.

Table 1-9. Estimated Heavily-Lightly Unionized Wage Differentials, 1955-1979*

Year	*D4*	*D5*
1955	−10.7	
1956	−8.7	
1957	−6.8	
1958	−1.4	
1959	−2.2	
1960	−0.8	
1961	1.3	
1962	1.3	
1963	2.3	
1964	0	0
1965	−1.9	−0.3
1966	−3.4	−1.7
1967	−4.9	−3.1
1968	−7.1	−3.4
1969	−7.6	−3.9
1970	−6.3	−4.8
1971		−3.2
1972		−0.8
1973		0.3
1974		0.6
1975		2.0
1976		3.6
1977		5.1
1978		5.8
1979		6.2

*1964 = 0

Explaining Movements over Time in the Union-Nonunion Differential

I now move to the question of what causes the union-nonunion differential to change over time. Even if some (or, for that matter, all) of the pure rent component of the increase in the differential is erased by quality adjustments, it is still interesting to ask why rates in unionized industries increased so much more rapidly than in nonunionized industries.

The overall picture that emerges from each of the five indices is that λ increased steadily until 1963, fell during the rest of the 1960s, and then increased again throughout the 1970s. This does not conform to a strictly cyclical pattern, but the unemployment rates were generally high in both the 1955–1963 and the 1971–1979 periods and generally low in the 1964–1970 period.

There are several hypotheses in the literature concerning movements in λ. First, Lewis advanced a "wage rigidity" hypothesis to explain his results. Union wages are, by this hypothesis, less sensitive than nonunion wages to both aggregate demand conditions and inflation. λ would thus tend to increase when the unemployment rate is high and when the rate of price inflation is low. (Note from table 1–2 the large increase in λ from the late '20s into the early '30s and the virtual elimination of the differential through World War II and the inflation of the late '40s.)

A second view, which I will call the COWPS (Committee on Wage Price Stability) hypothesis, is that unions tend to damage wage increases that match the rate of inflation, often through formal escalator provisions.[5] This means that the union-nonunion differential may increase in periods of rapid inflation, especially if the inflation is associated with low labor productivity growth due to increases in the prices of other factors (specifically, for the 1970s, energy).

A third hypothesis is that a large value of λ may tend to mitigate union wage demands because of a "pricing out of the market" phenomenon. Similarly, nonunion wages might rise faster when λ is high because of threat effects.[6] Both these arguments imply that the change in the union-nonunion differential in a given year should be negatively related to its value in the preceding year.

Table 1-10. Determinants of Year-to-Year Changes in Union-Nonunion Wage Differential

Index	*Period*	*Di(t − 1)*	*ΔP(t)*	*U(t)*	*Constant*	R^2	*D.W.*
*D*1	1956–1970	−.239	.143	2.49	−8.75	.80	2.37
		(−2.6)	(0.4)	(5.1)			
*D*4	1956–1970	−.247	.407	1.20	−4.36	.79	2.55
		(−3.7)	(3.7)	(4.2)			
*D*2	1965–1979	−.129	0.36	1.61	−4.63	.51	1.26
		(−1.2)	(0.2)	(3.1)			
*D*3	1965–1979	−.107	.064	1.81	−5.33	.55	1.37
		(−1.1)	(0.4)	(3.3)			
*D*5	1965–1979	−.068	.024	.96	−2.33	.47	1.18
		(−0.7)	(0.2)	(2.9)			

These hypotheses are tested by regressing the annual change in each index on the previous year's value ($Di\ (t - 1)$), the percentage rate of change of consumer prices ($\Delta P(t)$), and the unemployment rate ($U(t)$).[7] The only result consistent for all five indices is that the union-nonunion differential tends to increase when the unemployment rate is relatively high. The expected effects of $\Delta P(t)$ and $Di\ (t - 1)$ are observed only for index $D4$, the heavily-lightly unionized differential for manufacturing in the earlier period. For the later period, however, the impact of these two variables on the change in the differential is both small and insignificant.

Will λ continue to rise in the 1980s or will it fall to a more "reasonable" value the way it did during the 1970s? The results in table 1–10, especially those for the more recent period, suggest that it will decline only if the United States experiences a period of sustained low employment. The unemployment rate, however, would have to fall considerably below the 5.7 percent rate observed at the peak of the past business cycle.

Notes

1. See for example R. E. Hall (1975).
2. The wage data are from BLS, *Employment and Earnings in the U.S.*, (1980) and the unionization data are for the years 1968–1972 from R. B. Freeman and J. L. Medoff (1979).
3. This statement refers only to production workers; very highly skilled persons (physicians, attorneys, and the like) are not represented in trade unions (as such). Indeed, in 1970 the breakdown of income distribution among year-round full-time workers showed that only 4.9 percent of unionized workers earned over $15,000 per year versus 10.5 percent of those not in labor unions. Similarly, 10.7 percent of unionized workers earned less than $5,000 per year versus 25.0 percent of those not in unions.
4. See G. Johnson and K. Youmans (1971).
5. This hypothesis is set out (along with several other hypotheses) in D. J. B. Mitchell (1980 chap. 5). Mitchell concludes that unions are perpetuators of an inflationary process, a view that is neither confirmed nor refuted by the results in this chapter.
6. See R. Flanagan (1976) and G. E. Johnson (1977).
7. The unemployment rate used in the regressions was that for males between the ages of 35 and 44 rather than the overall unemployment rate. Although the two rates are highly correlated, the latter has risen relative to the former by about one percentage point per decade since the mid-fifties because of compositional shifts in the labor force.

References

Bulletin of Labor Statistics. 1980. *Employment and Earnings in the United States*.

Flanagan, R. 1976. "Wage Interdependance in Unionized Labor Markets." *Brookings Papers on Economic Activity* 3.

Freeman, R. B., and Medoff, J. L. 1978. "The Percent Organized Wage (POW) Relationship for Union and for Nonunion Workers." *NBER Working Paper 305*, December.

______. 1979. "New Estimates of Private Sector Unionism in the United States." *Industrial and Labor Review*, January.

Hall, R. E. 1975. "The Rigidity of Wages and Persistence of Unemployment." *Brooking Papers on Economic Activity* 2.

Johnson, G. E. 1977. "The Determination of Wages in the Union and Nonunion Sectors." *British Journal of Industrial Relations*, July.

Johnson, G. E., and Youmans, K. 1971. "Union Relative Wage Effects by Age and Education." *Industrial and Labor Relations Review* (February).

Lewis, H. G. 1963. *Unionism and Relative Wages in the United States*. Chicago: University of Chicago Press.

Mitchell, D. J. B. 1980. *Unions, Wages and Inflation*. Washington: Brookings Institution.

A Comment on Johnson, by John T. Addison

In his paper Professor Johnson seeks to chart the course of the aggregate (logarithmic) union-nonunion wage differential in the postwar interval, in effect starting out where Gregg Lewis (1963) left off. In actuality, of course, Gregg Lewis's study of union relative wage effects still continues, and to preface some of my subsequent remarks, I note that he is now of the opinion that the worth of aggregative exercises of the type conducted by Johnson is questionable at the outset.

Johnson himself is clearly aware of the difficulties surrounding aggregative estimates, and, indeed, the bulk of his paper is devoted to a justification of his basic series. We do, I believe, get some indication from the author's introductory comments that the main purpose in erecting time-series estimates of the union-nonunion differential has not been achieved or followed up in the present chapter. That purpose I take to be the estimation of the impact of unionism on the natural rate of unemployment—others might find the term NAIRU more congenial.

What Johnson does do in the present paper is to provide a description of the course of the aggregate union-nonunion differential (estimated over 20 two-digit manufacturing industries) over the period 1964–1969. Strictly, the differential is estimated from 1958, with 1964 chosen as a base year to provide continuity with the Gregg Lewis estimate of a logarithmic differential of around .15 in 1955.

As we have seen, there are three basic indices—$D1$, $D2$, and $D3$—covering the periods 1955–1970, 1964–1979, and 1964–1979, respectively. All are obtained from the basic estimating equation

$$\log W_{it} = \alpha_{it} + \beta U_{it}.$$

For $D1$, the Douty estimate of the extent of collective bargaining in 1958 is employed, while for $D2$ and $D3$ Freeman and Medoff's estimates of unionism for 1968–1972 are used.

The three indices constructed from the β-estimates point to a steady increase in the differential to 1963, a fall in that differential in the 1960s, followed by a large rise in the decade of the 1970s. As intimated above, the rest of Johnson's chapter, with the exception of the final two pages in which he attempts an explanation of observed movements in the differential (see below), is taken up with a justification of the time-series values.

Johnson's principal concerns with the aggregate series are twofold: first, that his β-estimates will be biased by unobserved movements in unionization from the base period; second, that the estimated differential will mask quality adjustments that may in the limit eliminate efficiency unit differentials. In the former context, the very construction of the $D2$ and $D3$ series (identical except for the absence of construction in the $D2$ sample) is geared toward the examination of potential negative bias in the $D1$ series the further away in time the β-estimate from 1955. The downward trend in the differential shown in the $D1$ series is shown to be of similar magnitude in the $D3$ series, although the narrowing is altogether less pronounced in the $D2$ series. (A change in the relative performance of the construction industry is hinted at but nowhere taken up.)

I do not quite understand Johnson's comments on movements in the differential in the 1970s. I simply understood him to mean that changes in the distribution of unionism in this period might imply the presence of some upward bias in the reported figures. Nevertheless, it would have been useful to have had the Douty and Freeman-Medoff estimates of coverage-unionism across the two-digit industries.

But Johnson is much more concerned with the possibility that unionized employers responded to the pronounced widening of the differential in the 1970s (by 1979 union wages relative to nonunion wages were some 5 percentage points above their 1964 value compared with 11 percentage points below that value in 1970) by hiring better quality workers. He first uses less aggregate data than those employed in the construction of his differential series to provide a rough check on the possible overstatement of the differential induced by quality adjustment. Specifically, he regresses the change in the logarithm of average hourly earnings for 1972–1979 on the level of unionization and the change in the fraction of total employment composed of women (the control) inter alia for 195 three-digit industries. He then compares the coefficient on unionism (measured note in a different way from Douty and Freeman-Medoff) multiplied by 100 with the change in the standardized β-values in the $D2$ and $D3$ series over 1972–1979. The quality control variable is shown to but modestly reduce the estimated impact of unionism.

A second check is attempted using micro data proper from the Michigan Income Dynamics study. Standard earnings functions are run for two groups (males and females) in 1969 and 1977 and quality adjusted and unadjusted estimates of the effect of union status provided for the two years. The results are viewed by Johnson to be consonant with the data revealed in the aggregate estimates of the differential and the findings obtained from the somewhat less aggregative data. (Interestingly, Johnson's interactive procedures might have caused him to modify his opening comments on the distortions introduced by unions in industrial relations systems where unionism is more entrenched than in the United States.)

Frankly, I am not overly impressed by the "corroborative" tests suggested by Johnson, although, in fairness, I though it appropriate to summarize some British results (Layard, Metcalf, and Nickell, 1977), which, as can be seen from table 1–11, also point to a pronounced widening of the union-nonunion differential in the 1970s.

My reservations are as follows. First, one cannot directly compare estimates of the differential produced from the various data sets employed by Johnson. For example, biases are introduced into estimates of the differential when α_{it} is replaced by a vector of variables hypothesized to determined the nonunion wage. Again, Johnson's estimating equations treat β as the mean for all i. But there is no reason to suppose that the differential will be the same for all i, thus implying that the coefficient on U_i will be biased and inconsistent. In fact, Johnson recognizes that the differential will vary according to union density. He includes a nonlinear term in U_i to capture this effect in his less aggregated BLS data tries. But his point appears to be that the D series is an accurate reflection of *movements* in the differential. To establish this point, he constructs two new D series—$D4$ and $D5$—corresponding in periodicity and coverage to $D1$ and $D3$, respectively. The new series, which computes changes in the differential between heavily and lightly unionized sectors, emerges as highly correlated with the basic series ($r_{D1,D4} = .79$; $r_{D3,D5} = .96$). But Johnson has, I submit, already gone a long way toward recognizing that the size of the differential may be considerably overstated.

A further difficulty concerns the very merit of constructing an aggregate series of the union-nonunion differential. Thus Gregg Lewis (1980) argues persuasively that estimation of the differential requires two types of unionism variables, namely *union status* and *extent of unionism*. In macro equations the distinction between the two variables frequently is lost. Moreover, even employing macro equations that are exact aggregations of the correctly specified micro equations, Gregg Lewis finds that the distinction between the two unionism variables is so obscured that estimates of the differential from macro data bear little resemblance to their counterparts derived from micro data. Gregg Lewis reports that where the aggregation is by industry, the use of extent of unionism variables by industry leads to large upward biases in the estimates of the differential, while the converse appears to be true of aggregation by occupation. The scope for yet further biases along other possible dimensions of aggregate leads Gregg Lewis (1980), with what I take to be characteristic understatement, to conclude: "Thus, at least for the moment, I am dissuaded from trying to extract estimates of relative wage effects of unionism from studies reporting wage equations fitted to macro-data" (p. 27).

Table 1-11. British Estimates of the Effects of "Coverage" on Industrial Group-Hourly Earnings, 1961-1975

Year[e]		Partial Regression Coefficients[a]	
		Unadjusted Coverage Data[b]	*Adjusted Coverage Data*[c]
1961	A	.17 (2.5)[d]	−0.2 (0.6)
	O	.17 (2.5)	−.01 (0.2)
1962	A	.15 (2.2)	−.01 (0.2)
	O	.19 (2.8)	−.01 (0.3)
1963	A	.19 (2.7)	−.01 (0.3)
	O	.15 (2.2)	.00
1964	A	.17 (2.5)	.00
	O	16 (2.3)	.00
1965	A	.20 (3.0)	.00
	O	.19 (2.6)	.00
1966	A	.21 (3.1)	.02 (0.5)
	O	.17 (2.4)	.00
1967	A	.17 (2.4)	.02 (0.5)
	O	.17 (2.5)	.02 (0.5)
1968	A	.18 (2.5)	.06 (1.1)
	O	.20 (2.8)	.08 (1.5)
1969	A	.21 (2.8)	.12 (2.0)
	O	.21 (2.9)	.13 (2.1)
1970	O	.26 (3.4)	.19 (2.6)
1971	O	.26 (3.1)	.22 (2.8)
1972	O	.31 (3.8)	.29 (3.6)
1973	O	.31 (3.7)	.31 (3.7)
1974	O	.25 (3.2)	.26 (3.4)
1975	O	.31 (3.3)	.31 (3.5)

Source: Layard, R., Metcalf, D. and Nickell, S. (1977, table 6 and annex table, pp. 25, 28).

[a]Holding constant proportion skilled, proportion unskilled, proportion aged 20–24, proportion aged 25–54, proportion working in the South East and Midlands, and proportion working in conurbations.

[b]Coverage level in each industry assumed constant at its 1973 level throughout.

[c]Coverage data adjusted for changes in unionization over time.

[d]Absolute t-values given in parenthesis.

[e]A = April; O = October.

But let us accept for argument's sake that the D series does consistently pick up movements in the differential through time and turn to the last part of Johnson's paper, which seeks to explore the determinants of such movements in the D series. Specifically, he tests whether annual movements in the differential are related to the unemployment rate, the rate of price inflation, and lagged values of the relevant index itself. The only result that is consistent across all five equations is that the differential widens with the level of unemployment.

It is rather surprising that Johnson's test procedures fail to take account of the long lags between wage change and its economic determinants. In any case, his conclusion that the differential will decline to the "reasonable" levels of the 1960s (he writes 1970s) only if the unemployment rate falls well below 5.7 percent (below the natural rate) is surely not substantiated. His regression analysis nowhere establishes this conclusion.

While Johnson's findings as to the sign of the unemployment variable strike a sympathetic chord, I feel a better treatment of the behavior of the differential over the cycle is available to us in the important though neglected study of Wachter (1974). Wachter regresses the coefficient of variation of interindustry wages in United States manufacturing on the reciprocal of the unemployment rate, the rate of price inflation, two dummies, and a time trend. His sample period is 1947–1974. Wachter's equations were estimated using Almon lags, and the coefficients reported in his study are the sum of weights: average lags being in the order of 3 years and the full lags of 5 years.

Wachter himself distinguishes between high-wage and low-wage sectors rather than unionized and nonunionized sectors, but for the purposes of the present discussion, we might perhaps treat the two as synonymous. The reason for the systematic movement in the interindustry–union-nonunion differential is said to be rooted in the fact that the high-wage union sectors have longer planning periods than the low-wage more competitive sectors. Longer planning periods generate lags of adjustment (= contract length) and lags in expectational effects. During periods of historically low unemployment and high inflation, such sectors tend to underestimate the economywide rate of wage change with the result that the dispersion narrows. Conversely, during slack.

I interpret Wachter's study as broadly conformable with that of Johnson but more soundly based. In particular, Wachter not only provides a very useful description of wage settlements in the 1968–1974 period (which suggests that after erring on the low side during the 1960s the high-wage sectors began to catch up as contracts expired during 1969–1971 and moreover projected into the 1970s the tight labor markets of the 1960s), but he is also able to identify when distortions of the differential became ironed out—in other words when relative wages were on target. This avoids the connotation of making unions the villains of the contraction and the heroes of the expansion.

Unfortunately, Wachter's study ends at 1974, and if we take it that the system was broadly in balance at that time, why have differentials continued to rise? One argument would be that the latter years of the 1970s were characterized by increasing uncertainty that made forecasting more difficult. My general point is simply that unions can have a major impact on the inflation problem in that they serve to lock important sectors of the economy into a given wage pattern that may run counter to strong cyclical swings in the economy.

Further investigation of the mid-to-late 1970s is clearly called for. Johnson has alerted us to the possibility of a pronounced widening in the differential. He has not, however, identified its causes but merely charted the familiar countercyclical behavior of the differential. A very much more sophisticated procedure is required before we can say whether the differential is, say, on or off target.

References

Layard, R., Metcalf, D., and Nickell, S. 1977. "The Effect of Collective Bargaining on Wages," presented to the International Economic Association Conference on *Personal Income Distribution*. Noordwijk-aan-Zee, Netherlands.

Lewis, H. G. 1963. *Unionism and Relative Wages in the United States*. Chicago: Ill.: University of Chicago Press.

______. 1980. "Interpreting Unionism Coefficients in Wage Equations," (mimeographed). Duke University.

Wachter, M. L. 1974. "The Wage Process: An Analysis of the Early 1970s." *Brookings Papers on Economic Activity*, no. 2: 507–524.

2 STRIKE COST AND WAGE RATES: *Cross-Industry Differences*

Melvin W. Reder

The basic hypothesis underlying this chapter is simple: An important part of the effect of a union on the wage rates of its members derives from its ability to impose cost on employers by striking. While this conjecture will not occasion surprise, it has not, as far as I am aware, been utilized heretofore in explaining union impact on wage rates.

A Theory of Union Wage Effects

Union-Nonunion Wage Rate Differential: Long Run

To simplify drastically, assume that all employer-worker bargaining pairs consist of one employer and one worker, who works a fixed number of hours per period. Assume further that workers are identical in all respects except for unionization. These assumptions eliminate complications resulting from

---

Research support for this paper has been provided by the Ontario Economic Council and the National Science Foundation grant number DAR–7826690. This support is gratefully acknowledged.

factor substitution, divergence of interests among union members, and differences in hours and weeks worked. Indisputably, the behavioral determinants from which I abstract are very important in other contexts, and for other theories of union wage effects. I abstract from them only because they are inessential to the theory I am proposing.

The long-run union-nonunion wage differential (in hourly wage rates) arises from the quasi-entitlement to continued employment that is conferred on *current* employees of a given firm *when they are unionized*. Unless satisfied with their terms of employment, the union of a firm's (current) employees can declare a strike and thereby halt production. The ability of the employer to replace striking workers is severely limited both by the legal protection given to the right of workers to engage in lawful strikes and by the de facto permission granted by the courts and the legislature to permit quasi-legally striking workers to harass strikebreakers and their employers. It is the permission to impede replacement of strikers that creates the quasi-entitlement.

Impeding the use of strikebreakers imposes an (appreciable) cost on an employer who wishes to replace striking workers. Because only unionized workers can (effectively) strike, the cost of replacing strikers drives a wedge between the cost of employing nonunion workers and the cost of employing otherwise identical union workers. Thus, union workers can demand a wage premium on threat of commencing or continuing a strike. In effect, the act of granting workers "nonprobationary status" confers on them a conditional property right—the right to require their union's agreement to the terms of employment as a condition for carrying on production—in the employer's business; the only condition of this right is joining a union.

To avoid adverse contingencies, firms often attempt to "preposition" themselves in various ways. In this context, one such technique might be to require contractually, as a condition of employment, that workers remain nonunion (yellow dog contracts); another technique is selection of workers who are likely to be averse to unionizing. But the legal barriers to requiring a nonunion commitment as a condition of employment, and the associated legal protection given to the right of current employees to unionize regardless of prior commitments, render such strategies of little value in curbing the effect of unionism on wage rates.

In effect, the risk of being unionized is an unavoidable hazard of starting a business that employs hired labor services. As a result, the long-run equilibrium wage rate is a weighted average, with the weights being the respective probabilities, of (1) the expected wage rate if hired workers remain nonunion and (2) the expected wage rate if the workers unionize. The weights are exogenous, and the expectations are taken as of the moment of starting the business. Recognition of the unavoidable risk of unionization, and the attendant increase in labor cost, ultimately leads to mutual adjustment of the (long-run) equilibrium wage rates of union and nonunion labor and of product prices. In this chapter, however, I focus on the effect of unionization on the difference between union and nonunion hourly wage rates (i.e., the union differential) and abstract from these further repercussions.

Absent a difference in productivity between union and nonunion workers, which I assume to be the case, the ability of union employers to pay a higher wage rate than their nonunion competitors is conditional on their earning rent on some endowed nontransferable assets. It is this rent that the union compels them to share; i.e., union employers earn less rent than nonunion employers.

In a nutshell, the legal privilege of impeding employment of strikebreakers gives a union a club with which to bludgeon an employer unless that employer purchases immunity by transfer of an acceptable quantum of rent. No other characteristic of a union need be invoked to explain the source of a long-run union wage differential. Since, in this theory, the source of the differential is simply the union's power to hold the employer's production and/or delivery hostage for satisfactory terms of employment, I term it the "Blackjack Theory of Unionism."[1]

Blackjack Theory of Unionism

In its simplest form, the blackjack theory explains the union wage differential in a model in which all employers are assumed to be identical and all workers are also assumed to be identical except for unionization. Any employer is assumed to be faced with an exogenously given probability of being unionized, Π. If not unionized, the hourly wage rate is w; if unionized, the wage is $w' > w$; employer rent (per hour of employment) is z if not unionized and $z' < z$ if unionized. Thus, unionization transfers $z - z'$ of rent per manhour of employment to unionized workers: $w' - w = (z - z')$.

Part of the gain from unionizing is used to defray the cost of union organization and part to offset any disutility of unionizing (which may be positive or negative). If $w' - w > 0$ (which is plausible), a complete model would have to explain why some workers choose to unionize while others do not. But such an explanation is unnecessary for the present purpose and, moreover, would require abandonment of the assumption that workers are homogeneous and would greatly complicate the argument. Accordingly, I assume that the unionization of an employer is determined entirely by chance with the probability of being unionized equal to Π.

Given these assumptions, one can readily construct a model in which all union workers receive the same wage, as do all nonunion workers, but with a differential between the wage paid to union workers and to nonunion workers. I shall not elaborate on this model because it is not germane to the measurements reported in the next section.

These measurements describe the (differential) effect on wage rates, among unionized firms, of differences in the expected cost of strikes; I interpret these differences as due to differences in the "size of the union blackjack." Assume unionized employers to be homogeneous except for their differential sensitivity to delay in production and/or delivery; for short, delivery delay. For convenience assume that an employer's loss from delivery delay arises from the sensitivity of customers to such delay. Let this sensitivity be reflected in the price the employer is able to command for output; that is, an employer is assumed to take orders for future delivery at a specified price and to make a commitment, implicit or explicit, as to the percentage, α, of a given order that will be delivered on time ($\alpha \leq 1$). The (profit maximizing) price charged for any given quantity of output (size of order) is $p = p(\alpha)$, $p' > 0$.

To command a price, p^0, requires not only a promise that $\alpha \geq \alpha^0$, but some behavioral indications that make the promise credible. Credibility depends on past performance and currently observable indications of delivery reliability. One important negative indicator of such reliability is strikes; thus, a history of strikes and/or a threat of strikes reduces the credibility of a promise that $\alpha \geq \alpha^0$. Recognizing this, a union can demand a wage premium on pain of interrupting delivery by striking. I assume that the employer and the customers are equally well informed as to the probability that the union will carry out any strike threat.

Given that a firm is unionized, its ability to promise $\alpha \geq \alpha^0$, and price accordingly, is conditional on the union's implicit agreement to limit strike activity. The extent to which the union wage reflects a simple transfer of employer rents, and the extent to which it is offset by a transfer of customer rents to the employer via an implicit three-party bargain, is not germane to this discussion. All that I am contending is that the wage the union can obtain for an implicit promise not to strike "more than some (loosely) specified amount" increases with the expected cost of a strike to the employer.

Put differently, the threat of a strike can be manipulated by the union (ex ante) to extract a union wage premium. Ceteris paribus, this premium will be greater, the greater the loss to the employers' customers from the interruption to production occasioned by a strike. The greater the premium that can be charged to customers for (credibly) promising a delivery schedule described by $\alpha \geq \alpha_0$ (i.e., α_0), the greater the wage premium that the union can obtain for agreeing to a style of collective bargaining—i.e., a level of expected strike cost (see below)—that is compatible with α_0.

The premium that customers will pay for α_0 depends on the sensitivity of their own production process to interruptions and the facility with which they can obtain substitute sources of supply during a strike. The greater this facility, the less important is the level of α and the lower the premium the employer can obtain for the promise of α_0, and hence the smaller the union wage the employer will pay.

Given the premium customers will pay for α_0, the more that it costs the union (in sacrificed wages) to interrupt production and delivery by striking, the smaller the wage premium it can extract from the employer. This is because the larger the loss of wages implied by a strike, the lower the willingness of union members to strike and therefore the smaller the wage premium necessary to induce them to avoid striking. Recognizing this, the greater the prospective wage loss to strikers, the more employers will resist a demand for a given union wage rate. As a result, across firms or negotiating units, the cost to union members in sacrificed wages (per manday of strike) is assumed to vary inversely with the availability of alternative employment for striking workers and their family members.

A further word on the relation of product prices to α: Customers are not interested in avoiding strikes per se, but in avoiding delivery interruptions, which can occur for many reasons other than strikes. Therefore, the theory of interunion wage differentials that is proposed here implies that these differentials should be correlated with other characteristics associated with worker behavior suggestive of reliability. Thus worker characteristics associated with low absenteeism, willingness to work overtime, and the like should be positively correlated with expected strike cost (per strike). Similarly, quality of equipment, availability of "backup facilities" in the event of unanticipated performance failure either of manpower or equipment, etc., should be positively correlated with expected cost per strike. The presence (or absence) of these correlations will provide further tests of the blackjack theory.

The customer is conceived as paying a premium for delivery reliability, which is related, in part, to the absence of strikes. The importance of such absence increases with the expected cost per strike, as alleged above. But it will also vary with number of strikes per unit of time (e.g., per year). That is, in paying for α^0, the customer is paying for the inverse of expected strike cost per year, rather than for (the inverse of) expected strike cost per strike.

Cost of a Strike

For simplicity, I shall assume that the cost of a strike to its participants is proportional to the reduction in net output that it causes. Reduction in net output is equal to the algebraic sum of (1) the reduction in output during the period of the strike and (2) any net increase in output during the periods preceding and following the strike that offset reduction in output during the strike. The cost of shifting output through time is also reflected by increased inputs per unit of output, and by higher interest charges. However I assume that, *across firms*, differences in strike cost due to intertemporal substitution of output are small relative to those resulting from differences in net output lost. Accordingly, I shall focus on the latter.

The net output loss from a strike is divided between the loss of wages to workers and of quasi-rents to employers. Varying from one firm to another, lost wages may be offset by earnings from alternative employment and (occasionally) from strike benefits that do not reflect disbursement of previously paid union dues. Division of strike cost (between workers and employer) varies with the extent to which the strike is anticipated and the parties are able to make cost saving adjustments. In this discussion, I assume the parties to be experienced bargainers who make informed judgments (1) as to the probability that a strike will occur on any given bargaining occasion and (2) as to the expected cost of the strike, conditional on its occurrence.

Across bargaining pairs, the expected cost of a strike varies with the expected net loss of output. If the negotiating unit is viable, the net loss of output will parallel a net loss of purchased inputs to the firm's customers. (If this does not hold, at least approximately, then the customers are assumed to have alternative sources of supply and, as argued below, the negotiating unit will not be viable.) The net loss of inputs per strike to the customers is indicative of, but does not measure, the expected cost of a strike to the customers. Therefore, the greater the expected cost of a strike to the bargainers, the higher the price they will pay an employer to adopt a bargaining strategy that leads, ceteris paribus, to a low probability of a strike, thus making possible higher product prices and higher union wages.

I assume further that the bargainers have achieved a "viable negotiating unit." The significance of this assumption is as follows: In a substantially competitive industry where the output of one firm is a good substitute for that of another, no employer can afford either (1) to take on a strike when many other firms continue to operate or (2) to agree to terms of employment unless they are similar to those of its product market competitors. One possible resolution of both problems is explicit multi-employer bargaining, in which all firms either agree to settle with the union or agree to a strike. An alternative solution is bargaining by single employers, or by groups less inclusive than the totality, but with implicit agreement not to exploit partial settlements (where some firms are struck and others not) so as seriously to worsen the long-run market positions of the struck firms. Failing either solution, unionized firms would not be viable in the long run. Thus, in the long run, either all firms will be nonunion or their bargaining and strike behavior will be coordinated.

Deferring details to another occasion, I assume that any *viable* negotiating unit has the following characteristics: (1) A strike will impose some cost on any included employer, but not so great a cost (i.e., permanent loss of customers) as to force the employer to make a (transitory) settlement incompatible with long-run survival, and (2) a strike will impose a cost on the workers sufficient for the employer to feel they will accept contracts compatible with employer survival, and without making the employer's expected cost of a strike so great as to warrant restructuring of the negotiating unit. I abstract from the (still greater) complications of the short run in which negotiating units may be nonviable and assume that union wage rates reflect the long-run adjustment to the threat of delivery delay.

Unfortunately, since measuring strike cost per year is not yet possible, we must be content, for the present, with cost per strike. I do not consider this limitation "too serious" in analyzing U.S. manufacturing industries because (1) "wildcat" or unauthorized strikes, which are a major cause of cross-industry differences in strike frequency, are of minor importance in manufacturing and (2) across industries, greater probability of a strike on any given contract negotiation is counterbalanced by contracts of longer duration so as to limit the effect of differences in expected frequency of strikes on expected cost of strikes per annum. In effect, differences (across bargaining pairs) in expected strike cost *per annum* are assumed to be captured by differences in expected cost *per strike*.

The Effect of Strike Cost on Wage Rates: Some Preliminary Results

As stated, the blackjack theory of unionism refers to bargaining between one-firm unions and individual employers. For the present, data limitations (affecting the estimate of strike costs) require that application be made to industries rather than firms. Accordingly, the following (crude) simplifications are made:

1. In each of the industries studied, all firms are assumed to be identical in

the marginal price increment they can collect from customers as compensation for a given increment in α;
2. In each industry the effect of a marginal change in the expected cost of a "unit of strike activity" on the equilibrium premium for credibly promising $\alpha = \alpha_0$ is the same for all firms;
3. In each industry the expected cost of striking is the same for all workers of given personal characteristics;
4. N.B. across industries, the expected cost of a unit of strike activity to the "typical worker" is equal; implying
5. Cross-industry differences in the expected cost of a unit of strike activity are reflected solely in differences in costs to *employers*.

Assumptions 1 through 3, while crude, are conventional simplifications. Assumptions 4 and 5 require comment. First, their purpose is to rationalize the assumption that industries with greater expected strike cost per unit of strike activity are those from which the union can obtain higher wage rates as a payoff for not striking (frequently). Obviously, if interindustry differences in expected strike costs reflect primarily differences in lost wages of strikers—and only negligibly differences in lost quasi rents of employers—greater strike costs would not be associated with a bigger union blackjack and consequent higher wage rates. Second, the ability of strikers to replace wages lost *during the strike* through alternative employment is the main source of interindustry difference in the cost of one strike day to union members. Availability of such employment depends upon the characteristics of workers and the structure of local job markets. Across manufacturing industries—upon which empirical work has thus far been focused—these differences would not seem to be either large or systematically related to levels of strike cost. Moreover, strike benefits appear to be neither large nor systematically variable across manufacturing industries. Accordingly, I posit assumptions 4 and 5, although the subject requires further research.

Given these assumptions, George Neumann and I (forthcoming) have estimated the effect of expected strike cost on hourly wage rates across three-digit manufacturing industries in the United States. As a first step, we have estimated the average cost per strike in each of 69 three-digit manufacturing industries for the period 1953–1976. The details of the estimation procedure are complicated and are presented in Reder and Neumann (in press a). The essence of the procedure is to estimate what output would have been in each month of the period, absent a strike. We then measure output in those months during which strikes occurred, as well as in an interval preceding and following the strike; the difference between estimated output in the absence of a strike and actual output summed over the strike period, and the intervals before and after the strike, is considered to be the cost of that strike. Averaging the cost of all strikes in a given industry over the 23-year period gives an average cost per strike for that industry. This average is the expected cost per strike that is used in our wage regression.

The reason for including output gained or lost during the intervals (before and after a strike) in the strike cost calculations is that the effect of a strike on output is normally anticipated and partially offset in the months preceding it and/or is made up in the months following its termination (Reder and Neumann, 1980). Thus the net loss of output from a strike is normally smaller than that which occurs during the strike period per se; this net loss is what is relevant to the effect of strike cost on wage rates.

The estimate of cost of strikes per strike by industry is then treated as a personal characteristic of all workers (i.e., the same for all) in that industry. This estimate is included in a vector of other personal characteristics (age, sex, occupation, region, years of schooling, race, weekly hours worked, and membership in a union) for individuals in the pooled Current Population Surveys (CPS) of the U.S. Bureau of the Census for 1973–1975, which are the independent variables in an OLS regression.

The sign of the coefficient of hourly wages on expected strike cost per strike(s) is used as a test of the blackjack theory of union wage effects. If the theory is valid, the coefficient of wages on strike cost should be positive; i.e., workers in industries with higher expected strike cost per strike should be able to obtain higher hourly wage rates by threatening strikes, other variables being constant. And this is the case: In preliminary results, Neumann and I have found that, among workers belonging to unions, 1*n* (hourly wage rate), increases (across industries) by .5 percent per $1 million increase in average net loss per month of strike; the *t*-ratio is +6.02.

To interpret this result properly requires some elaboration:

1. The three-digit industry classifications used in estimating strike costs come from the U.S. Department of Commerce data on "Output and Inventories in Manufacturing Industries" and are not the same as those used in the CPS from which measurements of the other variables are obtained. The required merging of the data sets resulted in reduction of the "original" 65 industries to 40.

2. The measurements of strike cost obtained are almost certainly biased downward (i.e., strike cost is underestimated); (Reder and Neumann). This bias is due primarily to aggregation (within each industry) across many bargaining pairs. As a result of this aggregation bias, only 21 of the 40 merged industries show strike costs to be greater than zero. We would

not suggest placing great credence in a coefficient that depends on variations in strike costs that are measured as negative. Accordingly, the reported results are based solely on observations from those industries in which strike costs are positive; for all 40 industries the coefficient is positive, but smaller than reported and with a lower *t*-ratio.

3. The reported coefficient reflects observations on both union and nonunion members. Running the regression separately on union and nonunion members generates positive and significant coefficients for both groups, but for the nonunionized subsample the coefficients are larger. The fact that a significant and positive coefficient is found for the nonunionized group raises an obvious question: If nonunion workers do not strike, how can fear of the cost of their strikes motivate higher wage payments?

Two answers are possible. First, employers' fear of workers' unionizing and subsequently engaging in costly strikes causes them to relate pay to the expected cost of their strikes. This explanation is a variant of the familiar "threat effect." Second, as already noted, greater concern with avoiding delivery delay not only gives unions a "heavier blackjack" (reflected in a larger coefficient of wages on strike cost), but also motivates employers to be more selective in order to obtain workers whose attendance, diligence, and general cooperativeness in fulfilling delivery commitments are above average. Such selectivity is likely to be associated with above average wages. While the characteristics on which employers would select are in principle observable, they are not measured in our data set, so that in the present context they are omitted variables whose effect on wage rates of nonunion workers is captured by the coefficient on strike cost. The separate effects of these explanations on wage rates are not distinguishable on the present data set. Inclusion of the omitted variable discussed under the second explanation may cause the wage coefficient on strike cost to be biased upward. Consideration of this possibility is a task for future research.

4. A competing, though not mutually exclusive, explanation of union-caused interindustry wage differentials is the effect of percentage of workers organized (POW) on hourly wage rates. This theory, first proposed by Lewis (1963) and most recently developed by Freeman and Medoff (1979) implies a positive coefficient of w on POW across industries. Preliminary work shows that introduction of POW into our regressions reduced the coefficient on strike cost negligibly, but left the coefficients on both variables positive and statistically significant at the 1 percent level. However the coefficient on strike cost is appreciably larger than that on POW. Further work in comparing the relative importance of strike cost and POW on wage rates is in progress, but no definitive statement on results is yet possible.

Note

1. The blackjack theory should be distinguished from the Marshallian argument relating the effect of unionism to the elasticity of derived demand for the services of union members. Marshall's argument refers to the technical possibilities of substitution, given employer freedom to move across its production function. The blackjack theory refers to the ability of a union to raise wages by halting production by impeding access to facilities regardless of the production function.

References

Freeman, R. B., and Medoff J. L. 1981, "The Impact of the Percentage Organized on Union and Nonunion Wages," *Review of Economics and Statistics* 63(4): 561–72.

Lewis, H. G. 1963. *Unionism and Relative Wage Rates*. University of Chicago Press, Chicago.

Reder, M. W., and Neumann G. R. 1980. "Conflict and Contract: The Case of Strikes." *Journal of Political Economy* 88, no. 5(October): 867–886.

———. (In press a). "Output and Strike Activity in U.S. Manufacturing: How Large are the Losses?"

———. (In press b). "The Effect of Strike Cost on Wage Rates in U.S. Manufacturing."

A Comment on Reder, by John Burton

The ability of trade unions to raise the wages of their members, via their influence in or on pecuniary markets, rests on two types of economic power.[1] These two dimensions of union economic power are related and reinforcing. Both rest, ultimately, on the control exercised by unions over labor supply. However, the two are analytically separable.

The monopoly power of a trade union resides in its ability to restrict supply or prevent entry to a labor market by long-term means (e.g., by the enforcement of lengthy apprenticeship regulations). Such a constriction of supply produces a response in the market: The price of unionized labor is caused to rise. Strike-threat power also rests on the ability to withhold labor, but in the *short* term, in such a way that the plans of the employer (and usually also of other economic agents, such as his customers) are disrupted thereby. To avoid such disruption the employer of union labor may be induced to pay a premium wage. Thus, union monopoly power works through the medium of the market process, whereas strike-threat power works through the (potential) disruption of market (or other) economic relationships.

I know of no research that has yet been done that identifies the relative importance of these two separable sources of union wage gains. To date, studies of the union-nonunion wage differential have been concerned with estimating its size and the netting out of other influences on the determination of relative wages (such as personal characteristics). They have not (yet) been concerned with the question of the decomposition of the net union-nonunion wage differential into a monopoly effect and a strike-threat effect (amongst others).[2]

Reder's paper does not directly confront that question either, although it certainly moves us in the direction of an answer to it. In the empirical part of his study, he is concerned to test the hypothesis that the (potential) costs of taking a strike, in terms of disruption, contribute to the explanation of cross-industry differences in wages, independently of other factors, such as union density by industry—the standard explanatory variable in studies of the union-nonunion differential.[3] He finds the hypothesis to be corroborated, using U.S. cross-industry wage data. The coefficient on his strike costs

---

This paper was written while the author was a social science research fellow, sponsored by the Nuffield Foundation. The foundation's financial support is gratefully acknowledged, although, of course, the analysis is attributable to the author alone.

variable is found to be both of the expected positive sign and statistically significant on the standard criteria.

I will comment here only marginally on the empirical aspects of Reder's study, reserving more room for discussion of the framework of theory underlying it. First, this study represents the first-ever attempt to estimate empirically the independent contribution of strike-threat power to the explanation of interindustry wage differences, and is to be applauded on these grounds. Second, and because of this (as yet) solitary status of Reder's study, its empirical results must be accepted with due reserve. There is, as the author suggests, clearly much room for experimentation with the specification of his estimating equation and the variables therein.

Reder builds on a framework of analysis developed jointly with Neumann (1980). Although complex when fully elaborated, the basics of the model may be presented very simply.

Reder assumes a scenario of long-run equilibrium, of full employment of all resources, and of competitive markets in nonlabor inputs. This assumption clears the deck, as it were, of certain (inessential) complications. The question to be answered is, What determines the wage level in a unionized firm, when strike disruption is possible? Reder's analysis suggests that it will be determined by the division of strike costs between the employer and the union; that is, the respective costs to each side of agreeing and not agreeing on a price for the delivery of unionized labor services.

Costs, by definition, are things to be avoided. Why do employers accept any such share of strike costs? Why don't they hire nonunion labor and avoid these costs? Reder's (brief) answer is that the "special legal and institutional position of labor unions" prevents this. It allows them to impose difficulties on substitution by employers—to attach a cost to the utilization of cheaper substitutes. Given this assumption, a union can impose a premium above the nonunion wage—a premium that the employer will be willing to pay in order to avoid strike costs. Unionization, in this view, thus represents a hazard, rather like the (British?) weather, that is one of the costly conditions of undertaking production in such environs.

In effect, in Reder's analysis, the employer acts as its customers' agent in limiting delivery delay. The premium that the employer is willing to pay will be limited by what its customers will accept. Union strike-threat power thus rests on a "pass-forward ability": the ability to extract increased payments from customers, via their potential for inflicting costs (delivery delays).

This brief resume of Reder's analysis sets the scene for some pertinent questions, and suggestions for development:

1. Ostensibly, the bargaining scenario in the Reder model is one played between unions and employers. However, as we have seen, this is but a veil

over the real game, which is one between the union and customers. The central question thus becomes why customers accept the situation. Why do they not turn to purchasing from nonunionized firms, who are not charging a premium for the avoidance of unwanted and union-imposed delivery delays? Reder especially notes that, if the latter occurs, then in the long run the union wage cannot exceed the nonunion wage.[4] The question remains: Why does this happen?

The implication is that union strike-threat power can persist in the long run only if the union has the ability to somehow prevent the consumers from turning to nonunion firms or to prevent emergence of the latter. A statutory monopoly granted by government to the current employer(s) would be one such device. Thus the strike-threat power of unions is ultimately founded on the ability of unions to obtain regulatory measures from government that inhibit or prevent consumer evasion of unionized production. The Reder analysis of strike costs ultimately leads to questions about the workings of the political market in regulation, and the influences of unions therein.

2. Reder's analysis assumes a world of commercial, profit-maximizing enterprises. The analysis needs to be extended to cover other important categories of organizational environment, such as bureaucracies, regulated firms, and state-owned enterprises.

Taking the latter case, nationalized industry, as an example, some indication of the extra complications for the analysis are as follows. The constraint on the union wage premium is no longer determined simply by what customers are prepared to pay in order to avoid or reduce delivery delays. There is the possibility of financing higher wages out of government revenues, and of using the strike-threat to acquire these payments. The costs of avoiding delivery delays will in this case not be borne alone by the consumers of nationalized industry output, but shared with taxpayers, including inflation taxpayers (if money creation is resorted to by government) and future taxpayers (in the case of bond finance of nationalized industry losses).

Notes

1. They may also be able to raise wages via actions in the political market. For example, getting government to stipulate that firms supplying it must accept union rates.

2. There may also be, for example, productivity and political effects.

3. Union density might be taken as a crude proxy for union monopoly power.

4. In this case trade unions would survive only if their members had a taste for membership, or if they could utilize other means of generating a positive wage differential over non-union wages.

Reference

Reder, M. W., and Neumann G. R. 1980. "Conflict and Contract: The Case of Strikes." *Journal of Political Economy* 88, no. 5 (October): 867–886.

3 CYCLICAL STRIKE ACTIVITY AND MATURE COLLECTIVE BARGAINING: *Evidence from Canadian Data: 1960–1976*

George R. Neumann

Students of collective bargaining have long known that the cutting edge for testing theories about trade union behavior is strike activity. If strikes are costly events, a "datum" that seems universally accepted, systematic patterns in strike activity become a large stumbling block for explanations based on rational—i.e., joint maximizing—behavior on the part of workers and firms. All explanations of union strength that I am aware of rest ultimately on the withdrawal of labor services, including, as a special case, the oftentimes sub rosa threat of violence. To the extent that strikes remain incapable of explanation, the logical foundation for other aspects of union behavior—for example, wage differentials or turnover—is correspondingly weakened.

Empirical research on strike activity has not been lacking in the past two decades,[1] indeed it is fair to say that just about every possible measure of strike activity has been regressed upon a wide assortment of variables. What has been absent is a careful integration of strike activity findings with the underlying model of union-employer interaction. The most obvious example of this is the widely found correlation of strike activity with measures of business cycle activity. Rees (1952) provides an early example of this finding, and Ashenfelter and Johnson (1969), whose work has been replicated on several different countries, provides the most comprehensive statement. That strikes could be correlated with business activity seems at first glance an obvious proposition, regardless of what sign the correlation is alleged to be. Historical analysis rooted partially in Marxist thought would stress the militancy of unions, a response to the worsened living conditions of workers, as the cause of an increase in strike activity during a downturn.[2] Labor economists in more recent periods have argued that the cost of a strike varies countercyclically to labor and procyclically to employers.[3] The observed correlation in strike activity and business conditions is explained then solely by economic factors, namely, shifts in the costs of strike activity.

These explanations of strikes and business present a rather one-sided view of the collective bargaining process in that they ignore the fact that it takes two parties to disagree. In particular, employers having expectations about the future and acting in such a manner as to maximize the value of an ongoing concern should be willing to make unusual concessions during economic booms and demand unusual concessions during economic lulls. Unless there is some deeper aspect to the business cycle that manifests itself in economic conditions being buoyant in just those periods when bunches of contracts come up for renewal, there is little reason to expect strikes to be related to business cycles per se.[4]

Observed patterns of studies and business activity present a paradox for the conventional view of firms as efficient agents who form "rational" expectations and attempt to maximize intertemporal profits. There are two possible avenues to pursue in inquiring whether this paradox is real or only apparent. The first, and more difficult one, is to investigate models of contracting based on asymmetric information wherein the uncertainties that affect the bargaining process are specifically related to aggregate demand conditions. The second avenue, the one pursued in this chapter, is to examine how much of the observed correlation can be attributed to nonbusiness cycle related factors. For example, it is well known that business failures and, by extension, business starts are related to economic conditions. To the extent that bargaining behavior has a specific capital component, inexperienced bargaining pairs will be more likely to find themselves in a strike than others, and to the extent that the number of inexperienced bargaining pairs is related to the business cycle, there is potential for an explanation of cyclical effects that is consistent with maximizing behavior. In addition to providing information of patterns of strike activity, this avenue also provides evidence about an aspect of bargaining that has been hypothesized frequently: Does mature collective bargaining lead to fewer strikes? "Mature collective bargaining" can, of course, mean different things, including being defined by the absence of strikes, but as it is generally used, the meaning of maturity is that of length of time in the relationship, and that is a measureable item.

This chapter begins with a brief discussion of strike patterns and economic activity. The empirical model used in this study is then presented and the major findings are discussed. The chapter then closes with a summary of the results.

Empirical Issues in Strike Activity

Economists have examined strike activity in two different ways.[5] One approach has been to focus on interindustry differences in strike activity—presumptively due to differences in the cost of strikes across industries—with an attempt to relate these differences to a plethora of variables. Examples of this approach would be Canada (Maki and Strand, 1980); United Kingdom (Bean and Peel, 1974; Knowles, 1952; Shorey, 1976); United States (Reder and Neumann, 1980).[6]

Most of the cited studies offer only a vague theoretical justification for the empirical work performed, but they all can be interpreted as following from Hicks's (1963) observation that strikes are accidents: Where the costs of accidents are large, bargainers will proceed in a manner that makes strikes less likely. If one believes, as I do, that the regressors included in strike activity equations are reasonable proxies for the costs of a strike to one or both parties, then the empirical resuts do not offer evidence against the view of rational joint maximizing behavior.[7]

The alternative to disaggregated studies of aggregate relationships, possibly because of greater data availability, has been the most common. Early work by Griffen (1939) and Rees (1952) in the United States and Knowles (1952) in the United Kingdom sparked some interest in the pronounced relationship of strikes with the business cycle.[8] But the subsequent flood of empirical work was motivated primarily by publication of the justly celebrated Ashenfelter-Johnson paper in 1969, in which an economic finding without an explanation, and one of uncertain ancestry, was legitimized by an " . . . essentially political model of the function of a strike . . . " (Ashenfelter and Johnson, 1969, p. 37). Moreover, this marriage of theory and evidence has great hopes for posterity: Studies by Cousineau and Lacroix (1976), Smith (1972, 1976), and Walsh (1975) for Canada; by Pencavel (1970) and Sapford (1975) for the United Kingdom; and by Farber (1978) and Roomkin (1973) for the United States.[9]

Yet the very success of this political model of strike activity should make one pause, for it runs counter to the way one normally thinks about employer behavior. If workers' "demands" are temporarily high, due to a low level of unemployment, and if it pays the firm to reduce these demands by taking a strike, then it seems equally appealing that the firm would beat down workers' "demands" when unemployment is high. Absent some institutional arrangement such as a minimum wage law—a detail I find irrelevant at least for the Canadian and U.S. experience—it is difficult to see how an asymmetric response could occur. Since collective bargaining arrangements have a degree of (at least expected) permanence, this apparent lack of intertemporal profit maximizing seems odd.

Evidence is evidence, however, and the consistency of the findings both over time and across countries is compelling: There is a relationship between strikes and economic activity. The important question is, What is the source? As I indicated in the introduction, there are two possible explanations: (1) strikes occur when economic activity is high because uncertainty about the future state of events is high, and (2) strikes occur when economic activity is high because there are more inexperienced bargaining pairs in existence. The first explanation seems a promising route, but little has been done on this topic.[10] The second explanation is essentially an aggregation argument about the composition of bargaining pairs at various stages of the business cycle. This argument can be illustrated simply. Suppose there are two types of bargaining pairs, with associated probabilities of striking (by accident) of λ_1 and λ_2, with $\lambda_1 > \lambda_2$. Let $k_1(\mu)$ be the fraction of high strike probability pairs, and suppose that it depends positively on some index of economic activity, μ. Then, aggregate strike activity frequency is:

$$\bar{\lambda} = \lambda_1 \cdot k_1(\mu) + (1 - k_1(\mu)) \cdot \lambda_2, \tag{3.1}$$

and the effect of an increase in economic activity on strike frequency is:

$$\frac{\partial \lambda}{\partial \mu} = k_1'(\mu)\,(\lambda_1 - \lambda_2) > 0. \tag{3.2}$$

If there were a way of identifying this simple sort of heterogeneity, it would be straightforward to make adjustments. Obviously, many factors could affect the propensity for strikes to differ among bargaining pairs, and a complete analysis would take all such factors into account, but the predominant factor that has been cited is the length of time the parties have dealt with each other. For want of a better term, I will call this measure "maturity." The empirical question I wish to pose is: Can the observed cyclical pattern of strikes be explained by differences in the maturity of the bargainers? In the following section an empirical model that focuses on this question is presented and the data on which it is estimated is discussed.

Model, Data, and Results

Model

To say anything about maturity and strike activity, one must have data on the history of specific bargaining pairs, data that is all too often nonexistent. Even when such data are available, questions arise as to what is the appropriate measure of strike activity: frequency, length, number of workers involved, or perhaps some transformation of all three?[11] These questions are off the mark. What is important is whether a particular pair is in the strike state at any time. How long they last in that state, and whether they are more frequently in that state, or whether both elements are related to the size of the bargaining group depends upon a host of factors—perhaps all cost, perhaps not. In any event, the bargaining history of the pair describe completely these elements. Thus, a complete model of strike activity can be stated by specifying the stochastic process governing transitions between the strike state, S, and the nonstrike state, P.[12] Since strike status is a discrete event, regression analysis is not a very convenient, and often not correct, way to analyze longitudinal data such as bargaining histories. As an alternative, consider the following continuous time representation of strike activity.

Define B_k as the bargaining history of pair k as the set of dates at which a transition from state i to j occurred. Let $\lambda_{ij}(i, j = P, S)$ be the instantaneous hazard rate of transitions from state i to state j. Furthermore, assume that the state dependent hazard rates are functions of fixed, exogenous characteristics, X, and time-varying characteristics, $V(t)$. Then the distribution and density functions of a spell in state i that starts at time τ_0 and lasts t^* is:

$$F_i(t^* \mid t_0, X_1, P_{t_0}^{t_0+t^*} V(t)) = \exp\left(-\int_{t_0}^{t_0+t^*} \lambda(\tau)\, d\tau\right), \quad (3.3)$$

and,

$$f_i(t^* \mid t_0, X, P_{t_0}^{t_0+t^*} V(t)) = \lambda(t_0 + t^*) \exp\left(-\int_{t_0}^{t_0+t^\circ} \lambda(\tau)\, d\tau\right), \quad (3.4)$$

where $P_{t_0}^{t_0+*} V(t)$ is the sample path of the time varying variables, $V(t)$.

The likelihood function for a particular bargaining history B_k is given by:

$$L_k = \prod_{s \in B_k} {}^{f}S^{(.).(d(s))} . {}^{f}(P)^{(s)(1-d(s))}, \tag{3.5}$$

where $d(s)$ takes on the value 1 when a transition from state S to P occurs and 0 elsewise.

The likelihood function for a collection of K bargaining histories is similarly defined as:

$$L = \prod_{k=1}^{K} L_k. \tag{3.6}$$

With an appropriate, i.e., empirically tractable, specification of the hazard function, one can maximize (3.6) to obtain estimates of the parameters governing the transition process between strike and nonstrike activity.

One attractive specification is the proportional odds model of Cox (1972):[13]

$$\lambda(X, V(t)) = \exp(BX + \delta V(t)), \tag{3.7}$$

with the density function given as:

$$f_i(t^*) = \exp(BX + \delta V(t^*) \exp\left(- \int_0^{t^*} \exp(BX + \delta V(\tau))d\tau) \right) \tag{3.8}$$

Note that the explicit time dependence of the event probabilities requires a separate integration for each observation for each iteration of the maximum likelihood function estimator. It is somewhat of an understatement to remark that extensive exploration of nonstationary behavior in a nonparsimonious way can be can expensive. For this reason I have investigated only the most commonly shared sorts of nonstationarity—namely, variations in the business conditions, measured by unemployment rates, and in maturity, measured by length of bargaining relationship.[14]

Data

The foregoing model is, to my eye, a neat way of describing strike activity, particularly since it has commonalities with the analysis of unemployment, a closely related subject.[15] Unfortunately, a data set that will allow its application does not exist. In principle, the model described in equations

(3.2) through (3.8) requires the complete history of a bargaining pair, including its initial conditions. This is a particularly severe requirement, and I know of no data that can meet it. Indeed, in part, it has been the absence of such comprehensive data that has led to the concentration of attention on aggregate data by economists and, essentially, on case studies by non-economists. The data set that closest approaches those requirements is, to my knowledge, the Canadian Work Stoppage data tape.

Since 1960 this record contains:

1. The starting date of the strike;
2. The ending date of the strike;
3. The number of workers involved;
4. The three-digit (SIC) industry of the strike;
5. The union involved;
6. The firm's employer identification number.

Taken literally—which, with a few adjustments, I intend to do—this data source provides the only record of employer-union bargaining interaction that exists.[16] Because of the nature of this data set, it is useful to consider the problems that may arise in interpreting any empirical results.

The critical aspect of this data set is its ability to identify bargaining pairs over time. Compared to the alternatives (a null set), this ability is of overriding importance. Yet even in the Canadian data, the identification is not perfectly done. Employer identification numbers can change for a number of reasons, as can union identifiers. If such changes have occurred, has the bargaining unit changed? The answer is a question mark. Plants may merge, as may unions, either may die out, and both may be reborn in a different (numeric) reincarnation, and yet still have the same bargaining relationship. Little can be said about the possible biases that may result from this possibility of misidentification.

A further problem of these data is that they are conditioned on the occurrence of at least one strike. For example, a bargaining pair that did not experience any strikes during the period 1960–1976 would not be included. For this reason, the results reported herein should be interpreted as applying to bargaining pairs that strike. One consequence of the strike conditioning aspect of the data is that one cannot infer maturity with complete accuracy. Employer identification numbers are given starting in 1960, and it is possible, indeed likely, that some bargaining pairs were formed earlier. Moreover, nothing that can be done about this, so January 1960 was arbitrarily set as time zero, the earliest point that a bargaining pair could have formed. A particular bargaining pair's maturity is dated then from the first appearance in the sample. This again causes some difficulty since, other things the same, a pair that has a high strike probability is more likely to enter the sample earlier, and hence to have greater maturity, as I measure it. This will produce a downward bias in the effect of maturity in addition to that which would be generated by simple measurement error. How substantial is the effect of this bias is, of course, problematical. Since we know so little about experience effects on strike activity, there is no work to which these estimates can be compared. I am hopeful that this situation will be changed in the near future.

Empirical Results

The likelihood function defined in equation (3.6) was maximized using a Newton-Raphson procedure. There were 5.669 spells of strike activity, and spells of nonstrike activity. These spells were generated by distinct bargaining pairs. Table 3–1 contains the estimated parameters of the hazard function for entering strike activity—the counterpart of the strike frequency equations estimated on aggregate data—and table 3–2 contains the estimates of the hazard function for leaving strike activity—the counterpart of strike duration equations.

Both tables show evidence of substantial differences in strike frequency and in duration of a strike. All else the same, a bargaining pair in the mining industry has a monthly probability of striking that is twice as high as the other industries category.[17] However, the probability of exiting the strike is about 50 percent greater for a pair in the mining industry. This finding is indicative of a general feature of Canadian strike data: that those industries with a low frequency of strike activity tend to have long strikes. Indeed, the simple correlation of the industry coefficients in the duration equation with the coefficients in the strike frequency equation is .633, which would be judged statistically significant at greater than the 95 percent confidence level. This rather interesting result suggests that unidimensional views of strike activity, e.g., looking only at the number of strikes, can be misleading.[18]

Turning to the major issue, in both strike frequency and duration there is evidence of a beneficial effect of maturity on strike activity, although in the latter case, the effect is not very strong, judging both by statistical significance and by the effect on strike duration of the mean level of maturity. Apparently, the effect of whatever learning goes on between bargaining pairs is to reduce the likelihood of getting into a dispute, but once a strike occurs, it pretty much has a life of its own.

Table 3-1. Strike Frequency Hazard Rate*

Industry	*(1)*	*(2)*
Forestry	−3.1391	−3.1261
	(31.6)	(30.3)
Mining	−2.730	−2.4112
	(36.0)	(33.1)
Construction	−2.9165	−3.1021
	(38.4)	(34.2)
Transportation	−3.1498	−3.1496
	(36.1)	(35.4)
Trade	−3.3126	−3.3211
	(43.8)	(44.0)
Durable manufacturing	−2.9884	−2.6143
	(58.6)	(56.2)
Nondurable manufacturing	−3.1962	−3.1704
	(60.4)	(60.3)
Government	−2.9901	−2.9912
	(46.0)	(44.7)
Other	−3.3935	−3.3701
	(26.9)	(25.6)
Unemployment	−0.3302	−0.3641
	(34.2)	(35.1)
Maturity	−0.0022	—
	(7.8)	
In(L)	−29,157.3	−29,161.5

*Asymptotic *t*-ratios in parentheses.

Even with this effect of maturity, however, that cyclical effects are still present is clear. The allowance for maturity in table 3–1 reduces the effect of unemployment, but only by about 9 percent. Thus we are left with the result that even on micro data evidence exists that both the frequency of strikes and their duration respond to aggregate economic conditions.

Conclusion

The results presented here provide some evidence that the collective bargaining processes are affected by maturity, but whether this is the result of

Table 3-2. Strike Duration Hazard Rate*

Industry	*(1)*
Forestry	0.2969
	(2.0)
Mining	0.2538
	(3.3)
Construction	0.9730
	(9.2)
Transportation	−0.0389
	(0.6)
Trade	−0.1104
	(1.5)
Durable manufacturing	0.0701
	(1.3)
Nondurable manufacturing	0.0124
	(0.2)
Government	0.6867
	(6.2)
Other	−0.1767
	(1.8)
Unemployment	−0.0404
	(4.6)
Maturity	0.0004
	(1.2)
Number of workers on strike (000's)	0.0041
	(1.2)
In(L)	−6,006.8

*Asymptotic t-ratios in parentheses

greater learning or just the survivorship principle at work cannot be determined. Yet, while these effects are real, they only partially offset the influence of cyclical variations in economic activity, reducing the overall responsiveness by only about 9 percent. This rather modest change may be due to the fault of the measurement of maturity, but given the magnitude and rather precise determination of the cyclical effects, it seems overly hopeful to expect that better measures of bargaining experience would eliminate all of the cyclical movement. I believe that what is needed is a deeper understanding of strikes as information-revealing mechanisms in the presence of private information.

Notes

1. A complete review of the empirical literature on strike activity would entail a discussion, or at least a mention, of well over 100 articles, a task beyond the scope of this paper.

2. Union militancy may have nothing to do with this argument, for as Shorter and Tilly have documented, strikes occurred in France before, and independently of, unions. I use the term "union militancy" only as a shorthand expression for longer and more complex statements.

3. This argument is an old one in economics, yet I have not been able to find the originator. Ashenfleter and Johnson (1969) employ it, as does Chamberlain (1955),but it is surely older.

4. There are reasons why strike activity might appear to be related to business cycles, owing to greater uncertainty in the bargainers' information sets, but these arguments are essentially statements that strikes are correlated with errors, i.e., the relationship between, say, strike activity and unemployment is spurious, with unemployment acting as a proxy for the variance in expectations about the future.

5. I am ignoring here the substantial body of work by sociologists and historians on strike activity. This omission should not be construed as a comment on the merits of their works; rather, it is a statement about focus. Most work outside of economics has focused on the extremes of strike activity—long, bitter, often violent events—or on the unusual conditions that led to particular strikes. Since there does not appear to be an element of universality to these studies, I find it difficult to relate them to any consistent model or body of data.

6. There is a subgroup of studies that model the duration of time in a strike but, because of a lack of data on characteristics of strikes or firms, were constrained to model only the stochastic structure, as opposed to the systematic part, of strike length. See Kennan (1980) and Lancaster (1972); both of these studies have influenced my thoughts about empirical work on strike activity, as will be evident in the last section.

7. There is ample room for skepticism about the meaning, or even the propriety, of some of the regressors that have been used, but that is a different story, whose unravelling would take a chapter in itself.

8. I may be doing a disservice to earlier authors who noted correlation of strikes and economic activity, but in criss-crossing the literature of the '50s and '60s on strikes in Canada, the United States, or the United Kingdom these names are referenced most. I am indebted to Mel Reder for the Griffen reference.

9. Roomkin (1973) updates the Ashenfelter-Johnson model to 1973, but what was done is difficult to understand. In work on a related project, I have reestimated the Ashenfelter-Johnson model on data up to 1979, with the finding that essentially all the model's results held even with the addition of 50 quarters of exceptionally, relative to the U.S. historical experience, turbulent times. Moreover, and this is particularly surprising,the model exhibits a fair amount of predictive ability, conditional on the exogenous variables, outside the sample period, and does not show obvious signs of deterioration such as would be implied by Lucas's critique (1972) of econometric models in a rational expectations framework. In other words, the Ashenfelter-Johnson model is not just a concealed Phillips curve.

10. See, however,the interesting papers on asymmetric information by Azariadis (1980) and Phelps and Calvo (1977). Both papers deal with the problems of inference when one party to a contract has private information about the state of the world.

11. Arguments as to the "appropriate" unit of measurement of strike activity can be found in several places, e.g., Vanderkamp (1970) and Smith (1972). These arguments are motivated primarily by regression analysis of aggregate data, and they have no particular relevance to its issue of what is strike activity.

12. This statement should alert the reader to the fact that I will henceforth be treating collective bargaining as an absorbing state—one is either at war or at peace—there is no limbo such as withdrawing from bargaining. Obviously this is counterfactual: How serious a problem it occasions is speculative. In any event, it is necessitated by the data.

13. Lancaster (1972) provides an early example of the use of this statistical model to strike activity.

14. The easiest form of nonstationarity to handle is a deterministic pattern. For example, if a trend term were added to the constant part of this hazard note, the density would be:

$$f_i(t^*) = \exp(BX + \delta t^*) \cdot \exp(-\exp(BX)) \cdot (\exp(\delta t^*) - 1)\delta^{-1}).$$

Extensions to higher-order approximations are immediate. Where the time variations are completely idiosyncratic—for example, length of union or management leader's tenure as bargaining agent—the costs of estimation become enormous. In this chapter, I have restricted the range of nonstationaryity to those costs that have a common origin—i.e., the integration can be done by a simple table look-up.

15. See Keifer and Neumann (1981) for an application of the state space approach to unemployment.

16. John Kennan has informed me that the same information is available for the United States but even that a Freedom of Information Act suit has been unsuccessful in making the data available.

17. The monthly probability of striking for industry I is $\lambda_I = \exp(B_I + B \cdot V)$, where V is the set of time varying factors. This ratio of monthly probabilities between industries is then:

$$\frac{\lambda_I}{\lambda_J} = \exp(B_i - B_J).$$

Comparison of the mining and other industries yields:

$$\exp(-2.73 + 3.3935) = 1.942.$$

18. This point was made early on by Vanderkamp (1970), but seems to have been ignored in the economic literature on strikes. Reder and Neumann (1980) investigate various dimensions of strike activity but no precise interaction is posited or examined.

References

Ashenfelter, O., and Johnson, G. E. 1969. "Bargaining Theory, Trade Unions, and Industrial Strike Activity." *American Economic Review*, 59, no. 1 (March): 35–49.

Azairiadis, C. 1980. "Employment with Asymmetric Information." CARESS Working Paper #80–22.

Bean, R., and Peel, D. A. 1974. "A Quantitative Analysis of Wage Strikes in Four U.K. Industries, 1962–1970." *Journal of Economic Studies* 1, no. 2:88–97.

Cousineau, J. M., and Lacroix, R. 1976. "Activité économique, Inflation et activité de grève." *Relations Industrielles* 31; no. 3:341–358.

Cox, D. R. 1972. "Regression Models and Life Tables." *Journal of the Royal Statistical Society*, Series B., vol. 34:187–220.

Farber, H. 1978. "Bargaining Theory, Wage Outcomes, and the Occurrence of Strikes: An Econometric Analysis." *American Economic Review* 68, no. 3: 262–271.

Griffen, J. I. 1939. *Strikes*. New York: Columbia University Press.

Hicks, J. R. 1963. *The Theory of Wages*, 2nd ed. New York: MacMillan.

Kalbfleisch, J. D., and Prentice, R. L. 1980. *The Statistical Analysis of Failure Time Data*. New York: John Wiley.

Kennan, J. 1980. "Pareto Optimality and the Economics of Strike Duration." *Journal of Labor Research* 1 (Spring):77–94.

Kiefer, N. M., and Neumann, G. R. 1981. "Wages and the Structure of Unemployment Rates: Evidence on the Bailey-Tobin Proposal." In *Labor Market Tightness and Inflation*, ed. Martin N. Bailey. Washington, D.C.: Brookings Institution.

Knowles, G. J. C. 1952. *Strikes: A Study in Industrial Conflict*. Oxford: Basil Blackwood.

Lancaster, T. 1972. "A Stochastic Model for the Duration of a Strike." *Journal of of the Royal Statistical Society*, 135, Series A:259–271.

Lucas, R. E., Jr. 1972. "Econometric Testing of the Natural Rate Hypothesis." In *The Econometrics of Price Determination*. Washington, D.C.: Board of Governors of the Federal Reserve System, pp. 50–59.

Maki, D. R., and Strand, K. 1980. "The Determinants of Strike Activity: An Inter-Industry Analysis." Mimeo, *Simon Fraser University*.

Pencavel, J. 1960. "An Investigation into Industrial Strike Activity in Britain." *Economica*, n.s., vol. 37, no. 147 (August):239–256.

Phelps, E. S., and Calvo, G. 1977. "Indexation Issues." In *Stabilization of the Domestic and International Economy*, ed. Brunner and Meltzer. Amsterdam: North-Holland.

Purdy, D. L., and Zis, G. 1974. "On the Concept and Measurement of Union Militancy." In *Inflation and Labor Markets*, ed. D. Laidler and D. L. Purdy. Toronto: University of Toronto Press, pp. 38–60.

Reder, M., and Neumann, G. R. 1980. "Conflict and Contract: The Case of Strikes." *Journal of Political Economy* 88, no. 5 (October).

Rees, A. 1952. "Industrial Conflict and Business Fluctuations." *Journal of Political Economy* 60, no. 3 (October):337–382.

Roomkin, M. 1973. "The Ashenfelder-Johnson Model of Strike Activity: Update and Extensions." Mimeo, University of Chicago Labor Workshop Paper.

Sapford, J. 1975. "A Time Series Analysis of U.K. Industrial Disputes." *Industrial Relations* 14, no. 2:242–249.

Shorey, J. 1971. "Interindustry Differences in Strike Activity." *Economica* 43 (November):103–109.

Skeels, J. W. 1971. "Measures of U.S. Strike Activity." *Industrial and Labor Relations Review* 24 (July):515–525.

Smith, D. A. 1972. "The Determinants of Strike Activity in Canada." *Relations Industrielles* 27, no. 4:663–678.

______. 1976. "The Impact of Inflation on Strike Activity in Canada." *Relations Industrielles* 31, no. 1:139–145.

Vanderkamp, J. 1970. "Economic Activity and Strikes in Canada." *Industrial Relations* 9, no. 1 (February):215–230.

Walsh, W. D. 1975. "Economic Conditions and Strike Activity in Canada." *Industrial Relations* 14, no. 1 (February):45–54.

Weintraub, A. R. 1966. "Prosperity vs. Strikes: An Empirical Approach." *Industrial and Labor Relations Review* 19 (January):231–238.

Comment on Neumann, by Göran Skogh

In section I, I briefly comment on Neumann's maturity theory of strikes and on his empirical results and in section II I give an accident- or maturity-theoretical explanation of the cyclical variation in strikes. Section 3 points out the similarities between the exit-voice and the maturity theory of strikes. I will extend my comment, in section 4, to include some comparisons between the North American and the Swedish collective bargaining systems. At an international conference like this, it is important to bear in mind that we may think of quite different systems when talking about labor unions. Moreover, the Swedish experience supports Neumann's maturity theory. The final section is a short summary.

Section I

Empirical studies following the work by Ashenfelter and Johnson (1969) show fewer strikes when unemployment is high. The common explanation of this phenomenon is that the cost of strikes varies countercyclically for labor and procyclically for employers. Neumann argues, however, that this is a one-sided view of the collective bargaining process, that there are always two parties in a conflict, where the strikes may well be caused by either side. Employers may very well bring about strikes by not accepting the demands of the workers. Thus, Neumann finds no obvious reason why strikes should be related to the business cycle per se.

Instead Neumann advocates an information-accident theory of strikes. In this theory strikes are costly mistakes in the negotiation process that would not occur if the negotiating parties knew fully equilibrium wages or the bargaining strenth of the counterparty. The number of strikes, or mistakes, depends therefore on the experience and competence of the negotiating pairs.

Using Canadian data, Neumann tests the hypothesis that maturity (measured by length of the bargaining relationship) decreases the number of strikes. He estimates the maximum likelihood of strikes, given industry characteristics, unemployment, and maturity. The result gives evidence for the hypothesis that longer bargaining relationships reduce the number of strikes. Maturity has, however, no significant effect on the length of the strikes.

So far, the maturity theory of strikes appeals to me, but I become sceptical when Neumann argues that the observed cyclical variation in strikes can be explained by cyclical variations in the maturity of the bargaining pairs. His argument is that during increasing economic activity new firms start and inexperienced negotiating pairs appear, thus increasing the probability of strikes. To test for this business-cycle effect on maturity, Neumann compares maximum likelihood estimates in which maturity is included and then excluded as an explanatory variable. Including the maturity variable decreases the impact of unemployment on strike frequency, but only by 10 percent. Thus, the cyclical variation in strike activity is hardly explained by the maturity theory. One reason is, I believe, that Neumann overemphasizes the incompetence of the bargaining pairs that emerge in booms. New firms are either small with relatively good information channels between workers and employers or result from mergers. In the merger case, both employers and unions have previous negotiating experience.

Section II

The theory that the more inexperienced bargaining pairs in existence during booms result in more strikes seems of limited value, both from a theoretical point of view and from Neumann's own empirical results. How then can we explain the cyclical variation in strikes with the accident theory? Neumann mentions that strikes may occur when economic activity is high because uncertainty about the future is high. He presents, however, no explanation of why uncertainty should be more important when unemployment is relatively low, except for the hypothesis on the maturity of bargaining pairs. I think, however, that there is a straightforward explanation of why uncertainty is higher in booms than in recessions, given the maturity of the bargainers. In the theories of strikes as accidents in the negotiating process, the number of strikes depends on the bargainers' information. As long as the negotiation concerns minor and relatively frequent changes in wages, layoffs, non-pecuniary benefits, etc., both parties at the negotiation table will be fairly well informed about the strategies used by the counterparty as well as about the range of realistic changes. In a boom with a large increase in the derived demand for labor and a general increase in prices, uncertainty would be relatively great and, consequently, the risk of strikes is high. The same would be true in depressions such as in the 1930s with large declines in demand for labor, many layoffs, and deflation. Note, however, that the low incidence of strike in periods of unemployment relates to recession periods during the postwar years. These recessions are characterized by relatively small price increases, slowdown in economic growth, and decreased mobility in the labor market. Hence, the possible changes are small and the information seems to be better for both parties as compared to booms and deep depressions.

Section III

One branch of the economic literature on collective bargaining and trade unions assumes that the union is a rent-seeking cartel. Another branch argues that important economies of scale may exist in the bargaining process, as well as in the enforcement of collective or individual agreements. Experience in bargaining, knowledge of implicit contract, information on the firm's derived demand for labor, as well as the employer's negotiating strategy, seem to include fixed costs. Neumann's paper belongs to the second branch. The exit-voice theory of strike is of the same type, in which the union reduces the numbers of quits by being a representative voice for the workers. Freeman's study (1980) gives evidence of fewer exits in firms with unionized workers. It is interesting to note the similarities between the maturity and exit-voice theories. The first reaction by unsatisfied workers is not necessarily to quit, but perhaps to stop work or to strike. Moreover, strikes may take place when there is no union. Or, if the union is not representative of the workers, the strike may be wildcat or voted for in opposition to the union leaders. In this case, the strike is primarily a result of dissatisfaction with the union. Hence, a strike-voice approach gives additional arguments as to why competent leadership in the unions results in fewer strikes.

Section IV

It is interesting to compare the North American experience of labor market negotiations with the Swedish system. A study such as Neumann's could hardly be undertaken in Sweden. The reason is that practically all workers are organized in unions, which are affiliated with the same confederation (LO). At least since the 1950s, power has been centralized in the confederation, and the unions would hardly start a strike without consulting LO. Independent firms usually follow the agreements made by LO and SAF. Negotiating experience is thus well established. The maturity of the bargainers is also the most common explanation of why numbers of strikes or manhours spoiled by strikes in Sweden are low by international standards.

Note that since it was founded in 1902, SAF has been an instigator of collective agreements. It started as an insurance pool to protect member firms from losses due to lockouts and strikes. To control the moral hazard problem within the pool, SAF was, by its constitution, given considerable power over its members. That is, separate firms had no right to settle collective agreements themselves and were not allowed to start lockouts without permission from SAF. Many employers disliked the centralized power in SAF. They submitted to the rules, however, to obtain protection in conflicts with workers. After the accession of the Metal Trades Employers Association in 1917, SAF had gained control of the most important areas of the Swedish industry. As an insurer of the separate firms, SAF wanted to end all small conflicts around the country. Many employers also argued that collective agreements should be made with the unions and that the agreements should include labor discipline, the obligation to preserve industrial peace, negotiations procedures, etc. In 1909, 15 unions had made agreements on a national basis with the separate employers' associations.

LO, on the other hand, did not have the same power to enforce central agreements as SAF. To increase obedience to the agreements that LO had achieved, SAF supported a centralization of power within the former organization. SAF also supported the reorganization of the labor unions according to the industry principle.

Since the 1950s bargaining between LO and SAF has started at the national level. The two sides present their view of the expected economic future and their claims; if they fail to reach an agreement, the government appoints an official mediator. Unions' and employers' associations negotiate on the implementation of the central agreement and on the wages that should apply within the limits already imposed by the central agreement. When these negotiations are completed, negotiations on the details of wages and fringe benefits are taken over at the company level.

After a long period of negotiation during the recession year 1966, a commission was set up composed of the leaders of the research branches of SAF, LO, and the Central Organization of Salaried Employers (TCO, founded in 1944). The objective was to reach a common view of the economic constraints of the economy and to reduce negotiation time. Inflationary wage increases would also result in governmental intervention in the bargaining procedure. The commission presented a model, accepted by both parties, of the relationship among terms of trade, productivity changes in the export-orientated private sector, and productivity changes in the protected domestic sector.

During the postwar period, up until the beginning of the 1970s, there was peace in the labor market, which may be explained by the centralized and strictly organized negotiating procedure. Note that the labor confederation which covers the whole of the private export-orientated sector has become more interested in productivity-increasing activities, which make general wage increases possible, rather than in rent seeking. One reason is that it is hard to gain monopoly rents on the competitive international market. Acceptance of monopoly wages by strong unions does not increase efficiency in the economy and may result in conflicts between different unions. These two points may explain why LO demanded high wage increases in branches with low wages. The expressed policy was to promote structural change to increase general productivity by accepting bankruptcy in firms that could not pay.

In the 1970s the situation in the Swedish labor market changed considerably, and strikes became more frequent. One contributing factor was the 1965 legislation that granted public workers the same right to strike as workers in the private sector. In 1966 upper-level primary school teachers started a strike after a lockout by the governmental negotiation body; around thirty thousand employees were involved in the four-week conflict. Despite its limited dimensions, it was the most extensive labor conflict since 1945. Today, most Swedes would agree that this strike was due to the inexperience of the bargainers. By including the whole public sector in the bargaining system, the outcome of the negotiations has direct macroeconomic consequences. Thus, the bargainers in the private sector have to consider not only the strategy of the counterparty, but also the strategies and the outcome in the public sector as well as the economic-political measures taken by the government. This intricate strategy has complicated the negotiations and presumably contributed to the large conflict in 1980, in which eight hundred thousand workers were involved. In 1981 LO and SAF rapidly came to an agreement, arguing that they wanted to avoid the confrontation of 1980.

Section V

My main conclusion is that Neumann's learning-by-doing approach is interesting and the test of maturity on strikes a good starting point. The Swedish experience of collective bargaining also supports the idea that strikes are failures in the bargaining process. One problem with the accident approach, however, is that it leaves us without any deeper understanding of why strikes actually occur. To learn more about strikes, we need information on the bargaining process, including the strategies and threats chosen by the bargaining pairs. Game and bargaining theory is, however, not of much help since it gives no simple solutions to labor conflicts.

References

Ashenfelter, O., and Johnson, G. E. 1969. "Bargaining Theory, Trade Unions, and Industrial Strike Activity." *American Economic Review* 59 (March):35–49.

Freeman, R. B. 1980. "The Exit-Voice Tradeoff in the Labor Market: Unionism, Job Tenure, Quits and Separations." *Quarterly Journal of Economics* 94 (June): 643–673.

4 THE RELATIVE WAGE EFFECT OF FRENCH UNIONS

Jean-François Hennart

Have labor unions succeeded in raising the wages of their members above those of nonunion labor? A considerable number of studies have sought to answer that question. American and British economists have used a variety of methods and data bases to obtain precise estimates of the impact of unions on relative wages. In the United States, single-equation models arrive at a differential of 10 percent (Schmidt and Strauss, 1976) to 40 percent (Ashenfelter and Johnson, 1972). There are fewer empirical studies on British data, and they estimate a differential that ranges from 10 percent (Pencavel, 1974) to 25 percent (Mulvey, 1976).

There have been even fewer empirical studies of the relative impact of French unions on wages. Bonety (1961) looked at collective bargaining in the iron and steel sector and concluded that unions had no effect on wages.

The author gratefully acknowledges comments by Jean-Jacques Rosa and by the staff of the Fondation Nationale d'Economie Politique. Jacques Généreux and Frédéric Jenny provided some of the statistical sources, and Michel Picot helped with the programming. As specific acknowledgments show, I am especially indebted to Bernard Lentz for many insights, and for a considerable number of helpful comments and criticisms. I wish also to thank Jacqueline Frisch, of the Centre d'Etudes Sociologiques, for letting me use some of the data of the 1970 FQP survey tape.

Parodi (1963) compared negotiated wage minima and effective wages in the building trades of the Marseille region. He observed actual wages to be much higher than minima and concluded that collective bargaining had no impact on wage determination. Frederick Myers (1965) compared wage minima, as determined by collective bargaining, to average wages paid in seven industries in the Paris region. Myers found that average wages for a given occupation were higher than negotiated minima in six out of seven industries and concluded that French unions do not seem to exert any impact on wages, at least in the Paris region.[1]

Frederic Jenny and André-Paul Weber (1975) have conducted the only systematic study, beside the present one, of the impact of French unions on wages. Jenny and Weber tested the proposition that concentrated industries pay higher wages than do competitive industries. They regressed average wage rates in each industry on the labor characteristics of that sector (percentage male, percentage of managers and administrators, etc.), on a proxy for unionization in the sector, and on the sector's concentration ratio. Jenny and Weber also regressed individual wages on educational level; professional experience; sex; the size of the city of residence; and the concentration ratio, the capital intensity, and the level of unionization of the sector where the individual is employed. The authors found that human capital variables were significant determinants of the wage, but that it was difficult to separate the influence of unionization on wages from that of concentration, for both variables were highly correlated. They therefore partitioned the industries in two groups according to their level of concentration and unionization. They found that unions had a very small (.007 percent) but significant impact on wages in industries with low concentration ratios, but no impact in highly concentrated industries. Jenny and Weber explain their findings by the fact that managers of highly concentrated industries share their rents with their employees, either because of the high level of unionization or in order to forestall the development of unionism in their enterprise. This factor tends to reduce wage differences between union and nonunion firms in oligopolistic industries. In more competitive sectors, on the other hand, unionization brings higher wages.

Jenny and Weber's specification can be criticized for its inclusion of a concentration variable in the wage equation. For, as Jensen and Meckling (1976) have shown, competition in the product market has no influence on the ability of managers to indulge in managerial discretion. Managers of oligopolistic industries are thus no more likely to increase wages at the expense of stockholders than their counterparts in more competitive industries. The probability that unions will obtain wage increases, however, is higher in concentrated industries, and we would therefore expect concentration to be a determinant of unionization.

Every one of the empirical studies we have just discussed treats unionization as exogenous. It can be argued, however, that unionism is not truly exogenous, and that union density is itself a function of the wage rate in that industry. Unions present themselves as organizations that seek to better the welfare of the workingperson, mainly by increasing wages. The decision to join the union, or to vote for unions in elections, should hence depend on the union record on that score, and we would expect to find a positive relationship between union density and the level of relative wages. Note that this relationship can hold even if wage increases won by unions are not caused by union pressure, but correspond to increases in the level of effort or in the qualification of the work force. To neglect consideration of the unionization variable as endogenous will lead to a simultaneity bias and to the tendency to overestimate the union coefficient.

Besides unionization, the average level of labor quality and the industry's capital-labor ratio should also be considered endogenous, because employers can respond to union-won wage premiums by raising hiring standards and by substituting capital for labor. An employer can recoup union wage increases in two main ways: (1) The wage premium won by the union will incite candidates to queue to obtain employment in the firm, which can therefore pick more highly skilled workers to replace the present work force. This capability depends on turnover within the firm and on the ease with which employers can be fired. (2) Employers can also reduce the impact of wage increases by substituting capital for labor. A correct specification should therefore consider the average level of labor quality and the industry's capital labor ratio as endogenous.

The Model

The model is broadly similar to that of Ashenfelter and Johnson (1972) and consists of four equations that are simultaneously determined. One major difference is that the technique of production, as described by the capital-labor ratio, is considered endogenous.

The four equations are:

$$\begin{aligned} \text{LNHW}_i = a_0 + a_1\,\text{SYN}_i + a_2\,\text{AE}_i + a_3 \\ \text{AEX}_i + a_4\,\text{HOM}_i + a_5\,\text{KL}_i + a_6\,\text{LIC}_i + e_1; \end{aligned} \qquad (4.1)$$

$$\text{SYN}_i = b_0 + b_1 \text{ WVA}_i + b_2 \text{ DKL}_i + b_3 \text{ LNHW}_i + b_4 \text{ HOM}_i + b_5 \text{ CON}_i + e_2; \quad (4.2)$$

$$\text{AE}_i = c_0 + c_1 \text{ URB}_i + c_2 \text{ SYN}_i + e_3; \quad (4.3)$$

$$\text{KL}_i = d_0 + d_1 \text{ SYN}_i + d_2 \text{ STAB}_i + e_4. \quad (4.4)$$

Where for each industry i:

LNHW_i = logarithm of the average hourly wage in 1969;
SYN_i = percentage of an industry's total labor force voting for a union candidate at the comité d' entreprise elections of 1969–70;
AE_i = average number of years of schooling for all employees in 1969;
AEX_i = average number of years of experience for all employees in 1969;
DKL_i = increase in capital per head between 1959 and 1974;
WVA_i = share of labor in value added;
KL_i = assets per employee in 1969 (in thousand francs);
HOM_i = percentage of male employees in the labor force in 1969;
LIC_i = average annual number of layoffs (1970–1975) per thousand 1970 employees;
CON_i = four-firm concentration ratio in 1969;
URB_i = percentage of employees living in urbanized areas in 1969;
STAB_i = ratio of total number of employees hired in 1969 to December 31 employment.

Equation (4.1) is a standard wage equation in which the logarithm of an industry's hourly wage depends on characteristics of the employees (their schooling, AE; their experience, AEX; percentage of men, HOM), characteristics of the industry (capital-labor ratio, KL; and instability of employment, LIC), and on the union variable (SYN). The effect of unions on relative wages is given by $\exp(\hat{a}_1) - 1$.

Equation (4.2) is a reduced form of the supply and demand of union services. The demand for union services is a function of the value of unionism to the worker (W), the price (D) of unionism (the level of dues), the worker's income (Y), the worker's taste for unionism (T):

$$U_D = U_D(W, D, Y, T).$$

The supply of unionism is a function of the price of union membership, D; the cost of providing services, C; and the employer's taste for unionism, Z:

$$U_S = U_S(D, C, Z).$$

Under equilibrium conditions, $U_D = U_S = U$ and the model can be written as:

$$U = U_D(W, D, Y, T);$$

$$U = U_S(D, C, Z).$$

Solving for the equilibrium values of D° and U° yields the reduced form:

$$U = U(W, Y, T, C, Z).$$

Let us look at all these variables in turn.

To a typical worker, the value of unionism consists in the potential relative wage advantage brought by unions and in the provision of private union services such as grievances or job security. In France most private job-related services, which in the United States are supplied by unions to their members, are provided by the state to everyone. To obtain a relative wage advantage is therefore the main reason to join or to vote for a union in France.

The ability of a union to obtain durable wage increases is itself a function of the elasticity of the demand for labor. That elasticity depends on the four Marshallian rules—viz, (1) the relative share of labor in production costs, (2) the ease of substitution between labor and capital, (3) the elasticity of supply of cooperant factors, and (4) the elasticity of final demand for the product.

To measure the share of labor in total production cost, I have chosen the share of wages and social security contributions in total value added (WVA). I expect this variable to enter the union equation with a negative sign. Finding variables that describe the ease of substituting other factors for union labor is difficult. The only way to ascertain the possibility of substitution is to look *ex post* at the substitutions that have taken place. I have therefore chosen as proxy for this Marshallian condition the rate of growth of capital per worker between 1959 and 1974 (DKL). This variable should be negatively correlated with our unionization variable.

Lastly, the elasticity of final demand for the product can be proxied by the industry's four-firm concentration ratio (CON), since the elasticity of demand depends on the availability of substitutes. The higher concentration is, the higher unionization, *ceteris paribus*.

The rate of unionization should also be a function of the level of sectoral wages, LNHW, because (1) the demand for unionism should vary with income and (2) because workers are likely to attribute their wage gains to union pressure. The prestige of unions, and therefore their ability to obtain votes and members should be greater, *ceteris paribus*, the higher the industry's wage rate.

Among the determinants of the workers' taste for unionization, the size of the establishment may be the most important. It can be argued that in large firms, direct contact between boss and employee becomes difficult. Unions play the role of go-between, and substitute in part for a personnel department (Freeman and Medoff, 1979). I would therefore expect the demand for unionism to vary positively with the average size of the firm in the sector.[2] As a proxy for the size of establishment, I use the concentration ratio (CON).[3]

Turning now to the determinants of the supply of union services, it is reasonable to expect the cost of providing these services to vary inversely with the average number of employees per establishment (proxied by CON). Organizing is more costly in small, geographically dispersed establishments (Pencavel, 1971). Large establishments have lower turnover rates, which means that the union does not have continually to recruit new members (Barbash, 1956).

Among the determinants of unionization, I also include the percentage of men in the work force. Many authors in the United States and in Europe (Moore and Newman, 1975; Bain and Elsheik, 1979) have advanced that the percentage of men among an industry's labor force (HOM) affects SYN negatively since women tend to be less attached to the labor market and have higher turnover rates.

According to Richard Lester (1941), employees' taste for unionism is likely to vary across industries. He points out that employers in industries in which labor constitutes a high proportion of total cost may be less opposed to unions than their counterparts in more capital-intensive sectors. Labor-intensive industries are characterized by low barriers to entry. Unions can be of considerable benefit to employees in such industries because they can reduce competition by equalizing cost conditions (Bain and Elsheik, 1979). WVA should therefore be positively correlated with unionism.

The third equation attempts to explain average labor quality (as measured by schooling, AE) in the industry. Ashenfelter and Johnson (1972) have shown that the optimal level of labor quality is achieved when a proportionate increase in the productive efficiency of labor with respect to labor quality is equal to the proportionate increase in wages that results from an increase in labor quality. The influence of labor quality on efficiency is therefore likely to depend on the characteristics of the firm's production function. The more complex the tasks and the greater the need for decision making on the part of the employee, the higher the marginal contribution of labor quality to efficiency.

How do we empirically measure a sector's need for high-quality labor? Ashenfelter and Johnson (1972) use the percentage of each industry's employees living in urbanized areas. They argue that city dwellers are generally more highly schooled than people who live in rural areas, because better educated people have a higher taste for urban life and therefore seek opportunities for education that are more available in urban areas. Thus, firms that can use qualified manpower productively will settle in urbanized areas, where the price of highly educated labor is lower than in the countryside. I have therefore used the percentage of each industry's work force living in urbanized areas (URB) as an ex-post proxy for the factors that determine the profitability of increasing labor quality.

As Kalachek and Raines (1980) have shown, employers in the United States "respond to wage premiums by raising the educational component of hiring standards." Union density (SYN) should therefore be positively correlated with the average educational level of the labor force.

In the last equation, the industry's capital-labor ratio is explained by union-density, SYN, and by seasonal instability in the industry, STAB. Union density, through its effect on wage premiums should lead the firm to substitute capital for labor, and therefore union firms should have a higher capital-labor ratio, *ceteris paribus*, than do nonunion firms. Another major influence on the firm's choice of capital-labor intensity is the stability of the firm's final demand. Since capital is generally more of a fixed factor than is labor, seasonal industries will have a lower capital-labor ratio than industries in which demand is more stable. I proxy the instability of demand by the ratio of employment on December 31, 1969, to the total number of employees hired in 1969 (STAB).[4]

The Data

The model was tested on 39 goods-producing industries. Mining and tobacco and match manufacture were excluded, the former because of the unreliability of unionism data, and the latter because it is a state monopoly and its employees then had civil service status. Sectors 33 and 34, 47 and 48, and 56 to 61 were consolidated. A complete description of the variables and of the statistical sources is given in the appendix to this chapter. It may be useful, however, to discuss here our measure of union bargaining power.

No data exist in France on union membership at the national or at the industry level, as well as no data on collective bargaining coverage. One possible proxy, used by Jenny and Weber (1975), can be built with the results of the elections to the "comités d'entreprise." These committees are composed of members elected for two years from those plants with more than 50 employees; only candidates from the four representative labor confederations can run for these elections. If less than 50 percent of the workers cast valid ballots, the election is held again, and lists of nonunion candidates can then be put on the ballot. Seats are attributed in proportion to the number of votes received. Comités d'entreprise manage social activities, which are financed from mandatory contributions by the employers, and also must be consulted on proposed changes in working hours, holidays, and on any change in the organization of work. Comités have access to all of the firm's accounting documents, but they play no role in wage negotiation.

My unionization variable, SYN, is the ratio of total votes cast for union candidates in each industry to total industry employment. Jenny and Weber have used a different variable since they have taken the ratio of union votes to registered voters. Jenny and Weber's variable fails to reflect union bargaining power for two main reasons. According to the law, comités d'entreprise must be created in establishments of more than 50 employees. In fact, more than half of these establishments did not have comités in 1970–71. Thus, since a mere complaint by one of the firm's employees to the labor inspector usually results in the setting up of a comité, the absence of a comité in an establishment subject to the law indicates the absence of union influence. Moreover, French labor legislation grants to unions a certain number of benefits, such as employer-paid time allowances and office space for union delegates, which must be provided in establishments with over 50 workers. Consequently, union penetration is much lower in firms with less than 50 employees than in large establishments.

By dividing union votes by total employment in the industry, I am taking these two factors into account.[5] I believe that this variable is a good proxy for trade union bargaining power since it reflects the strength of union organization and, where unions are organized, the size of their following. Most union experts believe that union members or sympathizers follow union directives and vote for union sponsored candidates. Furthermore, both unions and management consider the results of Comité d'Entreprise elections as representative of relative levels and trends of unionization at the firm and at the industry level.

Empirical Results

Each equation was first estimated by weighted ordinary least squares. Then the complete model was estimated by weighted two-stage least squares. The weights used were industry employment. The results of equations (4.1a) to (4.4a) using ordinary least squares are presented in table 4–1.

The first equation explains more than 80 percent of the interindustry variation in wage rates. All coefficients have the expected sign. The coefficients of education and experience are significant at the 99 percent confidence level. All other variables are not significant at the 90 percent confidence level. The coefficient of the union variable is large, implying a relative wage impact of about 20 percent, but it is not significantly different from zero at a 90 percent level of confidence. The coefficient of the education variable implies an average rate of return on schooling of approximately 25 percent. This figure is somewhat higher than that found by Riboud (1978), but the difference can be accounted for by differences in the sample. Our sample is limited to wage earners in industry, who have a lower level of schooling than average, and who should therefore receive a higher rate of return (Riboud, 1978, p. 138). She excludes women but includes civil servants, who, in France, seem to receive lower pecuniary returns on their human capital (Riboud, 1978, p. 153), and self-employed individuals, who take some of their return in the form of leisure.

The rate of return on an additional year of experience, AEX, is similar to that found by Riboud. Equation (4.1a) also suggests no significant differences between male and female wages when differences in the level of schooling and experience are taken into account, a conclusion also reached by Riboud (1979) from regressions on individual data. Lastly, KL and LIC have both the expected sign but are not statistically significant.

In equation (4.2a), the wage rate, LNHW, and industry concentration have both a positive and significant impact on unionization. The coefficient of DKL, the long-term increase in the capital-labor ratio, is negative, as expected, and significant at the 90 percent level of confidence. The proportion-male variable, HOM, has a very small negative coefficient (significant at the 90 percent level of confidence).[6] The size of the coefficient suggests no sex-based differences in the propensity to vote for union candidates, not a surprising finding given the nature of our union variable. The lower propensity of women to join unions can be explained, in the U.S. or British context, by a lower benefit-cost ratio; women have to pay the same dues (and the same cost in foregone wages during strikes) as do men but can expect a lower discounted return to such investment, because their tenure in the firm or in the industry is usually shorter. The cost of casting a ballot in a comité d'entreprise election is, however, negligible, as elections are held during working hours and on company premises. We would therefore expect no major sex differences in our SYN variable.[7]

The sign of the WVA variable reflects two offsetting effects. Unionization should be a positive function of labor's share in value added because

Table 4-1. Ordinary Least Squares

Equation	*Dependant Variable*	*Constant*	*SYN*	*LNHW*	*AE*	*AEX*
(4.1a)	LNHW	−1.130	.210	—	.247	.029
		(−2.78)	(1.22)		(7.73)	(4.31)
(4.2a)	SYN	−.268	—	.289	—	—
		(−1.61)		(4.05)		
(4.3a)	AE	7.665	1.920	—	—	—
		(41.05)	(3.90)			
(4.4a)	KL	−42.25	85.03	—	—	—
		(−.44)	(.85)			

Note: t-values in parentheses.

managers of labor-intensive industries have more to gain from unionism than their counterparts in more capital-intensive industries. Unionization should be negatively correlated with WVA because of the "importance of being unimportant." In the French, as in the British case (Bain and Elsheik, 1979), the positive effect tends to predominate.

Equation (4.3a) explains 63 percent of interindustry variations in the average level of education of the work force. Both the percentage urbanized (URB) and the percentage unionized (SYN) have the expected sign, and both are significant at the 99 percent level of confidence. The signs of SYN and

Table 4-2. Two-Stage Least Squares

Equation	*Dependant Variable*	*Constant*	*SYN*	*LNHW*	*AE*	*AEX*
(4.1b)	LNHM	−1.989	.029	—	.325	.035
		(−3.16)	(.12)		(6.07)	(4.38)
(4.2b)	SYN	−.439	—	.388	—	—
		(−2.24)		(4.24)		
(4.3b)	AE	7.660	1.990	—	—	—
		(40.95)	(3.82)			
(4.4b)	KL	−103.62	3.96	—	—	—
		(−.93)	(.32)			

t-values in parentheses.
$\bar{R}^2$ and standard errors are only asymptotically valid for 2 SLS.

HOM	*KL*	*LIC*	*WVA*	*DKL*	*CON*	*URB*	*STAB*	$\bar{R}^2$
.001 (1.30)	.0004 (1.19)	.001 (.13)	—	—	—	—	—	.83
−.001 (−1.81)	—	—	.003 (2.03)	−.0007 (−1.88)	.003 (4.06)	—	—	.71
—	—	—	—	—	—	2.621 (4.80)	—	.63
—	—	—	—	—	—	—	.904 (.53)	.11

STAB in equation (4.4a) conform to our expectations, but the coefficients of both of these variables are not significantly different from zero.

Turning to the 2SLS estimates in table 4–2, where wages, unionism, labor quality, and capital intensity are endogenous variables, we notice, in equation (4.1b), that the unionism coefficient drops to .029 and its asymptotic *t*-value to .12. To this decline in the coefficient of SYN corresponds the expected increase in the coefficient of our schooling variable, and, to a smaller extent, in the coefficient of the experience variable. The coefficients of the other variables are unchanged.

HOM	*KL*	*LIC*	*WVA*	*DKL*	*CON*	*URB*	*STAB*	$\bar{R}^2$
.001 (1.36)	.0005 (1.07)	.007 (.55)	—	—	—	—	—	.80
−.001 (−1.87)	—	—	.003 (1.71)	−.0006 (−1.60)	.003 (3.27)	—	—	.69
—	—	—	—	—	—	2.587 (4.69)	—	.63
—	—	—	—	—	—	—	2.09 (1.04)	.06

In equation (4.2b), there is a small increase in the value of the LNHW coefficient, but all other coefficients are basically unchanged. The coefficients of equation (4.3b) are not affected by simultaneity. In equation (4.4b), the coefficient of the union density variable is reduced, while that of STAB increases.

To assess the sensitivity of the results to the particular specification chosen, I have experimented with an alternate list of variables. Following Weiss (1966) and Jenny and Weber (1975), I have introduced a concentration ratio into the wage equation. Inclusion of this variable does not change the sign and the value of the coefficients of the OLS estimates. When we move to the 2SLS estimates, the coefficient of SYN becomes negative (−.018) but remains insignificant, with a t of −.061. The coefficient of the other variables are basically unchanged.

Conclusion

I have attempted in this study to evaluate the relative wage effect of French unions. To measure this impact, a four-equation model has been specified, in which unionism, wage, labor quality, and capital intensity are simultaneously determined. The empirical finding is that unions have not succeeded in obtaining a wage differential in French industry. When differences in the level of education and experience, in the sex composition of the labor force, in the degree of employment security, and in the capital per head in the industry are taken into account, workers in highly unionized industries receive the same money wages as their counterparts in nonunionized industries.

This result is quite plausible, given the particular characteristics of French unions. As Olson (1965) has shown, a labor union (or any group supplying a public good to a large number of potential consumers) can only survive if it provides "selective incentives" to its members. These incentives can be negative (such as "union shop," "closed shop," or "agency shop" arrangements, which make dues payments more or less compulsory) or positive (such as wage and nonwage benefits restricted to union members, seniority privileges, or the redress of individual grievances). French unions provide fewer of these incentives to their members than does the typical American union. French law does not recognize the union shop or the closed shop and forbids management to check off union dues. Closed shops are only found in the docks and in some printing trades.

Furthermore, French unions do not supply their members with the type of private benefits provided by their North American counterparts. In France, representation of workers is granted by statute to an elected works council (comité d'entreprise). Only representative unions can present candidates in the first ballot, but council members, once elected, speak for the entire work force.

Collective bargaining takes place at the industry level, and the resulting contract is applicable to all workers, union or nonunion. Contracts are also often extended by the state beyond the original unit. Many of the nonwage benefits obtained by unions for their members through collective bargaining (such as paid vacation and leave, severance pay, unemployment, and retirement benefits, overtime pay, health insurance, and job safety and health) are granted by statute to all French workers. One does not have to be a union member, or even to be in a strongly unionized industry, to benefit from these advantages. French workers are also free to negotiate their own wages, which may be superior to those established by collective agreements.

Perhaps the two most important private goods supplied by unions in England and in the United States are the handling of grievances and seniority. Unions do not control the grievance procedures in France. Grievances are brought to management's attention by the "delegué du personnel" elected by all workers at the plant. If the grievance is not settled to his or her satisfaction, the employee may sue in a state labor court or appeal to the government labor inspector. Membership in a union, therefore, does not significantly increase one's chances of obtaining redress. Similarly, union membership in France does not confer any seniority privileges: Management has so far retained the right to decide on the order of layoffs. For all these reasons, one would expect French unions to have limited impact on wages.

How can this finding be reconciled with the continuous support of unions by an overwhelming majority of French workers?[8] As Olson (1965) argues, it is perfectly rational for an employee to support union activities, and to wish that everyone would join unions, and yet to fail to become a union member himself. Another explanation of that apparent paradox is that the absence of a relative wage effect is compatible with the existence of a global effect on wages. Possibly, French unions have increased wages in all sectors in the same proportion. This result could happen even if unionization varies between sectors, because managers in nonunionized industries may be willing to pay union wage rates in order to forestall unionization in their industries (Lewis, 1963). French unions also seem to have been quite successful in having legislation enacted to extend to wage earners of all sectors the benefits gained in highly unionized firms or industries.[9] Furthermore, French law stipulates that collective agreements can be extended beyond the original bargaining unit to all firms in the same industry. Since some bargaining units are very large (for example "métallurgie" includes transportation equipment, electrical and nonelectrical machinery, ferrous and nonferrous metals, miscellaneous metal products), wage increases obtained in any particular firm or subsector are sometimes extended to other sectors. This result would tend to reduce the correlation between union penetration and relative wage effects of unions.[10]

Another possible explanation is that wage increases obtained by French unions were dissipated because unions were unable to restrict entry into occupations. Except in a few industries, such as the docks or the printing trades, French unions have no control over hiring. This factor may have been crucial in reducing the union relative wage effect in the postwar period, when women and immigrants were entering the labor force in large numbers.

The model suggests, however, a third explanation: Equation (4.3) indicates that unionism is a positive and significant determinant of labor quality. This suggests that employers offset, as hypothesized, union-secured wage gains by raising their hiring standards and hiring more highly educated employees. Thus, a 100 percent increase in unionization rates at the mean level leads to a 10 percent increase in years of schooling.

The process of increasing the average quality of the labor force must have been facilitated by the high growth rate of production in the postwar period, which has allowed managers to upgrade their labor force with new hires. Between 1954 and 1975, for example, the number of upper- and middle-level managers more than doubled, whereas the number of blue-collar workers only increased by 25 percent.[11]

French union workers thus seem to be paid their opportunity wage. This confirms Pettengill's (1980) hypothesis that, when managers can adjust to union wage increases by raising hiring standards, union and nonunion workers within a given ability class will be paid in the long run the same wage. The main impact of unions will then be to increase the wages of all high-ability workers (union and nonunion) relative to those of medium- and low-quality workers.[12]

If French unions do not have any impact on wages, equation (4.2) tells us that the level of wages is a powerful determinant of the rate of unionization. This is consistent with the findings of Ashenfelter and Johnson (1972), Schmidt and Strauss (1976), and Burkitt, Bowers, and Armstrong (1978).

In interpreting the results, however, keeping in mind some of the limitations of the study is necessary. First, DKL and WVA should probably be considered endogenous to the system. If unions succeed in raising wages, they will tend to increase the share of labor in value added and will incite management to increase the capital-labor ratio. When DKL and WVA are made endogenous, our model becomes underidentified. Left to a further study is the task of specifying equations for these two variables, or of finding variables that proxy for the Marshallian rules and that are truly exogenous.

Second, one must also be aware of the limitations of our wage variable. We do not have good measures of the actual length of work. That is, the data do not reflect interindustry differences in absenteeism, in paid personal leave (such as is granted for family events, for maternity, etc.), and in the intensity of effort. This fact is unfortunate, for it is highly likely that French unions, like their U.S. counterparts, also have an impact on these components of "real wages."[13]

Third, the results may be sensitive to the choice of union variable. Although it is highly probable that the percentage of union votes in comités d'entreprise elections is a good proxy for the union monopoly power in that industry, further research should explore the sensitivity of the results to the choice of alternative union variables. Lastly, this study is a cross section for the 1969–70 period. This period was one of rather low unemployment rates. Lewis (1963) has shown the union differential in the United States to be higher in recessions than in booms. Another study using more recent data may therefore reach different conclusions.

Notes

1. Myers compares wage minima for particular occupations as set by collective agreements to average wages effectively paid for the same occupation. It is possible, however, that negotiated wages are higher than measured by Myers because unions succeed in upgrading jobs, i.e., in having unskilled laborers (grade 100) reclassified at a higher grade. This point was brought to my attention by Bernard Lentz.
2. The size variable is also an important control since comités d'entreprise exist only in establishments of more than 50 workers. This point was brought to my attention by Bernard Lentz.
3. The (weighted) correlation coefficient between the average size of establishment and the four-firm concentration ratio is .64.
4. Bernard Lentz suggested to me the use of this variable.
5. Bernard Lentz contributed to the definition of this variable.
6. An industry with a completely male work force would have a unionization rate .1 percent lower than an industry with a 100 percent female work force.
7. I owe this point to Bernard Lentz.
8. In a recent poll, 83 percent of French workers declared that they considered joining unions useful. See *L'Expansion* (1979).
9. For example, the four weeks of paid vacation given by Renault to its employees were later extended by statute to all wage earners.

10. I am indebted to Bernard Lentz for this point.

11. See *Economie et Statistique*, July–August 1977.

12. Bernard Lentz brought this reference to my attention.

13. A study of 5,000 American families shows that union workers receive higher money wages, but have less desirable working conditions than nonunion workers (Duncan, 1974).

Data Appendix

LNHW is the logarithm of the average hourly wage in 1969 in each two-digit NAE sector. The wage used is the average annual wage of full-time workers, as reported in N. Chabanas and S. Volkoff (1973).

This figure includes money wages and income in kind, but excludes contributions to social security, to unemployment compensation, and to retirement funds. Average hourly wage was obtained by dividing the yearly wage by an estimate of the average annual hours of work in each industry, which we have obtained by multiplying average weekly hours in 1969 by an estimate of the average number of workweeks. Average weekly hours in each industry are published in the *Bulletin Mensuel de Statistiques Sociales* of the Ministère du Travail. The only available estimates of paid holidays in each industry are for 1976. We have used these data for our 1969 estimates.

The unionization variable SYN is the ratio of the number of votes received by union-sponsored candidates in comité d'entreprise elections of 1969–70 to total industry employment as of December 31, 1969. Representatives to the comités d'entreprise serve a two-year term, with half of the comité votes held each year. For these reasons we have added the results of the 1969 and 1970 elections, as published in the *Revue Française des Affaires Sociales*. Since data are partially or totally missing for the mining and the match and tobacco sectors, we have excluded these sectors. The industrial classification used for comités d'entreprise elections is more aggregated than that used for our other variables. I have therefore attributed to each sector the corresponding unionization average. Total industry employment on December 31, 1969, is published in Chabanas and Volkoff (1973).

The average number of years of schooling in each industry (AE) has been obtained from the sample of the Formation, Qualification Professionnelle survey of 1970. I have calculated these averages from a subsample made up of employed wage earners not presently in school ($n = 23{,}905$). The average number of years of work experience of the labor force (AEX) and the percentage of workers in each industry living in cities of more than 200,000 (URB) were calculated from the same sample.

The share of men in total employment (HOM) was calculated from unpublished INSEE data. The four firm concentration ratios (CON) are those presented by F. Jenny and A.P. Weber (1974). The share of labor and social security payments in value added in 1969 (WVA) and DKL, the index of capital per head in 1974 (1959 = 100), were obtained from "Emploi, Qualification and Croissance dans l'Industries," *Les Collections de l'INSEE*, Serie E, nos. 58, 63, 66, and 68. The industry's capital-labor ratio, KL, is the ratio of assets to employment and is computed from corporation tax data of the Ministry of Finance.

LIC is the ratio of the average annual number of layoffs in each sector over the 1970–1975 period to total sectoral employment in 1970. Layoffs are calculated from ministry of labor data as published in the *Bulletin Mensuel de Statistiques Sociales*. The STAB variable is December 31, 1969, employment divided by the total number of people hired during 1969, and is obtained from Chabanas and Volkoff (1973).

References

Ashenfelter, O., and Johnson, G. 1972. "Unionism, Relative Wages, and Labor Quality in U.S. Manufacturing Industries." *International Economic Review* 13, no. 3 (October): 488–508.

Bain, G., and Elsheik, F. 1979. "An Inter-Industry Analysis of Unionization in Britain." *British Journal of Industrial Relations* 17 (July): 137–157.

Barbash, J. 1956. *The Practice of Unionism*. New York: Harper and Row.

Bonety, R. 1961. *Pour une politique des salaires: Rapport sur les orientations de la CFTC en matière de salaires.* Paris: Confederation Francaise des Travailleurs Chretiens.

Burkitt, B., Bowers, D., and Armstrong, K. J. 1978. "The Relationship between Money Wages and Unionization: A Re-Appraisal." *Bulletin of Economic Research* 30, no. 2 (November): 95–107.

Chabanas, N., and Volkoff, S. 1973. "Les salaires dans l'industrie, le commerce, et les services en 1969." *Les Collections de l'INSEE*, Série M, no. 29.

Duncan, G. 1974. "Non Pecuniary Work Rewards." In *5,000 American Families*, ed. J. Morgan. Ann Arbor: University of Michigan Survey Research Center.

L'Expansion. "Les Français et leurs syndicats," 1979. 7/20, December, pp. 109–117.

Freeman, R., and Medoff, J. 1979. "The Two Faces of Unionism." *The Public Interest*, 57 (Fall): 69–93.

Jenny, F., and Weber, A. P. 1975. "Concentration, syndicalisation et rémunération salariale dans l'industries manufacturière française." *Revue Economique* 16, no. 4 (July):622–654.

———. 1974. *Concentration et politique des structures industrielles.* Paris: LaDocumentation Française.

Jensen, M., and Meckling, W. H. 1976. "Theory of the Firm: Managerial Behaviour, Agency Costs and Ownership Structure." *Journal of Financial Economics* 3:305–360.

Kalachek, E., and Raines, F. 1980. "Trade Unions and Hiring Standards." *Journal of Labor Research* 1, no. 1 (Spring): 63–75.

Lester, R. 1941. *Economics of Labor*. New York: Macmillan.

Lewis, H. G. 1963. *Unionism and Relative Wages in the United States*. Chicago: University of Chicago Press.

Moore, W., and Newman, R. 1975. "On the Prospects for American Trade Union Growth: A Cross Section Analysis." *Review of Economic and Statistics* 57, no. 4 (November): 435–445.

Mulvey, C. 1976. "Collective Agreements and Relative Earning in U.K. Manufacturing in 1973." *Economica* 43 (172):419–427.

Myers, F. 1965. "Deux aspects du rôle des négotiations collectives en France." *Sociologie du Travail*, no. 1 (January–March):1–33.

Olson, M. 1965. *The Logic of Collective Action*. Cambridge: Harvard University Press.

Parodi, M. 1963. "Wage Drift and Wage Bargaining: A Case Study of the Building Industry in Marseille." *British Journal of Industrial Relations* 1, no. 2, (June).

Pencavel, J. 1971. "The Demand for Union Services. An Exercise." *Industrial and Labor Relations Review* 24: 180–190.

______. 1974. "Relative Wages and Trade Unions in the United Kingdom." *Economica* 40 (162): 194–210.

Pettengill, J. 1980. *Labor Unions and the Inequality of Earned Income*. New York: North Holland.

Riboud, M. 1978. L' *Accumulation du capital humain*. Paris: Economica.

______. 1979. "Une analyse économique du salaire des femmes." *Cahiers de Recherches*, no. 7. Paris: Fondation pour la Nouvelle Economie Politique.

Schmidt, P., and Strauss, R. 1976. "The Effect of Unions on Earnings and Earnings on Unions: A Mixed Logit Approach." *International Economic Review* 17, no. 1 (February): 204–212.

Weiss, L. 1966. "Concentration and Labor Earnings." *American Economic Review* 56 (March): 96–117.

5 TRADE UNIONS AND RESTRICTIVE PRACTICES

John T. Addison

In this chapter, my main purpose is to examine the impact of trade union practices at the place of work. Although the chapter title refers to "restrictive practices," I propose to range more widely than a literal reading of that term may imply, since I interpret my remit as fundamentally one of assessing the impact of trade unions on productivity and efficiency.

I begin with a fairly conventional, general treatment of the job regulatory practices of trade unions. My intention here is simply to indicate that human capital theoretic considerations provide a common thread linking such practices as the closed shop, occupational licensing, featherbedding, and, indeed, even such practices as seniority provisions that need not necessarily be thought of as cost increasing. Besides providing a useful backdrop to what follows, this treatment introduces a dynamic element often missing in standard discussions of trade union impact.

I next turn to what might be termed the Harvard view of reality, which is based on an application of Hirschman's (1970) exit-voice paradigm to the labor market and collective bargaining. This approach seeks to shift attention away from what its adherents would term the monopoly view of trade unionism toward recognition of the wider goals of unionism and the likely productivity-enhancing nonwage effects of organization. According to this view, the process of unionization not merely involves shock effects (to management) but offers the prospect of introducing worker behavioral changes conducive to enhanced efficiency.

There follows a review of the empirical evidence on the effects of unions on resource allocation and productivity, with special emphasis placed on a critical assessment of the research findings of the Harvard School. Space constraints dictate that certain aspects of the resource allocative effects of unionism, and in particular those flowing from union impact on the intra-industry wage structure, will be neglected. In a concluding section, thc threads of the preceding analysis are drawn together, certain additional lacunae of the literature addressed, and a number of policy issues raised.

The Conventional Analysis of Job Regulation

The job regulatory practices of trade unions are basically threefold. First, we may identify those practices that control entry into an occupation or job—i.e., the various forms of closed shop, restrictions on apprenticeship, and controls over job assignment. These predominantly union-initiated practices have a long history and apply in the main to craft rather than industrial unions. Second, there are make-work practices that encompass overmanning and/or the rejection of modern machinery. While this category sometimes shades into the first, the distinction is worth preserving because of the intrafirm allocative inefficiencies introduced by make-work practices.

Third, there are the practices associated with the use of seniority to assign priority in such matters as promotion, demotion, and layoff. Seniority practices are associated mainly with industrial unionism. They merit separate identification to the extent that they are more a *joint* creation of management and unions than are the former two categories. Thus, training and screening investments can be shown to create a "natural" precedence for senior workers, which would imply that seniority practices need not be cost increasing.

Licensing and Job Assignment Rules

Let us first consider the behavior of the union (or professional association) as a monopoly supplier of labor. The lower the "costs" in reduced job opportunities for union members, the more willing are those members to collude to raise their average level of pay, ceteris paribus. The circumstances under which these costs can be expected to be low are indexed by the

Marshallian rules for the elasticity of derived demand. In its simplest form, the theory argues that, if such monopoly power exists, its exertion in raising wages will yield a once-for-all gain.[1] Moreover, that gain will be restricted to the current membership. It is a once-for-all change because the union is supposed to move quickly to exploit its monopoly power once it has been recognized. Its benefits accrue to existing members alone because the resulting improvement in relative pay over occupations requiring similar training is presumed to attract new entrants. Thus job slots will have to be rationed. Assuming that no favoritism is extended to particular classes of applicants, then, in equilibrium, new entrants are likely to pay for access up to the point at which there is no advantage to entering this unionized occupation over any other. (Note that this argument is analogous to the argument that real resources are consumed in order to obtain and maintain monopolization of labor markets—see conclusions section.) However, if favoritism is practiced, those so favored will be able to enter the profession at a lower cost and will consequently receive a higher rate of return on capital invested than is available in alternative occupations.

According to this view, union members are held to have a capital investment in their occupation, for which they hope to obtain a competitive return. The erection of higher licensing standards thus yields a windfall capital gain to incumbents—providing these standards are not imposed on the existing membership (the so-called "grandfather clause"). Accordingly, there is an incentive to follow this course of action. A corollary of this result is that any influx of qualified applicants—occasioned, say, by a change in immigration patterns or in work assignment rules— will tend to bring about a capital loss for incumbents. Thus, those who seek to enter the occupation will tend to be regulated via the closed shop or work permit. Also, the definition of the occupation itself will be continually policed by enforcing work assignments and by demarcation rules. Finally, there is an obvious incentive to discriminate in favor of members' relatives when considering applications for entry. Such a policy is consistent with the goal of family income maximization. Indeed, evidence exists to suggest that "self-recruitment" is pervasive in professional occupations and craft unions (Becker, 1959).

Human capital theoretic considerations thus provide a common thread linking the closed shop, high occupational entry standards, favoritism, careful job definition via work assignment rules, and opposition to technical change. This is not to say that human capital theory requires that such practices develop; rather, it indicates that they will prove difficult to remove once established. This is because individuals invest in an occupation on the expectation that income flows, buttressed by the rules, will be maintained. In a very real sense, these union workers can thus be seen to have "property rights in the form of inherited protective practices" (Flanders, 1964, p. 10). The major factor in the development of these rules is likely to be organization.

As noted earlier, the problems of occupational licensing and jurisdictional rules apply in the main to industries employing members of craft or professional associations. American industries that involve the craft system have been estimated to represent about 10 percent of total employment (Stinchcombe, 1965, p. 166), whereas in the United Kingdom the figure approximates 25 percent. To these figures must be added the professional associations, which perhaps account for a further 10 percent of the work force in both countries.

To raise entry standards over time and to guard and even extend the areas of work restricted to union members (the union's jurisdiction) is clearly income maximizing. Higher entry standards and tighter demarcation of union boundaries can be defended on the grounds of increasing safety or standards of service to the public. Indeed, this will inevitably be the argument advanced by union leaders. For example, increased training of doctors or teachers would raise standards as well as improve the earnings of incumbents. Thus, evidence of pressure for additional training does not of itself support the hypothesis that craft-type organizations manipulate entry rules so as to maximize earnings. But, clearly, the "public interest" can hardly be invoked to justify other protective practices, such as nepotism or the closed shop, which involve the rejection of qualified applicants.

Consider those policies that regulate entry to the craft union. We observe a tendency toward rising entry requirements in a number of associations, including the medical profession on both sides of the Atlantic (Friedman, 1951; Siebert, 1977) and barbers (Rottenberg, 1962). However, one can also discern contrary tendencies, insofar as periods of apprenticeship have been shortened. Having said this, the latter development has been accompanied by a rise in the apprentice-journeyman wage ratio (Slichter, Healy, and Livernash, 1960, p. 84), making it less possible for apprentices to bear the cost of their own training. As such training is general in form, the rising ratio may be seen as an attempt to shift the costs of apprenticeship on to the employer, who has responded by reducing the number of training places available. Indeed, much of the so-called "crisis in apprenticeship" would appear to stem from employer reluctance to make training places available.

Further, the closed shop has been maintained despite periodic legislative attacks on it. Thus, the prohibition of the closed shop under Taft-Hartley appears simply to have "driven it underground" (Miller, 1976, p. 887). Similarly, the curb placed on closed shops by the British Industrial Relations Act of 1971 has had to be lifted. This lack of success might reasonably have been predicted on human capital grounds: Neither measure involved any attempt to compensate the interest groups for the undoubtedly large capital loss they would have suffered through an influx of new entrants were the closed shop actually to collapse.

The problem of the closed shop is an intractable one but two policy options are available. One is to guard against further encroachment while ensuring the right of independent appeal against union action. The other is to solve what is a *genuine* free-rider argument (see next section) by a once-for-all buying out of union monopolistic distortions financed by the issue of public debt.[2]

The jurisdiction of the craft is also carefully guarded against competition. In the United States, for example, dentists and lawyers tend not to have arrangements that recognize qualifications granted in another jurisdiction. In addition, the states in which practitioners have high incomes are also those with high failure rates for applicants, thus indicating a successful attempt by incumbents to preserve their high incomes (Holen, 1956). And in the United Kingdom doctors are currently pressing for an arrangement whereby they, and not the hospital administrators, can set the standards for specialists, in addition to their long-standing licensing of junior doctors.[3]

An indication of the effect of occupational entry restrictions may be gained by comparing the present value of lifetime earnings for occupational categories with restrictions on entry with those for which there is none. A British study that compared lawyers and general practitioners with the generality of first-degree university graduates suggests that the internal rate of return for lawyers and general practitioners (at 23 and 18 percent, respectively) is much higher than we would expect if a competitive return were being earned on their extra investment in training (Siebert, 1977). An American comparison of general practitioners' lifetime earnings with those of college graduates also yields a high internal rate of return, namely 24.1 percent (Sloan, 1970, 1976). However, we cannot be sure that higher rates of return are in fact captured by entrants to such professions. Thus, the considerably higher relative earnings of such groups might simply reflect the higher ability and/or effort required of medical and law students, and thus represent equilibrium differentials. The answer to this particular question will depend on the extent of favoritism in medical and in law school entry procedures. There are grounds for believing that nepotism is in fact pervasive in these areas.

Jurisdictional issues have also been of importance within the manual crafts. Although there might be greater flexibility in the United States than in the United Kingdom, jurisdictional agreements are the subject of hard bargaining in both countries. In the chemical industry, for example, jurisdictional questions form the main subject of grievance committee meetings.[4] Flexibility could be a less important issue for the American craftsperson because of a stronger internal labor market orientation—i.e., it is the employer who tends to finance training. For example, one study of American construction craftspersons estimated that only 20 percent of the sample had experienced an apprenticeship, the rest learning the trade informally (Strauss, 1965). By way of contrast, a British study of various craft groups showed that 58 percent of craftspersons had served an apprenticeship (Robinson, 1970). Be this as it may, in both countries the bilateral monopoly situation of management and union will tend to result in bargaining over job assignment. Formal arrangements for settling such demarcation issues exist in both countries.

A final point to be covered is the propensity toward nepotism on the part of professional associations and craft unions. Evidence of this practice is widespread within American construction and other unions (Slichter, Healy, and Livernash, 1960; Strauss, 1965), and its presence has been well documented in the case of the British medical profession.[5] Nepotism is seen as a way of inheriting favorable job opportunities, and for this reason it must be reduced if minority groups, including women, are to have their employment prospects improved.

Featherbedding

Make-work practices, or featherbedding, can similarly be interpreted as an attempt to protect (or enhance) a human capital investment. Indeed, in a number of cases, the connection between the rules described earlier and featherbedding will be a very close one. For example, the British practice of forbidding the craftsman's "mate" to perform skilled tasks, or the prohibition on foremen doing the work of bargaining-unit (that is, union) employees, can sometimes give rise to featherbedding. However, it is more usual to regard featherbedding not as a preconceived strategy but as resulting from attempts to balk technological change—"the carrying forward of a set of practices appropriate for one technology to another where it is alien" (Weinstein, 1964, p. 147). An American example is the rule (since modified) in West Coast longshore operations that prohibits the lifting of loads heavier than 2,100 pounds (Killingsworth, 1962). Once a safety measure, this became a make-work practice. As in the case of licensing rules, featherbedding tends to be more a problem with craft than with industrial unions because industrial unions generally comprise a number of diverse groups, some of which will be helped and others harmed by a given technological change. Accordingly, concerted opposition is less easily practised.

Featherbedding, contrary to what one might expect, need not always reduce an industry's output and raise the price of its product. Here one must distinguish between *level* and *ratio* featherbedding. The former relates to a featherbedding rule that specifies a minimum level to the labor force (the negotiation of a work force stabilization or "no redundancies" clause). The latter specifies that labor shall be employed in a given ratio to some other factor (say, a fixed number of men per machine) (Weinstein, 1960). The importance of the distinction is that in the case of level featherbedding the marginal cost of labor is zero and thus the marginal costs of production are lower (but average costs are higher) than in the no-restriction example, up to the stipulated minimum labor force. Ratio featherbedding, on the other hand, causes marginal costs of production to be higher than they would otherwise be at all levels of output. If increasing average costs is possible without driving the firm out of business (that is, if the industry is monopolistic), it follows that level featherbedding increases output while the ratio variety reduces output. Within a competitive scenario, of course, the imposition of either variant will drive some firms out of business (Simler, 1962).

The implication of this analysis is that featherbedding will certainly increase unit cost. Generally it will also increase prices, except in the case of a monopoly where featherbedding takes the form of a minimum labor force requirement. Because of its likely smaller impact on prices (and thus employment) in monopolistic industries, we would expect featherbedding to be more prevalent in precisely such industries. However, to overemphasize the distinction between market structures is possible. Political theory would suggest that union policies tend to reflect the demands of some average of workers (the median voter model), who will be relatively less mobile and have greater specific training than the marginal worker, who is most likely to lose employment. To this extent, the long-term unemployment consequences of protective practices are less of a deterrent, and they can be expected to affect the more competitive as well as the monopolistic sectors.

The point here is that an important strand in the explanation of "*X*-inefficiency" would be protective labor practices. Having said this, labor productivity varies for many reasons other than union action. A recent comparative study of British and American plants found that output per worker was on average some 50 percent higher in the latter. Of this difference, 35 percentage points were tentatively attributed to factors such as scale, technology, and product mix, and 15 points to such "behavioral" factors as strikes, restrictive practices, and overmanning (Pratten, 1975). On the basis of this study, a case can be made for arguing that labor practices are of importance in determining lapses from X-efficiency. Further evidene of this adverse impact will be reviewed in the discussion of empirical evidence. At this point we might usefully note that most protective practices are to be viewed as a rational response to potential job loss.

Examples of featherbedding abound, most significantly in areas such as printing, rail transportation, and harbor work. The fact that the latter tend to be monopolistic industries would tend to bear out the theoretical implication that featherbedding occurs in those circumstances in which a sharing of monopoly gains is possible. One important gap in the case studies relates to the investigation of overmanning in government service. The growth in collective power of government workers, allied with the monopoly nature of government, would appear to provide an ideal environment for the growth of featherbedding practices.

The circumstances in which featherbedding has resulted in an increase in output to the consumer have not been investigated. Possibly, the short-run effect of featherbedding in rail transportation has been to improve services to the consumer. Over the long run, the resulting increase in average costs has permitted undercutting by other forms of transport. In these circumstances, it might appear as though the rail unions had overestimated the degree of monopoly possessed by the industry—featherbedding causing a "perverse" effect on employment. Such apparently suboptimal decision making would be explicable if union democracy were such that marginal workers, those most likely to become unemployed, had less voice in union councils.

A novel alternative explanation for this behavior has been advanced by Hirschman (1970), whose exit-voice paradigm will be commented upon in greater detail in the next section. Hirschman's argument runs in terms of the lack of stimulus to good management in industries such as railroads, which are neither completely monopolistic (because of competition from trucking) nor competitive. In such industries, poor management is penalized neither by the "exit" of dissatisfied customers nor by their complaints (or "voice"). This is because, even if customers switch loyalties, the government usually stands ready to make up the loss. In such circumstances, the making of a loss is little deterrent, particularly in view of the likely political costs of, say, rooting out overmanning. Moreover, since it is perhaps the most concerned customers (those who would "raise hell" if there were poor service) who leave first, the voice channel to management is correspondingly muted. This line of argument serves to emphasize that featherbedding requires management complicity.

Although featherbedding is outlawed under Taft-Hartley, the provision appears to have been singularly ineffective (Gomberg, 1972). Given the power of the union to oppose, and their "interest" in so doing, this outcome is less than surprising. On the other hand, dockworkers on both sides of the Atlantic have been able to receive compensation; here, real progress has been made (Goldberg, 1973; Mellish, 1970). The compensation principle has either taken the form of a direct cash payment, as in the case of the Pacific Coast Longshoring Mechanization and Modernization Agreement, or indirect remuneration through the provision of job security via "decasualization," as in the East Coast and British dock industry cases. The main point is that to enable technical change to proceed, some measure of job security or its equivalent seems to be necessary.

Labor Force Adjustment

The development of seniority practices implies that unions are likely to affect the entire pattern of labor force adjustment (their impact on quits will be considered in the discussion of empirical evidence). The origins of the seniority principle appear to be partly the result of union-political processes and partly the consequence of economic forces such as firm size and internal labormarket structuring. Whatever the reasons for its development, the application of the seniority principle means that longer-service workers are the last to be laid off. Given that senior members exercise a disproportionate influence in union councils, the implication is that layoffs will be the preferred method of the labor force and that adjustment mechanisms available to the unionized firm will be limited. Where seniority is applied, the quit rate will be reduced since separating from the firm will entail the loss of substantial privileges. The greater wage inflexibility in unionized firms thus suggests that the layoff becomes the dominant form of adjustment.

Methods of regulating promotion within a firm may be classified under the heading of seniority practices. A basic point to be made at the outset is that seniority, unlike the job regulation practices considered above, is to some extent employer initiated. In other words, seniority practices need not be cost increasing. But once seniority systems are widely implemented, it becomes costly for individuals to enter the more skilled jobs. Thus, human capital analysis once more becomes applicable to problems of capital loss consequent upon technological change or plant closure. At the same time, a system of seniority allied to bumping rights confers job security. This practice protects workers and makes them less likely to block technological change to the extent that it is the younger and more easily reemployable of their number who tend to bear the burden of work force reduction.

One of the initiating forces behind seniority is said to be a union desire to avoid the arbitrary exercise of authority by management (Ross, 1958). This factor is reinforced by arbitrators' concepts of equity—"the ethics of the queue" (Slichter, Healy, and Livernash, 1960, p. 104; Reder, 1960, p. 358).

As intimated earlier, forces on the side of the employer also promote seniority. Because a seniority system ties workers to the firm, this outcome is in accord with the interests of the employer, who has specific training investments in these workers. To some extent specific investments must accumulate in workers as they serve with the firm and come to know its methods. The firm in recession will thus attempt to postpone the layoff of experienced workers, and to this extent there is a "natural" seniority system built on profit maximization. This aspect should not be overemphasized, however, because we would expect the firm to have a wide capacity for adjustment to different degrees of emphasis on seniority. A system without seniority rules and consequently more interfirm mobility would simply have, in equilibrium, workers who finance more of their own training, that is, training that would tend to be less specific. Conversely, in a system with seniority rules, specific investments will increase in relation to general ones. Training that would ordinarily be general has to be financed by the firm; screening expenses are also greater since workers at the bottom of the ladder must be of suitable material to eventually fill the spaces at the top. Firms or industries emphasizing seniority are thus more likely than other firms to screen carefully their job applicants (Slichter, Healy, and Livernash, 1960, p. 195). Since screening is so important, moreover, employers might prefer that current employees bring along relatives to fill vacancies; thus giving rise to the possibility of nepotism in industrial as well as craft occupations. On balance, we would expect the main impetus to seniority systems to be provided by unions. Because screening and training costs can be suitably adjusted, however, and perhaps also because of the certainty introduced into industrial relations by an "objective" decision rule, management may be expected to accept such provisions.

As to the beneficial effects of seniority rules for the economy, we can say that positive benefits will more likely accrue if it is the firm rather than the craft that marks the jurisdictional boundary. In such circumstances manning would be more flexible. We have noted that adjustment to technological change might also more easily be accommodated, although large industrial changes—plant closure, merger, or subcontracting—which menace the survival of the seniority unit will tend to be impeded. We note here that the enforcement of seniority has not been accompanied by any marked acceptance of technological change in U.S. rail transportation. Yet, possibly, this industry is atypical for the reasons cited earlier. In general, the proposition that seniority systems reduce the dislocation caused by labor-force reductions appears to be a valid one. Thus, perhaps, severance pay schemes appear more fully developed in the United Kingdom, where seniority is less prevalent and enterprise markets less well developed than in the United States.

Unionism and Productivity—The Harvard View

The conventional view of the impact of unionism on productivity stresses in roughly equal measure the allocative inefficiencies that result from distortions in the relative wage structure (the redirection of higher quality labor and capital from higher to lower marginal product uses) and the nonwage induced inefficiencies attributable to job regulation.[6] Drawing on Harberger's (1954) method for evaluating the welfare losses of enterprise monopoly, and assuming a relative wage impact of 0.15 and an elasticity of demand for labor in the union and nonunion sectors of −1, Rees (1963) calculated the output loss of unionism to be a mere 0.14 percent of U.S. national output. Adding in the loss attributable to the intra-industry relative wage effects of unionism, Rees doubles this output loss estimate to approximately 0.3 percent. Although he does not provide a guesstimate of the output losses that result from direct restrictions of output through control of manning requirements, the work pace, and work practices, Rees argues that such losses probably exceed the latter value—implying that the overall loss in output due to unionism approximates 1 percent of GNP.[7] This relatively modest magnitude, coupled with a perception of the socially constructive role of trade unions, influenced many labor economists to argue that on balance the economic losses imposed by unions were not too high a price to pay for the successful performance of their social and political role on behalf of workers (e.g., Rees, 1977).

The Harvard interpretation of the noneconomic characteristics of trade unionism has to be placed in this context. The new view, associated with the work of Freeman and Medoff and their students at Harvard, while not denying the monopolistic role of labor unions, maintains that the monopoly view of unions (i.e., organizations whose chief function is to raise wages) is seriously misleading. Unions, they would argue, have significant nonwage effects that influence diverse aspects of modern industrial life. By providing workers with a "voice" at the work place, for example, unions can and do affect positively the functioning of the economic system. Indeed, it is a central tenet of the new view that unions have the potential to more than offset, via enhanced productivity, the cost increases that result from application of their monopoly (= wage) function.

The essence of the Harvard view is contained in Freeman (1976). His analysis draws heavily on the exit-voice paradigm of Hirschman (1970) and is linked to the internal labor market literature of the 1950s and 1960s, as developed and extended by Doeringer and Piore (1971), and to the idiosyncratic exchange variant of the "new-new" microeconomics (Williamson, Wachter, and Harris, 1975). Having said this, the theoretical content of the Harvard model is somewhat meager, and its further development awaits refinement of the internal labormarket construct (see, for example, Miyazaki, 1977).

In Freeman's labor market analogue of the Hirschman product market case, quits are the expression of exit and unions are treated as the expression of collective voice. Freeman then contrasts the efficiency properties of the two mechanisms for transmitting to employers worker desires for conditions of employment, compensation packages, and rules of the work place.

Freeman's starting point is the familiar internal labor market argument that because of on-the-job skills specific to the firm and the costs of mobility and turnover, gains are to be had from regular employment, a continuing relation between firms and much of their work force, in which allocative and remunerative decisions are not directly controlled by the price mechanism. The contracts that result are complex and multidimensional, involving numerous issues other than wages, because workers care about nonpecuniary conditions of employment and the rules of the work place, and because different conditions, rules, and methods of organization have different costs. Also, because workers have some control over their own activities and can influence the productivity of others, particularly in "team" settings in which the monitoring of individuals is expensive, their attitudes, or morale, are potentially important inputs into the production process.

The "public goods" nature of the work place, therefore, arises from two sources. First, there are shared working conditions, which imply restrictions on individual behavior or an imperfect matching of an individual worker's preferences with plant policy. These shared working conditions raise questions about possible mechanisms, such as labor unions, for choosing levels of the goods and compensation for workers. Second, the public goods potential of the work place can also arise from nonseparability of effort input of each worker. Without a collective organization, the incentive for each individual to take account of the effects of his or her actions on others is too small. Note that for this public goods aspect of the work place to be relevant, two other conditions have to be met. First, there must be substantial costs to the firm in using the market in the form of search costs in finding new workers and mobility costs for workers who quit. Second, the production unit needs to be subject to a number of imperfectly foreseen, exogenous shocks that will require adjustments to meet efficiency conditions.

After Williamson, Wachter, and Harris (1975), Freeman argues that the complex, multidimensional, and continuing nature of the employment relation creates a substantial information problem in the labor market; his concern is to focus on the type of information about conditions and preferences conveyed by the exit and voice mechanisms.

Taking quits (exit) first, he argues that the amount of information to be inferred from quit data is small relative to the costs of processing that data. Thus, inferences about the preferences of workers who quit may yield incorrect information due to "selectivity bias." The wider the variation in tastes among workers, reflecting differences in preferences and position in the work place, and the greater the different modes of quit, the greater will be the difficulties of the inferential process.[8] On the other hand, obtaining direct information from interviews runs into the problem of motivating the quitter to detail workplace problems. In short, labor quits contain a high noise-to-signal ratio. Despite the well-known efficiency properties of marginal decisions, the point is made by Freeman that the extent of quitting to convey information may be suboptimal since workers who do quit will not benefit from the improvement in conditions that may result from their actions. But the *key* question is not one of whether individual mobility provides enough information to enable the employer to find the optimal labor contract but rather one of whether it outperforms the alternative information-acquisition mechanism arising from collective voice (which Freeman takes to be synonymous with trade unionism).

Voice is seen as a collective institution because the communal nature of work conditions and rules, which apply to all workers, creates a "public goods" problem of preference revelation and because of the need to police or monitor the *long-term* contractual agreement. The advantages of collective voice (again taken to be synonymous with unionism) over individual quits are taken to lie in the very different information about workers' preferences that is conveyed, namely specific facts about areas of discontent and actual trade-off (between wages or other conditions for desired improvements) possibilities. Perhaps more important is the role of voice as an institutional mechanism for innovation in labor contracts. Managerial attention and effort thus tends to be focused on labor issues on a regular basis.

Freeman argues that by providing a mode of expressing discontent beyond exiting, collective voice can be expected to reduce quit rates and absenteeism inter alia. As a result, labor turnover and training costs will be reduced and firm-specific investments in human capital will be increased. He also suggests a possibility of *efficiency* gains, although he clearly recognizes, in the spirit of previous section, that the reduction in quits engineered in this way may be excessive.

While resisting the standard monopoly view of unionism, Freeman nonetheless accepts that unions unequivocally set wages above and employment below competitive levels. He thus pursues a dual model of union behavior, in which monopoly gains are offset by other benefits to management. Specifically, by providing information and a mechanism for potentially complex bargaining among workers and between workers and management that is more efficient than quits, collective bargaining is likely to yield a better mix among wages, work conditions, rules of the work place, and a reduction in turnover costs and increased firm specific human capital. Bargaining among workers and potential worker demands for public or lumpy goods could then offset the inefficiency losses that inevitably result from the switch from a marginal to a median supply calculus (although the potential for manipulation of the union political organization is not addressed other than in passing).

In sum, Freeman presents a view of unionism with "two faces," each of which leads to a different view of the institution. As a voice institution, unions enable management to learn about and improve the operation of the work place and the production process. Collective voice can thus improve managerial efficiency. Equally, Freeman argues, a negative response by unions to reorganization can have adverse consequences for the performance of the firm. In fact, the new analysis tells us little of the direct, productivity-enhancing contribution of unions. Rather, the entire argument is couched in terms of collective voice, which, as noted above, is taken to be synonymous with trade unionism.

Interestingly, the idiosyncratic exchange literature contains little mention of trade unionism in its discussion of efficient market contracting. Major emphasis is placed on the job evaluation process, whereby wages attach to jobs rather than to individuals, thereby forestalling individual bargaining, and to internal promotion ladders that encourage a positive attitude toward on-the-job training and enable the firm to reward cooperative behavior. The role of grievance procedure with arbitration and orderly contract renewal is also stressed.[9] But Williamson, Wachter, and Harris (1975, p. 277) note that these results, while commonly facilitated by trade unions, do not strictly require trade unions (especially in small organizations). The authors also recognize that there are degrees of idiosyncracy, but fail to consider the corollary of whether there are varying requirements for unionism. Freeman (1976, p. 361) himself simply notes that his analysis is not directly applicable to the case of craftsmen.

The important question that arises is whether trade unions are actively or passively associated with productivity, accepting in part the basic public goods argument advanced by Freeman. Might it not be the case that *part* of the union-nonunion differential *is* a compensating differential reflecting conditions of work, such as a structured work setting, inflexibility of hours, employer-set overtime, and a faster work pace. While accepting that working conditions are public goods, the public goods dimension of nonseparability of effort input, and that voice can be more efficient for intrafirm resource allocation than exit, this interpretation differs in emphasis from that employed by Freeman. Specifically, one might postulate that certain working conditions—proxied by, say, work effort, proportion of time on job working with machines, and difficulty of taking time off work—will be positively related with union membership. Some support for this hypothesis is provided by Duncan and Stafford (1980). Interestingly, their analysis succeeds only in explaining two-fifths of the quality adjusted union-nonunion differential. One obvious implication is that the other three-fifths are indeed rents to union members. Another is of course that the residual is attributable to unmeasured personal skills. But the difference in emphasis of the two approaches remains. The role of working conditions is nowhere considered in the empirical test procedures adopted by the Harvard School, and reviewed in the next section.

At this point, it is perhaps useful to remind ourselves after Pencavel (1977, p. 139) that there is nothing novel in recognizing that the terms of exchange in the market for labor are not well defined. The typical labor contract does not enumerate exactly how each party will behave in different circumstances simply because it is prohibitively expensive of time, effort, and money to draw up and enforce such detailed contracts even if all future contingencies could be foreseen. But where an individual has the occasion to pursue his or her own interests at the expense of others and where it is costly to enforce contractual arrangements, the standard problem of shirking will arise. As Pencavel points out, the firm's response to informational problems of this type will involve a mix of incentives and penalties that take the form of combining aspects of various wage-payment systems with the use of supervisors to monitor employees' work effort. Thus, the trade union may be viewed as the employees' auditor of management or, when the union is given a role in overseeing work performance, as monitors of the employees. The efficiency of the organization will presumably depend on the extent to which these monitoring activities achieve a close association between productivity and rewards. While the activities of trade unions may on balance enhance productivity, the result is clearly not guaranteed. One casual test would be to investigate whether firms actively encourage the unionization of their workers. The conventional treatment of trade unionism implies that this will not be the case; as Pencavel (1977, p. 140) notes, the increased security from disagreeable management decisions secured by organization will tend to induce greater malfeasance on the part of unionized labor. Indeed, the conventional approach argues that trade unions will in fact formalize this misconduct via work rules and act in a conventional cartellike fashion by restricting output.

Before turning to the empirical evidence, let us enter one final remark on the use of the term "public good" in the foregoing. This should not be taken to imply that trade unions require the support of the closed shop, since the context is one of a demand-revealing process (though the evident disproportionate role of a particular group of members in collective decision making is ignored). Moreover, in light of the cautionary comments made above, it is more fitting to consider the services of trade unions as providing a club good for its members.

Empirical Evidence

As noted earlier, union-won wage increases cause a misallocation of resources by inducing newly unionized firms to hire fewer workers, to use more capital (and supervisory inputs) per worker, and to hire higher quality workers than is socially efficient. Ignoring for the moment those specific union contract provisions discussed earlier, and focusing upon net productivity effects, what evidence is there to support the Harvard view that unions raise productivity sufficiently to offset the cost increases of higher wages? (We shall assume for the purposes of the present discussion, and consistent with these and other research findings, that unions, having adjusted for quality differences, do secure a positive differential in favor of their members.)

Harvard School estimates of the impact of trade unions on productivity for a variety of industries are presented in table 5–1. As we shall see, the studies in question control for capital labor ratios and diverse other factors that may influence productivity. All the results, with the exception of the final line, show a positive effect of unionization on productivity that in most cases exceeds the monopoly (wage) effect.

Let us consider the studies in a little more detail, however, beginning with the path-breaking analysis of Brown and Medoff (1978)—a cross section study of the relationship between unionization and productivity of "otherwise comparable" union and nonunion workers across 20 two-digit U.S. manufacturing industries in 1972. Consider first the labor quality adjustment

Table 5-1. Selected Estimates of the Net Impact of Unionism on Productivity

Sample	Estimated Change in Output per Worker Due to Unionism (cet. par.)
Wooden household furniture[a]	+15%
All 2-digit SIC manufacturing industries[b]	+ 20 to + 24
Construction, all sectors[c]	+ 29 to + 38
Cement[d,e]	+ 6 to + 8
Underground bituminous coal[f]	
1965	+ 25 to + 30
1975	− 20 to − 25

Sources: [a]Frantz (1976); [b]Brown and Medoff (1978); [c]Allen (1979); [d]Clark (1980a); [e]Clark (1980b); [f]Freeman, Medoff, and Connerton (in process).

that is used to purge the estimates of those productivity effects that do not in any way reflect effects attributable to unions. Brown and Medoff estimate a wage equation (earnings function) over May 1973–1975 CPS (Current Population Survey) data to establish the value of observable labor quality indexes (age and education) in the sample. Dummies for a sector of regions are included as controls. The coefficients of the wage equation are then used to calculate a predicted wage ($\hat{q}_m$) for each worker, m, in each state by industry cell. Thus the labor quality variable for state i in industry j equals:

$$Q_{ij} = \sum_{m \in i, j} \hat{q}_m w_m / \sum_{m \in i, j} w_m,$$

where w_m is m's CPS sampling weight.

This measure is included as an independent variable in some equations and to weight the dependent variable in others.

Brown and Medoff also report the coefficients of the wage equations when union membership (a dummy variable) is included as an independent variable. These results indicate a sizable union wage effect—24 percent and 21 percent for females and males, respectively. Not surprisingly, perhaps, the wage equations explain less than 40 percent of the variance in log earnings.[10]

Having obtained a labor quality adjustment factor, Brown and Medoff estimate a production function of the form:

$$ln(Y/L) \simeq ln\, A + \alpha ln\, (K/L) + (\alpha + \beta - 1)\, ln\, L + \beta\, (c - 1)\, P, \quad (5.1)$$

where

Y = output, measured in value added terms;

K = capital;

L_u = union labor;

L_n = nonunion labor;

$L = L_u + L_n$;

$P = L_u/L$;

α = elasticity of output with respect to capital;

β = elasticity of output with respect to labor;

c = ratio of marginal product of union to nonunion labor.

Equation (5.1) is then run for labor unadjusted and adjusted for quality. A comparison of the two estimated equations reveals that virtually none of the union productivity effect is attributable to measured quality differences. In the regression for which labor was not adjusted for quality, the coefficient obtained was 0.237, thus implying that unionized establishments are 24 percent more productive than nonunionized establishments when the quality of the labor forces is not held constant. With the quality adjustment, the coefficient points to unionized establishments being 22 percent more productive which, if entirely attributable to labor, implies a union labor productivity effect of around 30 percent (measured by the coefficient divided by 1 minus the K/L coefficient).

One basic difficulty with the study lies in its use of value added labor as a dependent variable (as opposed to, say, physical labor output). Clearly, if unions have a wage effect and relative cost differences are fully reflected in prices, the estimated union coefficient identifies only a price effect. Another difficulty is the production function assumption:

$$Y_n = AK_n^\alpha\, L_n{}^{1-\alpha}$$

$$Y_u = AK_u^\alpha\, (BL_u)^{1-\alpha,}$$

namely, that the production functions of the two sectors are identical, with the exception of the productivity of labor parameter, B, in the union sector. This raises the possibility of specification bias in the estimation of the productivity parameter, c. Brown and Medoff themselves show the ambiguities introduced by potential differences in technology.

Some advances are reported in the interesting study by Allen (1979) of the craft-oriented construction industry. Allen's methodology is almost identical to that employed by Brown and Medoff, but he does include the state price index as an independent variable in his production function to test whether the percentage unionized, P, is merely a proxy for price differences. The inclusion of this variable does indeed reduce the coefficient on the unionization variable (from 0.33 to 0.29), but it remains significant at the 1 percent level. Recognizing the possibility of errors in his price index, Allen reestimates his equation with the constraint that the coefficient of the state price index equals unity. The union coefficient now falls to 0.150 with a standard error of 0.091, leading Allen to conclude that part, though not all, of the reported union productivity effect (see below) represents a price effect.

Allen also attempts to control for differences in technology by including two industry and eight region dummies. More importantly, he attempts a simple test of the null hypothesis $(\alpha_u - \alpha_n) = 0$. His regression results confirm that the hypothesis cannot be rejected at the 5 percent level, although the possibility of specification error remains.

Overall, Allen's coefficients on P yield values in the range 0.29 to 0.38, which, in association with the estimated capital-labor ratio coefficients, imply that union workers (in each industry) in each region are between 38 percent and 51 percent more productive than their nonunion counterparts. Corresponding coefficients for the union dichotomous variable in the quality adjusted wage equation (estimated over both men and women) indicate a 43 percent differential.

Taken at face value these results are perhaps somewhat surprising in view of the fact that make-work rules and policies are likely to be more prevalent in construction than elsewhere. Technical issues apart, some qualification to Allen's study is provided by the analysis of Mandelstamm (1965), who concluded that the greater efficiency in unionized firms detected in his own construction industry sample was due to the rejection of those workers who could not be paid the union rate.[11] Mandelstamm tentatively concluded that factors not associated with the unions have been the primary causes of the superior efficiency of the unionized (Ann Arbor) labor market, while noting that the unfavorable (intrafirm allocative) aspects of union behavior, associated with working rules and suppression of new techniques, had little effect.

The final analysis to which I refer in detail in the particular context of the general productivity augmenting effects of unionization (I shall comment on the negative productivity value cited for bituminous coal mining in 1975 below) are those of Clark (1980a, 1980b). The two studies cover much the same ground, and I shall base the burden of my comments on the former study. Conceptually, Clark's study marks an advance on the earlier investigations, but, as we shall see, his results even when viewed in their most favorable (half) light suggest a union-induced productivity-augmenting effect of between 6 and 8 percent coupled with a monopoly (wage) effect of between 12 and 18 percent.

Clark investigates some six plants within the U.S. cement industry that changed their union status in the 1953–1976 period. The strengths of his time-series analysis are as follows. First, the dependent variable is measured in physical output (per manhour) of production workers, thus sidestepping the price effect difficulty noted earlier. Second, differences in technology are controlled for by comparing plants of the same vintage. Third, an attempt is made to control for "firm effects," such as inherent differences in the quality of management. (Note that without direct measures of the organizational factors, productivity effects specific to the firm cannot be held fixed in cross-sectional data.) Fourth, changes in the supervisor-production worker ratio are controlled for. This is potentially most important since we might expect the firm to respond to a price change by altering the ratio upward in an endeavor to monitor work effort more thoroughly, in addition to altering the labor-capital ratio. Finally, Clark also attempts the qualitatively valuable exercise of ascertaining what changes in the internal operations of the firm followed the change in union status.

Clark first estimates the standard Cobb-Douglas production function, constraining the production process in the union-nonunion sectors to be identical (but see below). Here his primary focus is on the analysis of firm fixed effects. In the absence of other data, he controls for these effects by assuming that the errors in his basic equation have the following structure:

$$\begin{aligned} \upsilon_{it} &= \mu_{it} + \varepsilon_{it}; \\ E\,\upsilon_{it} &= \mu_i; \\ \operatorname{cov}(\upsilon_{it}, \upsilon_{is}) &= E\varepsilon_{it}\,\varepsilon_{is} \\ &= \sigma_\upsilon^2 \text{ when } i = j \text{ and } t = s \\ &= 0 \text{ otherwise.} \end{aligned}$$

Thus the firm specific component (μ_i) is fixed and ε_{it} is uncorrelated across establishments and through time. Under this specification, consistent estimates of the basic equation can be obtained with pooled data by introducing individual establishment intercepts. Tests for additional serial correlation are also presented by the author.

What does the introduction of improved measurement and controls reveal?

The upshot of a fairly sophisticated estimating procedure produces union-induced productivity effects in the 6 to 10 percent range (though labor quality is not controlled for at this stage). Clark fails to comment on the fact that none of the union coefficients is significant at conventional levels (on a two-tailed test). Rather, importance is attached to the broad stability (and positive sign) of the coefficients themselves with changing model specification. In subsequently attempting a rather novel correction for unmeasured labor quality differences, Clark notes the monopoly (wage) effect to be in the range of 12 to 18 percent. The disparity between the productivity-augmenting union effect and the monopoly effect is apparently insufficient to raise unit costs.[12]

What I would interpret to be the same, essentially modest results are reported by Clark (1980b) in a more refined analysis, again of the cement industry but now cross section in form. Here he allows the production function to differ as between union and nonunion plants and to allow for regional differences in the union effect. The union productivity differential is again shown to lie in the 6 to 8 percent range, irrespective of the technology constraint. Interestingly, negative values for the union coefficient now appear.

Summarizing the evidence thus far, I would argue that improved methods of isolating the effect of unionism yield ambiguous results for the collective voice model of trade unions. Most importantly, the evidence does not establish that unionized firms are on average more productive because they are unionized. In this latter context, the notion that unions make firms with workers of given personal characteristics more productive would be more persuasive if the *mechanics* by which productivity is improved were isolated in empirical tests. While Clark's (1980a) study describes in some detail the changes in the labor contract and the operation of the firm consequent to the change in union status, he is unable to chart a clear picture of workers' behavioral changes (*e.g.*, exit behavior and, more important, work group effectiveness). What he is able to do is detect a consistent pattern of management adjustments on the lines of the shock effect model. Here his qualitative analysis suggests evidence of lapses from X-efficiency but has no dynamic content. Also in such circumstances there is no guarantee that the consumer will be the beneficiary of positive net changes in productivity.

The only quantitative evidence of the mechanisms by which trade unions improve productivity is contained in Brown and Medoff (1978) and Freeman (1980). The former offer a relatively simple test procedure. First they regressed the (state/industry) quit rate and then the wage rate on their regional and industry dummies, labor quality, and fraction unionized. Their results indicate that unionized establishments had annual quit rates substantially lower than those of nonunionized establishments even when the rate was held constant. They next reestimated their production function, first including fraction unionized, then omitting fraction unionized and substituting the quit rate, and finally including both variables. Their hypothesis is simply that if unionization worked exclusively through the mechanism of quits to improve productivity, then the fraction unionized coefficient should fall to zero in the final iteration. It emerges that quits, despite their statistically significant effect on output (value added per worker), reduce the importance of fraction unionized by only one-fifth. Brown and Medoff conclude that other factors, such as better management, morale, motivation and communication inter alia explain (in some unmeasured way) the residual four-fifths. Another interpretation would be that, even if we can accept the implicit direction of causation employed by the authors (see below), a specific productivity variable explains a modest amount of the variance in labor's value added. How far this construction takes us becomes starkly evident when we recall from table 5–1 that Freeman, Medoff, and Connerton detect a "perverse" productivity effect of unionism in coal mining for part of their sample period.

Also to be noted is the point, recognized by Brown and Medoff, that if workers with low propensities to quit due to large investments in firm-specific capital are more prone to unionization, the coefficient on fraction unionized will be an upwardly biased measure, with additional ramifications for the production function itself.

Freeman's (1980) study casts some light on the direction of causation issue; that is, he asks whether his main results, which point to a strongly negative effect of unionism on quits and a strongly positive effect on tenure, ceteris paribus, (see table 5–2) are the result of unions organizing inherently more stable workers, as opposed to his postulated mechanism whereby the union institution itself causes workers' behavior to change. Using longitudinal data from the Michigan Panel Study of Income Dynamics, he attempts to standardize for the stable worker using a fixed effect logit model (Freeman, 1978). Controlling for the individual propensity to quit has no effect on the unionism coefficient in his previously estimated turnover equation, while the coefficient on wages changes in sign and becomes insignificant at conventional levels. This interesting result requires fuller investigation. In the interim, it is necessary to emphasize that Freeman does not have a direct measure of the voice component of unionism. Rather, he adduces support for the voice model from the failure of other factors to explain the union effect. If collective voice does not require the presence of a union, then Freeman's test procedures are ambiguous. Perhaps most

Table 5-2. Estimates of the Effect of Unionism on Quits and Tenure, Wages Held Constant

Sample	*Percentage Reduction in Quits Due to Unionism*	*Percentage Increase in Tenure Due to Unionism*
Michigan panel study of income dynamics, all workers	45%	36%
Current population surveys, 1973–75, all workers	86	—
National longitudinal survey,		
older men (48–62 in 1969)	107	38
younger men (17–27 in 1969)	11	15
Bureau of Labor Statistics, industry-level turnover rates, manufacturing workers	34–38	—

Source: Freeman (1980).

important of all is the fact that Freeman conducts his analysis in a setting divorced from the determinants of unionization.

What of the evidence of nonwage *inefficiencies* introduced by trade unions? Systematic empirical evidence in this area is sparse, the bulk of the material either taking the form of case studies of establishments (Slichter, Healy, and Livernash, 1960) or somewhat casual empiricism (Haber and Levinson, 1956). Much interesting British material came to light as a result of the deliberations of the Donovan Commission (1968), most notably in the context of productivity agreements. Unfortunately, although this evidence is suggestive of the importance of restrictive/protective practices, it is not directly relevant (at least in the short run) to the question of assessing the contribution of unionism to productivity since the workers in question were unionized both before and after the introduction of productivity agreements. It is well known that unorganized workers themselves practice restriction of output (Mathewson, 1931), and the influence of informal work groups on output and performance has been a subject of intensive study by social scientists since Roethlesberger and Dickson's (1939) pioneering study. Yet, as noted in the previous section, it might reasonably be argued that union structure is likely to effect a more effective policing of the cartel (Pencavel, 1977). Accordingly, we shall have again to confine our comments to net effects. Earlier we noted that Freeman, Medoff, and Connerton detected a "perverse" (to them) impact of unionism on productivity in U.S. underground bituminous coal mining for 1975. However, the authors "balance" this result in reporting a positive 25 to 30 percent productivity effect in the same industry for 1965. The unfavorable movement is attributed to deteriorating industrial relations in the union sector in the late 1960s and 1970s, associated with the internal problems of the United Mine Workers on one side and the employment of inferior supervisory personnel on the other.

The only other systematic study is that of Pencavel (1977), relating to the performance of the unionized sector of the British coal mining industry from 1900–1913. Having failed to detect a union relative wage effect at this time—his analysis thus uncontaminated by price effects—Pencavel postulates that production technology in coal mining is characterized by a CES production function and tests the argument that the production frontier of unionized coal fields lies parallel to and everywhere inside that of nonunionized coal fields. In other words, he tests whether the neutral efficiency parameter, A, varies with the extent of unionism, every other parameter of the function being unaffected. The efficiency parameter is specified as a function of time (to incorporate technological progress), the mean width of coal seams (to account for geological elements in coal production), and the fraction of the work force belonging to trade unions.

The equation was estimated in both logarithmic and semilogarithmic form; the latter reflecting the possibility that the effect of unionism on output is also a function of the level of unionization. For his logarithmic specification, Pencavel obtains a significantly negative coefficient on fraction unionized of -0.110 (0.033). Given that the fraction unionized in coal mining rose from 66 percent to 80 percent over the period in question, it follows that this development was associated with a reduction in coal output of 2.3 per cent (-0.110×21.2 percent). For his semilogarithmic specification, the coefficient on proportion unionized is again significantly negative at -0.217 (0.053), thus indicating a depressing effect of unions on productivity of 3.1 percent (-0.217×14). Taking this latter value, production of coal at the end of the sample period would have been 9 million tons above what it was had the fraction of miners unionized remained at its 1900 level. Indeed, if we are entitled to extend the results beyond the range of sample observations, it emerges that a totally unionized coal field would produce some 22 percent less output than its completely unorganized counterpart.

Interestingly, Pencavel's findings lend support to the assertions made at that time (e.g., Pratt, 1904) that the growth of unionism did contribute to the declining productivity of British coal mining because of increased absenteeism, a rising disputes trend, a cut in hours, and the reduced fear on the part of miners, in the wake of unionization, of the disciplinary actions of employers.

If any one single conclusion has to be drawn from the empirical evidence surveyed above, it is that the behavioral productivity enhancing facets of this "second face" of unionism have yet conclusively to be established, even within the short run. Indeed, the empirical evidence suggests an impact (short-run) of unionism that is not many standard deviations away from the basic analysis of the impact of a minimum wage law. Most of the interesting questions thus remain unanswered.

Conclusions

Conventionally, the effects of unions on productivity are measured by adding together intrafirm allocative inefficiencies associated with job regulation and interfirm allocative costs associated with the union-nonunion wage differential. The view of the Harvard School is that the former costs are in general negative (though their underlying collective voice model presumably applies only to industrial unions) and of sufficient magnitude to more than offset the increase in costs resulting from the higher wages of unionized labor. Thus union and nonunion firms can compete alongside one another in competitive product markets. The empirical evidence supplied in support of this hypothesis, when viewed in its most favorable light, does little more than suggest evidence of a shock effect. The direct contribution of unions is unclear, and, moreover, the dynamic aspect of unionism is ignored. In the absence of other explanatory variables (e.g., participation, achievement, and reward), one might well conclude that future offsetting opportunities, both in the areas of economic substitution and institutional response, will diminish. Here, the human capital theoretic explanation of the job regulatory practices of trade unions presented in the second section has both more dynamic content and policy prescriptive content. Though the latter has not been commented upon in the paper, we refer here to the buying out of restrictive-protective practices and the closed shop, the consideration of severance payments to ease the resistance of labor to technological change, and the possibility of amalgamating the best features of productivity bargaining with those of payment-by-result schemes.

Also pertinent is the Harvard School failure to establish that unionization (rather than collective voice per se) is necessary to the efficient contracting mode of internal labor markets. The upshot is that the few empirical tests geared toward isolating the *mechanisms* by which productivity is supposedly increased (namely, reduced quits) are flawed. In other words, and as noted in the second section, quits could be "artificially" reduced by unionization of a "given" internal labor market structure, which the authors have no way of standardizing for.

On a related issue, the implicit direction of causation employed by the Harvard School is ambiguous. Their thesis is of course that unionism leads either directly or indirectly to increased productivity. Yet higher-than-average productivity could be associated with certain working conditions—for example, structured work settings, inflexibility of hours, and a faster work pace—that cause unionization (or simply collective voice). According to this view, unions are a passive rather than an active agent in improving productivity. More importantly, empirical tests should seek to identify an association between working conditions/productivity and unionization, not simply the converse. We alluded to certain empirical evidence favoring this interpretation in the previous section, and noted that three-fifths of the union-nonunion differential (standardized for labor quality) remained unexplained.

Unions in the Harvard School view of reality suffer from split personalities. On the one hand, they behave like monopolies on the wages front and on the other (admittedly in the limit), engage in a collaborative exercise with management. They appear rather like certain public utilities that maximize profits by output restriction on the one hand and subsequently engage in other, nonprofit maximizing pursuits. The difference is of course that public utilities behave in this way (i.e., cross subsidize) because they are constrained by the regulatory agency. Unions face no such constraint. Nor are we told of the industrial relations variables that presumably mediate the association between productivity and rewards.

In short, whether the Harvard thesis constitutes a model of trade union behavior is questionable. Certainly the analysis fails conspicuously to consider public choice theory. Thus, perhaps not surprisingly, the test procedures implemented are more closely geared to show the inability of other factors to explain the union effect rather than to provide positive support for their collective voice hypothesis, with the possible exception of Freeman (1980). This lacuna becomes most starkly evident on the odd occasion that a "perverse" effect of unionism on productivity is detected (Freeman, Medoff, and Connerton, in process). Here recourse is made to ad hoc industrial relations variables.

In concluding this chapter, it is appropriate to consider what might be termed the "third face" of unionism (Troy, Koeller, and Sheflin, 1980). We refer here to the exertion of political power by trade unions to extract, maintain, and enhance the monopolization of labor markets, and indeed to expand state intervention in labor markets and generally to increase the level of public expenditures. The first point that should perhaps be made here is the simple though often neglected one that real resources are consumed in order to obtain and maintain monopolization of labor markets. In the limit, the costs of competing for the additional earnings received by union members would be equal to the value of those additional earnings. This consideration will clearly inflate the real costs of trade unionism over and above those conventional estimates reviewed in the previous section based on the price and nonprice effects of unionism.

Economists in general have eschewed investigation of this third dimension of trade unionism, despite the fact that no monopoly in the economic marketplace has much chance of sustaining itself in the long run against the processes of market competition and innovation unless it can achieve some protection via the apparatus of the state. Recently, however, there have been signs of a shift in research resources toward investigation of the political dimension of trade union power. For the United Kingdom, Burton (1979) has presented an interesting analysis of the way British unions have used their economic power to obtain legal immunities that have in turn buttressed their power in the economic marketplace. In other words, economic power and political power are seen as reinforcing/interacting. Clearly, unions in the United States have also sought the regulatory benefits of the state, particularly in situations in which organizing workers into monopolies has proved difficult. Thus the Railway Act in 1926 enforced collective bargaining in interstate transportation; the 1930s saw the introduction of the Davis Bacon Act to protect union wages in construction, the Norris-LaGuardia Act to restrict court injunctions against union violence, the Walsh-Healey Act to spread union wages among federal contractors, and the Fair Labor Standards Act to fix minimum wages, overtime premiums, and working hours. Perhaps most important of all in this context was the Wagner Act of 1935. This act supplied the government services demanded by unions in the form of government determination of bargaining units, representation elections, monopoly bargaining rights (which, incidentally, has had the effect of *artificially* creating a public goods element in the services provided by trade unions), and machinery for enforcement.

Recently, in an effort to stem the ebb of union power in the private sector, U.S. unions lobbied vigorously for the ill-fated Labor Reform Act of 1977, an attempt to be seen as but one aspect of a continuing quest for more decisive governmental intervention to facilitate the organization of those groups that unions find most difficult to organize.

The lobbying activities of U.S. unions have recently come under scrutiny by Heldman and Knight (1980), whose analysis casts doubt on the assertion of Freeman and Medoff (1979) that unions are political institutions that represent the will of their members. Using data on the surveys of leading pollsters, Heldman and Knight detect wide discrepancies between members' preferences and AFL-CIO lobbying goals before Congress, most concretely in the cases of union security/compulsory membership and so-called "common-situs" picketing.

We raise these issues simply to confront the Freeman-Medoff view that union monopoly power and political power can safely be divorced because of the *assumed* benign nature of the latter. Analysis of union lobbying activities is a useful though partial analysis of this wider question. Freeman and Medoff ignore the monopoly aspect of the exertion of political power, simply lumping together assumed beneficial political activities along with the productivity-enhancing characteristic of collective voice within their second face of unionism.

Now it may well be that there are profound economic benefits attaching to the closer integration of trade unions into decision making at the highest level, but this has to be demonstrated and not merely asserted or assumed away. A positive development in this area has been the focus of political theorists and sociologists on the sociopolitical nature of the inflationary process. By positive, I mean the welcome shift of attention in inflation analysis fundamental as opposed to proximate determinants rather than toward the analytical context of the sociopolitical analysis itself (on which, see Addison and Burton, 1981). One might refer to the corporatist version of the sociopolitical model, which postulates a relationship between corporatist-industrial relations, social democracy, and industrial conflict through to social democratic corporatism, trade union capacity for restraint, and inflation (e.g., Crouch, 1983).

Already I begin to range well beyond the remit of this paper. But this is a comment on the open-ended nature of the Harvard collective voice thesis. Although a thought-provoking and often useful treatment, that thesis is partial and but loosely specified. Having said this, one is aware of the limitations of the somewhat simplistic view of unionism offered in the present paper, and it is to be hoped that the conference proceedings will shed somewhat more positive, choice-theoretical light on the economics of trade unions that I have attempted here.

Notes

1. Olson (1979, pp. 37–38) would deny the effect is once-for-all, arguing that unions will choose successively higher points along the employers' labor demand curves as time goes on. His public choice theoretic rationale for this behavior is that the core of older-worker decision makers in the union is successively reduced by retirements and deaths.

2. See Burton (1978).

3. See, *Report of the Committee of Inquiry into the Regulation of the Medical Profession*. 1975. London: Her Majesty's Stationery Office, Cmnd. 6018, para. 151.

4. See, *Manpower in the Chemical Industry*. 1967. British Chemical Economic Development Council, London: Her Majesty's Stationery Office, pp. 10.

5. See *Report of the Committee* (1975).

6. See also Johnson and Mieszkowski (1970).

7. Rees (1963, pp. 775) does note that management in a single industry—railroads—claimed in 1959 that obsolete work rules were costing some $500 million a year or, equivalently, 0.1 percent of the national product.

8. In addition to separations, quit behaviour includes absenteeism, partial withdrawal of labor time, and the reduction of work effort in the form of malingering or slack or in extreme cases "quiet sabotage."

9. In the United States, 30 percent of nonunion firms have formal grievance procedures.

10. Observable characteristics, such as age, sex, race, education, inter alia may be poor indicators of the true attribute of interest, namely, mechanical aptitude. Accordingly, hedonic wage equations may be subject to serious bias due to omitted (i.e., unobservable) variables.

11. We also note that Mandelstamm avoids the chronic problem of measuring output in the heterogeneous product construction sector by having union and nonunion contractors cost out an identical product.

12. In general, however, unit costs are increased by unionism because the higher productivity (sic) under unionism is not large enough to offset higher compensation *plus* higher capital intensity.

References

Addison, J. T., and Burton, J. 1981. "The Sociopolitical Analysis of Inflation," *mimeo*. University of South Carolina.

Allen, S. G. 1979. *Unionized Construction Workers Are More Productive*. Washington, D.C.: Center to Protect Workers' Rights, November.

Becker, G. S. 1959. "Union Restrictions on Entry." In *The Public Stake in Union Power,* ed. P. D. Bradley. Charlottesville, Virginia: University of Virginia Press, pp. 209–224.

Brown, C., and Medoff, J. L. 1978. "Trade Unions in the Production Process." *Journal of Political Economy* 86, no. 3 (June):355–378.

Burton, J. 1978. "Are Trade Unions a Public Good/Bad?" In *Trade Unions: Public Goods or Public 'Bads'*? L. Robbins et al. London: Institute of Economic Affairs, Readings 17, pp. 43–52.

———. 1979. *The Trojan Horse—Union Power in British Politics*. Leesburg, Virginia: Adam Smith Institute.

Clark, K. B. 1980a. "The Impact of Unionization on Productivity: A Case Study." *Industrial and Labor Relations Review* 33, no. 4 (July):451–469.

———. 1980b. "Unionization and Productivity: Micro-Econometric Evidence." *Quarterly Journal of Economics* 95, no. 4 (December):613–639.

Crouch, C. 1983. "The Conditions for Trade-Union Wage Restraints." In *The*

Politics and Sociology of Global Inflation, ed. L. Lindberg and C. Maier. Washington, D.C.: The Brookings Institution (forthcoming).

Doeringer, P. B., and Piore, M. J. 1971. *Internal Labor Markets and Manpower Analysis*. Lexington, Mass.: Heath.

Donovan Commission. 1968. Royal Commission on Trade Unions and Employers' Associations. *Report*, London: HMSO (Cmnd. 3623).

Duncan, G. J., and Stafford, F. P. 1980. "Do Union Members Receive Compensating Differentials?" *American Economic Review* 70, no. 3 (June):355–371.

Flanders, A. 1964. *The Fawley Productivity Agreements*. London: Faber and Faber.

Frantz, J. R. 1976. "The Impact of Trade Unions on Production in the Wooden Household Furniture Industry." Senior Honors Thesis, Harvard University, March.

Freeman, R. B. 1976. "Individual Mobility and Union Voice in the Labor Market." *American Economic Review, Papers and Proceedings* 66, no. 2 (May): 361–368.

______. 1978. "A Fixed Effect Logit Model of the Impact of Unions on Quits." *NBER Working Paper*, no. 280.

______. 1980. "The Exit-Voice Tradeoff in the Labor Market: Unionism, Job Tenure, Quits and Separations." *Quarterly Journal of Economics* 94, no. 4 (June):643–673.

Freeman, R. B., and Medoff, J. L. 1979. "The Two Faces of Unionism." *Public Interest* (Fall):69–93.

Freeman, R. B., Medoff, J. L., and Connerton, M. L. " Industrial Relations and Productivity: A Study of the U.S. Bituminous Coal Industry" (in process).

Friedman, M. 1951. "Some Comments on the Significance of Labor Unions for Economic Policy." In *The Impact of the Union*, ed. D. M. Wright. New York: Harcourt Brace, pp. 204–234.

Goldberg, J. P. 1973. "Longshoremen and the Modernization of Cargo Handling in the United States." *International Labor Review* 107, no. 3 (March):253–279.

Gomberg, W. 1972. "Featherbedding: An Assertion of Property Rights." In *Readings in Labor Economics and Labor Relations*, ed. R. L. Rowan. Homewood, Ill.: Irwin, pp. 350–359.

Harber, W., and Levinson, H. 1956. *Labor Relations and Productivity in the Residential Construction Industry*. Ann Arbor: University of Michigan.

Harberger, A. 1954. "Monopoly and Resource Allocation." *American Economic Review, Papers and Proceedings* 24, no. 2 (May):77–87.

Heldman, D. C., and Knight, D. L. 1980. *Unions and Lobbying—The Representative Function*. Arlington, Virginia: Foundation for the Advancement of the Public Trust.

Hirschman, A. O. 1970. *Exit, Voice, and Loyalty*. Cambridge, Mass.: Harvard University Press.

Holen, A. S. 1965. "Effects of Professional Licensing Arrangements on Interstate Labor Mobility and Resource Allocation." *Journal of Political Economy* 73, no. 5 (October):492–498.

Johnson, H. G., and Mieszkowski, P. 1970. "The Effects of Unionization on Distribution of Income: A General Equilibrium Approach." *Quarterly Journal of Economics* 84, no. 4 (November):539–561.

Killingsworth, C. C. 1962. "The Modernization of West Coast Longshore Work Rules." *Industrial and Labor Relations Review* 15, no. 3 (April):295–306.

Mandelstamm, A. B. 1965. "The Effects of Unions on Efficiency in the Residential Construction Industry: A Case Study." *Industrial and Labor Relations Review* 18, no. 4 (July):503–521.

Mathewson, S. B. 1931. *Restrictions of Output Among Unorganized Workers*. New York: Viking Press.

Mellish, F. 1970. *The Docks After Devlin*. London: Heinemann.

Miller, R. L. 1976. "Right to Work Laws and Compulsory Union Membership in the United States." *British Journal of Industrial Relations* 14, no. 2 (July): 186–193.

Miyazaki, H. 1977. "The Rat Race and Internal Labor Markets." *Bell Journal of Economics* 8, no. 2 (Autumn):394–418.

Olson, M. 1979. "An Evolutionary Approach to Macroeconomics," *mimeo*. University of Maryland.

Pencavel, J. H. 1977. "The Distributional and Efficiency Effects of Trade Unions in Britain." *British Journal of Industrial Relations* 15, no. 2 (July):137–156.

Pratt, E. A. 1904. *Trade Unionism and British Industry*.

Pratten, C. F. 1975. *Labour Productivity Differentials Within International Companies*. Cambridge: Cambridge University Press.

Reder, M. W. 1960. "Job Scarcity and the Nature of Union Power." *Industrial and Labor Relations Review* 13, no. 3 (April):349–362.

Rees, A. 1963. "Effects of Unions on Resource Allocation." *Journal of Law and Economics* 6 (October):69–78.

Rees, A. 1977. *The Economics of Trade Unions*. Chicago, Ill.: University of Chicago Press.

Robinson, D. 1970. "External and Internal Labour Markets." In *Local Labour Markets and Wage Structures*, ed. D. Robinson. London: Gower Press, pp. 28–67.

Roethlesberger, F. J., and Dickson, W. J. 1939. *Management and the Worker*. Cambridge, Mass.: Harvard University Press.

Ross, A. M. 1958. "Do We Have a New Industrial Feudalism?" *American Economic Review* 48, no. 5 (December):903–920.

Rottenberg, S. 1962. "The Economics of Occupational Licensing." In *Aspects of Labor Economics*, National Bureau of Economic Research. Princeton, N.J.: Princeton University Press, pp. 3–20.

Siebert, W. S. 1977. "Occupational Licensing: The Merrison Report on the Regulation of the Medical Profession." *British Journal of Industrial Relations* 15, no. 1 (March):29–38.

Simler, N. J. 1962. "The Economics of Featherbedding." *Industrial and Labor Relations Review* 16, no. 1 (October):111–121.

Slichter, S. H., Healy, J. J., and Livernash, E. R. 1960. *The Impact of Collective*

Bargaining on Management. Washington, D.C.: The Brookings Institution.

Sloan, F. 1970. "Lifetime Earnings and Physicians' Choice of Speciality." *Industrial and Labor Relations Review* 24, no. 1 (October):47–56.

______. 1976. "Real Returns to Medical Education—A Comment." *Journal of Human Resources* 11, no. 1 (Winter):118–126.

Stinchcombe, J. G. 1965. "Social Structure and Organization." In *Handbook of Organizations*, ed. J. G. March. Chicago, Ill.: Rand McNally, pp. 142–193.

Strauss, G. 1965. "Apprenticeship: An Evaluation of the Need." In *Employment Policy and the Labor Market*, ed. A. M. Ross. Berkeley and Los Angeles: University of California Press.

Troy, L., Koeller, C. T., and Sheflin, N. 1980. "The Three Faces of Unionism." *Policy Review* 14 (Fall):95–108.

Weinstein, P. 1960. "Featherbedding: A Theoretical Analysis." *Journal of Political Economy* 68, no. 4 (August):379–387.

______. 1964. "The Featherbedding Problem." *American Economic Review* 54, no. 2 (May):145–152.

Williamson, O. E., Wachter, M. L., and Harris, J. E. 1975. "Understanding the Employment Relation: The Analysis of Idiosyncratic Exchange." *Bell Journal of Economics* 6, no. 2 (Autumn):250–278.

A Comment on Addison, by John H. Pencavel

John Addison's paper on restrictive practices and on recent studies of the effect of trade unions on productivity induced me to consider whether restrictive practices might be a predictable feature of a particular class of employment contracts. I discuss this first and then offer a few comments on Brown and Medoff's (1978) influential paper.

Restrictive Practices and Employment Contracts

What are "restrictive practices"? Some writers appear to define restrictive practices in the labor market as behavioral rules that reduce the level of an individual's or a firm's output below its maximum. This definition is unsatisfactory for the simple reason that output is never maximized: An employee's choice not to work any overtime may well mean that this individual has forfeited an opportunity to raise his or her output at the place of work, but has not failed to maximize his or her utility.. A more satisfactory approach rests on the understanding that the voluntary transfer of property rights over goods and services, including labor services, always involves the explicit or tacit negotiation of the terms under which the exchange is to take place. To focus attention exclusively on conditions placed on the employment contract that result in a lower level of production than would obtain in the absence of these conditions is to ignore the substitutability among different dimensions of the contract. If such "output-reducing provisions" on the employment contract restrict the employer's exclusive discretionary authority over the range of activities to which these workers may be assigned, then these labor services are less valuable to the employer. Consequently, in a competitive market in which each individual worker freely maintains such provisions in the employment contract, these "output-reducing provisions" will be associated with lower remuneration paid to the workers. In this case, as far as the allocation of resources is concerned, the situation is no different analytically from one in which workers in accident-prone industries are compensated by higher wages for the risks they take. In each situation, the worker trades some pecuniary for nonpecuniary income.

It is no wonder, then, that "output-reducing provisions" of the employment contract are found in nonunionized as well as in unionized markets. Indeed,

*I have benefitted from discussions with Orley Ashenfelter on some of the issues addressed here.

in a number of cases, unions surely do no more than register (in perhaps a better publicized fashion) the attitudes of its members and the existence of the union makes no essential difference to the terms of the employment contract. Turn now to noncompetitive labor markets, and, in particular, consider the determination of the employment contract in a labor market in which a trade union exercises some monopoly influence. As is the case in competition, particular provisions of the employment contract cannot be detached and analyzed separately from the rest, and, consequently, we cannot avoid the issue of how wages, employment, and other aspects of the exchange are settled in unionized labor markets.

Two major classes of explanation describe contract determination in unionized markets, in each of which the wage rate of union members and their number employed are arguments of the union leader's objective function. One explanation is what I have called in my paper at this conference the "modified Fellner-Cartter model," a special case that characterizes the employer's profit-maximizing labor demand function as a constraint on the union's simultaneous attainment of high wages and high employment. According to this model, at each wage rate management selects the number of workers to employ such that the marginal revenue product of labor equals the wage rate. When the union leader selects a wage above the transfer price of labor, then some mechanism must be adopted to ration employment among those offering themselves for work. Rationing schemes include long apprenticeship programs, high initiation fees, seniority rules, and nepotism. Because employment adjusts so that the marginal revenue product of labor equals the wage rate, this sort of employment contract should not be characterized by restrictive work practices such as make-work and featherbedding.

A second model describing the resolution of labor contracts in unionized labor markets has the employer and union leader entering into agreements such that the wage-employment combination lies somewhere on their contract curve and, from the point of view of the two parties (but not of society), the contract is Pareto efficient. As Leontief (1946) and Fellner (1947) pointed out over 30 years ago, this outcome is consistent with a powerful union presenting management with an "all-or-nothing" wage and employment package. Here employment will be set at a level such that the wage rate exceeds the marginal revenue product of labor. Expressed differently, the union's monopoly position is obliging the firm to employ more workers than it would otherwise choose to at the negotiated wage, and these superfluous workers will be accommodated through minimum crew rules, featherbedding, make-work practices, and other manifestations of the inefficient use of labor. In this way, a natural definition of restrictive practices suggests itself: namely, monopolistic rules that maintain the marginal revenue product of labor below the wage rate. Also, because the transfer price of labor will fall short of the wage rate, as in the case of the Fellner-Cartter model, some mechanism must be adopted to ration employment among those offering themselves for work. Therefore, these efficient contracts will be characterized both by devices to restrict entry into union employment and by rules that serve to absorb the excessive number of workers employed (excessive, that is, given the relationship of the marginal revenue product of labor to the wage rate). According to this interpretation, the presence of restrictive work practices is not some haphazard and incidental element of various labor contracts, but rather a distinguishing feature and an integral property of a particular class of models of wage and employment determination in unionized markets.

Unionism and Productivity

How do the studies of what John Addison calls "the Harvard School" on the comparative efficiency of unionized and nonunionized establishments fit into this? It is by no means clear primarily because, as Addison correctly notes, the emphasis in this research has been on generating empirical results rather than on presenting a precisely articulated statement of the determination of the employment contract in unionized labor markets. The "rule-making process" (Flanders, 1970) of collective bargaining figures prominently in the Harvard School's perception of unionized labor contracts; in particular, they stress the channels of communication set up within the firm by well-functioning grievance procedures. No serious student of trade unions was ever unaware of the considerable value that workers say they attach to grievance procedures, but no one would have guessed that this system of industrial jurisprudence (or some other related attribute of unionism) induces unionized manufacturing establishments in the United States to be some 22 percent more productive than comparable nonunionized establishments. This provocative finding of Brown and Medoff (1978) calls for an explanation. (I agree with Addison that Clark's [1980] results are appropriately interpreted as indicating that no significant difference in productivity exists between union and nonunion plants in the cement industry, hardly a surprising inference given that the nonunion establishments constitute only some 6 percent of his sample of observations.)

Putting aside the well-known problems of identifying and estimating Cobb-Douglas production function parameters from cross-section observations, I submit two explanations for Brown and Medoff's findings, both of which derive from the wage-raising ability of trade unions. First, when unions raise wages above levels in comparable nonunion establishments, it is essential in fitting production functions to both union and nonunion establishments to control for the wage-induced substitution in the unionized plants of the services of physical capital and of the services of nonunion labor inputs (such as managerial supervisors). Brown and Medoff are aware of this point, but I am unconvinced that they have avoided all measurement error in these other inputs. Therefore, what appears as greater output for any given level of inputs in unionized establishments is, more precisely, a relatively greater use of the services of physical capital and of nonunion labor inputs that have not fully been incorporated into the regression equation and that are correlated with their unionism variable. This is why I have argued on a previous occasion (Pencavel, 1977) that the best situation for a study of the effect of unionism on productivity is one in which "there are no union-related wage differentials either because the union wage scales operate in the nonunionized as well as the unionized sector or because the presence of the union makes no essential difference (appearances notwithstanding) to the wages of their members." In this situation any productivity differences between union and nonunion establishments would not be attributable to relative price-induced differences in input usage that, in turn, are not measured accurately.

A second explanation for the Brown and Medoff result is a sample selection argument. Assume that, prior to the great union organizing drives of the 1930s and 1940s, the frequency distribution of productivity across establishments in what will subsequently be the union and the nonunion sectors is identical. (So unions are not organizing the most productive firms in each industry, a possibility entertained by Brown and Medoff.) Now one part of the industry becomes unionized, and the union effects a higher wage in the firms it organizes. As a consequence, some firms in the union sector reduce their output and some are forced out of business, the least efficient firms and those least able to absorb this union-induced increase in wages. It is as if the left-hand tail of the frequency distribution of productivity in the union sector has been truncated as a result of the union's wage policy. Therefore, the average efficiency of the unionized firms left in business will naturally be higher than those in the nonunion sector—not because unionism "causes" firms to operate more efficiently, but because unionism forces the least efficient out of business.

Finally, although it is evident that I am not inclined to accept their interpretation of their results, I feel that Brown and Medoff have been subject to far more cheap criticism than their paper deserves. They have done the hard work of collecting and organizing the data and of computing and presenting their estimates, and I hear too often the sort of armchair sniping that dismisses their results out of hand and that does not try to account for their findings or, even better, to test competing explanations. Any day, give me the scholar who undertakes the arduous labor of empirical work to support various conjectures that I do not accept rather than the carping, sedentary critic whose judgments I share.

References

Brown, C., and Medoff, J. 1978. "Trade Unions in the Production Process." *Journal of Political Economy* (June): 335–378.

Clark, K. 1980. "Unionization and Productivity: Micro-Econometric Evidence." *Quarterly Journal of Economics* (December): 613–640.

Fellner, W. 1947. "Prices and Wages Under Bilateral Monopoly." *Quarterly Journal of Economics* (August): 503–532.

Flanders, A. 1970. *Management and Unions*. Faber and Faber.

Leontief, W. W. 1946. "The Pure Theory of the Guaranteed Annual Wage Contract." *Journal of Political Economy* (February): 76–79.

Pencavel, J. H. 1977. "The Distributional and Efficiency Effects of Trade Unions in Britain." *British Journal of Industrial Relations* (July): 137–156.

II THE NATURE OF UNIONS

6 THE ECONOMIC ANALYSIS OF THE TRADE UNION AS A POLITICAL INSTITUTION

John Burton

Recent years have witnessed a resurgence of research into the economics of trade unionism. The agenda of this research has been, largely, the application of more sophisticated econometric analysis to the study of the *effects* of trade unions on economic variables (such as relative wages, wage inflation, etc.). A survey of this recent research (Johnson, 1975) noted the point:

> [T]he problem of modeling trade union behaviour has proved to be virtually intractable. [Pp. 23–24]
>
> [M]y major conclusion is that while little progress has been made in modeling the behavior of trade unions . . . there has been a great deal of sound empirical work on the economic effects of unionism. [P. 27]

This chapter, in contrast, is concerned with some basic theoretical issues in the modeling of the union and does not pretend to surmount the deficiencies noted by Johnson. The limited objective is to abstract something constructive

---

This paper was written while the author was a social science research fellow, sponsored by the Nuffield Foundation. The foundation's financial support is gratefully acknowledged, although, of course, the analysis here is attributable to the author alone.

out of earlier theoretical discussion about the modeling of the union, and to suggest some further lines of theoretical inquiry.

Concern with the nature, and appropriate paradigm for modeling, the trade union is hardly new. The Ross-Dunlop controversy of the '40s and '50s was, of course, centrally concerned with the nature of the union as an institution, the identity of the closest institutional analogy of the union (viz, a private business enterprise or a political agency), and the most relevant disciplinary paradigm—economics or politics—to be adopted in analyzing union behavior. The issues and consequences of the controversy are reviewed briefly in the second section.

The economic theory of the trade union has not been entirely neglected in the current resurgence of research into unionism. An important development, if not yet widely known, has been the application of the property rights paradigm by Martin and Rosa to the analysis of the union.[1] The positive aspects of this paper are premised on a different theoretical perspective: public choice theory, or the economic analysis of political institutions.

The earlier theoretical debate about the trade union—the Ross-Dunlop controversy—revolved around the issue of whether trade unions are to be regarded as economic or political entities. A primary purpose of this chapter is to suggest that this question is a nonissue. More positively, it suggests that trade unions are political entities, in even a more general sense than that argued by Ross (1948), but that economic analysis may be usefully applied to the understanding of political entities, such as trade unions. To this end, the Ross political model of the trade union is set out in terms of an economic analysis in the third section. This leads on to the outlining of some potentially fruitful avenues of further inquiry into the union as a political institution, as suggested by public choice theory in the fourth section.

The "Ross-Dunlop Controversy"—A Review

Historically, the long-established tradition in orthodox economic thought was to consider the trade union as a rent-maximizing monopoly/cartel in labor supply.[2] However, Dunlop (1944) presented an array of economic models of the union of which the union monopoly model was but one variant.[3] Indeed, Dunlop's preferred model was one in which the union maximand was that of the wage bill of the membership, not that of their collective wage rents.[4] Other theorists have suggested economic models of the union in which the objective is the maximization of per capita membership income (Simons, 1944), membership utility defined over the two dimensions of wages and employment (Fellner, 1949; Cartter, 1959), the residual between union receipts and expenditures (Berkowitz, 1954), and monopoly rent net of monopolizing costs (Lewis, 1959).

While the goal functions specified in these economic models of the union thus show variety, the models also possess two common properties. First, all employ the rational choice paradigm as their fundamental analytical basis: Behavior is seen as resulting from a maximizing choice subject to constraints. Second, all view "the" trade union as the relevant decision-making unit for analysis, acting as a "corporate individual" analogous to "the" business enterprise in the orthodox theory of the firm.[5]

A. M. Ross (1948) challenged the relevance and empirical content of this economic modeling approach to the study of the labor union. His argument was based upon two main struts, in counterpoint to the two characteristics of the economic models of the union noted above. First, Ross rejected the value of the rational choice paradigm as a tool for analyzing union behavior: "Among all the participants in economic life, the trade union is probably least suited to purely economic analysis" (p. 7). More positively, Ross argued that the paradigm more suited to the task at hand was "a broader frame of reference" incorporating political, sociological, psychological, as well as economic, analysis. However, in the subsequent elaboration of his own analysis of the union, Ross was to draw the most heavily on concepts borrowed from political science (as it was then constituted): concepts such as power, conflict, cross-cutting pressures, and the process of social comparison making. This latter predilection relates to the second main theme in Ross's attack upon the economic approach to the modeling of the union.

This second theme was that Ross rejected the validity of an analogy between the business enterprise—to which, he accepted, economic analysis may be properly applied—and the trade union:

> [T]he union is not a business enterprise selling labor. It is a political institution representing the sellers of labor. [Ross, 1948, p. 22]

> [I]t [the labor union] is a political agency operating in an economic environment. [Ross, 1948, p. 12]

This visualization of the trade union as an essentially political entity Ross (1948) based on two observations: first, "the trade union is preeminently a group, a collectivity," and second, that "it is not only a group, but an institution as well; it leads a life of its own separate and distinct from its members" (p. 7).

These insights led Ross to argue, furthermore, that the political nature of union behavior essentially involved the reconciliation of three separate objectives: (1) the provision of a certain minimum level of acceptable benefits (both of the wage and nonwage variety) to rank-and-file members, this level being determined by the comparisons made by the latter with selected comparator groups; (2) the institutional aim of the maintenance of the size, survival, and growth of the union organization; and (3) the personal ambitions of the union leaders. Ross also noted that in the usual case objective (3) is attained by the satisfaction of objective (2).

The controversy over the nature of the union proceeded for a number of years in the literature. In the introduction to the second edition of his *Wage Determination under Trade Unions*, Dunlop (1944) defended stoutly the economic modeling of the union. He attacked the political approach as a mere 'fad,' based upon "a preoccupation with the very short run to the exclusion of more persistent factors [in wage determination] . . ." that ". . . neglected the stubborn factors of the external world" (Dunlop, 1955, pp. iii–iv).

Later reflection on the issue appears to have produced a more conciliatory attitude from Dunlop (1955), arguing that ". . . it does not advance understanding of decision making in organisations to label the process as either 'political' or 'economic' " (p. 14). A related view to be observed in the '50s literature on this topic was the argument that neither the economic model of Dunlop (et. al.) or the political model of Ross provided a general analysis of trade union behavior. The two models need to be blended in some fashion for a proper appreciation (e.g., Brochier, 1955). One particular "compromise" view that has found some favor flows from the writings of Reder (1952) and Levinson (1966). This view concedes the point that the union is an essentially political agency but places greater stress on the constraints imposed by the economic environment, within which trade union political forces must operate, than Ross (1948) accorded to them in his original treatment.

However, in hindsight it is apparent that such a compromise approach was not successful in uniting labor economists and industrial relations analysts on the issue of the nature of the trade union. The controversy was, in fact, never satisfactorily and clearly resolved. Neither the political model, nor any of the various economic models, or the compromise model have been generally adopted, developed, applied, and tested widely by labor economists and industrial relations analysts. The political model of the union, married with a profit-maximizing analysis of the firm, has for example, been applied with some empirical success to the explanation of strike activity (Ashenfelter and Johnson, 1969), but with little empirical payoff or theoretical progress in the study of the wage transmission process or wage inflation (Burton and Addison, 1977). Dunlop's wage-bill maximization model has generated even less research and application; it has, however, been subjected to searching (economic) theoretical criticism by Atherton (1973). Only one study of wage determination and inflation, for example, has employed it: De Menil's (1971) integration of the wage-bill maximization hypothesis with a Nash bargaining model to provide an econometric model of wage movements in densely unionized American industries.[6] The cartel model of the union retains a certain residual attraction for some economists (e.g. Reynolds, 1980), but, once again, it has not exactly been the vehicle of substantive theoretical and economic progress in the analysis of unionism over the past two decades. Nor has the compromise model of Reder and Levinson been the focus of research over this period. The reality is that the latter approach has provided no more than a temporary means of papering over the schism in thought about the nature of the trade union that opened up in the Ross-Dunlop controversy. Progress on the modeling of the trade union has, apparently, been stultified, for some considerable time, in both labor economics and industrial relations analysis.

The important point is how we proceed from here in the construction of a more fruitful theory of the trade union. This chapter makes a number of suggestions. First, I shall argue that perhaps the long controversy over the nature of the trade union was unfruitful because it was wrong-footed. Both sides—the protagonists of the economic and political models respectively—were making useful theoretical contributions that were mixed with erroneous points. Specifically, I shall argue that Ross was half right and half wrong in the balance of his analysis. In the following section I shall seek to show that Ross was misled by his important insight that trade unions are a collective entity into an unfortunate and unnecessary rejection of economic analysis in the modeling of the trade union.

An Economic Version of the Ross Political Model

One of Ross's central arguments was that it is incorrect to analyze the trade union "as if" it were a corporate individual. A recognition of this institutional characteristic would indeed seem crucial for the understanding of many important facets of trade union behavior. In this sense, the economic models of the union of Dunlop, et al., are deficient.

Ross's other major theme was that economic analysis cannot be applied to the behavior of such political institutions as the union. With the benefit of hindsight, we may now see that Ross was clearly wrong in this contention. The development of public choice theory—otherwise known as the economics of politics, or the new political economy—has demonstrated amply that the rational choice paradigm can be applied to the study of political institutions. Indeed, the literature on this topic is now massive. If, as is evident, economic analysis can be applied fruitfully to the study of political institutions proper, then there is at least a theoretical presumption that it might also be applied to other social organizations, such as the trade union, that exhibit elements of collective decision making.

This section seeks to justify that contention, by erecting an economic model of the trade union that incorporates the main "political" characteristics of the trade union as detected by Ross (1948). The purpose of this exercise, it should be emphasized, is not to present a model that the present author regards as adequate, or fruitful, as it stands. Some reasons for rejecting this revised Ross model as an adequate explanatory framework for analyzing union behavior are advanced toward the end of this section and in the next section. The concern here, rather, is to demonstrate that Ross did not need to throw out the baby of economic analysis with the bathwater of the corporate individual assumption. This at least sets the stage for a more positive, public choice perspective on the trade union, entertained in the next section.

Some Background Analytical Perspectives from Modern Economics

Ross claimed that the essence of the political nature of the union lies in the reconciliation of three objectives: (1) a minimum acceptable level of benefits to members, (2) the institutional goal of size and growth, and (3) the personal goals of union leaders. He also argued that such a situation could not be handled with economic analysis. But a little reflection suggests that this is the sort of multiple-interest situation that the "managerial" theories of the firm—notably those of Baumol (1958, 1959) and Marris (1963, 1967)—have sought to elucidate, while yet retaining an economic mode of analysis. For example, in Baumol's model of the managerial enterprise, the managing executives—having a degree of discretionary power arising from a divorce of ownership and control in the modern corporation—are viewed as pursuing a policy of sales-revenue (size of firm) maximization, subject to a minimum profit constraint (necessary to satisfy stockholders). As with the union executive in Ross's analysis of the trade union, the assumption underlying Baumol's analysis is that the private interests of business managers will normally be promoted by the pursuit of the "institutional objective" of size maximization. This analogy with the theories of managerial corporations thus suggests a means of formalizing Ross's analysis in economic terms.

A second perspective on Ross's analysis of the union to be drawn from contemporary economics may be drawn from Niskanen's (1971) work on the economic theory of bureaucracy. As further remarked upon later, a trade union cannot be regarded as economically equivalent to a public bureaucracy; there are important distinguishing features between the two types of organization. However, the two types of organization do share one important characteristic: Bureaucracies are not-for-profit organizations and so too—in the usual case—are trade unions.[7]

Niskanen's analysis of the behavior of chief executive officers under a zero-profit constraint has relevance to the union leader as well as to the bureaucrat. Economic reasoning would lead us to predict that the union leader, like the bureaucrat, will seek to substitute goals other than maximization of pecuniary surplus of his organization, under such a constraint. In the Niskanen model, this leads the bureaucrat to maximize the size of the budget. Similar economic reasoning applied to union leaders would suggest—because the status, power, and income of the leadership are likely to be positively related to union size—that their adopted goal would be that of the "institutional objective" of the maximization of the size of the membership of the union.

In both the Baumol model of the managerial corporation and the Niskanen model of the bureaucracy, executives are constrained to provide some minimum acceptable level of benefit to the purchasers (stock owners and government, respectively) of their services. In the Baumol model, managers have to provide a minimum acceptable rate of return to the equity holders; in the Niskanen model bureaucrats cannot expand the size of the budget beyond that point at which the government's consumer surplus on the services provided is completely negated. Similar considerations would lead to the argument that, in pursuing their own goals, union leaders would be constrained by the need to provide some minimum acceptable level of services or benefits to their members. Failure to meet this requirement might be argued, on grounds of economic reasoning, to imply a utility loss to union leaders, via two routes. First, failure to meet the constraint could lead to membership loss, the opposite of the union leader's proximate goal. Second, it might mean a threat to the union leader's security of office, by enhancement of the likelihood of challenges to the leadership from aspiring union leaders.

It is clearly possible to interpret Ross's "political" approach to the modeling of the union in these lights. His arguments about the behavior of the union do show some overlap with later economic theorizing about the conduct of organizations in which managerial discretion exists, such as the large joint stock company and the public bureaucracy. As I would interpret Ross, he was not actually erecting the foundations of a political/non-economic model of the union. Rather, he was implicitly suggesting a *different sort* of economic model of the union to that of Dunlop et al.; and one which has some consanguinity with later and more refined economic analysis of "managerial organizations."

A Formal Specification of Ross's Implicit Economic Model of the Union

It is unfortunate, therefore, that Ross chose to jettison an economic mode of analysis together with the corporate individual assumption. This would seem to have misled debate over the modeling of the union. Formal economic analysis of any social organization—be it a business enterprise, family, or trade union—does at least have the advantage of providing a clear statement of the analysis and predictions, for the simple reason that the logical structure of the underlying paradigm—the rational choice paradigm—is the most well developed of any currently on offer in social science. Ross's advocacy of the importation of political concepts to economics and industrial relations analysis for the purpose of understanding union behavior was, in retrospect, a blind alley. There was no body of positive political theory, at the time of which he wrote, on which to draw. Such positive political analysis as has later emerged has largely resulted from importations to politics from other disciplines, notably sociology and, more latterly, economics.

To clarify the nature of Ross's "political" model of the union, setting out his analysis of the trade union in a formal economic manner seems useful and valid. The forementioned analogies with the economic theory of the managerial corporation and the public bureaucracy suggest a means of doing this. As I would interpret Ross, the skeleton of his implicit economic model of the trade union might be described in terms of the following set of equations:

$$V = V(R, S, Y, J) \quad V_r, V_s, V_y, V_j > 0, \tag{6.1}$$

$$R = R(M) \qquad R_m > 0 \tag{6.2a}$$

$$S = S(M) \qquad S_m > 0 \tag{6.2b}$$

$$Y = Y(M) \qquad Y_m > 0 \tag{6.2c}$$

$$J = J(W, W^*) \quad \begin{aligned} &J_{w^*} = 0 \text{ for } W \geq W^* \\ &J_{w^*} < 0 \text{ for } W < W^* \end{aligned} \tag{6.3}$$

$$\begin{aligned} M = M(W, W^*, U, x_1, \ldots, x_n) \quad & M_w \gtrless 0 \\ M_u < 0;\ & M_{w^*} = 0 \text{ for } W \geq W^* \\ & M_{w^*} < 0 \text{ for } W < W^* \end{aligned} \tag{6.4}$$

$$U = U(L, E) \qquad U_1 > 0; \qquad U_e < 0 \tag{6.5}$$

$$L = L(W, P^e) \qquad L_w > 0; \qquad L_{p^2} < 0 \tag{6.6}$$

$$E = E(W, P^e) \qquad E_w < 0; \qquad E_{pe} > 0 \tag{6.7}$$

$$W^* = W^*(W_i, P^e, T, Z_1, \ldots, Z_n) \quad W^*_{wi}, W^*_T, W^*_{pe} > 0 \tag{6.8}$$

where:

V is union leadership utility;

R is an index of union leadership power;

S is some index of the social status of the union leader;

Y is trade union leader income;

J is a measure of union leadership job security;

M is the number of members of the trade union;

W is the actual wage rate;

W^* is the minimum acceptable wage rate for the membership;

E is membership employment;

L is the supply of labor to this subsector;

W_i is the wage of the ith comparator group (i = 1, . . . , k);

P^e is the expected level of prices over the contract period;

U is the amount of membership unemployment;

T is the rate of income tax;

$x_1, \ldots, x_n$ are a set of other variables (e.g., government legislation) affecting union membership;

$Z_1, \ldots, Z_n$ are a set of other variables (e.g., nonwage benefits) affecting W^*.

The structure of this formal economic version of the Ross model in verbal terms is as follows. Equation (6.1) is the assumed union leadership utility function; utility depends (positively) on power, social status, income, and job security. Equations (6.2a) through (6.2c) link the first three of these arguments to the size of union membership. Equation (6.3) specifies union leader security of tenure as a function of the relation between the negotiated wage rate and that minimally acceptable to members. Equation (6.4) is a particular version of what Dunlop (1944) called the "membership function," which is consanguine with Ross's analysis. Equation (6.5) assumes membership unemployment to be a function of the difference between total labor supply and the amount of membership employment; equations (6.6) and (6.7) are the total labor supply and membership employment equations, respectively. Finally, (6.8) defines the minimally acceptable wage rate to the rank-and-file members, in a Ross-type model.

We return to a discussion of the membership function—equation (6.4)—and its rationale. Ross (1948) did not employ the concept; it had been put forward by Dunlop (1944). However, the concept of a membership function does not, on close reading, seem to be inconsistent with Ross's analysis; what he appears to be advocating is a different form of the membership function to that initially expressed by Dunlop. Dunlop (1944) defined the membership function as a relationship

> showing the total amount of labor that will be attached to the labor organization at each wage rate . . . [it] must be regarded as the appraisal by the leadership of the amount of labor that will be allied to the union at each wage rate. [P. 33]

The membership function here specified retains the Dunlopian feature of relating total union membership to the wage rate. There are, however, a number of differences between equation (6.4) and the membership function of Dunlop. First, Dunlop argued that the union membership is either a positive function of the wage rate, for all levels of W, or that union membership may be of zero elasticity with respect to W—as shown by the curves M′ and M″ in figure 6-1, respectively. It is possible to follow Galloway (1971, p. 92), however, in assuming that the membership function is backward-bending, as shown in figure 6-2. This is so because membership unemployment may be a determinant of trade union size, as Ross seemed to argue, on the reasoning that unemployed workers are less likely to retain their membership than are employed workers. But unemployment, as we see from equations (6.5), (6.6), and (6.7), is determined partly by the wage rate. That is, differentiating (6.4) with respect to W, we obtain:

$$\frac{dM}{dW}=\frac{\partial M}{\partial W}+\frac{\partial M}{\partial U}\left\{\frac{\partial U}{\partial L}\cdot\frac{\partial L}{\partial W}+\frac{\partial U}{\partial E}\cdot\frac{\partial E}{\partial W}\right\}. \tag{6.9}$$

Thus, even assuming that the first term on the RHS of (6.9) is unambiguously positive, we cannot sign the expression as a whole, because the second term on the RHS of (6.9) is unambiguously negative. It is plausible, however, that above some level of wages—W' on figure 6–2—the second

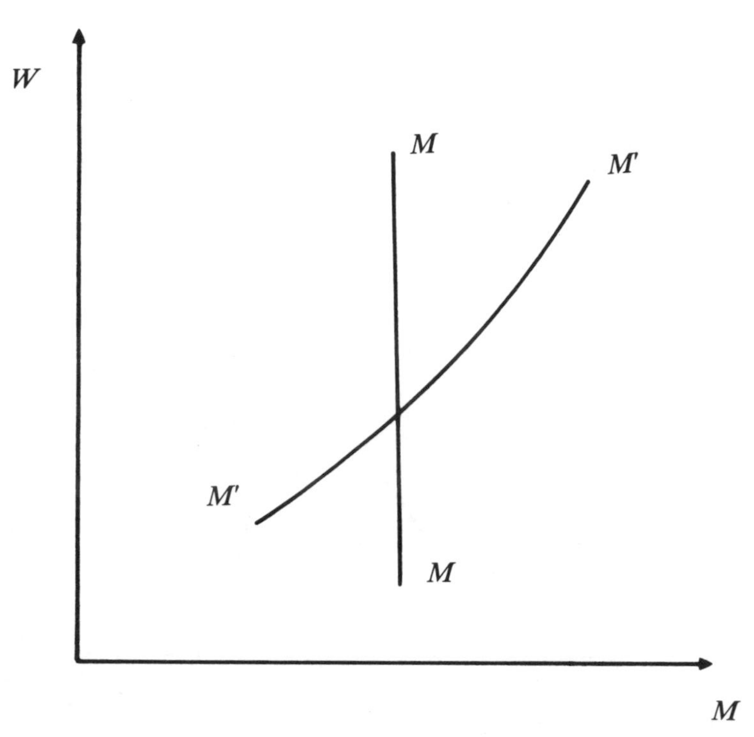

Figure 6-1. Dunlop's Alternative Membership Curves

effect will dominate over the first, and the curve will turn back toward the vertical axis. Following Ross (1948, p. 28), we may refer to the first term on the RHS of (6.9) as the "membership effect" and the second as the "employment effect"; Ross noted that they may well move in opposite directions.

A second difference between the specification of (6.4) and Dunlop's original membership function relates to the inclusion of W^* as a determining variable of M in (6.4). This is included, in respect to Ross's (1948, p. 28) argument that a wage rate that fails to satisfy minimal membership expectations is likely to bring about a wave of resignations. According to the formulation of the model, this effect will fail to operate if $W > W^*$; but for $W^* > W$, then, in the long run—if the situation maintains for a considerable period of time—the entire membership curve will shift to the left. Other variables, such as changes in the legal environment, might also shift the M function; these other variables are left unspecified as the $x_1, \ldots, x_n$.

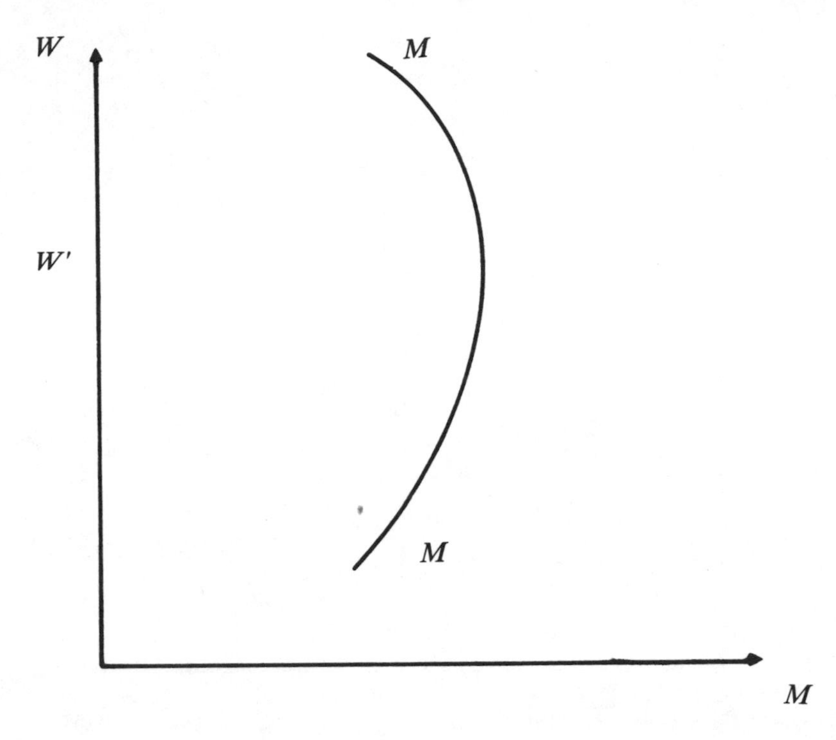

Figure 6-2. The Backward-Bending Membership Curve

Some more words are also called for regarding the specification of equation (6.7), which is also constructed along the lines of Ross's indications. Ross (1948) argued that rank-and-file wage expectations would be affected by three variables, in particular:

> One is strain upon established standards of living brought about by an inflation in the price level or by a reduction in take-home pay. . . . The other is an invidious comparison with the wages, or wage increases, of other groups of workers. [P. 38]

These arguments are represented by the inclusion of the P^e, T, and W_i variables in equation (6.8).[8] In summary, the economic version of the Ross political model of the union here presented visualizes his implicit economic model as being one in which the union leadership maximizes (6.1), subject to the rest of the relationships in the model. Fortunately, the model may be compressed into a simple diagram, as shown in figures 6–3(a) and 6–3(b).

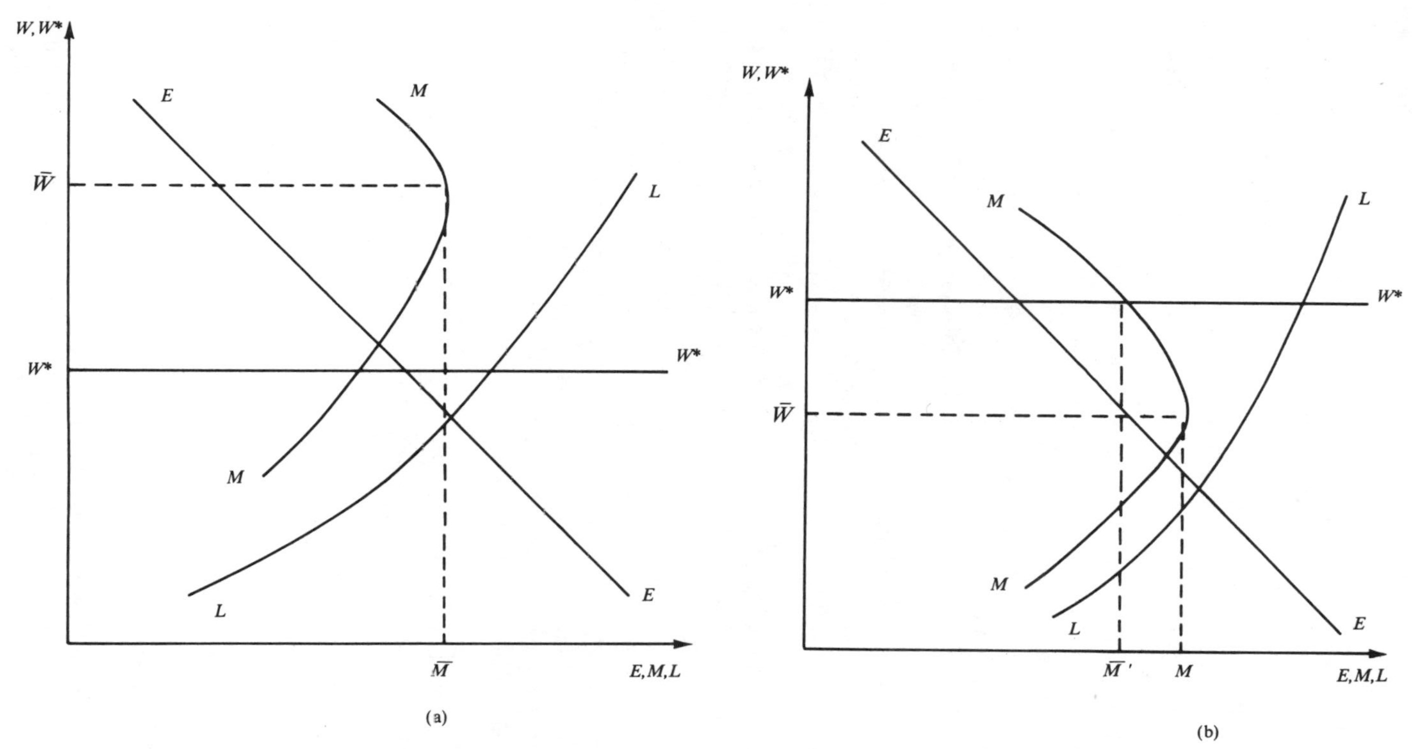

Figure 6-3. Ross's Implicit Economic Model of the Trade Union

Here (for both diagrams) MM is the membership function, and EE shows the employment level of union members at various wage rates, while LL is the (total) labor supply curve. W^*W^* represents the minimum level of wages acceptable to the membership, as determined by (6.8). In the situation described by figure 6-3(a), union membership would be maximized at $\bar{M}$ with a wage rate of $\bar{W}$. However, in the case shown by figure 6-3(b), $\bar{W}$ — the wage that would (temporarily) maximize membership, given the current position of the membership function—is below W^*. If the leadership were to indulge in short-run membership maximization, the result, from equation (6.4), would be that the membership function would shift inward, threatening the organizational survival of the trade union. The union leadership will in this case pursue as strategy of long-run membership maximization by seeking a negotiated wage equal to W^*. This would result in a total membership size of $\bar{M}'$.

This economic model and graphical apparatus can be used to illustrate the propositions about union behavior advanced by Ross. Consider, for example, a situation of jurisdictional competition between two unions, A and B, for the same group of workers. Initially, we shall assume that a situation of "political wage equilibrium," as Ross (1948, p. 64) called it, exists between the two; i.e., the wages of their members are such that neither union is gaining or losing members. Now assume that union A attempts to expand its membership (i.e., to gain members from B) by upsetting the political wage equilibrium and by increasing the wage rate of its own members. The consequences of this situation for union B are shown in figure 6–4. If the members of B make wage comparisons with the members of A, as they are likely to, then the increase in the latter will raise their minimally acceptable wage rate. This is shown in figure 6–4 by upward shift of $W_1^*W_1^*$ to $W_2^*W_2^*$.

The existent wage, $\bar{W}_1$ is now less than the rank and file's minimally acceptable wage rate, W_2^*. Failure of the leadership to placate the coercive comparisons of the rank and file would invite membership loss; the membership function would start shifting inward, from M' to M' and would continue to do so (according to the formulation of the model) as long as $\bar{W} < W^*$. Consequently, the optimal wage rate for the leadership of union B to negotiate is that of $\bar{W}_2$. This minimizes the hemorrhage of members, although it does entail some loss of members $(\bar{M}_2 - \bar{M}_1)$.

The Interpretation of Ross's Analysis

This section has sought to demonstrate that Ross was wrong to reject economic analysis as a means of formalizing his political model of the trade

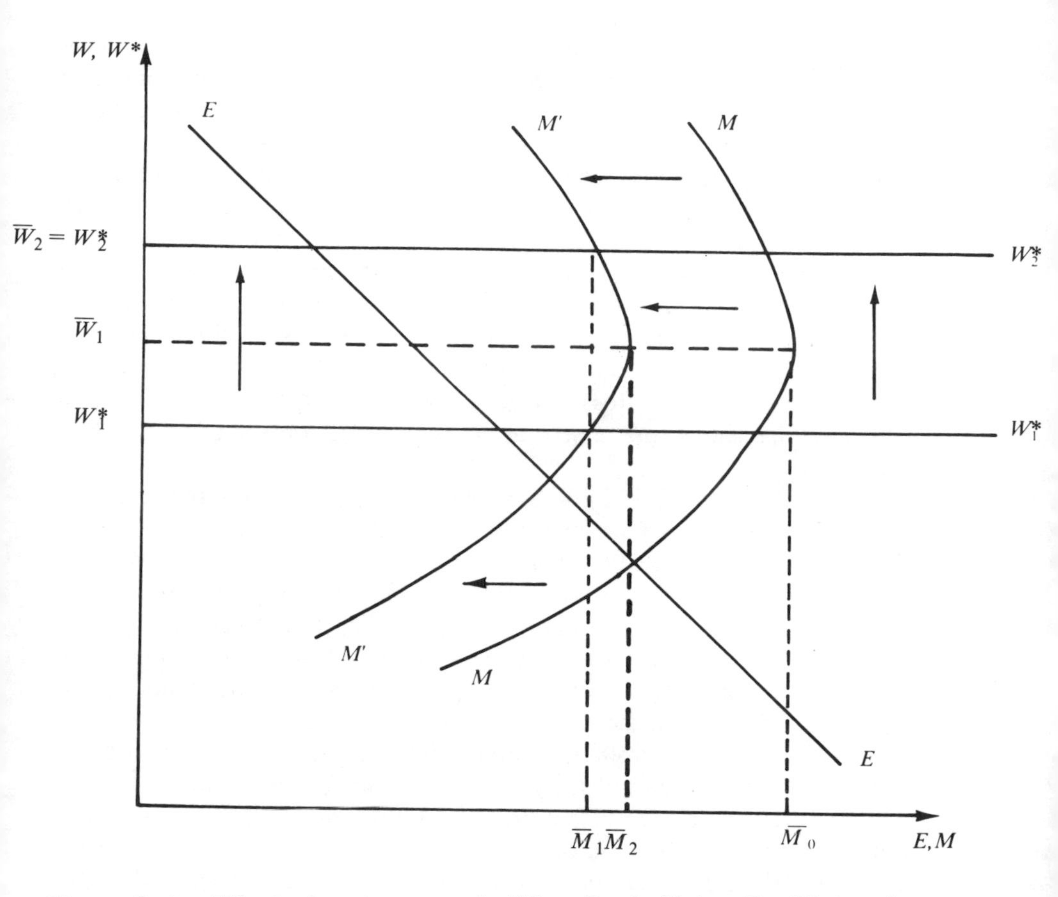

Figure 6-4. Effect of an Increase in W*on Trade Union Equilibrium in the Ross Model

union. Furthermore, it has been argued that Ross was implicitly specifying a particular sort of economic model of the trade union, as a not-for-profit organization in which the managers have some discretion to pursue their own goals. This implicit economic model clearly has some family resemblance to modern economic models of the managerial enterprise and the public bureaucracy. A convenient means of formalizing Ross's model along these lines has been presented.

It is interesting to inquire why Ross did not take up this line of approach himself—why he did not dress out his implicit economic model of the union in the style of economic analysis. One possible reason, that has been suggested to me, is that perhaps Ross did not have the necessary training in formal economics to perform this task. Whatever the truth of this allegation, I would argue that there was a further reason for Ross's mistake.

It merits emphasis that Ross (1948, pp. 24–31) considered at some length the question of the similarities of the trade union and the contemporary managerial enterprise. Indeed, he concluded that the goal structure of both institutions is fundamentally similar. In both cases, he alleged, chief decision makers pursue their own goals via the institutional goal of size and growth, subject to the provision of a minimum level of benefits for the voters, who nominally control the organization (union members and stockholders, respectively). Why did Ross not develop this insight further and erect an economic model of the union as a managerial organization, as here presented?

Ross (1948, pp. 27–31) was apparently turned away from such an approach by his various arguments that significant differences exist between the two forms of organization. Space is not here available for a consideration of the numerous points raised by Ross. Suffice it to say that none of the points raised by Ross sustains the claim that economic analysis is inapplicable to the trade union. For example, one of Ross's major arguments is that performance criteria are more difficult to apply to a trade union than to a business firm because the services provided by unions to their members are inherently vaguer than profit measured in dollar units. However, as Niskanen (1971) notes, the vague and nonquantifiable nature of bureaucratic outputs is a characterizing feature of state-financed bureaucracies. This in itself does not prevent the construction of an economic theory of government bureaucracy. Nor does it prevent the erection of an economic analysis of the labor union.

This is not to deny the fundamental economic differences between trade unions and business firms. Ross failed to identify in his analysis, however, the basic differentiating characteristic of these two types of organization. Although both are notionally controlled by vote process, stockholders can sell their voting rights and union members cannot. There is no second-hand market in union voting rights, as there is with stock voting rights. Or, to put it another way, the business firm is a proprietary organization, while the trade union is a form of nonproprietary organization. This fundamental difference in the property-rights structuring of the two institutions may be predicted to give rise to significant differences in their behavior. Be that as it may, there is no reason why economic analysis cannot be applied to the behavior of the not-for-profit, nonproprietary organizations such as the trade union.[9]

Some Deficiencies of Ross's Implicit Economic Model

One advantage of specifying Ross's political model of the union in formal economic terms is that it clarifies its strengths and weaknesses. The political approach or model has a number of attractive features, when so presented. Foremost is its recognition that the possibility of managerial discretion exists in the trade union. Previous (economic) models of the union had analyzed the union "as if" a corporate individual and supressed questions concerning the potential conflict of interest between the managing officers of the union and its rank-and-file members. Furthermore, the union executive officer utility function that is implicit in Ross's treatment would seem to foreshadow later developments in the economic theory of the managerial corporation and the economic theory of bureaucracy.

However, some deficiencies are also apparent. For example, there is no subsystem in the model concerned with the determination of union financial variables—the flows of receipts and outgoings. Ross ignored this important aspect of the trade union, as did, also, the earlier economic models of the union.[10] A second deficiency of Ross's implicit economic model is that the behavior of the union leadership and of the rank and file are not analyzed in a consistent choice-theoretic manner. The union leadership are visualized as utility maximizers; the rank and file are not. The behavior of the latter is merely summarized in two reaction functions: the membership function and the (minimum) wage expectation function. These reaction functions have not been derived from any underlying choice-theoretic analysis of the membership decision and the wage expectation decision, in the same way in which (for example) the labor supply curve of standard theory is derived from an analysis of the work-leisure choice.

This lacuna of the Ross model is essentially the same as that in Baumol's (1958, 1959) theory of the manager-dominated corporation, with which the formalized Ross model has considerable resemblance. In Baumol's model, business executives maximize their utility by maximizing the size of their organization subject to a "vaguely-defined" minimum profit constraint, stipulated (somehow) by stockholders. In the Ross model of the trade union, the union executive maximizes utility by maximizing the size of the membership, subject to an equally vaguely defined minimum returns constraint stipulated by the rank and file.

A more general deficiency of Ross's implicit economic model of the union is that it is not very rich in predictive implications—a most serious weakness for any theoretical apparatus, if it is to contribute to the possibilities of empirical testing and knowledge.

Enough has been said to indicate the weaknesses of Ross's political approach to the union, when analysed in economic-theoretic terms. The more important issue, however, is how to proceed positively from here, in terms of the evolution of a more fruitful theoretical framework. This matter is taken up in the next section.

The Trade Union as a Political Institution, from a Public Choice Perspective

One line of positive theoretical development has been provided by Martin (1980), and Rosa (1980) in particular. This line of development builds on property rights analysis, and the economic analysis of agency relationships in particular, to provide an economic model of the trade union as a nonproprietal organization. This is certainly a positive way of building on some aspects of Ross's seminal insight, drawing on developments in modern economic theory. Another potential line of development for the theory of the union is to consider more fully Ross's suggestion that trade unions should be understood as a political institution, drawing theoretical input from the modern economic analysis of political institutions, or public choice theory. This is the approach considered and advocated here.[11]

A Public Choice Perspective on the Nature of the Trade Union

A useful starting point here is to consider the common and differentiating characteristics of trade unions and bureaucracies. As earlier noted, both types of organization, with the exceptions of racketeering unions and corrupt bureaucracies, have the feature of being not-for-profit institutions. However, a further defining characteristic of the bureaucracy, as analyzed by Niskanen (1971), is that it is financed by a single sponsor (government) by means of a block (usually annual) grant. Trade unions, by contrast, produce a package of services (e.g., wage negotiation, contract policing, grievance handling) for a multiplicity of sponsors—their members. Both in the West and in the Soviet Union, the bulk of union finances derive from membership contributions in the form of dues and initiation fees, and not from government.[12]

The trade union may thus be viewed, drawing upon public choice theory, as a Buchanan (1965)-type club in the production and consumption of union services. The defining feature of a club good is that, although there is jointness in consumption (or production, in the case of a club-type factor input), exclusion is possible. A club good lacks the nonexcludability characteristic of a public or collective good.

Some analysts, however (e.g., Olson, 1965), have visualized trade unions as providing services that are typically of a collective-goods nature. The union is seen as beset, therefore, by the free-rider problem that is endemic in the provision of collective goods, because noncontributors (here, nonunionists) cannot be excluded from consumption of the collective services.

Closer examination of this issue reveals the need for considerable qualification of the collective goods view of the trade union (Burton, 1978). First, it becomes apparent that the services typically produced by trade unions are not collective goods in any *technical* sense; exclusion would be technically possible in the usual case. For example, it would be technically possible for trade unions to limit the results of their wage negotiation services to their own members by restricting the coverage of their collective agreements to their own members. Yet, typically, trade unions do not do this. Why so?

Two cases need to be distinguished, which I will label as the A (or American) case and B (or British) case, respectively. In the A case, trade unions could technically exclude nonmembers from consuming their services, but are required *by law* (specifically, section 9(a) of the Wagner Act) to extend these representation services to all nonunionists who work in the situations in which they are the recognized bargaining agent. Here, trade unions are providing services that are technically of a club goods character, but are caused by law to provide a "collective" good.

In the B case, a trade union has not only the technical ability to exclude nonmembers from consumption of their services, but also the legal ability to do so. They could sign collective labor contracts with employers that restrict the coverage to their own members, but choose not to do this. In the United Kingdom, for example, the work force is (just over) 50 *percent* unionized, whereas union contract coverage extends to (just over) three-quarters of employees. Why do our B case unions act like this? An incentive lies in the fact that if nonunion employees were not covered by the union-negotiated rates (and other conditions), they would be free to undercut. Any rent-seeking institution, such as a trade union, has a natural incentive to avoid or prevent such competition. Thus our B case unions may be seen as the suppliers of "impure" club goods: Noncontributors could certainly be excluded (both technically and legally) but only at some probable cost in terms of sustainable club size, and the rent accruing to it.

Consideration of the trade union as a clublike entity, in terms of economic analysis, does not necessarily imply that the club will be operated purely in the interest of its members; the club managers have their own interests, differentiated from those of the members. Two types of club model of the trade union are thus potentially worthy of investigation: one in which club policy is determined purely by the views of its members, and one in which the club managers have some discretion to pursue their own interests. I shall term the first type of model that of the *member-dominated union club*, and the second as one of the *union club with executive discretion.*

The Member-Dominated Union Club

Assume a scenario in which all issues of union policy are determined by a referendum of union members, in which all vote. The policies of the trade union would then be determined by the membership. The nature of the outcome will depend on two things: the nature of the collective decision rule by which union policies are decided, and the nature of union members' preferences in respect to these policies.

Ross (1948), in fact, emphasized the heterogeneity of union members' preferences and the variety of distinct interest groups present among the typical union's rank and file (e.g., young and old; employed and unemployed; skilled and unskilled; etc.). However, he provided no technical apparatus for examining these matters and for producing a determinate theoretical model. Herein lies one of the advantages of a public choice approach, compared to that of Ross, to the analysis of the trade union as a political institution. The analysis of the effects of voter interest diversity and cleavage has been extensively developed in the literature on the economic analysis of politics,[13] and there would be no difficulty in erecting a member-dominated model of the union along these lines.

The outcome in such a model will also, as noted, depend upon the nature of the voting rule by which union policies are decided. Decision by simple majority voting, the standard case in trade unions, has been exhaustively examined in the public choice literature. If, for example, we assume that union member preferences can be depicted along a single dimension, and have the property or single-peakedness, then the member-dominated model of the union club produces an equilibrium outcome at the peak preference of the median union member. If such assumptions are breached then, as is well known, majority rule decision making in the trade union may not produce any stable equilibrium outcome; it could be cyclic over successive collective decisions.

Hopefully, enough has been said to indicate that the construction of a member-dominated model of the union club presents no new theoretical problems. To the contrary, the theoretical basis for such an approach has been elaborated extensively in the public choice literature. The more important question concerns the value of such an enterprise. I would offer the guess that such a model would certainly have some applicability to trade unions in their initial emergent phase, when these organizations were small and localized. Under such circumstances, the potential for executive discretion is perhaps small, and a member-dominated model of the union club has some plausibility. Trade unions might be here visualized as a "collective voice" institution, *pur et simple.* As regards the typical large-membership union of today, however, the applicability of such a model is subject to considerable theoretical question, for reasons examined below.

The Union Club with Possibilities of Executive Discretion

Unlike the scenario entertained in the foregoing member-dominated model, policy issues in contemporary trade unions are not typically decided by a referendum of all members, compulsory or otherwise. According to the union's constitution, balloting of members takes place only regarding certain selected issues. The cost of continuous referendums in a large trade union on all issues of trade union policy and action would be astronomical. It is for this reason that any large trade union "club," as with the operation of "mass democracy" in modern liberal-democratic polities, is necessarily a sentative institution.

Elected representatives, be they politicians, union officers, or the elected executive officers of a corporation, are of necessity given some freedom of action in decision making, to act as the occasion warrants in the interest of those whom they represent. However, all representatives have an incentive to pursue their own interests, and possibly these interests are not in perfect alignment with those of their electors.

What is the nature of this conflict of interest between the leadership of the union and the membership, and how will it be resolved? We may make with Ross the plausible assumption that, in the absence of the possibility of acquiring profits, union managers may well seek to maximize the size of their 'club,' in order to enlarge their power, status, and income. This is of course not the only possibility. For example, it is quite conceivable that some union leaders may maximize their utility by seeking to use any discretionary power to pursue ideological goals (e.g., "wrecking the capitalist system"). However, the larger the union organization behind the union leader, the more effectively pursued are ideological/revolutionary goals. Thus, the size maximization postulate appears to be a plausible assumption applying to a wide class of union leadership behavior.

However, the size of union organization that maximizes union leadership utility may well differ from that preferred by the median union member. The optimal size of union club for the median member is that which maximizes the per capita rent accruing to the membership. At any size of union less than the latter, the interests of the median union member and the union leadership are in harmony, in the sense that it is in the both of their interests to increase the size of the union club. However, once the per capita rent maximizing volume of membership has been achieved, a divergence of interest emerges between the median union member and the union executive. It is in the interest of the median member to restrict further growth and entry to the union: it remains the interest of the union leader to pursue an expansive policy on further membership growth.

How is this conflict of interest resolved? Different analysts have responded with different assumptions. Simons (1944), in his classic treatment of the long-run consequences of trade unionism, noted that such a conflict of interest existed between union leaders and members, but went on to argue that this conflict of interest will usually be reconciled in favor of the interests of the rank and file. He thus arrived at his vision of an economic system slowly being strangulated by a member-dominated, restrictive union movement. The Ross model discussed in the foregoing section makes the opposite assumption to that of Simons. It presumes that the conflict of interest will be resolved in favor of the union leadership. They are presumed to have sufficient managerial discretion in union decision making to pursue their membership expansion goal to the limit (checked only by the need to observe some minimum-returns-to-the-membership constraint).

I have argued elsewhere (Burton 1980a) that both the Simons and Ross assumptions are in fact oversimplifications. Once again, public choice theory throws light on this issue and points the way to the construction of theory allowing the matter to be analyzed.

The potential for the union leadership to exercise discretion to pursue their own goals will depend on the *alternatives* open to union members when the leadership's actions fail to reflect their interests. In discussing these alternatives, Hirschman's (1971) "exist-voice" taxonomy of responses to organizational malfunction may be fruitfully employed. That is, when any organization fails to achieve the performance desired or expected by its members, two broad classes of response are potentially open to the latter. First, they may make use of the exit option: withdrawal from the organization, and search for a preferential arrangement. Second, they may employ the voice option: participating to a greater extent in the internal affairs of the organization in order to make dissent felt, and to change behavior from within.

The operation of these exit and voice mechanisms, in the presence of union-manager discretionary behavior, are discussed below.

The Operation of the Exit Mechanism in Trade Unions

Within the class of exit possibilities, disgruntled union members have two general possibilities. First, they may exit from the union into a nonunion status. Second, they may enter another union, the performance of which is perceived as superior, that is organizing in the same employment area.

I discuss the operation of the latter type of exit/entry process first. Two scenarios are compared: a world with many competing unions with no inter-union agreements restraining competition for new members, and a world of tight jurisdictional agreements between trade unions.

In the first-mentioned scenario, the world of zero jurisdictional constraints on competition for members, perceived descrepancies between the membership desired and actual policies of a union could lead to "voting with feet." Trade unions that expanded beyond that preferred by members or exploited executive discretion in some other way would suffer a threat of membership loss. The Tiebout (1956) model of local government and interjurisdictional citizen mobility has clear applicability to such a scenario. Under the Tiebout model assumptions of low costs of interjurisdictional mobility and awareness of alternatives, economic agents will move so as to take advantage of being in a more desirable fiscal environment, or trade union. In the long run, such a process would bring about a redistribution of members such that the potential for executive exploitation of discretion would disappear.

The other scenario assumes a world of tight jurisdictional agreements between trade unions, with each union being allocated a particular category or sphere of employment in which it may recruit.[14] The costs of interunion "voting with feet" would be much higher, ceteris paribus, in this scenario than in the first because to switch union affiliation would be to imply an interindustry or interoccupation move as well. Thus, we would expect that the potential for the pursuit of executive discretion, in the conduct of union policy, would be greater in the latter scenario than in the first. We may also make the prediction from our analysis that the average size of trade unions will, ceteris paribus, be larger, and the number of unions fewer, in the presence than in the absence of interunion restrictions on competition for members.

The costs of using the exit option into nonunion status will depend, among other things, on the extent of the closed shop in the employment sector concerned. If many nonunion employers exist in the industry, or those that do not have union membership agreements with the union from which the member wishes to exit, then the disgruntled member may transfer to nonunion status in the same line of employment. If, at the other extreme, closed shop agreements are prevalent throughout the entire employment sector, then exit from the union to nonunion status will mean entry to another linc of employment or even into unemployment. In other words, exit from the union in this latter situation will mean the foregoing of the returns stream on such human capital investments made by the exiting member that are specific to his or her current type of employment.

The conclusion is that the extent of closed shop agreements in an employment sector will affect the costs of exiting to a nonunion situation. Thus, the more extensive the closed shop, the greater will be the potential for the exercise of union executive discretion. We may thus predict that, all other things being equal, a trade union will tend to be larger if it has extensive union membership agreements with employers than if it does not.

The foregoing prediction is not as obvious as it may seem at first sight. A member-dominated union, in which executive discretion does not exist, would use such devices as the closed shop to ration and restrict union membership to that level which maximizes the per capita rent of the membership. This may be, for example, the purpose for which the institution of the closed shop is employed by small craft unions of highly skilled workers. But, in a large trade union, the device of the closed shop may be used, as we have analyzed, to increase the cost of exit and thus to enlarge the limits of executive discretion in the conduct of union policy. In this latter case, the closed shop may be used to increase attainable union size.

Voice in the Trade Union

Two means of recourse to the voice option are potentially available to union members, and thereby to constrain executive discretion. First, members may invest their own time in greater direct participation in union affairs; in attending more meetings; voting on more union resolutions, and so on. Second, they may throw their voting and lobbying support behind an aspiring candidate for union leadership who promises a performance more in accord with membership preferences than that of the incumbent leader. We shall examine the implications of these two types of voice process for union executive discretionary power in turn.

A proposition that has been enunciated in the public choice literature, known as the paradox of participation, has application to the individual's decision to participate in union affairs. The proposition is based on the fact that each individual has but the tiniest expected benefit to gain from participation in a collective decision when the number of others involved in the decision is very large, because the influence of his or her vote on the outcome of the collective decision is statistically minute. There are, however, definite costs to be borne by voting and thus exercising voice: attending boring and lengthy union meetings, for example. The *paradox* of participation, when the number of voters-union members are large in number, is that anyone bothers to participate at all in the collective decision-making process.

It follows that the larger the trade union, the smaller the incentive for each individual member to participate in union affairs, and thereby to exercise some policing of leadership behavior. Conversely, the smaller the union, the more influential each member's vote, and thus the incentive to participate. We therefore obtain the prediction that, ceteris paribus, the larger the trade union, the greater the leeway for the union leadership to pursue its own interest. More concretely, we should expect that the larger the union, the more expansion-minded will be its membership policy. A related implication of this line of analysis concerns the applicability of the so-called "law of proportionate effect" to trade unions. The law states that the probability of an organization growing at a rate of x percent is independent of its size. Some observers claim that the law holds for the population of business enterprises (e.g., Simon and Bonini, 1958; Hart and Prais, 1956; Hymer and Pashigian, 1962). However, the testable implication of our foregoing analysis is that the law will not apply to trade unions: We should expect the growth rate of trade unions to be dependent on their size. Although this proposition has yet to be formally put to the test, there are some indications from the statistics on union size in Britain that give credence to the proposition.[15]

The foregoing analysis requires no major qualification in respect to the other means of expressing voice within the union—giving support to competitors to the union leadership. As Martin (1980) and Rosa (1980) emphasize, the aspiring union leader cannot aggregate voting rights by purchase from members. An electoral contest for a union executive position thus resembles competition in democratic political markets rather than a takeover bid for a business enterprise. Such a leadership contest is subject to the same paradox of participation described above with respect to individual participation in union affairs. The larger the union, the smaller the incentive for the individual member to vote in the leadership election. If other things were equal, this factor would harm the vote support of the incumbent and aspirant leader equally. However, other things are typically not equal in such contexts. The incumbent is usually much better known to the membership than the aspirant and has the extra advantage of controlling the trade union machine, including its channels of communication with the membership. If, as is plausible, union members perceive this inherent incumbent's advantage, it will reduce the expected benefit of voting for the aspirant, and thus the likelihood of voting for him or her. All of this is perhaps only to record that new contestants for union executive office, like new political parties, face a very uphill task in seeking to win an election. Our analysis does, however, afford a theoretical explanation of the well-known paucity of effective challenges, and thus of the very existence of challenges, to an incumbent union leadership. The extent of union executive (ab)use of their discretionary power to further their own interest may have to be very large for it to significantly tip the calculus of membership voting in favor of a new challenger for union office.

Trade Unions and the Political Market

The public choice approach to the study of unionism here advocated inevitably invites consideration of the operation of trade unions in the political market. Neglect of this matter constitutes an important lacuna in Ross's (1948) analysis of the trade union as a political institution. His model was one in which the union was visualized as acting primarily within an "economic" environment, that is, an environment of pecuniary markets. It is true that he noted: "No group can maintain significant economic power in present-day society without political influence."[16] He failed, however, to develop this important insight and to apply it to his own analysis of unionism. He failed to appreciate sufficiently that trade unions are political institutions in quite a different sense from his own use of that term; that is, unions operate not only in the pecuniary market but the political market as well. Over recent years a number of economists have sought to analyze the neglected aspect of the behavior of trade unions (e.g., Gärtner, 1979; Rosa, 1980; Burton, 1979, 1980a, 1980b).

A full analysis of trade unions as a political institution requires the examination of this political market dimension of trade union activity. Here, again, I would suggest that existent public choice theory provides some potentially fruitful foundations for this study.

Down's (1957) theorem suggests that we should find a predominance of producer lobbying over consumer lobbying in the political arena. This result would suggest that organizations such as trade unions, businesses, nationalized industries, and bureaucracies hold greater sway in the political market than do consumer groups. Perhaps the bulk of evidence would support this view, but sometimes we do find consumer influence winning out against producer groups (as in the recent airline deregulation in the United States). Stigler's (1971) economic theory of regulation would seem to provide a more general and fruitful framework to explore the involvement of trade unions (and other groups) in the political market. For example, an important implication of the economic theory of regulation is that the amount of regulation is likely to be greater in large-numbers industries than in small-numbers industries because of factors operating on both the demand and supply sides of the market in regulatory activities. The demand for regulation is likely to be higher in the large-number case because of the higher costs of private cartelization than associated with small numbers. Furthermore, from the supply side, government is likely to supply larger amounts of regulation where the voting rewards are greatest (i.e., the large-numbers case).

The manner in which the theory of regulation may be employed to understand the political market activities of trade unions may here be only briefly illustrated, but the foregoing analysis appears to throw light on British trade union political history. The "new model" unions that emerged in the United Kingdom from 1851 onward were composed largely of a "labor aristocracy" of skilled craft workers that pursued economic rent primarily through the tactic of private-sector cartelization (restriction of membership to apprenticed craftsmen, high membership fees, etc.) Their involvement in the political market was relatively low. However, following the emergence of the mass "new unions" after 1889, which were organizing large numbers of lower-paid and unskilled workers, the scale of trade union activity in the political market was to increase markedly in Britain. One aspect of this was the establishment of the distinct Labour group in Parliament in 1900, subsequently to become the (union-financed) Labour party. The nature and timing of these developments are thus in conformity with the propositions of the economic theory of regulation.

These remarks should be taken as illustrative only. The topic of the regulation of the labor market and industrial relations has yet to be studied in depth from the perspective of the economic theory of regulation. Indeed, the theory itself is still in need of theoretical refinement and elaboration. This direction, however, is the one in which a public choice approach to the study of unionism will need to move in the future.

Retrospect and Prospect

Starting from a brief review of the old (Ross-Dunlop) controversy on the nature and appropriate modeling of the trade union, the body of this chapter has been concerned with the contention (of Ross) that the trade union is best viewed as a political institution and with whether economic analysis is a useful tool for studying the behavior of such an institution.

One underlying presumption of the discussion has been that it was a valuable insight of Ross to visualize the trade union as a collective decision-making entity, analogous to political institutions proper. However, another theme of the discussion has been that acceptance of this first postulate does not preclude an economic analysis of the trade union as a political institution.

To justify the latter contention, two possible approaches from economic analysis to the modeling of the trade union as a political entity have been presented. One approach (elaborated in the third section) takes for granted Ross's own conception of the trade union as a political institution but clothes the Ross model in (what seems to be) congenial economic methodology. Construed in this light, Ross appears to have offered us not a political model of the trade union as a political institution, but rather an implicitly economic model of the trade union as a type of "managerial" organization. If this is a valid interpretation, then the Ross model is to be seen as the forerunner of later developments in the economic theory of the firm and of bureaucracy and, today, of some important current developments in the study of unionism from the perspective of the economics of nonproprietary organizations.

The alternative economic approach to the analysis of the trade union as a political institution presented (and, indeed, advocated positively) here builds on existent public choice theory. The Ross approach, reduced to its bare essentials, seems to visualize the trade union as a manager-dominated organization acting in an environment of (primarily) the pecuniary market. The alternative, public choice, approach, visualizes the trade union under some circumstances as an instrument of collective voice, and under others as a representative institution, beset with the problems of controlling representatives that pervade large-scale organizations of this nature. Furthermore, the public choice approach visualizes the trade union as (potentially) an actor in the political market as well as in the pecuniary market.

The Ross analysis of the trade union as a political institution, when formalized in economic analysis, exhibits some attractive features, and others less so. Regarding the latter there is, for example, no clear microtheoretic analysis embedded in the Ross model as to what determines the "strength" of membership-imposed constraints on union executive officer discretion.

The public choice analysis of the trade union does have a number of advantages over the Ross model. First, it allows us to draw on a large body of existent theory concerning the behavior of collective decision-making processes. Second, we are able to specify from this approach some of the factors that theoretically will determine the potential for discretion by elected representatives in a trade union, and to derive related predictions regarding the determinants of the size, and membership policies, of trade unions. It thus provides us with an agenda for the empirical testing of refutable predictions about trade unions.

Notes

1. See the papers by Martin and Rosa in this volume for further references.
2. Dunlop (1944, pp. 41) argued that this maximand was "of analytical interest but without any readily discernible counterpart in trade union policies."
3. Some commentators (e.g., Mulvey, 1978, pp. 19 and 32) appear to believe that Dunlop's preferred model was one in which the trade union seeks to maximize its total membership. In fact Dunlop did not even consider such a model; he stated categorically that "the most suitable general model of the trade union for analytical purposes is probably that which depicts the maximization of the wage bill for the total membership" (Dunlop, 1944, pp. 44).
4. Dunlop (1944, pp. 44) did note that the component of the total membership whose total wage income the union will seek (according to his hypothesis) to maximize "will vary with the orientation of political control within the union." He did not, however, develop intra-union group goal conflict as a central part of his subsequent analysis.
5. De Menil (1971) does not, to be precise, employ the wage-bill maximization hypothesis, but rather his variant of it, which he calls the wage-surplus (maximization) hypothesis of the union. This latter assumes that the union's goal is to maximize that portion of the total wage bill that is union-induced.
6. With the honorable exception of Atherton (1973), who does attempt to visualize the union as a collective entity.
7. I here ignore the case of racketeering unions, which are probably best analyzed via a profit-maximizing model.
8. The profit rate—often argued to be an important argument in wage demands—has not been included here, as a consequence of Ross's (1948, p. 38) claim that this variable is too "remote" to have much effect on wage expectations. It bears repetition that the main purpose of the model presented in this section is to show how Ross's "political" view of the union can be fruitfully constructed along the lines of economic analysis.
9. See, for example, Clarkson and Martin (1980), Martin (1980), and the contributions by Martin and Rosa in this volume.
10. For some analytical treatment of this issue, see Berkowitz (1954).
11. Rosa's (1980) analysis also builds on aspects of the economics of politics. politics.
12. Of course, considerable differences exist between Western and Soviet trade unions, notably as regards the government-union relationship and the legitimacy of strike activity and overt wage bargaining. See Heldman (1977) for some comparisons between Soviet and American unions.
13. See Mueller (1979) for a survey of the literature.
14. The Soviet situation, in which each trade union is allocated a branch of industry, is perhaps the clearest example of this. The Bridlington Agreement between TUC-affiliated unions

in Britain, by contrast, allows for greater competition at the margin for members than does the Soviet model.

15. See Price and Bain (1976).

16. See, Ross (1948, p. 7).

References

Ashenfelter, O., and Johnson, G. E. 1969. "Bargaining Theory, Trade Unions and Industrial Strike Activity." *American Economic Review* 9:35–49.

Atherton, W. N. 1973. *Theory of Union Bargaining Goals.* Princeton, N.J.: Princeton University Press.

Baumol, W. J. 1958. "On the Theory of Oligopoly." *Economica*, New Series, vol. 25:187–98.

Baumol, W. J. 1959. *Business Behavior, Value and Growth.* New York: Harcourt, Brace and World.

Berkowitz, M. 1954. "The Economics of Trade Union Organization and Administration." *Industrial and Labor Relations Review* 7(July):575–592.

Bradley, M., ed. 1959. *The Public Stake in Union Power.* Charlottesville: University of Virginia Press.

Brochier, H. 1955. "An Analysis of Union Models as Illustrated by the French Experience." In Dunlop J. T., ed. (1955), pp. 136–47.

Buchanan, J. M. 1965. "An Economic Theory of Clubs." *Economica* 32(February):1–14.

Burton, J. 1978. "Are Trade Unions a Public Good/Bad? The Economics of the Closed Shop." In *Trade Unions: Public Goods or Public 'Bads'*, ed. L. Robbins et. al. London: Institute of Economic Affairs, pp. 31–52.

Burton, J. 1979. *The Trojan Horse: Union Power in British Politics.* London: Adam Smith Institute.

Burton, J. 1980a. "Some Further Reflections on Syndicalism." *Government Union Review* (Spring):42–56.

Burton, J. 1980b. "Trade Unions Role in the British Disease: An Interest in Inflation?" In *Is Monetarism Enough?* ed. Minford, P., et al. London: Institute of Economic Affairs, pp. 99–111.

Burton, J., and Addison, J. T. 1977. "The Institutionalist Analysis of Wage Inflation: A Critical Appraisal." *Research in Labor Economics* 1(March):333–376.

Cartter, A. M. 1959. *Theory and Wages and Employment.* Homewood, Ill.: R. D. Irwin.

Clarkson, K. W., and Martin, D. L., eds. 1980. *Research in Law and Economics; A Research Annual, Supplement 1: Economics of Nonproprietary Organizations.* Greenwich, Connecticut: JAI Press.

De Menil, G. 1971. *Bargaining: Monopoly Power versus Union Power.* Cambridge, Mass.: MIT Press.

Downs, A. 1957. *An Economic Theory of Democracy.* New York: Harper & Row.

Dunlop, J. T. 1944. *Wage Determination under Trade Unions*. New York: Macmillan.

______. 1955. *The Theory of Wage Determination*. London: Macmillan.

Fellner, W. J. 1949. *Competition Among the Few*. Republished in 1971. New York: A. A. Dropf.

Gallaway, L. E. 1971. *Manpower Economics*. Homewood, Ill.: R. D. Irwin.

Gärtner, M. 1979. "Legislative Profits and the Rate of Change of Money Wages: A Graphical Exposition." *Public Choice*, 36:3–4.

Hart, P. E., and Prais, S. J. 1956. "The Analysis of Business Concentration." *Journal of the Royal Statistical Society*, Part 2, pp. 150–191.

Heldman, D. 1977: *Trade Unions and Labor Relations in the U.S.S.R.* Washington, D.C.: Council on American Affairs.

Hicks, J. R. 1935. "Annual Survey of Economic Theory: The Theory of Monopoly." *Econometrica* 3(January):1–20.

Hines, A. G. 1964. "Trade Unions and Wage Inflation in the United Kingdom, 1893–1961." *Review of Economic Studies* 31, 88:221–252.

Hymer, S., and Pashigian, P. 1962. "Firm Size and Rate of Growth." *Journal of Political Economy* (December):556–569.

Johnson, G. E. 1975. "Economic Analysis of Trade Unionism." *American Economic Review* (May): Vol 65, 23–28.

Levinson, H. M. 1966. *Determining Forces in Collective Wage Bargaining*. New York: John Wiley.

Lewis, H. G. 1959. "Competitive and Monopoly Unionism." In P. D. Bradley, ed. (1959), pp. 181–208.

Marris, R. L. 1963. "A Model of the Managerial Enterprise." *Quarterly Journal of Economics* 77(May):185–209.

Marris, R. L. 1967. *The Economic Theory of "Managerial" Capitalism*. London: Macmillan.

Martin, D. L. 1980. *An Ownership Theory of the Trade Union*. Berkeley and Los Angeles: University of California Press.

Mueller, D. C. 1979. *Public Choice*. Cambridge: Cambridge University Press.

Mulvey, C. 1978. *The Economic Analysis of Trade Unions*. Oxford: Martin Robertson.

Niskanen, W. A., Jr. 1971. *Bureaucracy and Representative Government*. Chicago: Aldine-Atherton.

Olson, M., Jr. 1965. *The Logic of Collective Action*. Cambridge: Harvard University Press.

Price, R., and Bain, G. S. 1976. "Union Growth Revisited: 1948–1974 in Perspective." *British Journal of Industrial Relations* 14(November).

Reder, M. 1952. "The Theory of Union Wage Policy." *Review of Economics and Statistics* 34(February):34–55.

Reynolds, M. O. 1980. "The Intellectual Muddle over Labor Unions." *Journal of Social and Political Studies* 4, no. 3.

Rosa, J. J. 1980. "Théorie de la Firme Syndicale." *Vie et Sciences Economiques* 86(Juillet) (Numéro Spécial: L'Économie des Syndicats), pp. 1–22.

Ross, A. M. 1948. *Trade Union Wage Policy*. Berkeley: University of California Press.

Simon, H. A., and Bonini, C. P. 1958. "The Size Distribution of Business Firm's." *American Economic Review* 48(September):607–617.

Simons, H. C. 1944. "Some Reflections on Syndicalism." *Journal of Political Economy* 52(March):1–19.

Stigler, G. J. 1971. "The Theory of Economic Regulation." *Bell Journal of Economics and Management Science* 2, no. 1 (Spring):3–21.

Tiebout, C. M. 1956. "A Pure Theory of Local Expenditures." *Journal of Political Economy* 64(October):416–424.

A Comment on Burton, by Melvin W. Reder

John Burton has written an interesting survey of possible methodological approaches for studying the behavior of trade unions. I have no serious argument with the details of his discussion, but some reservations concerning the utility of methodological prolegomena at this stage in the study of trade unions. There may well be some merit in all the various ideas on which Burton comments when considered as candidates for inclusion in a model used to explain one aspect or another of union behavior. I believe, however, that the main reason for the near quarter century of neglect from which the subject has suffered has not been a paucity of candidate theories but rather a lack of firm and interesting empirical findings seeking explanation.

At present the critical methodological questions for an investigator are (1) which aspects of union behavior are being considered and (2) what specific phenomena are we attempting to explain. At this juncture, to use disparate theoretical constructions for explaining different aspects of union behavior is likely to be appropriate (e.g., effects of unionism on wage rates, growth rates and steady state sizes of union organizations, range of activities in which unions engage). At a later stage, to integrate the various theories being used may be desirable (and even necessary). At that time the type of speculation that Burton offers will become more applicable than at present (to what I consider) the immediate research agenda of our field.

To give point to my remarks, I note the (lack of) use made by Ross of his "political theory" in the (scant) empirical work presented in his book, *Trade Union Wage Policy*. I refer especially to chapter 6 which attempts to explain the relation of unionism to interindustry wage differentials. Neither in this chapter nor in a subsequent empirical study by Ross and Goldner (1950) is any attempt made to see whether the empirical findings support the political model or some alternative theory. A similar accusation could be directed at Dunlop's "economic model."

In my opinion, our task is not to see how much theory we can deploy, but how little we require to explain the very complex phenomena that are the subject matter of our specialty. Burton has described some potentially useful tools; I look forward to his joining those of us who are trying to apply them.

Reference

Ross, A. M., and Goldner, W. 1950. "Forces Affecting the Inter-Industry Wage Structure." *Quarterly Journal of Economics* 64(May):250–281.

7 TOWARD A THEORY OF THE UNION FIRM

Jean-Jacques Rosa

Since Adam Smith economists have been divided on the trade union issue: With Henry Simons and Fritz Machlup, they have denounced union attempts to lower productivity. But with Stuart Mill and, in some cases, Marshall, they have seen unions as having positive influence on the welfare of wage earners, at least when the latter were free to join or not join unions. This debate is still raging today, with Freeman and Medoff (1979) arguing that unions not only tend to improve working conditions but also have a positive effect on the firm's productivity. Union activity would thus be Pareto-optimal. Other authors, such as Burton (1978), consider trade unions as negative externalities. Lastly, most economists who have dealt with unions look at them as monopolizing the supply of labor to the benefit of workers, or even, as argued by Maloney, McCormick, and Tollison (1979), as a help to producers' cartels.

I thank Laurence Porteville, Sylvain Gallais, Jacques Généreux, Jean-François Hennart, Christine Leblanc, Bernard Lentz, Patrick Messerlin, and Michel Picot for offering criticism and suggestions on a preliminary version of this paper. Jacques Généreux has helped me gather the data for the appendix. Jean-François Hennart translated the paper from French. Responsibility for the opinions and the errors remain my residual property.

Just as microeconomics does not explain the raison d'être of the firm but concentrates mainly on pricing and markets, these studies deal with the union behavior on labor markets, not with the nature of the union organization. We will show in a first section how these analyses cannot explain satisfactorily what we observe on labor markets and in the field of labor relations. In the second section, we will draw on the theory of organization to consider the union as a particular type of firm.

Recent progress in the economic theory of politics, in the theory of property rights, and in the theory of organization throws a new light on trade unions. A trade union can be seen as a firm that belong to its managers and acts on both the political and the labor market according to the respective costs and benefits of both type of activity. This explains why unions are more politicized in some countries while labor-market oriented in others.

This view of the multifaceted union throws a different light on the bases of union power, the varying political nature of this activity, and the differences in business attitudes toward them. Unions are forced on firms by the political market and they compel firms to adapt to their labor policies, for unions act as partial substitutes to a personnel department. Unions develop because of social legislation and because of managerially run monopolistic firms that benefit from such policies. Unions then spread, through external effects, to firms that have a lower preference for unions and hence a greater preference for their own personnel management. That enterprises differ in their attitude toward unions is therefore likely.

The Labor Market and the Demand for Union Services

Unions are usually analyzed in the economic literature as a cartel attempting to obtain a monopoly rent for wage earners. This theory is, however, too vague to explain the precise form taken by union behavior. The work contract includes many elements besides money wages, and the theory of monopoly rent unionism cannot tell us to which of these elements a union seeking a monopoly rent will direct its action. Most empirical work has sought to determine whether unions affect money wages and whether the capitalists or nonunion members are shouldering the corresponding losses.

More recently, some economists have hypothesized that union services are demanded not only by wage earners and that union services do not necessarily result in losses for firm owners. On the contrary, there would be demand by firms for union services, either as a substitute or as a complement to a personnel policy, or as a way to monopolize or to attain vertical control in an industry in order to escape antitrust legislation.

These two approaches correspond to the microeconomics of labor market wage determination but do not explain union behavior, just as the classical theory of the firm describes how prices are set without looking at the raison d'être and the workings of the enterprise. The union firm is a black box. For this reason, we will classify these traditional and recent theories as theories of the demand for union services on the labor market, by opposition to the still young theories of the union firm, which will be examined in the second part of this article.

The Demand of Union Services by Wage Earners

According to traditional theory, wage earners are supposed to perceive union services as a cartel restricting the quantity of labor in order to obtain a monopoly rent. But situations in which unions coerce employees to maintain their monopoly power raise the interesting problem of convergence or divergence between the goals and interests of workers and union leaders. This problem, which we will take up later, is implicitly reflected in the wage-employment point chosen in collective bargaining. Each worker wants a high wage, irrespective of total employment. Union leaders know that union dues go up with the total number of employees, and possibly with their average wage. The collective decision of both employees and union leaders cannot be known a priori. This theoretical indetermination does not exist in the usual theory of monopoly, for the latter applies to a capitalist firm, with a unique price-quantity optimum defined by profit maximization. The union monopoly cannot be described in such simple terms. One does not know who "owns" the union, i.e., the identity of the agents who control the union to attain their own objectives.

In these conditions, the theory of the demand of union monopoly services on the labor market assumes implicitly a compromise between the maximization of employment and that of wages. This incomplete theory predicts that there will be some impact of unions on wages and has been the subject of empirical work by many authors following Gregg Lewis. They have attempted to determine whether unions have had an effect on the relative wages of firms and on sectors in which they are strong. Lewis has calculated the nationwide differential between unions and nonunion industries and found it to fluctuate widely during the 1920–1958 period. It amounted to 15 percent in 1955–1958. Other studies report even higher figures for the United Kingdom, reaching a high of more than 36 percent in 1975.

There have been few empirical studies on the French case, probably because of the considerable problems of data collection. A study by Jenny and Weber (1975) found a positive and significant impact of union membership (proxied by the percentage of votes obtained by unions in works council election) on the average level of wages in the sector. A more recent and detailed study by Jean-François Hennart (1980), using a more appropriate estimation technique, did not find a significant influence of unionism on wages.

In this context, one must underline the limitations of most studies on wage differentials. The fact that one observes a wage differential does not mean that unions cause wages to rise; rather, unions may flourish where firms are able to pay higher money wages. Higher money wages do not mean higher "full" wages, for wages also include payment in kind, more or less pleasant work environment and conditions, and greater or lower job security and work effort. Comparison of the sole monetary elements can be misleading. A detailed study of 5,000 American families concluded that union membership is greater wherever monetary wages are higher and nonmonetary benefits are lower (Morgan, 1973). One can think of two reasons for this finding: (1) union activity, leading to an increase in monetary wages, incites firms to reduce nonwage benefits or, (2) as we argued earlier, unions develop wherever work conditions are the worst and monetary wages the highest.

The second explanation has been tested in a simultaneous equation model that seeks to explain unionization by the level of wages and the wage level by unionization. In the case of France, the findings of Hennart (1980) confirm U.S. results: While unionization is higher in sectors in which wages are higher, unionization has no net impact on wages. Workers who attribute to unions their higher wages would thus be subject to a "union illusion."

If this is true, and if unions can only modify the mix of monetary and nonmonetary wage elements without being able to affect the wage level, what is the usefullness of unions?[1] If they cannot bring monopoly gains to their members, what do they deliver? Do they bring benefits to the other economic agents? Some authors argue that unions bring advantages not to workers but to management and, at best, to both groups, at the expense of consumers and nonunion members.

The Demand for Union Services by the Firm

If unions do not provide their members with monopoly gains, what do they provide? A new view in the economic literature argues that negotiation and the monitoring of labor contracts are public goods and hence require collective decision. The union would be, like the state in some of its activities, a supplier of public goods to workers, and probably to employers as well.

Olson (1965) and Pulsipher (1966) have considered union activity to be a collective good. According to the authors, unions provide indivisible bargaining services to all employees of a firm or of a sector inasmuch as the firm makes a single decision concerning pay and working conditions. Since the final bargaining decision will apply to all, a collective decision is necessary. When the union speaks for all employees, it should reach a solution that reflects their preferences, just as political parties influence government policies so as to reflect the views of their voters. Freeman and Medoff (1979) argue this case.[2]

This analysis would justify the desire of unions to monopolize the representation of employees and to have the right to coerce them, even if they cannot bring them monopoly rents—for public goods provision is subject to the free-rider problem. If this is true for union services, it would warrant forcing employees to join unions and to pay the corresponding union dues. Olson argues that if one grants employees the right not to join unions, one also grants any citizen the right not to pay taxes and not to be inducted for military service.

Burton (1978), however, argues that to consider union services as collective goods is erroneous. Unions perform four types of functions: (1) collective bargaining with employers, (2) the monitoring and implementation of collective or individual contracts (whether implicit or explicit), (3) lobbying and propaganda, (4) private services to members such as retirement houses, cooperatives, strike benefits. Categories (3) and (4) are not collective goods, for they can be individually performed or purchased outside the firm. Even (1) and (2) do not have characteristics of collective goods, for unions could very easily negotiate agreements that would apply only to their members.

Morever, one can object to the second reason for collective action presented by Freeman and Medoff—the fact that the voice-exit alternative presented by Hirschmann (1977) does not correspond to the opposition between collective bargaining and individual bargaining. The direct voicing of demand by parties without termination of contract or interruption of the exchange is part of the usual process of private bargaining. It was a basic feature of all markets before the rather recent introduction of set prices. The mix of voice and exit on markets is a function of the relative cost of both actions for the traders involved in a multifaceted complex transaction. If they like some aspects of the services but not others, they would probably find it costly to abandon the whole set of characteristics that constitutes the service.

Instead, they may find it more advantageous to negotiate a modification of the portfolio characteristics in a way that suits their preferences.

Morever, it is not obvious that the result attained by collective bargaining is always more advantageous than that obtained by individual bargaining. Lastly, maximum demands are not always optimal. Thus, in spite of what the theoreticians of the publicness of union services say, union services could be privately produced. The nature of union activity does not justify the right to monopoly on coercion. On the contrary, it is the law that, by granting to unions a monopoly on bargaining, has created a public good out of a service that wasn't.[3]

In fact, unions find it advantageous to ask for egalitarian wage and working conditions so as to justify their presence. They are opposed to personnel policies that seek to individualize wages and working conditions, such as performance-related pay schemes, flexible hours, part-time work, and workplace dispersion. The role played by unions in the leveling of wage differences within the plant has been underlined by Farber and Saks (1980). By bargaining at the sectoral level, unions also equalize wages between firms.

The role played by unions in equalizing wages explains in part why firms demand unions. As Slichter, Healy, and Livernash (1960) point out, union presence results from the equilibrium between supply and demand for union services by employees, union officers, and employers. Employers do demand unions, even if their demand remains implicit.[4] Managers can reduce the union presence within the firm by an active social policy if they accept its cost in time and efforts. Such a policy can be an "individualized, social policy," as a recent meeting of the French employers' association put it,[5] which contributes to reduce the public good attributes of union services and therefore the usefulness of unions—for the usefulness of the union is a function of the degree to which it can make public a contract that could be private. When the firm replaces uniform agreements by an individualized personnel policy, it weakens union influence, as shown by the many recent experiments reported in a recent *l'Expansion* article.[6]

The firm is therefore able to counter the union. When management doesn't act, one must assume that it deems the union to be preferable to an active and individualized personnel management. Uniform rules are cheaper than individualized ones. The union shoulders part of the cost by trying to formulate the workers' average preferences to bargain with management.

The union thus becomes a substitute to a personnel department, its role being the monitoring and enforcement of the work contract.[7] The savings thus attained allow the firm to pay union dues. This view, when pushed to the limit, leads to the "transmission belt" union such as exists in the Soviet

Union—or a substitute for the personnel department. Membership is mandatory, and the union has a legal monopoly. The firm cannot choose the optimal mix between union and personnel department; demand for unions is determined by the state.

In other countries, such as France, the situation is more complex. Company unions are probably little different from a personnel department, whereas national unions, which benefit from a legal monopoly of representation, are able to impose to the firm a cost—of acceptance or rejection—that the latter cannot escape.[8]

Given market competition between firms, cross subsidization favors firms that allow union representation and penalizes those that restrict union action and seek to develop their own personalized personnel policy. Since union organization in France is especially strong in a few large nationalized firms, the development of national unions introduces a bias toward those firms and against all other firms.

We can thus explain why the firm often opposes a union that imposes a method of management that is not optimal, and yet accepts in practice this division of labor and the method of personnel management it implies: because the alternative, the fight against the unions and the development of an effective personnel policy, is even more costly. Thus the internal policies of the firm are in part influenced by union legislation. The fact that management demands unions does not mean that the observed rate and characteristics of unions are optimal for the enterprise, because the legal provisions that favor the union are equivalent to a public subsidy to unions. Furthermore, the union presence in a firm can be seen as a negative external effect, a pollution for the firm because unions are national in scope, and not limited to the firm. The development of national unions in other industries or in the public sector provides resources that unions can devote to sectors in which conditions are less favorable. This cross subsidization within the union raises the cost of resistance to unionization in nonunionized industries. The nature of social legislation can thus push firms to adopt a degree of uniformization of work contracts that does not necessarily correspond to their first choice.

An opposing view argues that a firm should maintain a rigid and uniform wage structure so that workers can expect to obtain wage increases only as a result of a general increase in the profits of the enterprise, rather than at the expense of other employees.[9] This argument is perhaps valid in the case of small groups, but loses its validity in the case of medium-sized or large firms. In that latter case, the impact of each employee on the sales and the productivity of the enterprise is so small that the individual cannot hope to increase his or her own salary by increasing the productivity of the whole firm. This is the argument developed by Olson in *The Logic of Collective Action*, and it allows us to doubt the efficiency of such a policy of uniform wages.

Another theory seeking to explain the presence of unions in firms has been recently expounded by Maloney, McCormick, and Tollison (1979) and by Faith and Lentz (1979). According to Maloney, McCormick, and Tollison, the existence of national unions allows all managers of a given sector to reduce production simultaneously through strikes, wherever they so desire, and thus to form a cartellike agreement, in spite of the Clayton and Norris-La Guardia Acts. They can thus obtain monopoly prices for their products. The authors cite a similar analysis by Simons (1944).[10] Faith and Lentz develop this theory by hypothesizing that strikes can help maximize a firm's profits by spreading production through time in response to the business fluctuations.

These hypotheses have not yet been empirically tested. In the French case, their validity seems a priori doubtful, given the weakness of French antitrust legislation. On the contrary, the government has almost always encouraged collusion and cartels in industry. One could then say that during a long period, trade associations and then the plan commissions and the ministries have provided a good substitute to trade unions for that specific task. Increased international competition is changing the old links between industry and the state and may lead to a different situation in the future.

The Union Firm

The study of union effects on the labor contract cannot really throw much light on their objectives. There seems to be as many different union types as specific situations, from the journeyman, craft unions, and industrial unions, to the politicized national confederation and the internal confederations. This diversity in organization reflects differences in behavior and in services supplied and seems to prevent us from making any generalizations. It explains the relative lack of success of economic research up to this day. As D. L. Martin (1980) points out:

> The biggest stumbling block for economists, however, has been the answer to the deceptively simple question asket by Dunlop (1950) some thirty years ago: "What do unions maximize?"
>
> . . . The response to Dunlop's question by economists and students of industrial relations has been disappointing, to say the least. The profession has generated an embarrassingly large number or maximands. From time to time, it has been suggested that unions maximize the wage bill (Dunlop [1950]), the wage rate per member (ibid and Simons [1944]), the utility of membership (Fellner [1949],

> Cartter [1959], and Atherton [1973]), the size of the membership" (Ross [1948]), and the difference between union receipts and expenditures (Berkowitz [1954], Atherton [1973]). Still others have suggested that unions are satisfying rather than maximizing institutions (Reder [1960]).

Similarly, Dertouzos and Pencavel (1980) argue that "although empirical studies measuring the effect of trade unions have multiplied in the last few years, the behavioral underpinnings of unionism remain poorly understood." These authors see this situation as arising from an excessive development of theoretical models to the detriment of empirical testing, in opposition to what, in their view, is taking place in the economics of the firm or the family.

The modern theory of the union is also built on such extreme simplifications, especially since the controversy between Ross (1948) and Dunlop (1950), most economists being now aligned with the latter. Ross criticized the traditional approach of the union as an economic agent seeking to maximize one or many variables on the sole labor market. Ross argues that the union brings together a large number of individuals and of heterogeneous groups. Union leaders must therefore play a crucial role and draft a compromise to keep their position. The problem is one of internal politics. Unions should therefore be more easily explained by political scientists than by economists. Atherton (1973) later subscribed to such a view.[11]

Dunlop rejected Ross's arguments for four reasons. First, the role played by political factors was large in only a few unions, where internal dissensions had taken place. Second, political factors had only a short-term impact on policy, whereas long-term policy was influenced by those economic forces that determine wages and employment. Third, union leaders, as any other economic agents, reacted to economic constraints, which cannot be changed, and not to political considerations, which are only transient. Lastly, Dunlop showed that membership was a function of the wage increases obtained by the union and that internal political questions were therefore dependent on the labor market and on collective bargaining.

Until recently, economists have sided with Dunlop and have looked at unions through wage and employment determination and through a few other labor market variables. They have ignored the internal organization of unions and the role played by unions on the political market. The union is therefore seen as a labor monopoly with a behavior similar to that of the monopolistic firm in traditional microeconomics.

But while the firm has a specific statutory goal of profit maximization and whereas its peformance on that score is easy to measure, such is not the case with a union. In this sense Dunlop is right in asking his preliminary question.

One cannot use monopoly theory if one does not know what is the precise statutory objective pursued by the organization.

The second reason why this approach is unsatisfactory follows from Ross's discussion, but goes further. The union is a political entity, not only because of its internal workings, but also because of the type of activities it undertakes in the outside, on the political market. In all countries unions play a political role and have links with political parties. They play a part in the regulatory game and are officially recognized in many laws. Atherton (1973) underlines this fact:

> A . . . limitation of this study is that it is concerned with only one part of union activity: the formulation of goals which the union will try to achieve by bargaining with and putting economic pressure on the employer. Unions also seek to advance their member interests in other ways: for example, by securing favorable legislation. But this and certain other aspects of trade unionism lie beyond our concerns.

In fact, this does not constitute just one aspect of union activity, but one of the most important elements of union power. The union can control labor supply and earn monopoly rents only if it obtains official recognition. A union must therefore act on both the labor and political markets. As G. Warren Nutter (1959) wrote:

> Perhaps union power is best thought of as "organic" in nature: successful collusion leads to successful exclusion, and conversely. In a very real sense, "success breeds success," and "power feeds on itself." We must immediately add that this is true only within limits set by relevant economic conditions, the established mores, and law, but for the moment we shall not try to specify these limits. The point being made here is that union power is not derived from a logical sequence of causes, but from the interaction of many factors, reinforcing each other. If any one factor is to be considered as antecedent, it is the right to organize and collude, which has as its corollary the right to strike.

Thus the union must be considered to be a political institution both because of its internal working rules (vote and absence of nonnegotiable property rights) and of its field of action. Thirty years later, the Ross-Dunlop controversy has become most interesting because of recent progress in two new fields of economic theory. With the school of public choice, political problems are now subjected to economic analysis. The economics of politics studies what had to be left aside in 1948. Moreover, the development of the theory of property rights and that of the agency contributes to an analysis of the workings of various organizations, including the family, the limited-liability company, government bureaus, and unions.

The Theory of Organizations

Following the now classical articles of Coase and Alchian-Demsetz, Jensen and Meckling (1976) generalize the new approach of the firm by showing its importance for the study of any organizations:

> It is important to recognize that most organizations are simply legal fictions which serve as a nexus for a set of contracting relationships among individuals.
>
> . . . The private corporation or firm is simply one form of legal fiction which serves as a nexus for contracting relationships and which is also characterized by the existence of divisible residual claims on the assets and cash flows of the organization which can generally be sold without permission of the other contracting individuals.
>
> . . . The firm is not an individual."

Queries on the "goal" or the "social function" of the firm are therefore meaningless. By "legal fiction," the authors mean an artificial legal construct that allows some organizations to be considered as persons. Within an organization, the goals of the individuals who are linked by contracts reach an equilibrium just as they do on a market. This is why the "behavior" of the firm is similar to that of a market: it is the result of a complex equilibrating mechanism. However, while we rarely make the mistake of thinking of markets as human beings, we often consider organizations as persons with goals and motivations. This is what we do when we ask, What do unions maximize?

The consequences of this analysis are quite important. As soon as one stops considering the organization as a person, one no longer has to ask questions about its objectives. Moreover, no longer has one to study the conflicts between groups within the organization, which are themselves made up of persons whose interests are not identical. When considering that the organization is a web of contracts, one is led to study the relationship between each member and the organization. One person, however, has a particular position in the legal fiction that constitutes the organization: the person who has the right to make decisions that bind the firm with other organizations, i.e., the manager. It is the manager who decides, given the constraints put on him or her by agency relationships with other members of the organization.

For this reason, analysis of the organization must start with the behavior of the manager and study how the contractual rules of the organization are constraining that behavior, to make it compatible with the interests of the other members of the organization.

In a private limited liability company, the goal of all the management team and of the manager himself is to obtain as high a personal income as possible. Such is also the case with employees and suppliers. Inversely, customers want as low a price as possible. Stockholders, who are taking the risk of having to pay creditors of the firm up to a given amount should the firm go bankrupt, are getting in exchange the residual income of the firm. Hence, stockholders are the only ones to seek to increase the difference between cost and receipts, whereas all the other agents seek to reduce it. For this reason, the law gives generally to stockholders the right to name and to fire ad nutum the managers responsible for monitoring the various contracts. This clause constitutes for the manager a strong incitation to act to maximize the interests of the stockholders and to make profits. Manne (1965) and Alchian (1969) have shown that the existence of a market in which the stockholders' property rights can be sold is crucial to the efficient management of the firm and to a reduction of agency costs.

This solution does not exist in organizations for which the law does not define (or forbids) profits and ownership in the organization is not freely and individually transferable. The managers of such organizations, which we will call "political firms," have more leeway, and their behavior is therefore different.

As De Alessi (1974) puts it:

> Property rights in political firms may be taken to be nontransferable. This rules out specialization in their ownership, and inhibits the capitalization of future consequences into current transfer prices (if such prices were available), thereby reducing incentives to detect and police managerial behavior which is inconsistent with employers' (the owners', i.e., the members') welfare. Among other things, this implies that the managers of political firms have greater opportunity to increase their own welfare by pursuing policies designed to increase noncapitalizable returns.

As we will attempt to show the analysis of political firms can be applied to the union.

A Political-Economic Theory of the Union

Just like any other social organization, the union is a web of social relationships of exchange and cooperation between individuals pursuing their own objectives. The union is a nonprofit organization, i.e. an organization that produces services without the stated goal of making profits. The list of services is not strictly defined. The union is therefore akin to a producer or consumer cooperative, or a mutual insurance company. It differs from these organizations by its products.

In France, the union is legally a nonprofit association (law of March 21, 1884), and in the United States a nonprofit organization. In such an organization individual members do not have transferable property rights. The control of managers is achieved through periodic elections, a feature that makes these organizations analogous to the political market.

The absence of transferable property rights on the residual and the a priori indeterminate products of the organization limit the ability of members to monitor managers. Further, measuring the performance of the managers is difficult. The controversy among economists as to what unions really achieve reflects this problem and that of the absence of a visible and synthetic index of performance. It is therefore difficult, i.e., costly, for a union member to evaluate the managerial performance of the union leaders. These conditions resemble those found on the political market and determine a similar degree of "rational ignorance" on the part of the voter. This is especially so since the benefit to be gained from better monitoring of the union manager is small. Given the absence of a residual and of property rights on the latter, union members cannot benefit from efforts devoted to increase the wealth of the organization in the medium and long terms. In contrast to stockholders in a private firm, they cannot sell at any point in time their property rights on the future wealth that will result from their past efforts and sacrifices. There is no capitalization of expected income, no transformation of past investment into a transferable present value. Because of this factor, changing the managers is harder, i.e., more costly.

Typical union members have no incentive to invest in such an action, for they will be in the same situation of limited control vis-à-vis the new managers. They are therefore forced to seek immediate gains, even if they are small, and even if they go against their own long-term interests. (The situation is the same as in the self-managed Yugoslav firm.[12] Union members cannot hope to cash in on their personal investment in the union if their investment is limited to the firm or to the sector, unless they stay for a significant period of time in the firm or in the sector, an improbable event in a mobile society.[13] Union members should therefore not invest in union activities, but ask for immediate gains. This results in inflated demands, especially from the younger members, who are more mobile and whose expected tenure in the firm is smaller.[14] Thus, even if a strike does not bring as much in terms of discounted wage increases as it costs in terms of reduced union finances, such a strike can be undertaken because the building up of reserves will not be shouldered by the present but by the future members.

Union members do not therefore exercise a tight control on their leaders, who thus benefit from a considerable degree of leeway. Union leaders can pursue their own objectives, which are not necessarily those of the membership; because the union is a managerial type of organization.[15]

Contrary to the usual conclusions of the theory of competitive markets, competition between unions does not lead to more satisfied consumers of "union services." One could think that open competition between unions, especially when entry is free, should lead unions to better satisfy the preferences of their voters. In this case, unions would be less managerial. But the union market, just like the political market, suffers from the same imperfections that cannot be remedied solely by free entry. On the contrary, as Gregg Lewis (1959) points out, the competitive union is likely to be unable to provide a real advantage to its members, at least as far as wages are concerned:

> Competitive unionism . . . produces no real wage effects; monopoly unionism, on the other hand, does produce such effects though in particular cases they may be imperceptible.

This last conclusion is also reached by Jensen and Meckling (1976) for every type of firm. Competition or monopoly in the product market has no influence on agency and monitoring costs within the organization. There are no grounds to say that the interests of the principal will be better defended in one case than in the other.[16]

It is therefore erroneous to argue with Gregg Lewis (1959) that high union dues are an indication of the monpoly power of the union and on its impact on wages. Moreover, as Becker (1959) has shown, a union can use other nonmonetary devices to make new members pay for their share of the monopoly rent. The level of dues will more probably reflect the degree of control of union members on new members, i.e., the level of service desired by new members when the union is less managerial. This level of services is not limited to the wage differential, which can be negligible.

Martin (1980) underlines the conditions under which the union cards can be privately transferred in the United States. In general, unions are opposed to the free transfer of union cards, such as may take place in a private firm. Nevertheless, such practices, although rare, sometimes exist,[17] although they are occasionally covert. In such a case, the union becomes a proprietary organization. When the union card is transferable, one can expect union leaders to favor medium- and long-term wage increases, which depend on technical progress and on labor productivity, rather than immediate wage gains, which tend to lower the firm's profits and investments and therefore future increases in income. Similarly, private transferability of the union card should lead union officers to supply differentiated private services to their members rather than uniform services with collective good characteristics. Lastly, the manager should be more tightly controlled by the membership.

In the opposite (and general) case, the union firm constitutes an extreme form of managerial enterprise. The members get a limited service, and are only ready to pay a small price. In this case, the interesting question is not What do unions do? but Who are the owners? As in the case of mutual insurance companies, one can argue that the members are not really the owners. As Hetherington (1969) puts it:

> To the extent that ownership means the ability to use and to make and implement decisions affecting a business, the owner of a mutual organization is its managerial establishment. To the extent that such an establishment is free of the possibility of outside interference or removal, it occupies a proprietary position to a degree not possible to its counterpart (hired management) in a stock corporation Realistically, the only aspect of ownership which a mutual management clearly lacks is the proprietary right to profit.

But, as Frech (1980) has argued, even this last type of property right can be indirectly obtained by the managers of a mutual company (and consequently a union) by such devices as wages, retirement plans, the use of the association's country and retirement houses, and the control of private corporations.

The independence of the manager, and its de facto ownership of the organization, will be stronger the smaller the need for the resources brought by the de jure owners of the association, the dues payers. This phenomenon is strictly similar to the attenuation of the property rights of stockholders when the firm raises capital through bonds or bank debt.[18] This attenuation, as Jensen and Meckling show, increases agency costs, and thus the freedom of the managers.

Furthermore, the independence of union officers explains the variety and range of union activities. When a union is tightly controlled by a homogeneous group of members, its decisions reflect the interests of its members, who are rather homogeneous and well defined. When property rights are attenuated, the membership is heterogeneous and managers have discretionary powers and can undertake all sorts of activities to bring them monetary or nonmonetary benefits. The leadership is not bound by constraints that might force it to maximize a unique goal. Union managers will seize all opportunities and enter those markets that appear profitable. They are no longer limited to the labor market, but can undertake an unlimited range of activities. For this reason, there are no limits to the scope of activities of a modern union and why those activities will differ across countries and across time. This is why some unions will develop their action on the political market: because the profitability to the managers of such endeavors is higher than on the labor market.

We have seen, however, that to be active on the political market is a necessary condition for successful union activity. In France, for example, representative unions have a legal monopoly. This monopoly has not allowed them to obtain a wage differential on the labor market, but it has been nevertheless profitable because it has subsequently brought political rents. The laws of 1959 and 1969 have forced firms to grant union delegates and elected workers representatives free time to perform their duties. This constitutes a rent, since these dispositions amount in fact to compulsary financing of unions by enterprises as long as the law remains in force. These rents are obtained on the political market since only the government has the power to impose regulations that amount to a tax and a transfer. In the present case, the tax is levied on firms, and the transfer benefits the unions. Unions can obtain such transfers because of their political and electoral power. One can argue that the goodwill and the distribution network controlled by unions constitute a considerable amount of intangible capital. This asset can be converted in monetary receipts through the sale of services: union publications, demonstrations, miscellaneous enterprises. It can also be used to the benefit of political entrepreneurs in exchange for privileges and rents.

Political rents play an important role in the financing of trade unions. As an example, the money equivalent of time allowances has been calculated (see the appendix to this chapter). The total is impressive and is comparable to the U.S. "closed shop." If workers in France are not forced to belong to the union, firms are forced to do so because they are legally obliged to pay wages to union officers, as shown in the appendix to this chapter.

These resources increase, moreover, the independence of union managers and reduce further the control that union members have on them. Consequently, union managers have less need to obtain wage gains for their membership. Nevertheless, in countries where political intervention has rapidly increased in the last ten years, collective bargaining on the labor market is often dependent on advantage obtained on the political market. Surveying the development of unions in France, Germany, Japan, Great Britain, and the United States since 1900, Dunlop (1978) concludes:

> The experience of these five countries since 1900 reflects an increasing role of governmental agencies employment. The method of legal epactment is an increasing alternative to the method of collective bargaining.

The chapters in this volume develop the relationship that exists between unions on political parties and their ideologies. The contrast between reformist and

> revolutionary unions, and the evolution of their political policies since the outset of the century, are decisive to the operation of these industrial relations systems.

He adds:

> In the mid-1970s in England and West Germany labor parties and their political allies constituted the governments; in France and Japan the unions were mainly allied with the parliamentary opposition to the elected governments; in the United States the unions were not as formally related to political parties as in the other four countries, but sought to use their considerable electoral and lobbying influence for particular candidates or legislation. In all these countries, unions had grown to be a power in the economy and polity.

Gärtner (1979) underlines also the interaction between unions, whose activity is theoretically on the labor market, and politics:

> Other union demands like those for equal educational opportunities for working-class children or extended industrial codetermination reach far into the political sphere.

The author attempts to explain union activity from the ideological preferences of the leaders, the phase of the political cycle, and the chances of electoral success of the political parties allied to the union. Gärtner contrasts "ideological " and "professional" unions. This distinction is often made when discussing the role of the union. One generally contrasts German unions, which are more concerned with wage increases and which cooperate with management, with French or Italian unions, which are more interested in political action. One can build with Gärtner a union activity function with these two objectives, W, wage increases, and PR, political rents:

$$U = U(W, PR).$$

A political union will be characterized by the indifference curves pertaining to its manager of the type shown in figure 7–1(a), whereas a union more interested in the labor market will be represented by figure 7–1(b).

In fact, the wage increases, or satisfying union members, can be thought of as the cost of capital for strengthening union power, which makes possible the manager's receiving rents on political markets. The flaw in this approach is that it explains economic choices by differences in tastes. But as Stigler and Becker (1977) argue, the nature of economic analysis is to explain choices by changes in prices and incomes. To determine the optimal level of union activity on both the labor and the political markets, we need a budget constraint (since union finances are limited) and a price ratio (the ratio of the

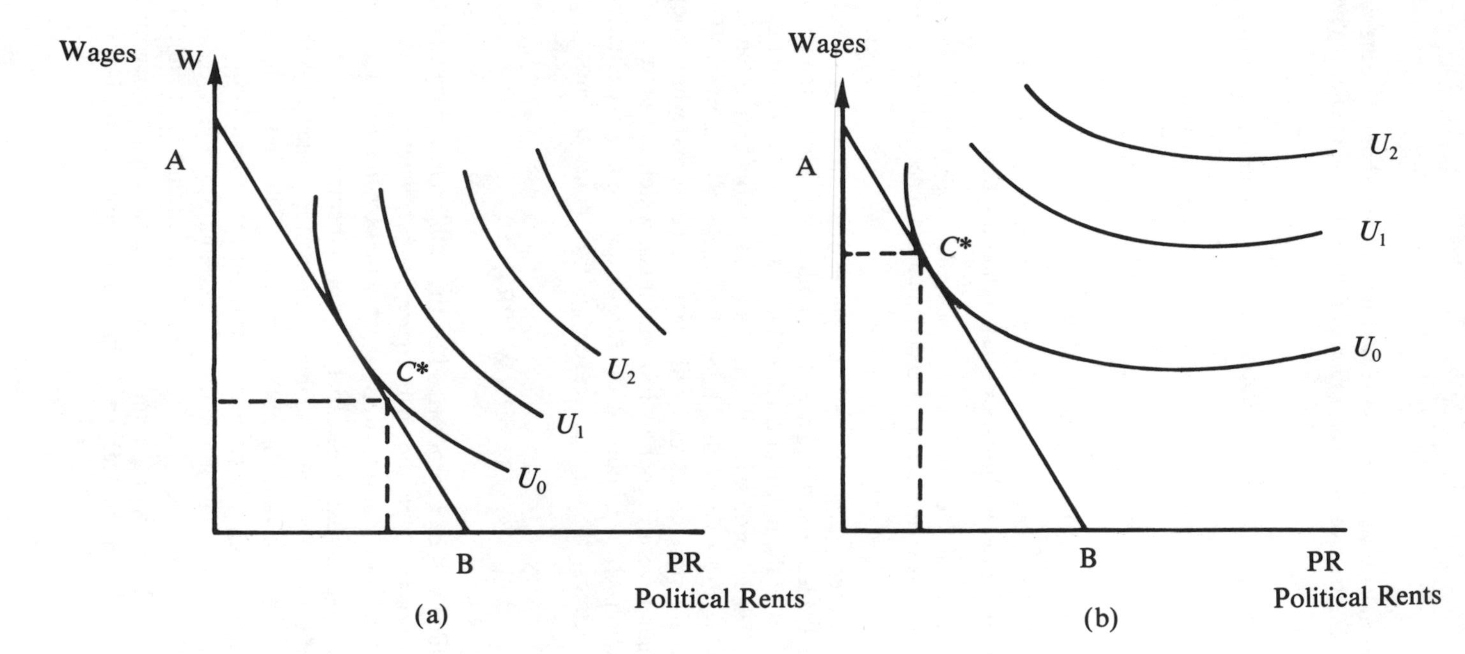

Figure 7-1. Labor Market, Political Market, and Union Manager Utility

wage gains that must be given up to obtain political rents to the political rents that must be sacrificed to obtain wage gains). When we introduce the AB budget constraint, we obtain different mixes of union activity, (C), with different union preferences. The analyses of Atherton and Martin can be incorporated in this model. Unions whose membership has strong property rights will prefer wage gains, figure 7–1(b), whereas the managerial union will prefer political rents, figure 7–1(a). Union organization, the content of property rights, and the political relationship between groups within the union influence the decisions of the managers, as represented by the utility function.

A different approach is possible, however, which seems more fruitful in understanding union dynamics. We can assume that all union leaders have the same utility function, but that they face different relative prices. Thus, in figure 7–2, the German union would obtain more wage increases than the French union not because it is less "ideological" and more "constructive" but because seeking wage gains is, in Germany, more efficient than political action, whereas the opposite is true in France.

This analysis leads to a new interpretation of observed facts. First, a union for which political action has a low cost (a high payoff) will devote itself entirely to the latter. It consequently has few members and will not depend on them for financing. Its managerial aspect will be reinforced. Thus it is not the initial preferences of unions leaders but the conditions of political action that determine its orientation and attract a particular type of members. We go from a psychological to an evolutionary theory of trade unions.

Second, the relative price of both types of action depends on the relative resistance of government and of employers to the union. The relative resistance (the relative demand for unions) of these groups will vary. Governments will be pushed to grant more political rents during periods of political uncertainty. The same is true before elections, with, as Gärtner does, a positive or a negative sign, depending on whether the government in power is favorable or opposed to unions. In this context, it is the present value of future political gains that must be taken into account in explaining the relative price of political market activities. This future value can be significantly affected by the decisive results of an election. One could cite the French legislative elections of 1978 and the ensuing decline of the most "politicized" unions.

This framework can therefore take into account the demand for unions by government and by employers. It can be developed along the lines of the traditional theory of wage bargaining, but with the addition of political business cycle variables to the economic business cycle variables. This is what Gärtner has started to do, but he so far has only introduced the electoral cycle.

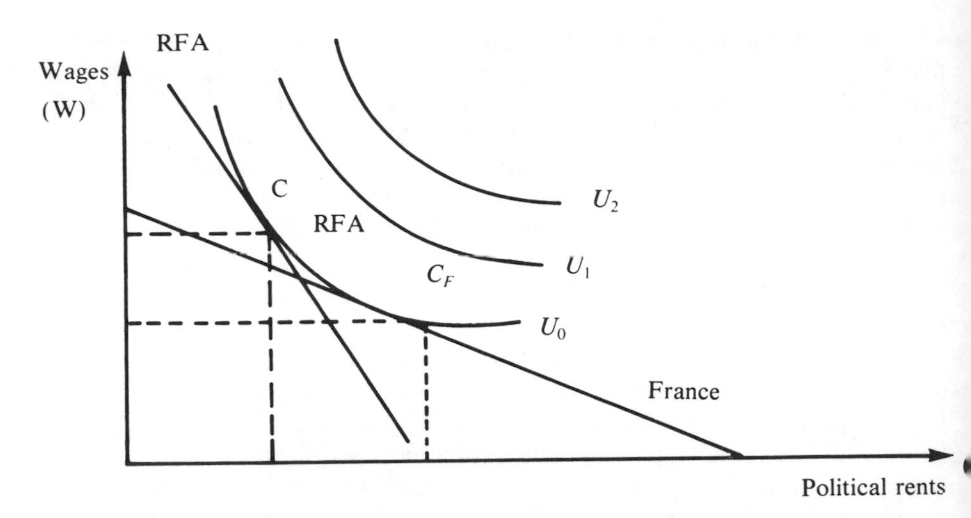

Figure 7-2. One Utility Function, Variable Relative Prices

Lastly, a fuller analysis cannot completely separate political rents and wage gains. Both can be complementary through time even if they are substitutable at any point in time. This is what could be called "political leverage." The intangible asset represented by the union "sales force" allows union manager-owners to obtain political rents, which make it possible in turn to obtain more easily wage gains or better working conditions when bargaining with employers either because the higher resources controlled by unions, such as free hours for union officers, allow them to impose higher losses on employers or because political rents result in government pressure on employers to accede to union demands.[19]

To the union managers, wage increases for workers are the equivalent of depreciation for maintenance of customers' goodwill. There is probably an optimal level for such investment, but the analysis of this problem is beyond the present study and will be developed elsewhere.

As a conclusion, the development of political leverage by the managerial union seems to correspond to observed trends, and especially to the effort of equalization of union gains, from enterprises where they are well tolerated toward enterprises that resist their presence. To quote again Dunlop (1978):

> Unions appear to have been generally stronger initially in blue-collar occupations and goods—producing industries and only more gradually have come to organize white-collar positions and service industries, which, outside the public sector,

often still remain relatively underorganized and weaker. Unions have tended to develop a strong hold among public employees, derived in part from the critical role of political processes in influencing their wages and conditions and from the character of public management and administration.

The theory of the trade union is thus particularly complex. It can be developed today thanks to recent progress in the theory of the firm and of contracts, of the theory of finance and property rights, of firms and political markets. The synthesis of all these contributions throws a different light on some aspects of union activities. It allows us to better understand the controversies that have marked the study of these organizations. It should allow us to systematically analyze comparable institutions, such as political parties and the state.

Appendix: An Evaluation of a Union Political Rent: Time Allowances

Beside direct monetary resources obtained from dues, unions receive funding by firms through the time allowances legally granted since 1968 to union representatives.

Union delegates are granted a time allowance of 10 hours per month in firms of 150 to 300 workers, and 15 hours in firms of more than 300 workers. Elected representatives are granted 15 hours per month. These hours are supposed to allow delegates to carry out their duties and are paid as work hours by the firm. It is interesting to evaluate the amount of this tax levied on firms, and especially to assess the relative importance of this source of funding in total union finances.

To calculate the total yearly number of hours benefiting the union, we make two hypotheses. First, we assume that the distribution of delegates within each firm size class is the same as that of union locals. Second, we assume that the distribution of delegates according to union confederation is similar to that of union locals. Tables 7–1, 7–2, and 7–3 show the total amount of hours obtained by the nonelected union representatives of each of the four main union confederations for 1971, 1972, and 1973. To this amount must be added the time allowances of delegates elected to the works council as workers' delegates. This figure is obtained by multiplying the

Table 7-1. Distribution of Union Locals According to Firm Size and Estimate of the Number of Delegates According to the Size of Firms

Distribution of Union Local	*1971*	*1972*	*1973*
(1) Firms with 150 to 299 employees	26	26.5	25.4
(2) Firms with 300 to 1000 employees	24.9	22.9	21.1
(3) Firms with over 1000 employees	6.3	5.8	5.1
(4) Total number of delegates	15,875	20,151	23,828
Estimated number of delegates			
(5) Firms with 150 to 299 employees	4,127.5	5,340	6,052.3
(6) Firms with 300 to 1000 employees	3,952.8	4,614.6	5,027.7
(7) Firms with over 1000 employees	1,000.1	1,168.8	1,215.2

Note: Firm size is in percentage. Numbers (5), (6), and (7) are obtained by multiplying (4) by (2), (3), and (4). We assume therefore that the distribution of delegates by firm size is proportional to that of union locals.

Table 7-2. Distribution of Union Locals by Main Confederations

	1971			*1972*			*1973*		
Confederations	*150 to 299 E.*	*300 to 1,000 E.*	*Over 1,000 E.*	*150 to 299 E.*	*300 to 1,000 E.*	*Over 1,000 E.*	*150 to 299 E.*	*300 to 1,000 E.*	*Over 1,000 E.*
CGT	46.4	40.8	32.2	43.9	40	30.1	43.8	38.8	30.3
CFDT	25.7	25.2	25.66	25.1	24.7	25	25	24.4	2.2
FO	10	10.5	12.7	10.6	10.4	12.6	10.6	10.9	12.7
CFTC	3.9	4.3	5.7	4	4.6	6.2	4.1	4.5	6.5

Table 7-3. Number of Delegates by Confederation and Firm Size[a]

	1971		
Confederations	*Delegates Firms of 150–300 Employees*	*Delegates over 300*	*Annual[b] Time Allowances*
CGT	1,915	1,935	578,100
CFDT	1,061	1,252	352,680
FO	413	542	147,120
CFTC	161	227	60,180

[a]The number of delegates is calculated by applying to the estimated number of delegates (5), (6), and (7) in table 7–1 the distribution by main confederation of table 7–2.

[b]*Annual time allowances:* 12 times to 10 hours, per delegate in firms of 150–300 employees plus 12 times 15 hours per delegate in firms over 300 workers.

number of delegates elected for each union by the legal maximum time allowance, viz., 15 hours. For example, the CFDT had 7,050 elected delegates in 1972 and therefore 105,750 hours per month, or 1,269,000 hours per year. If one adds this amount to that obtained by the CFDT union representatives (see table 7–3), 1,269,000 plus 418,560 hours, or over 16 millions francs at 10 francs an hour.[20] This would amount to over 32 million francs at the average 1980 wage.

The interest of such a calculation is to show the order of magnitude of one union's political rents. It is therefore important to compare this with their other financial resources. This comparison is difficult because we have data only on the budget of confederations, not on the budget of each national union. It is however possible to solve this problem. Union dues make up the quasitotality of explicit union finances, and we can estimate the proportion of these resources that is forwarded to the confederations. Thus, in 1972, the share of union dues received by the CFDT confederation is f 3,945,440 francs. The corresponding amount for total CFDT union dues cannot be directly known, for in 1973 the share of dues going to the national union was freely decided by each national union. However, this share can be calculated for the years 1974 to 1978; over these five years the confederate share varies between one-eighth and one-sixth of the total. If we apply these percentages to the dues received by the confederation in 1972, total union dues are between f 31,563,520 and 25,672,640 francs. When we compare this

1972			*1973*		
Delegates Firms of 150–300 Employees	*Delegates over 300*	*Annual[b] Time Allowances*	*Delegates Firms of 150–300 Employees*	*Delegates over 300*	*Annual[b] Time Allowances*
2,344	2,198	676,920	2,652	2,321	735,900
1,340	1,432	418,560	1,513	1,511	453,540
566	627	180,780	642	703	203,580
214	285	76,980	248	305	84,660

amount to the 16 million francs of time allowances, we find that time allowances make up between 71.3 and 53.5 percent of total resources.

Time allowances are therefore an important element in total union resources. The lack of data on the budget of national unions (federations) and regional unions (*unions departementales*) does not allow us to arrive at precise figures. However, one must mention that the data cover only the private sector and that time allowances have been calculated by using only the legal minimum. It is therefore likely that our figure on total hours is underestimated.

Notes

1. The mix between the monetary and nonmonetary elements (working conditions, intensity of effort, level of risk) of the wage in a firm depends both on the preferences of the employees and on the optimum for the firm. This last optimum is a function of the age of the equipments and of the case with which the employees' level of effort can be controlled. In tasks for which results are highly visible and where there is a high degree of standardization, it is easy to monitor effort. In such cases, a high monetary wage can be paid.

On the contrary, the firm should not pay high monetary wages for those tasks for which results are hard to measure. Such high wages will not necessarily incite a high degree of effort because effort is hard to monitor and because the mutation to shirk is strong. In this last case, the firm may expect a minimum effort on the part of employees and only grant a minimum wage to equalize the full wage to the market wage. The first case could correspond to highly "tailorized" enterprises, while we would find the second case in services or in firms that do not maximize profits. The firm can always increase monitoring and surveillance costs in those activities for which results are hard to measure.

One finds, of course, many examples that seem to counter these hypotheses: Some firms have both high monetary wages and excellent working conditions. But the level of effort may be higher there than elsewhere. Other firms may have bad conditions and low wages because work effort is lower there.

For any given competitive full wage, it is possible to observe a full range of monetary wages given the positive (pleasantness of the work) or negative (effort) components of the full wage. It is therefore erroneous to measure union monopoly power by comparing only the monetary components of the wage.

2. Freeman and Medoff (1979) wrote:

> Collective rather than individual bargaining with employee and employer is necessary for effective voice at the work place for two reasons. First, many important aspects of an industrial setting are "public goods," which affect the well-being (negatively or positively) of every employee. As a result, the incentive for any single member to express his preferences, and invest time and money to change conditions (for the good of all), is reduced. Safety conditions, lighting, heating, the speed of a production line, the firm's policies on layoffs, work-sharing, cyclical wage adjustment, and promotion, its formal grievance procedure and pension plan—all obviously affect the entire work force in the same way that defense, sanitation, and fire protection affect the entire citizenry. "Externalities" (things done by one individual or firm that also affect the well-being of another, but for which the individual or firm is not compensated or penalized) and "public goods" at the work place require collective decision making. . . . A second reason why collective action is necessary is that workers who are not prepared to exit will be unlikely to reveal their true preferences to their bosses, for fear of some sort of punishment. . . . Since the employer can fire a protester, individual protest is dangerous.

3. In the United States, the Wagner Act (section IX, a) states that "representatives elected by a majority of the plant employees will be the exclusive agents of all plant employees for collective bargaining." Similar clauses exist in France and in the United Kingdom.

4. Expressed differently, it is the converse of the aversion of employers for unions, just as a demand for risk is the converse of a preference for safety.

5. On February 18, 1980.

6. Christine Mital (1980), "le New Look de la lutte des classes: comment des patrons combattifs reprennent en main le jeu social." I am indebted to Jean-François Hennart for pointing out this reference.

7. Well after this paper had been completed, I became aware of the work of Fred K. Foulkes (1980) *Personnel Policies in Large Nonunion Companies*, (*Prentice-Hall, 1980*), which makes essentially the same argument.

8. *L'Expansion*, February 22–March 6, 1980. According to the annual report (1979) of the Center for the Study of Public Choice, Virginia Polytechnic Institute and State University (p. 13), Professor Reid, in his work in progress on trade unions, "finds that the company union of the 1920s were employer's agents, as well. These company unions did not enforce monopoly restrictions. Rather, the company unions aggregated and transmitted the preference and questions of workers to management, and explained directives of management to workers. A measure of the efficacy of company unions at raising productivity is the anathema in which they still are held by to called independant unions."

9. It is the thesis argued by Lester Thurow (1975). The author argues that a rigid wag

hierarchy can increase the dynamic efficiency of the firm because "individuals can only raise their own incomes by raising the productivity of the entire enterprise" (p. 84), while without fixed hierarchy employees "have every incentive to stop giving informal training . . . [and] to build their own little monopoly by hoarding skills" (p. 81).

10. Simon (1944) wrote:

> The obvious struggle within particular industries over division of earnings tends largely to obscure the more substantial identity of interest and functional complementarity of labor and employer organizations. Popularly regarded and defended as counterpoises to industrial concentration or enterprise monopoly, unions in fact serve mainly to buttress effective monopoly in product markets where it already obtains, and to call into existence when it does not. Labor leaders have, indeed, a quite normal appetite for monopoly prices and for monopoly profits which high bargaining power permits them to appropriate and to distribute among their members.
>
> While extremely ill-informed, I know of no instance where a powerful union has proposed reduction of a monopolistic product price or given real support, singly or in federations, to antitrust policy. On the other hand . . . the formal and enforced cartelization of the coal industry may be credited largely to the UMW. And, if some proposals of CIO leaders for labor participation in management are not pure cartel schemes, I cannot identify the beast when I see it. If some labor remains and becomes increasingly cartelized along industry lines, enterprises must be similarly organized for bargaining purposes—not only to present a united front and to recoup wage increases from consumers but because labor itself will prefer, demand, and, in many cases, compel such employer organization . . . .
>
> We must alter our labor policy or abandon our antitrust as English businessmen so urgently recommend. If one big union is a fait accompli in, say, the automobile industry, that industry is all through as a competitive sector of our economy—and damned to full cartelization, if not to General Motors.

11. Atherton (1973) wrote:

> Unions are often composed of groups whose preferences diverge in some respects. Furthermore, groups which find the union's policies to be insufficiently compatible with their own goals may leave it (or try to alter its leadership, or undermine its programs with greater or less difficulty, depending on the circumstances. Since the loss of affiliated groups will usually harm the union, its leadership faces the task of finding a compromise sufficiently satisfactory to most of its members to keep the union together. This aspect of union policy making has often been discussed—perhaps most effectively by Ross—but has not been treated formally. . . . Producer cartels and some cooperatives face similar problems. So do political parties and coalitions of such parties. Successful theorizing about the problems of one type of "cartleoid" organization may be helpful in dealing with another. We have not, however, attempted . . . to extend our analysis to any group other than labor unions. [Pp. 4, 5]

12. See Furnbotn and Pejovich (1972).

13. This probably constitutes a reason for the replacement of craft by national unions. A national union bargaining with all firms brings to an employee a kind of general insurance policy for the results of bargaining. Inversely, this leads to an equalization of work conditions, as we have shown earlier, thus reducing the relative gain of any particular employee. This could explain why unions seek to reduce mobility. A decrease in mobility favors investments by employees in union activities. It increases the intangible capital of the union, its goodwill, and the stability of its "commercial assets."

14. The coming of retirement reduces the professional horizon of older workers. But since retirement pay depends on pay for the last active years, behavior must be cautious, for the risk becomes very high.

15. Howard Rosenthal (1974) shows that union leaders stay in power by using various electoral strategies. This tends to show that their power is strong vis-à-vis the membership. I am indebted to Bernard Lentz for pointing out this reference.

16. This hypothesis seems confirmed by a recent article by Bennett and Johnson (1980). The authors compare five characteristics of union activities (union dues, services given to members, management costs, salaries of union officers, and investments) in right-to-work states and in other states. Contrary to their expectations, they find no significant difference between unions in both types of states.

17. See Martin (1972 and 1973).

18. One can argue that French capitalism, with its rather limited reliance on the stock market and its heavy indebtedness to the largely state-owned banking sector, is only partially "capitalist" and belongs in large part to the public sector. The Communist slogan of "state monopoly capitalism" is not without relevance.

19. See "Social Affairs: The New Rules of the Game," *le Nouvel Economiste*, July 7, 1980, "The employers have yielded more to the continuous pressure of government than to the demands of workers."

20. The average hourly wage rate for blue collar workers was 6.37 francs in 1972.

References

Alchian, A. A. 1969. "Corporate Management and Property Rights." In *Economic Policy and the Regulation of Corporate Securities*. Washington, D.C.: American Enterprise Institute.

Alchian, A. A., and Demsetz, H. 1972. "Production, Information Costs, Economic Organization." *American Economic Review* 62(December):777–795.

Atherton, W. 1973. *A Theory of Union Bargaining Goals*. Princeton, N.J.: Princeton University Press.

Becker, G. S. 1959. "Union Restrictions on Entry." In *The Public Stake in Union Power*, ed. P. D. Bradley. Charlottesville: University of Virginia Press.

Bennett, J. T., and Johnson, M. H. 1980. "The Impact of Right to Work Laws on the Economic Behavior of Local Unions—A Property Rights Perspective." *Industrial Labor Relations Review* 33(July):452–467.

Berkowitz, M. 1954. "The Economics of Trade Union Organization and Administration." *Industrial Labor Relations Review* 7(July):575–592.

Burton, J. 1978. "Are Trade-Unions a Public Good/"Bad": The Economics of the Closed Shop." In *Trade-Unions—Public Goods or Public "Bads"?* London: Institute of Economic Affairs.

Cartter, A. 1959. *Theory of Wages and Employment*. Homewood, Ill.: Greenwood Press.

Coase, R. H. 1937. "The Nature of the Firm." *Economica* (November)n:

De Alessi, L. 1974. "An Economic Analysis of Government Ownership and

Regulation: Theory and Evidence from the Electric Power Industry." *Public Choice* (Fall).

Dertouzos, J. N., and Pencavel, J. H. 1980. "Wage and Employment Determination under Trade Unionism: The International Typographical Union." *Mimeo*, April.

Dunlop, J. 1950. *Wage Determination under Trade Unionism*. New York: Augustus M. Kelley.

———. 1978. "Introduction." In *Labor in the Twentieth Century*, ed. J. T. Dunlop and W. Galenson. New York: Academic Press.

Faith, R. L., and Lentz, B. 1979. "The Intertemporal Impact of Strikes on Profits and Wages." Mimeo, Virginia Polytechnic and State University, July.

Farber, H. S., and Saks, D. H. 1980. "Why Workers Want Unions: The Role of Relative Wages and Job Characteristics." *Journal of Political Economy* 88 no. 2 (April):349–369.

Fellner, W. J. 1949. *Competition Among the Few*. New York: Augustus M. Kelley.

Frech, H. E. 1980. "Health Insurance: Private, Mutual, or Government." In *The Economics of Nonproprietary Organizations*, ed. K. W. Clarkson and D. L. Martin. Greenwich, Conn.: JAI Press.

Foulkes, F. K. 1980. *Personnel Policies in Large Nonunion Companies*. Englewood Cliffs, N.J.: Prentice-Hall.

Freeman, R. B., and Medoff, J. L. 1979. "The Two Faces of Unionism." *The Public Interest*, no. 57 (Fall):69–93.

Furnbotn, E., and Pejovich, S. 1972. "Property Rights and Economic Theory: A Survey of Recent Literature." *Journal of Economic Literature* (December).

Gärtner, M. 1979. "Legislative Profits and the Rate of Change of Money Wages: A Graphical Exposition." *Public Choice* 34:3–4.

Hennart, J. F. 1980. "L'effet es syndicats français sur lcs salaires." *Vie et Sciences Economiques* (Juillet).

Hetherington, J. A. C. 1969. "Fact vs. Fiction: Who Owns Mutual Insurance Companies." *Wisconcin Law Review* 196.

Hirschmann, A. O. 1970. *Exit, Voice and Loyalty*, Cambridge: Cambridge University Press.

Jenny, F., and Weber, A. P. 1975. "Concentration, syndicalisation et rémunération salariale dans l'industrie manufacturière française." *Revue Economique* (July).

Jensen, M. C., and Meckling, W. H. 1976. "Theory of the Firm: Managerial Behavior, Agency Costs and Ownership Structure." *Journal of Financial Economics* (October) 3:305–360.

Lewis, H. G. 1959. "Competitive and Monopoly Unionism." In *The Public Stake in Union Power*, ed. P. D. Bradley. Charlottesville: University of Virginia Press, pp. 181–208.

———. 1963. *Unionism and Relative Wages in the United States*. Chicago: University of Chicago Press.

Maloney, M. T., McCormick, R. E., and Tollison, R. A. 1979. "Achieving Cartel Profits through Unionization." *Southern Economic Journal* 46(October) no. 2, 628–634.

Manne, H. G. 1965. "Mergers and the Market for Corporate Control." *Journal of Political Economy*.

Marshall, A. 1920. *Principles of Economics*. London: Macmillan.

Martin, D. L. 1980. "Unions as Nonproprietary Institutions." In *The Economics of Nonproprietary Organizations*, ed. K. W. Clarkson and D. L. Martin. Greenwich, Conn.: JAI Press.

Mital, C. 1980. "Le New Look de la Lutte des Classes: Comment des patrons combatifs reprennent en main le Jeu Social." *L'Expansion*, 22 Février–6 Mars.

Morgan, J. ed. 1973. *5,000 American Families*. Survey Research Center, University of Michigan, Vol. 2.

Mulvey, C. 1978. *The Economic Analysis of Trade Unions*. Glasgow: Martin Robertson.

Nutter, G. W. 1959. "The Limits of Union Power," In *The Public Stake in Union Power*, ed. P. D. Bradley. Charlottesville, University of Virginia Press.

Olson, M. 1965. *The Logic of Collective Action*. Cambridge, Mass.: Harvard University Press.

Pulsipher, A. G. 1966. "The 'Union Shop': A Legitimate Form of Coercion in a Free Market Economy." *Industrial and Labor Relation Review* (July).

Reder, M. 1960. "Job Scarcity and the Nature of Union Power." *Industrial Labor Relations Review* (April) 73:349–362.

Rosenthal, H. 1974. "Game-Theoretic Models of Bloc-Voting under Proportional Representation: Really Sophisticated Voting in French Labor Elections." *Public Choice*. (Fall).

Ross, A. 1948. *Trade Union Wage Policy*. Berkeley: University of California Press.

Simons, H. 1944. "Some Reflections on Syndicalism." *Journal of Political* Economy (March) 52(1):8–25.

Slichter, S. H., Healy, J. J., and Livernash, E. R. 1960. *The Impact of Collective Bargaining on Management*. Washington, D.C.: The Brookings Institution.

Stigler, G. J., and Becker, G. S. 1977. "De Gustibus Non Disputandum Est." *American Economic Review* 67, no. 2(March):76–90.

Thurow, L. 1975. *Generating Inequality*. New York: Basic Books.

A Comment On Rosa, by Gordon Tullock

There is a widespread myth, which until recently I shared: A union is a union is a union. One of the results of attending a conference reported in this book is that I realize that the unions in France are so radically different from those in the United States that it is indeed, I think, a mistake to translate "syndicate" as union. A visit to Australia convinced me that there was at least a third category under the general term "union." It is Rosa's achievement to indicate that, in fact, there is a fundamental similarity in all of these organizations. Specifically, they are all examples of the managerial firm.

When the managerial firm was first invented by Berle Means, it was, of course, used to describe the American corporations. With time, and particularly the work of Henry Mann, it was realized that this was not a correct description of most American firms. It is certainly true that the average stockholder pays little attention to "his" firm and that the managers do, indeed, have some discretion, but the existence of the market for control means that this discretion is highly limited. The individual who is disappointed with his firm sells his stock rather than voting against the management, a more effective way of imposing efficiency on the management than voting would be.

If corporations in the United States are not examples of managerial firms, a good many nonprofit organizations are, and Rosa points out that unions, in general, are to be accounted among them. It is not, of course, true that managements are completely free of control from their members although there appears to be some hereditary union presidencies in the United States. It is, however, true that the control of the members over the union member, or of the union itself, is extremely weak for the reasons discussed by Professor Rosa.

We can then consider a union, either in the United States, France, or Australia, as an organization with a very straightforward objective function: It is attempting to maximize the well-being of its management. This simplifies many, many tasks. Although the unions in the United States, England, and Australia are genuine labor monopolists but nevertheless live in a competitive environment,[1] it is important for them to obtain as many dues-paying members as possible, and they must compete with other unions and with nonunion employment for this objective.

The idea that unions are actually run for the benefit of management has always seemed somewhat improbable in the United States because the amount that the union dues produced for management was always a very small part of the wage increase that the monopoly gave to the members of the union. On the other hand, the theory that the union was attempting to maximize the interest of its members was characteristically contradicted by the observation that wages were not kept so high that no new members entered. It appeared to be a cartel that was not maximizing the returns to its present members nor the returns to its managers. The managerial theory of the firm provides at least a partial explanation for the riddle.

The managers must provide enough gains to union members so that it is in the interest of the union people to join the union. Further, they have to bring new people in. Thus, in a way, the union is in a competitive situation in the labor market and, in a way, indirectly competes with other unions, even unions in totally different industries. It is important that young people just entering the labor market consider a particular union as a suitable place for them to move because, if they don't, with time that union will gradually die. Most members of the managerial staff are not in a position to sell their management control, but they do stay in office for astonishingly long periods of time and quite frequently either die in office or retire on luxurious union pensions.

Thus, from a personal standpoint, the union manager has to balance several factors. One of these factors is that the advantage of being employed in this union must be high enough to attract new people into it. The second is that it must not be so high that there are no openings for new people. The union, which was really attempting to maximize the well-being of its members, would continuously raise wages so that no new openings developed.[2] Solving this problem is no doubt hard for management, and they are, in fact, further constrained by the fact that, if their dues begin to look exceptionally high, they may inspire a workers' revolt. The workers have very little motive to engage in surveillance of the union, but they can hardly avoid knowing what dues they are paying. Thus, if this particular variable is set too high, ambitious people who would like to be president of the union are provided with an opportunity.

This institution, then, can be expected to function quite differently, depending on the environment. Whether it turns to the political marketplace or the economic marketplace to benefit its members would depend on the particular environment. I would guess from life in Australia that one characteristic that union managers must face is that their members actually rather like going on strikes now and then. One of the things union managers must provide then is a series of short strikes that do not cut too badly into the income of members but that provide them with entertainment.

But that is a mere detail. The basic model of unions provided in Rosa's paper seems to me an important new start in the study of the labor unions. It should inspire a great deal further research in the future.

Notes

1. I gather this isn't all that true in France and Italy. I don't know enough about other countries to make a judgment.

2. It has been pointed out that if a labor union is trying to maximize the well-being of a majority of its members, and if it uses seniority in its layoff policy, then, rationally, it should select a wage product which unemploys 49 percent of its members, and when they quite choose a higher one which unemploys 49 percent of the remainder, etc.

8 THE AGENCY PROBLEM IN A NONPROPRIETARY THEORY OF UNION BEHAVIOR

Donald L. Martin

The agency problem in unions was recognized relatively early in the modern American literature on the theory of labor organizations. Arthur Ross (1948) may have been the first to observe that union leaders, as the agents of union members, are not infrequently governed by interests at variance with their constituents. Later writers attempted to state this conflict more rigorously with varying degrees of completeness and success (Ashenfelter and Johnson, 1969; Atherton, 1973; Berkowitz, 1954; Weinstein, 1966). Although they recognized that preferences might not be identical, that information might be relatively more costly to members, and that the nature of political constraints on leaders endowed the latter with some discretionary powers, their analyses failed to adequately identify the mechanism that would permit or sustain a divergence of objectives between union management and union membership.

The purpose of this paper is to present an economic model that is capable of predicting and explaining the divergence of interests between leaders and members and that defines the agency problem in unions. The model is formally grounded in the structure of property rights that characterize conventional labor unions. This structure we define as *nonproprietary*. That is, we assume throughout that members and leaders, unlike shareholders of a corporation or seatholders on the New York Stock Exchange, do not hold private property rights in their membership status nor do they own alienable rights to the net assets of individuals, but are utility maximizers. Finally, abstracting from differences between craft and industrial unions, we also assume that the political regime within a union is such that we may treat the median voter-member as the unit of analysis for generating implications about the rank-and-file membership.

The rest of this chapter is divided into four sections. The first section discusses the agency function within unions and introduces the source of managerial discretion enjoyed by union leaders. The second section introduces a utility maximizing model of the median voter-member in a nonproprietary union and derives several implications that reflect membership interests in the formation of specific collective bargaining policies. The third section is the heart of the chapter. It introduces the union leader as a separate functionary who seeks to maximize his own utility subject to the constraints that operate on him in a nonproprietary union. Since this model of leader behavior incorporates his conflicts of interest with the membership, it should yield implications for collective bargaining goals that are closer to reality than experienced by earlier models of union organization. The last section offers some conclusions.

The Agency Function

The Collective Production of Monopoly Rent

The role of the trade union in society is often described in multidimensional terms. It is at once economic, fraternal, political, egalitarian, revolutionary, and educational. Yet, it is not unreasonable to argue that the source of a union's ability to serve these roles well is its comparative advantage in affecting the terms of trade in the labor market.[1] This capacity derives from the legally sanctioned, publicly and privately enforced, restriction on the contractual freedom of all individuals who would otherwise supply labor services competitively to employers of union members. These restrictions are defined by the *exclusivity* of bargaining rights held by the union within some appropriately specified jurisdiction. Such rights not only insulate the incumbent members from the competition of rival unions' representational claims (and the demands such claims would make on resources), but also from the threat to the collective posed by the independent bargains otherwise struck between employers and individual union members. In this sense, an exclusive bargaining right is a resource that facilitates the exercise of collusive behavior among workers, i.e., a monopoly.

Together with the strike (the ability to effectively and legally withhold competitive labor services from a given employer) and congenial market conditions, exclusive bargaining rights make the union an instrument for the production of monopoly rents that can be appropriated by its members. These rents are created by getting employers to agree to pecuniary and nonpecuniary compensations that exceed those available at market clearing terms.

Shirking

Like a publicly held corporation, a labor union owes much of its success to its ability to attract large members of "investor-members" who are willing to commit resources to the formation, maintenance, and goal achievements of the organization. These investments may take the forms of initiation fees and dues assessments as well as foregone income resulting from strike and picketing activities. Members expect these investments to yield a net return in the form of positive wage and nonwage differentials in labor markets.[2] Since the magnitude of this return (net of member resource commitments) is not fixed, members may be viewed as residual claimants, the counterparts of corporate shareholders.[3]

Abstracting momentarily from obvious ownership differences, both institutions face a common problem. If residual claims are distributed among large numbers of people, the gains or losses arising from unexpectedly good or bad decision making are widely dispersed, and each *individual* member (shareholder) has the incentive to *shirk* in the collective production of net returns. An esoteric relationship between rents (profits) and *individual* productivity is thus assumed so that it is costly to discover productivity differences among members, in order to police their behavior, by examining final products.[4] Conversely, the fewer the members (shareholders) and the closer is individual's productivity correlated with final outcomes, the smaller is the incentive to engage in shirking.

Even if it were costless to police employer performance in executing the provisions of collective agreements,[5] and even if participatory democracy within unions was so inexpensive to administer that each and every member voted on each and every union decision, economic theory suggests that it would be in the interests of most members to transfer some decision-making authority to a smaller group (managers or agents) whose main function would be to monitor or police the rent-producing activities of members, including the integrity of their individual relationships with the firm.[6] The important point is that the potential for widespread shirking inherent in such collective arrangements generates a demand for monitoring services. Union management, empowered with such disciplinary weapons as the power of expulsion, provides monitoring services by locating, exposing, and acting against shirkers on behalf of the rest of the residual-claiming membership.

Union managers are elected or appointed by the membership, not only because they provide an economical control over rank-and-file shirking, but also because they provide other services. Information about collective bargaining opportunities is costly to acquire and interpret, negotiations and planning are subject to economies of specialization, and the policing of collective bargaining agreements uses up resources. Managerial functions within unions include the formulation of collective bargaining goals, the negotiation and monitoring of collective bargaining agreements, the policing of jurisdictional boundaries, and the administration of internal union affairs. The latter include disciplinary actions against members who threaten the monopoly position of the organization; adjudicating differences among members; and husbanding strike, pension, and legal defense funds as well as general revenues. Union managers also perform valuable services in expediting and advocating the grievances of members and in administering and protecting seniority rights.

The effective conduct of these tasks often requires the sort of managerial discretion that is characteristic of the powers assigned to corporate executives. In general, it would be prohibitively costly to subject each and every problem or issue that confronts the union to popular discussion and vote. As a consequence, leaders are assigned or, by default, adopt for themselves decision-making powers that could be used to improve the welfare of the membership. This is their agency function.

But if the union manager monitors the behavior of the rank and file, who monitors the monitor? Stockholders of private property corporations, instead of devoting resources to the monitoring and policing of management's decisions (more costly with many stockholders than with only a few), can exercise the right to *sell* ownership claims. This right provides a lower cost alternative for each stockholder than seeking to alter disagreeable decisions (Alchian and Demsetz, 1972, p. 788). Moreover, "the policing of corporate managerial shirking relies on across-market competition from new groups of would-be managers as well as competition from employees within the firm who seek to displace existing management" (Alchian and Demsetz, 1972, p. 788). A *proprietary* union, similarly, would also be able to offer such safeguards. Members dissatisfied with the performance or policies of management would be able to withdraw their investment through the sale of union cards. Of course, this might constitute a costlier response than in the case of stockholders. But union managerial shirking would also be policed by interunion and intraunion competition for managerial positions, processes considerably attenuated in nonproprietary unions, as discussed below and more fully in the fourth section.

The policing policy that will maximize utility for members equates the marginal cost of detecting deviant agent behavior and controlling it with the marginal returns from such policies. However, nonproprietary unions, by definition, lack the institutions that would otherwise make the net returns to policing deviant union leader behavior as rewarding as they would be under proprietary assumptions. This suggests that there will exist a range of managerial discretion in union affairs where leaders may deviate from the interests of the rank and file. The magnitude of this range will depend on such things as the opportunities for rival unions and internal opposition, the costs of switching affiliation, the existence of *no raiding agreements* among unions, the geographic decentralization of the membership, the heterogeneity of member preferences, the total value of attainable rents, and the ownership characteristics of the union.[7] It is important to note that these constraints do not explain why leaders and members might be expected to have differing objectives; they merely define the range within which leaders may exercise discretion if they so choose. Before we offer an explanation for leadership objectives and examine how the above constraints operate on them, we must first present a model of the median voter-member in a conventional labor union. Abstracting from differences between craft and industrial unions, the next section presents the interests of the membership in a nonproprietary union. Following this we return to our analysis of the agency problem.

Membership Objectives

As discussed in the previous section, under the right set of conditions a union can be the instrument for the production of monopoly rents for its members. However, the opportunity to produce monopoly rent and the incentive to maximize that rent are not one and the same, as we shall see. Because the firm sometimes has a comparative advantage in providing some on-the-job or job-connected goods that are consumed or used by its workers, the employer is not indifferent to the composition of the remuneration package exchanged for labor services. This suggests that in addition to the "normal" cost unions face in attempting to improve their terms of trade with employers, the latter will offer differential resistance to alternative remuneration packages of equal *market* value. Resistance may take the form of prolonged negotiation, or willingness to sustain long strikes, or perhaps just lethargy in executing an agreement once it is signed. This, of course, implies added costs for the union. Some remuneration packages for which it might bargain will be more costly to secure and thus yield smaller rents than others. As a consequence, union monopoly rents may be expressed in both pecuniary and nonpecuniary forms.[8]

We define the total real value of union rents appropriable to incumbent members as a group to be ρ_m. This is the present value of the residual that is the difference between the discounted sum of pecuniary and nonpecuniary differentials resulting from the exercise of union monopoly power and the value of resources committed by the members to the exercise of that power. A formal statement of the rent definition may be found in the appendix to this chapter.

Rent creation by the union implies a relative scarcity of jobs, at the union wage, to those seeking employment or wishing to retain it in the unionized firm. The scarcity value of these jobs depends in part on the form(s) in which rents may be appropriated. Under closed shop or even union shop conditions, membership effectively represents an access right to employment. If rights to rent-yielding jobs—i.e., *job rights*—were assigned individually to incumbent members (e.g., in the form of union cards or positions in the hiring queue) and were both specified and enforced as their private *alienable property*, the cost to members of endorsing rent-affecting policies that *failed* to maximize the net present value of a job right would be greater than if transferability were prohibited. This follows because transfer rights imply the possibility of immediate capitalization and appropriation of expected future rents into the present, while an absence of such rights (the case of nonproprietary union) implies that rents can only be appropriated when and where they are generated. Unless life span and job tenure are known with certainty and the individual member does not plan to change employers, *nontransferability* suggests a lower opportunity cost to individual members of ignoring the *future* consequences of *present* collective action. To the extent that such actions affect the production of rent, it will be less costly than otherwise to ignore them for other activities.

Let α be an index of ownership in the union that measures the fraction of an *individual* member's potential rents, in present value terms (ρ_m), that he or she may actually appropriate in the current period. Let $\rho_m = \delta\rho_\tau$ (see appendix to this chapter). Where a given individual may fully participate in any and all union-generated rents immediately upon acquiring membership status, can transfer (for a consideration) the right to participate in union-generated rents, and where the costs of enforcing a claim are nonprohibitive, the proprietary or ownership index α takes on the value of 1. Under such conditions, the scarcity value of the union card is equal to the present value of the stream of rents a given owner can expect to appropriate over n periods, ceteris paribus. On the other hand, where rents are unassignable, or where enforcement costs are prohibitive and members may not even participate in rents as they occur at any moment in time, α has a value of zero; as has the scarcity value of a union card.[9] Between these two extreme values of α, lies a continuum of values reflecting numerous permutations and combinations of possible ownership configurations of union members. For example, between two unions that have virtually identical participatory rules for members in collectively generated monopoly rents, save for the fact that in one union incumbent members may bequeath their union cards to relatives while in the other union such transfers are prohibited, we can say that the value of α in the former is greater than in the latter. We can also say that the value of α in the former union is less than 1. For the purpose of the analysis that follows, we will assume that α is exogenous to the decision calculus of any given union member.[10]

Since most workers must be physically present on the job to deliver their work, the working environment (in both its tangible and intangible forms) is a source of utility to them, *irrespective of the nature of their ownership rights in the union.* Purely as a matter of taste, the set of utility-maximizing environmental characteristics for any given worker could be different from the set that maximizes rents. These characteristics include many of the nonpecuniary goods that contribute to the composition of rents, such as plant or office lighting and air conditioning, work tools, personal characteristics of co-workers, cafeteria, menus, work clothes, etc. This suggests that, where members can affect union decisions, a theory that accommodates preferences will yield a richer set of implications.[11] Toward this end, we introduce a twice differentiable utility function for the median voter-member:

$$\upsilon_m = \upsilon_m(G_0 G_1) = \upsilon_m(g_i, \ldots, g_j, \ldots). \tag{8.1}$$

Members derive utility from two classes of goods, G_0 and G_1. The vector, G_0, represents goods consumed off the job and acquired through general purchasing power (i.e., real wage payments).[12] The vector G_1 represents nonpecuniary goods consumed on the job. Assume that both the worker's contract hours and the price level are exogenous to the individual union member, and that relative prices among g_i elements in G_0 are fixed, so that G_0 may be treated as a Hicksian *composite good*. It can then be shown that members' choices between off-the-job consumption, G_0, and on-the-job consumption, G_1, reflect choices between w, the contract nominal wage rate sought by the union member, and g_j, elements of the latter vector. Given the constraints faced by union members, utility-maximizing choices by individuals, as expressed through a collective choice procedure, will yield unique values for nominal wage rates and G_1. We take as axiomatic that members behave as if they maximized utility irrespective of the ownership characteristics of their particular organization.

From the wealth constraint described in the chapter appendix and expression (8.1), utility is maximized, between G_0 and the jth good in the G_1 vector, for the median voter-member where:

$$\frac{\theta \partial \upsilon / \partial g_j}{\theta \partial \upsilon / \partial G_0} = \frac{P_j - \alpha \partial \rho_m / \partial g_j}{P_0 - \alpha \partial \rho_m / \partial G_0}. \tag{8.2}$$

This expression is a variant of the conventional condition for utility maximization. Conventionally, maximization requires that the ratio of the marginal utilities of any two goods must equal the ratio of their prices. The effective price for the marginal unit of the composite good G_0 is $P_0 - \alpha \partial \rho_m / \partial G_0$. The effective price of a marginal unit of the g_j good in the vector G_1 is $P_j - \alpha \partial \rho_m / \partial g_j$. When $\partial \rho_m / \partial g_j = 0$, the price of this good is P_j and utility maximization requires its equality with $\partial \upsilon / \partial g_j$. Assume for now that $\alpha = 1$. To the extent that the choice of g_j, in the bargaining package, increases the rent generated by union activity so that $\partial \rho_m / \partial g_j > 0$, the *effective price* of choosing more g_j is lower than its ostensible price, p_j. Imagine g_j to be cafeteria lunches at the work place. The average price for such a lunch is p_j. Assume, however, that the union would be successful in bargaining for a higher-quality lunch than would obtain in the absence of a union contract—i.e., than if the quality of lunches were determined by competitive market force alone. The higher-quality lunch, at p_j, is a nonpecuniary rent, the value of which must be deducted from the ostensible price p_j to reflect the effective price of consuming a cafeteria lunch at work. Consumption will proceed until the marginal utility of consuming lunch equals this effective price. As $\partial \rho_m / \partial g_j$ increases, the effective price of g_j falls, ceteris paribus. Likewise, a fall in $\partial \rho_m / g_j$ will *raise* the effective price of g_j. Note what happens to the effective price of g_i when $\alpha = 1$. The effective price of goods that increase rents rises as α falls below 1. Conversely, the effective price of goods that decrease rents falls as α falls below 1. Thus, *nonproprietary union institutions penalize rent maximization by union members.*

For some goods, g_n, the *onstensible* price facing the individual union member at the margin will be zero. These are public goods. For example, plant lighting is an object of collective bargaining, a potential source of nonpecuniary rent to representative union members. Yet, the ostensible price of consuming another unit of candlepower will be zero to them. Assume again that $\alpha = 1$. The effective price facing these members is therefore $-\alpha\partial\rho_m/\partial g_n$, the increment in rent associated with another unit of candlepower in the plant. Rent as a function of candlepower is subject to deminishing marginal returns. Therefore, the more candlepower demanded, the lower $\partial\rho_m/\partial g_n$. At some level of g_n, $|\partial\rho_m/\partial g_n| < 0$, and the effective price facing union members will be *positive.* Utility will be maximized at $\partial\upsilon/\partial g_n = -\alpha\partial\rho_m/\partial g_j$. This will occur where $-\partial\rho_m/\partial g_n > 0$.

The above analysis is also relevant for treating variations in the Hicksian composite good, G_0, the vector of goods that a union member consumes off the job with real earnings, and at constant relative prices. If we continue to assume that the price level and contract hours per worker are exogenous to members, an increase in members' demands for G_0 or in the quantity of G_0 demanded translates into a demand for higher wage rates, W, or general purchasing power. For any given union member, under a collective agreement, a wage increase will appear as if it were a public good; i.e., the ostensible "price" of securing that increase is zero for that union member.[13] By choosing to consume more G_0, until $\partial\upsilon/\partial G_0 = -\alpha\partial\rho_m/\partial G_0$, the union member will select a contract wage rate that maximizes his utility. Moreover, the lower is α below unity, the higher the wage rate the union member is inclined to demand, ceteris paribus, because the effective price of G_0 is lower than where $\alpha = 1$. Thus, constrained utility maximizing for the median voter-member, by choice of G_0 and G_1, implies a unique set of wage and nonwage bargaining goals.

A Change in the Demand for Labor

Now consider the response of the median voter-member to an increase in the demand for labor in the unionized firm. Assume initially that $\alpha = 1$. An increase in labor demand raises ρ_m for all $\partial\rho_m/\partial_g > 0$, causing the effective prices of all rent-enhancing elements in the voter's utility function to fall relative to the prices of nonrent-affecting activities. Thus, the quality of rent-enhancing elements demanded by members will increase. Two of these elements, where $\alpha = 1$, are wage rates *and* union membership. Revenues from the sale of new memberships under a proprietary regime are reflected in the capital value of membership rights in the union. This suggests that an increase in the demand for labor will not be rationed by wage increases that limit employment to the incumbent membership. Rather, employment-membership will be altered to expand to a point where the present value of rents are maximized.

Once we relax the constraint that $\alpha = 1$, we get a different result. If members do not have proprietary rights in the membership status—i.e., if

$\alpha < 1$—the full value of potential rents associated with an increase in labor demand will not be reflected in the wealth constraint of the median voter-member. As between increases in membership and increases in wage rages, rents may be captured only in the latter. This may be seen by reexamining a modified version of equation (8.2):

$$\frac{\theta \partial \upsilon / \partial g_j}{\theta \partial \upsilon / \partial G_0} = \frac{p_j - \alpha \partial \rho_m / \partial g_j}{-\alpha \partial \rho_m / \partial G_0}. \tag{8.2'}$$

Assume that g_j represents new members. We may interpret p_j as the maximum wage increment foregone, to a representative incument member, from allowing employment to expand to the rent-maximizing level. Equation (8.2′) differs from (8.2) in that P_0 has been removed to signify that the composite good G_0 is a public good as seen by the median voter-member. In the proprietary case, as discussed above, both goods contribute to the enhancement of rent. However, in the nonproprietary case, the value of α in the numerator is zero and less than unity in the denominator. The "relative price" of a wage increase to the effective price of increased memberships favors the former, and incumbent members will demand higher wages than they would have if $\alpha = 1$ for all sources of rent. In the limit, incumbents will demand increases that will constrain employment to their numbers. But, we rarely see unions rationing increased labor demands to the point where only incumbent members are employed. One explanation for the failure of this implication to square with reality may be that unions have a lot more proprietary rights than commonly believed. A more likely explanation focuses on the pursuit by union leaders of different objectives. We discuss this more fully in the next section.

Current Versus Future Payoffs

Some policy choices, as expressed in the utility function of the median voter, yield more of their benefits in future periods than do other policy choices. For the proprietary union member, these choices are made commensurate by equating the ratio of effective prices, discounted to the present, with the ratio of discounted marginal utilities. In equation (8.3) assume that $\alpha = 1$, that $P_j - \alpha \partial \rho_m / \partial g_j$ is the effective price of g_j benefits received currently, and that $P_i - \alpha \partial \rho_m / \partial g_i$ is the effective price, discounted to the present, of g_i benefits to be received in the future:

$$\frac{\theta \partial \upsilon / \partial g_i}{\theta \partial \upsilon / \partial g_j} = \frac{P_i - \alpha \rho_m / \partial g_i}{P_j - \alpha \rho_m / \partial g_j}. \tag{8.3}$$

Income tax incentives aside, the analysis suggests that collective bargaining goals will include both current and deferred payments as determined by the conventional conditions for utility maximization. Once we switch to the nonproprietary union, however, α does not retain the same value in both periods. Since members have no current *alienable* claims on future benefits, the value of α associated with future rents is relatively lower in the numerator of equation (8.3) and the effective price of g_i, discounted to the present, is relatively higher than it would otherwise be. The effective price of future-oriented goals is relatively higher than the effective price of present-oriented goals. The implication is that members of nonproprietary unions will seek collective bargaining goals that stress current, rather than deferred, benefits or payments, ceteris paribus. However, once the objectives of union leaders are introduced, this implication must be qualified.

The nonproprietary model of union behavior is capable of generating several other implications that have been derived and discussed elsewhere (Martin, 1980). Our analysis so far has implied that the median voter-member in a nonproprietary union will not seek to maximize the present value of the stream of available monopoly rents, that the member prefers to ration increased demands for labor with wage rates that limit employment to the incumbent memberships, and that the member prefers bargaining packages with relatively few deferred payments. It is now time to compare these interests with those of union leaders.

The Agency Problem

As discussed in the second section, nontransferability of membership rights precludes two sources of control or influence over managerial behavior in unions that are available to stockholders in proprietary firms. First, members may not withdraw the capitalized value of the rent stream expected from their investments as a strategic response to undesirable leadership policies. Second, voting power may not be concentrated in a few individuals for the purpose of changing managerial personnel.[14]

More importantly, however, the limited nature of an individual member's claim to rents (whether pecuniary or otherwise), and the collective nature of the gains arising from monitoring-errant management, lowers the returns to rank-and-file members of participating in efforts to detect, police, and change management. As a result, the nonproprietary character of most unions provides greater opportunities for managers or leaders, if they so choose, to increase their own utility "at the expense" of rank-and-file members. This suggests that rumors and accusations, as well as accurate information about poor union management, should instigate relatively little activity by rank-and-file members to reform such unions.

It also suggests that rank-and-file "apathy" on collective-choice issues will dampen the flow of reform candidates challenging incumbents for power. Still, leaders will anticipate competition for their jobs as long as holding a leadership office permits a significant degree of discretionary behavior (i.e., behavior inconsistent with median voter interests).[15] Officers would be willing to expend some of the rents implied by exercise of that discretion to secure their tenure in the management of the union. This implication is consistent with the control union leaders have been observed to exercise over their union's information-disseminating channels, making it difficult for potential opposition candidates to attract the attention of the membership.[16] Constitutional clauses outlawing "dual unionism" have been frequently used to silence opposition candidates and dissidents, as has the vague clause "conduct threatening to the security of the union".[17] Presidential powers to appoint committee members and fill staff positions have often provided the means to buy off opposition (Taft, 1956, pp. 36, 124–125). Finally, in an attempt to avoid political confrontation, many national unions have failed to hold regular conventions and many locals have failed to hold regular meetings (Seidman, 1964, p. 15).

These considerations lead us to expect that the tenure of officials in nonproprietary unions should be longer, and the frequency of contested elections fewer, than experienced in proprietary organizations (both unions and corporations) of similar size that elect their officers by shareholder or member vote.[18] Moreover, among nonproprietary unions, the tenure of officials should be longer and contested elections fewer where union leaders have more managerial discretion than where they do not.

The above discussion is not meant to suggest that union management is unfettered by its membership and has full discretion over union policy decisions. Rather, it is meant to convey the notion that the structure of rights in labor unions yields logically refutable implications concerning the incentives "owner-members" will have in order to detect, police, and censure union management discretion, competitive with rank-and-file interests. Unless every policy decision is subject to membership ratification, managerial discretion will be a part of union institutional life.

For each rank-and-file member, however, there is some nominal level of utility, associated with alternative union policy choices, below which it is worthwhile to join the union with other members and threaten the political survival of incumbent officials.[19] This critical level represents a survival constraint on managerial behavior and in a union of heterogeneous preferences is associated with the median voter. Its height is a function of the existence of rival unions, the costs of forming and maintaining internal opposition to current leadership, the costs of changing over from one union to another, the existence and enforcement of no-raiding agreements, and the personal benefits from changing administrations, which themselves are a function of the structure of rights facing members. Given a rival union and zero costs of monitoring and policing union leaders, the critical level of utility for the median voter would be identical to the maximum level attainable, consistent with his wealth constraint. This analysis suggests that variations in determinants of critical utility levels across unions should yield differences in the degree of managerial discretion exercised by union leaders.

To the extent that members anticipate excessive discretionary behavior on the part of management, it may be in their collective interest to devise bureaucratic procedures, rules, and requirements designed to constrain such discretion and reduce "mismanagement." For example, we would expect managerial decisions in unions to be subject to more frequent referendums than managerial decisions in publicly held corporations of similar size, as measured by voting shares outstanding. Decisions relating to the specification of wage rates and of working conditions negotiated in collective agreements, to strike calls, job actions, and slowdowns, to the purchase of assets and the issuances of indebtedness, and to the admittance of new members are not infrequently subject to the vote of the membership or of convention delegates.[20] On the other hand, decisions relating to the pricing of products, to their quality and level of production, to the issuance of indebtedness, and to the sale of additional stock certificates are rarely, if ever, subject to referendum in publicly held corporations.

The implication that is suggested by such rules is that the asset structure of nonproprietary unions will appear relatively more conservative when compared with the investment policies of proprietary organizations, including corporations. For example, compare pension fund investments wholly managed by a nonproprietary union with pension fund investments of nonunionized proprietary corporations (see Allison, 1975; Belfer, 1954).

The absence or attenuation, in nonproprietary unions, of a single all-encompassing criterion, such as the maximization of present value of union monopoly rent, implies a greater variety of bureaucratic constraints on leaders than would be observed under proprietary unionism. This follows because the range of *wealth-maximizing* rules or procedures, other things the same, is narrower than the range of rules and procedures consistent with maximizing the utility of rank-and-file members *across nonproprietary, heterogeneous unions*.

The question naturally arises, Why should the interests of the leadership differ from those of its constituency, the rank-and-file members of the union? Are not leaders also union members? Are they not most frequently, if not invariably, selected from the working environment of their constituency and therefore a reflection of that body? Earlier writers have offered answers in terms of the personal characteristics and role perceptions of those who lead or manage. Of course, such characteristics and role perceptions do not really "explain" divergences between the interests of leaders and members; they merely describe different types of behavior on the part of union managers. Although behavioral differences may certainly be affected by the particular preferences or personal motivations of different individuals, such differences are difficult to recognize ex ante. Less difficult is the identification of differences in the cost-reward structures facing individual decision makers. Even if the elements of the utility functions of union leaders and of members were identical, the two groups might still behave differently if they faced different constraints.[21]

Like rank-and-file members, union leaders have no negotiable right to their union cards or to managerial perquisites. As a result, they are unable to fully capitalize into current transfer prices the present value of future rents that would otherwise come about from current actions they might take. Consequently, those activities will have a smaller payoff relative to actions with more immediate effects. In this sense the constraints facing leaders are little or no different from those facing nonoffice-holding members. However, unless leaders are also employees covered by the collective contract, their salary is usually fixed, at least de jure, by constitutional provisions or convention referendum. Although these salaries may in part reflect rents expected by all members and past performances by leaders, they probably do not vary from contract to contract as rents change with strikes and negotiation costs. This suggests that, other things being equal, the behavior of union leaders will exhibit significant differences, depending on whether they derive most of their income from employment covered by collective agreement and function as union officials on a part-time basis,[22], or whether they are paid a full-time straight salary and are not covered or paid under the union's collective agreement. The former group will have objectives and exhibit behavior more in line with rank-and-file interests than will the latter group.

If leaders fail to share directly in current rents created by wage increments above market levels, they will find it less costly to emphasize other bargaining goals that tend to increase their own welfare. Earlier, it was suggested that, absent managerial discretion, the ownership characteristics of nonproprietary unions bias rank-and-file preferences for rents in favor of current as opposed to deferred payments. That is, the utility maximizing ratio of current payments to deferred payments for the median voter-member should be higher in nonproprietary unions than in proprietary union, ceteris paribus. Once managerial discretion is introduced, this implication is less obvious.

Current Versus Deferred Payments

If union managers administer union trust funds, they may and often do determine the interim use of these funds and/or the financial institutions in which they will be kept. This is, literally, a valuable responsibility, one that can be made to increase the welfare of managers either directly through pecuniary kickbacks from financial intermediaries or indirectly through favors, information, introductions to influential people, and other nonpecuniary rent diversions. But even if moral fortitude in managers is so great that such temptations are usually resisted, the salaries of leaders—like the salaries of managers of large corporations—normally are positively correlated with the size of the union's assets, including trust funds, which they administer. Thus managers of nonproprietary unions have the incentive to bias their choices toward contributions to capital accumulation relative to current payments. Although other things being equal, rank-and-file members may seek to bargain for a "higher" current payment—deferred payment ratio, to seek a lower one is in the interests of leaders.

Information about the responses of employers to alternative wage demands and to the composition of alternative bargaining packages is costly to discover away from the bargaining table. The leadership, therefore, is provided with an opportunity to change the membership's perception of the parameters that affect them.[23] Consequently, union bargaining goals are more likely to approach configurations consistent with, or closer to, leadership preferences. Even if members have the opportunity to compare their settlement with those obtained by other unions, managers likewise have the opportunity to influence those comparisons. The selection of suitable comparisons is not the only way leaders convince their membership that they have done a good job, but it is an important aspect of collective bargaining (see Estey, 1967).

Figure 8–1 describes the relationship between a union leader's preferences and those of the rank and file, as expressed by the median voter-member, for current versus deferred payment components in the bargaining package.

Panel A contains a maximum rent curve in terms of the ratio of deferred payments to current payments. Total rents, ρ_τ, are shown on the ordinate axis and the ratio of deferred payments (d.p.) to current payments (c.p.) is shown on the abscissa. Superimposed on the A panel is the leader's preference function. The preference direction is northeast, so that more rents and more deferred payments relative to current payments enhance the leader's utility.

If we assume that the union has a nonproprietary structure, and if the costs of detecting and policing deviations from rank-and-file objectives are positive, the relevant constraint facing the leader is the negatively sloped portion of the total rent curve in panel A. Utility is maximized for the union leader, at payment ratio a″. Note that a″ constitutes a higher ratio of deferred-to-current payments than at $\bar{a}$, where rents are maximized. Moreover, a″ is not consistent with utility maximization for the rank and file, as reflected in the utility function of the median voter-member in panel C. The point a″ in panel A may be projected onto panel C by means of the rent distribution function m (ρ_m), with slope 1/m located in panel B. The larger is m the more steeply sloped the distribution function and the smaller the amount of rent available to any given union member. The equivalent of a″ in median voter utility space, given the distribution function, is at c″. Constrained by the rent function, the median voter at c″ may reach only utility level U″U″.

Compare this result to one in which there are zero costs of detecting deviations by union leaders from rank-and-file objectives. Continue to assume that the union has nonproprietary characteristics. Information acquisition and enforcement are costless activities to members. As a consequence, payment ratios that conflict with utility maximization for the median voter-member will be rejected in the bargaining package negotiated by leaders and therefore constitute a threat to their incumbency. In panel C, utility is maximized at c′, at utility level U′U′. With costless monitoring, the slope of the constraint facing the union leader in panel A will be infinite at payment ratios beyond a′, limiting the leader to utility level I′I′. Returning to panel C, the median voter-member would be indifferent to payment ratios c″ and c′ if given a lump-sum payment sufficient to be placed on utility level U′U′ at c′. Thus, where monitoring costs are greater than the improvement in member welfare that would result from policing leaders, the latter may exercise full discretion in bargaining for a payment ratio that would leave the union member at c″.

For reasons just developed, members of a proprietary union are better situated to capture the improvement in welfare that would arise from policing the discretion of union leaders. This implies that members of such a union will be willing to devote relatively more resources to the monitoring function than their nonproprietary counterparts. This in turn suggests that leaders in proprietary unions will make collective bargaining choices more in conformity with the utility maximization interests of their membership. Thus, we should expect that current/deferred payment ratios will differ between the proprietary and nonproprietary union. Moreover, we can expect that the payment ratio in the proprietary union will be closer to the ratio that maximizes rents than the ratio to be found in the nonproprietary union. This can be seen from a further examination of panels A and C in figure 8–1. In panel C, the line BB represents the market rate for the sale or lease of membership rights in a proprietary union. If the preferences of a majority of members in this union differ from the payment ratio that maximized rents, they can always sell or lease their property to others having preferences more consistent with maximum rent. At a price such as BB, the median voter-member agrees to choose payment ratio $\bar{c}$, desired by a minority of members. The ratio at $\bar{c}$, however, is not the *effective* ratio of current to deferred payments consumed by median voters. Payments to them in exchange for their vote allow them to reach a higher level of utility, UU, than they could otherwise achieve without proprietary rights in membership status. Under these assumptions, utility is maximized for the median voter at c. Thus the payment ratio for which leaders in a proprietary union will be authorized to bargain will be closer to the ratio that maximizes rent than will be the case in a nonproprietary union. This is demonstrated by projecting the payment ratio in panel C at $\bar{c}$. Since members of proprietary unions may capture the gains from monitoring leadership discretion, the slope of the opportunity set in panel A is infinite for all payment ratios beyond $\bar{a}$. From panel A, it can be seen that nonproprietary unions imply a relatively higher ratio of deferred-to-current payments (a″) and smaller rents than are implied by the proprietary form of unionization (a).

Taking the analysis one step further, it may be argued that since proprietary rights in membership and voting permit the effective choice of *any* payment ratio, the median voter-member will be unwilling to sacrifice any rent for alternative ratios of current to deferred payments. In other words, the indifference curves will appear horizontal in panel C and utility will be maximized at $\bar{c}$. Leaders will face an infinite constraint, in panel A, at $\bar{a}$, where the present value of monopoly rent for the organization is maximized.

The above analysis also yields implications for comparisons between payment ratios in nonunionized firms and unionized firms organized by nonproprietary unions. Assume that nonunion workers and nonproprietary union members have tastes for current and deferred payments that, although

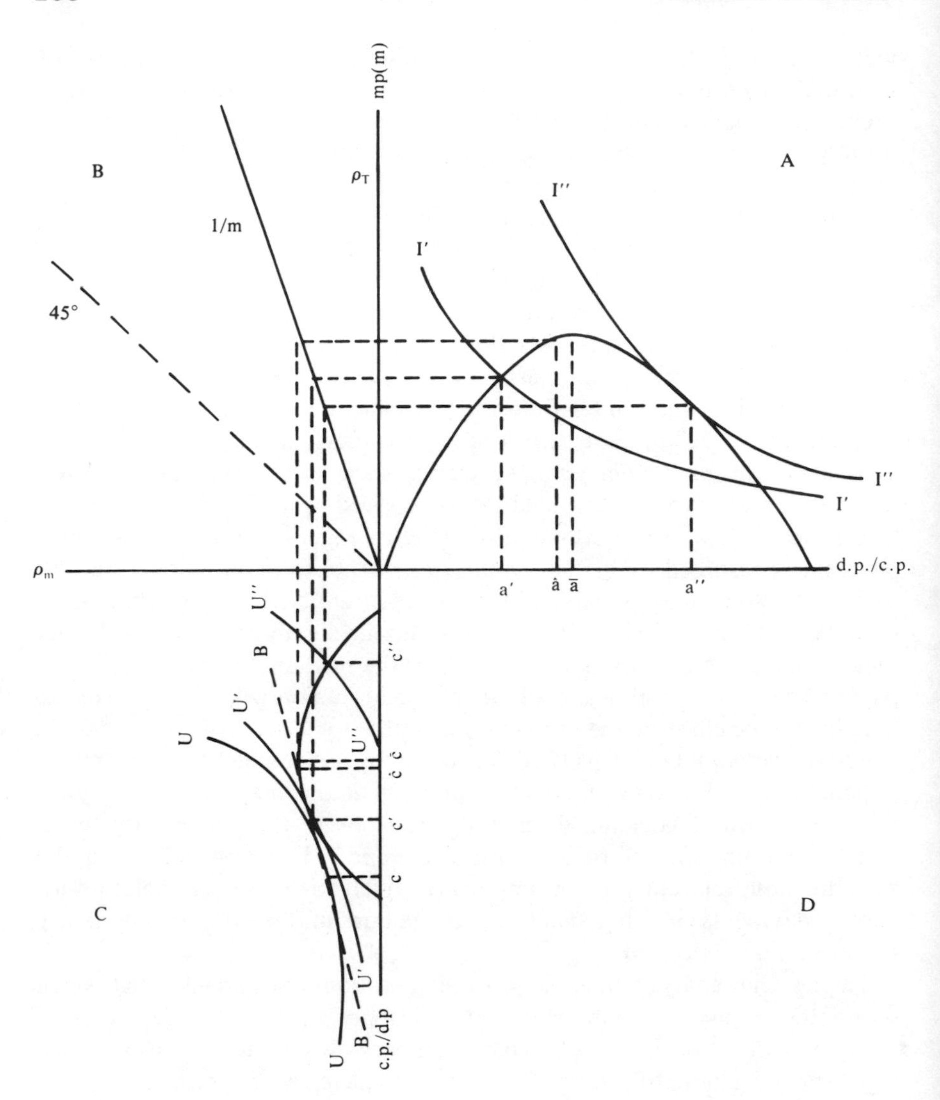

Figure 8-1. Relationship between a Union Leader's Preferences and Those of the Rank and File.

different in terms of absolute levels, are approximately the same in relative terms. Then, if the costs of monitoring union managers are positive, we should expect to observe a higher ratio of deferred payments to current payments among nonproprietary union workers relative to nonunion workers.[24] This follows from our analysis in figure 8–1 and from our analysis in the last section. Employers in nonunionized firms will purchase labor at competitive payment ratios, with the view of attracting the marginal worker, while employers in unionized firms will face the collective bargaining demands of union leaders seeking to shift current payments to deferred payments.

Wage-Membership Policies of Leaders

The discussion above has focused on current payments (usually in the form of money wage rates) *relative* to deferred payments. Analyses of managerial discretion in nonproprietary unions are also relevant in explaining changes in the *level* of remuneration per worker, whether it relates to money-wage payments or to the dollar value of supplements. Under the assumptions used in the third section, it was argued that incumbent members of nonproprietary unions would respond to an increase in the demand for labor by seeking wage levels that would encourage employers to limit employment at or near the existing membership. This appears to be contrary to observed behavior in most labor unions (Reder, 1960). Increases in demand appear to be positively correlated with the expansion of both employment and of union membership in unionized industries. Either it is the case that members of these unions own a great deal more proprietary rights than suspected (and therefore the returns to monitoring managerial discretion are "high"), or some other factors are operating. This section seeks to identify some of the latter.

Several factors encourage union managers, in the face of an increased demand for labor, to bargain for wage rates and other worker remuneration so that employment and membership may expand beyond existing levels. These factors include the effects of expanded employment and membership on leader salaries, union treasuries, tenure, and the leader's relationship with the employer. The salaries of union leaders are, in part, positively associated with the membership size of the unions they administer and the value of union assets Taft, 1956, pp. 105–11.). Since the initiation fees and dues in most unions are either fixed by constitution or subject to change only at the will of the majority of members managers have an incentive to expand membership when possible. "Large" memberships often mean "large" treasuries, from which to finance expense accounts and purchase assets. The large memberships sought by leaders are at the expense of higher wage rates for incumbents The sacrifice of potential rents in terms of foregone wage differentials does not directly constrain union managers, because they rarely share in them.[25] If salaries of managers did vary directly, with current rents obtained by members through wage differentials, managers would still find it attractive—at the margin—to trade *some* of this reward for both (somewhat) higher executive salaries associated with larger membership *and* the nontaxable benefits that come with control of larger treasuries and trust funds.

Union managers may also be expected to pursue wage policies that expand membership in response to increased labor demand if larger memberships raise the cost of forming voting blocs strong enough to threaten managers' political survival. The larger the membership, the smaller the returns to any one member of devoting resources to collective action. Moreover, the larger the membership, the more likely it is to have *heterogeneous* interests. Although this may make it more difficult for managers to identify the median voter, on any issue, it will also make it more costly to form coalitions of voting blocs.[26]

Of course, the foregoing arguments assume that the membership does not vote on each and every element in the collective bargaining package as a separate item. Otherwise, it would be extremely difficult for managerial preferences to overshadow the revealed sentiment of the membership. This kind of voting, however, is prohibitively costly. If ratification by members or by delegates is required before collective agreements may be executed, it is the entire package that is accepted or rejected. This makes less popular features of contracts more costly to oppose, giving leaders a freer hand. If membership ratification of collective bargaining agreements is not required,[27] leaders must at least be careful to adopt policies that yield utility to a significant proportion of members above some *critical* level.[28]

A relatively more moderate stance of the leader, in the face of growing labor demand, may yield the benefits of employer gratitude, in addition to larger employment and memberships. Collective agreements that tend to suppress wage rates and other payments per worker at the expense of at least some incumbent members have been termed, pejoratively, *sweetheart contracts*. The more notorious arrangements were exposed during the McClellan hearings of the 1950s (Senate Select Committee, 1959), revealing instances of employers' making pecuniary payments directly to union leaders in exchange for assurances against strikes and "excessive" wage demands. Yet, the incentives for such behavior differ only in degree from the incentives of union leaders to "get along" with their counterparts across the bargaining table and to "maintain good relations" with them (Ross, 1948).

"Good relations" are a source of utility to union managers because they indirectly yield both pecuniary and nonpecuniary rewards. Employers may be more willing to make "loans" to union managers, to introduce them to persons more willing to be their creditors, to introduce them to prestigious individuals with whom they will be able to socialize outside their work environment, or who will provide valuable information at favorable terms. Likewise, "moderate" and "responsible" behavior also appeals to politicians. It relieves political pressures to "do something" about "irresponsible" wage demands. The more costly it is for members to know just what is attainable, and the more costly it is for them to police or monitor managerial discretion, the greater the opportunity for leaders to trade off one source of utility—the rewards associated with higher wages for members—for another source—the rewards associated with maintaining "good relations" with management and government.

Conclusions

Although members and leaders have the same nonproprietary rights in membership status, differences in other costs and rewards facing these groups, respectively, suggest a divergence of interests that can be policed only at some positive cost to the rank and file. The higher this cost, the more discretion (up to some critical level) leaders may exercise in formulating and executing union policy. This is the agency problem in labor unions. This potential intra-union conflict, together with the nonproprietary nature of most union organizations, yields implications that are capable of refutation. For example, our analysis suggests:

1. Nonproprietary unions will adopt a relatively higher ratio of deferred to current payments in establishing bargaining policies when compared with unions possessing relatively more proprietary characteristics.
2. Nonproprietary unions will adopt a relatively higher ratio of deferred to current payments in their bargaining policies when compared to the deferred–current-payment ratios of workers in nonunionized firms.
3. In those nonproprietary unions where policing and monitoring costs of the union's leadership are relatively high, employment rigidities under conditions of rising labor demand will be relatively less pronounced than in other nonproprietary unions.
4. The tenure of officials in nonproprietary unions should be longer and the frequency of contested elections should be lower than experienced in proprietary organizations that elect their officers by shareholder or member vote.

5. Relatively more managerial activities and functions in nonproprietary unions will be monitored by formal rules and regulations than will managerial activities in proprietary organizations.
6. The asset structure and investment policies of most nonproprietary unions will appear very conservative when compared with proprietary organizations of similar ownership size (shareholders or members).

Appendix: Maximizing the Median Voter-Member's Utility Subject to a Rent Constraint

We define ρ_τ as the present value of total monopoly rents generated by the union. Where,

$$\rho_\tau = [\bar{W}(\overline{mH})/P^* - \hat{W}(\overline{mH})/P^* + (P_1 G_1) - P_1' G_1' - FX], \qquad (8.4)$$

and:

$\bar{W}$ = A vector of discounted *contract* nominal wage rates containing (w_i) wage rates over (n) time periods;

$\overline{mH}$ = Contract manhours. The product of contract employment for members, m, and contract hours, H, a vector containing h_i hours per worker-member discounted over (n) time periods;

P^* = Price deflator;

$\hat{W}$ = A vector composed of discounted *market* clearing nominal wage rates w_i, or wage rates in best alternatives, over (n) time periods;[29]

$P_1 G_1$ = A vector of discounted market values composed of g_j goods, valued at discounted p_j prices ($p_j g_j$) produced by union or firm under collective agreement and consumed by members *on the job*;

$P_1' G_1'$ = A vector of discounted market values composed of g_j' goods, valued at discounted p_j', prices ($p_i' g_j'$), produced by the firm and consumed by employees *on the job without union contract*;

F = A vector composed of discounted resource prices f_i faced by the union in producing rents over n time periods;

X = A vector composed of resources x_i employed by the union in seeking rents over n time periods;

n = Number of periods during which rents will be received.

Given that rents are composed of both pecuniary and nonpecuniary payments, their magnitudes are, in part, a function of the particular selection of W and G_1 made by the union, and of employer resistance associated with some selections. The production of rents is subject to the following constraints:

$$\beta(\bar{W}, G_1) = Z(X), \tag{8.5}$$

$$\frac{-dmH}{d\bar{W}} \cdot \frac{W}{mH} = \eta, \tag{8.6}$$

where (8.5) is a rent production function for all goods identified with rents, including the vector of the those goods (G_0) that general purchasing power will buy outside the firm and union. We substitute (W) in (8.5) since the union affects members' command over (G_0) through this variable. Equation (8.6) is a "wage" elasticity of labor demand in terms of manhours for members. More accurately (8.6) may be interpreted as a *variable labor cost elasticity* of labor demand to call attention to the fact that remuneration per manhour includes variable nonwage payments as well.

For each member, the choice theoretic structure that bears on union policy objectives may be derived from expression (8.1) in the text and written in expected utility form:

$$\begin{aligned}\text{Max } \phi = \theta \upsilon_m(G_0, G_1) + (1-\theta)\upsilon_m(G_0', G_1') = \\ \theta \upsilon_m(g_i, \ldots, g_j, \ldots) + (1-\theta)\upsilon_m(g_i, \ldots, g_j, \ldots),\end{aligned} \tag{8.7}$$

subject to:

$$0 < \theta < 1 \tag{8.7a}$$

and

$$(P_0 G_0)_m + (P_1 G_1)_m < \alpha \rho_m + (\hat{\mathrm{w}}\bar{\mathrm{h}})_m + (P_1 G_1)_m + Y_m \tag{8.7b}$$

if the union job is retained or

$$(P_0' G_0')_m + (P_1' G_1')_m < (\hat{\mathrm{w}}\bar{\mathrm{h}})_m + Y_m \tag{8.7c}$$

if the union job is abolished, where

$$\rho_m = \delta \rho_\tau.$$

Recall that

$$\rho_\tau = [\bar{W}(\overline{mH})/P^* - \hat{W}(\overline{mH})/P^* + (P_1 G_1) - P_1' G_1' - FX],$$

and that

$$G_0 = Z(X)$$
$$G_1 = Z(X)$$

or

$$\beta(G_0 G_1) = Z(X).$$

The symbol θ in (8.7) is the probability that a given cardholder will retain his or her job over some specified period as a result of union policy objectives. $(1 - \theta)$ is the probability that the union cardholder will be in a nonunion job as a result of collective bargaining. η is a function of the variable cost (or wage) elasticity of demand for labor, the percentage increase in variable cost attributable to union labor, and the seniority of the cardholder.[30]

In expression (8.7b), the constraint faced by a utility maximizing worker under union contract includes the variable ρ_m. This is the net present value of the stream of rents appropriable to any given union member. Recall that $\rho_m = \delta\rho_\tau$. If all employed members share rents equally, $\delta = 1/M$. It is more likely, however, that older and more skilled members enjoy a higher α than younger and less skilled members. The variable $(wh)_m$ is the segment of a member's total wage earnings attributable to competitive opportunity costs at union contract hours, h. Likewise, $(P_1' G_1')_m$ is the segment of nonpecuniary benefits that are obtained in competitive markets. In (8.7c), the constraint faced by a worker not under union contract, $(wh)_m$ represents earnings and hours under competitive conditions. The variable Y_m in both (8.7b) and (8.7c), respectively, is other income.

If we assume that θ is exogenous to the worker's choice decision, then G_0' and G_1' may also be taken as exogenous, since they are determined for the worker by the competitive sector of the labor market. Therefore, under this assumption, the choice problem facing the individual member is to maximize just $\theta\upsilon(G_0, G_1)$, subject to (8.7a) and (8.7b):

$$\text{Max } \phi = \theta\upsilon_m(G_0, G_1) = \theta\upsilon_m(G_0, g_j, \ldots,) \qquad (8.8)$$
$$\text{S.T.} \quad (5.1)$$
$$(5.2)$$

Using the Lagragian procedure,

$$\max \phi = \theta \upsilon_m(G_0, G_1) - \lambda[P_0 G_0 + P_1 G_1 - \alpha \rho_m - \hat{w}\bar{h}/P^* - P_1' G_1' - Y],$$

first-order conditions in G_0, a Hicksian composite good, and G_1 are:

$$d\phi / dG_0 = \theta \partial \upsilon / \partial G_0 - \lambda[P_0 - \alpha \partial \rho_m / \partial G_0] = 0 \qquad (8.7d)$$

$$d\phi / dg_j = \theta \partial \upsilon / \partial g_j - \lambda[p_j - \alpha \partial_\rho / g_j] = 0 \qquad (8.7e)$$

The first-order condition in (8.7d) identifies the effective price for the marginal unit of the composite good G_0. This is $P_0 - \alpha \partial \rho_m / \partial G_0$. The effective price of a marginal unit of the g_j good in the vector G_1, as defined in (8.7e) is $P_j - \alpha \partial \rho_m / \partial g_j$.[31]

Notes

1. To the extent that the union has a comparative advantage in the production of some goods, such as grievance services, contract policing, group purchase benefits, and others, the union itself will be a source of rents to the membership, completely independent of the benefits arising from any monopoly power it may exercise. This, however, should not suggest that rents arising from grievance services, etc., performed by the union are necessarily independent of that power. In fact, it should not be surprising to find unions with relatively more monopoly power providing relatively better or more services to their membership, ceteris paribus. Nevertheless, this explains why some unions survive even when their monopoly power in the labor market is nil.

2. For an interesting analysis of membership as an asset, see John Pencavel (1971).

3. To my knowledge, Ross was the first to discuss the analogy between shareholders and union cardholders. See Arthur Ross (1948, p. 7).

4. Although they did not devote much space to labor unions, the present analysis owes much to Alchain and Demsetz (1972), and Jensen and Meckling (1976). With respect to the union case, productivity refers not to members' performance in the work place, but to their contribution to the production of monopoly rents. This is one of the important characteristics of what Alchian and Demsetz call *team production*, a form of production in which output is larger if several people *cooperate* in completing a task rather than each working separately. By this definition, collective bargaining, strikes, and picketing activities to achieve wages above market-clearing levels are team production efforts.

5. Recently, the monitoring function of managerial services has been awarded special prominence in attempts to construct a general theory of organizational behavior, as contrasted with market behavior (Alchian and Demsetz, 1972). With regard to union-type organizations,

> some forms of employer performance [other than the payment of money wages] are less easy to meter and are more subject to employer shirking. Fringe benefits often are in nonpecuniary, contingent form; medical, hospital, and accident insurance . . . are contingent payments or performances partly in *kind* by employers to employees. [Rather than] . . .

"trust" the employer not to shirk . . . [employees] would prefer an effective and economic monitor of those payments. We see a specialist monitor—the union employee's agent—hired by them to monitor aspects of employer payments most difficult for the employees to monitor. [P. 790]

6. Some union institutions, like the closed and union shops, are designed partly to police competition among union members. It is interesting to note that Selig Perlman (1928) cites the closed shop as an innovation designed "as much to . . . 'conserve' the jobs as to make the bargaining solidarity with the employer *treason proof*." (p. 269). See also Taft (1956, p. 123).

7. Except for the last two, Atherton (1973) discusses the logical consequences of each of these factors on the behavior of union managers.

8. The notion that union monopoly rents include nonpecuniary elements is not novel. Earlier, Becker (*Union Restrictions on Entry*, p. 209) noted that "Most economists would agree that union power has been imperfectly estimated partly because the measure ignores union effects on *nonpecuniary and future income* . . . ." (Emphasis added). Moreover, empirical examination of the relationship between wage and nonwage supplements led Rice (1966) to conclude that "relative money wage differentials progressively understate differentials in compensation, as measured by the sum of money earnings plus wage supplement expenditures . . . it is clear that we should not examine money wage differentials assuming that private wage supplements are proportional to total wages" (p. 292).

9. This last case suggests the plight of rank-and-file members of a "racketeering" union making "sweetheart" contracts with employers. *Effective* wage rates to union members are not greater than levels determined by competitive forces. See Weinstein (1966).

10. Jensen and Meckling, in an important paper concerning ownership and control questions in the theory of the firm, use the notation α to identify the fraction of shares owned by managers in order to derive implications about managerial discretion or agency problems. See Jensen and Meckling (1976).

11. Note that so long as a member's utility is affected by job-related environmental characteristics, the transferability of job rights offers no guarantee that members will have tastes consistent with rent maximization. It does suggest, however, that tastes are more likely to be coincident with rent maximizing than where job rights are *not* transferable.

12. This particular formulation calls attention to what should be obvious, that persons do not bargain for wages qua wages, but for the utility associated with the market basket of goods money wages may purchase. Real wage payments are defined in the appendix as $\bar{w}(h)_m/P^*$, where the contract wage rate is $\bar{w}$, the contract hours per worker is $(h)_m$, and P^* is the price level.

13. It should immediately be objected that a wage increase will reduce employment for someone and that this fact destroys the collective good analogy. But the employment effects of a wage hike need not result in disemployment for incumbent workers. A common response to the higher cost of labor is employment cutbacks through attrition. Thus, it is not unreasonable to assume that incumbent members, individually, view increased wage rates as a collective good.

14. This is not to suggest that nontransferability is an undesirable feature of union membership. As discussed elsewhere, this rule may be perfectly rational and a net benefit for the union membership as a whole. See Martin (1980). Moreover, the above statement should not be construed to mean that management can't be voted out of office. Of course, a majority of members can accomplish this feat, if they can be persuaded to vote the same way. However, it may be more costly to accomplish this than to purchase additional voting rights.

15. For an excellent discussion of the expected limits on managerial discretion in proprietary firms with widely dispersed ownership and competitive markets for management, see Alchian (1960).

16. Before the Landrum Griffin Act (1959), incumbent officers could and did deny space in union publications and access to membership lists to candidates for union office.

17. This point seems to have been ignored by some earlier scholars. "Unions, even where the level of democratic life is low, are not less responsive to the will of their membership than corporations are to the desires of stockholders." See Taft (1956, p. 35). Taft's point is that the absence of opposition in union elections can be misinterpreted unless the difference between a labor union and other kinds of social organizations is recognized. This difference, he says, is based on the "need" for unions to present a united front to employers and members alike. Although this "need" may be obvious with respect to the former group, it is interesting to dwell upon Taft's explanation regarding the membership. "How are unpalatable compromises to be made and how are contracts, some of whose terms may not be attractive to the union membership, to be enforced when the intelligence or integrity of the leaders are questioned?" (p. 35). With relatively fewer avenues open to would-be managers in unions, as opposed to corporations, it seems particularly useful to examine the frequency of contested elections as a check on managerial discretion. Taft reports evidence that elections of union officers often go uncontested and that there is a tendency for contests for office to decline over time, suggesting that incumbents are able to build up barriers to competition (pp. 36–64).

18. Where size is measured by numbers of voting rights outstanding (i.e., union cards or corporate voting shares).

19. Such threats may manifest themselves through the generation of rival candidates for political office, contests for exclusive bargaining rights promoted by raiding unions, or referendums to decertify the existing union in favor of no union at all. If the assumption of identical rank-and-file preferences is retained, the nominal level of membership satisfaction consistent with the survival of existing management is identical for all members. Where heterogeneous preferences obtain, the minimal level relevant to survival is determined by the median voter-member. See Atherton (1973).

20. See National Industrial Conference Board, *Handbook of Union Government Structure and Procedure* (no date).

21. For students of union behavior, this appears to be a subtle point. Even Ross (1948), who repeatedly recognizes that constraints affect the behavior of leaders (see pp. 27, 30, 31), couches much of his discussion of leadership goals in terms of "the *instinct* for survival and the *impulse* toward growth" (p. 26, emphasis added).

22. See Sayles and Strauss (1967). Leaders of small union locals are more likely to receive most of their income from employment under collective contract than leaders in other organizations. See also Taft (1956, pp. 98–102). Note that there is some correlation between the salaries of local union business agents and their performance in terms of wage increments. See Ehrenberg and Goldberg (1977).

23. This was also recognized by Ross (1948, p. 41).

24. Some evidence supporting this implication is revealed in Goldstein and Pauly (1976, chap. 3) and Rice (1966). Earlier writers noted a tendency for union negotiators to favor benefit plans more strongly than rank and file members. See Mark Greene (1964, pp. 7–8) and Mendelsohn (1956). Researchers that have found worker preferences for benefit increases over money wage increases stronger among union members than among nonunion members have failed to hold money incomes constant and failed to account for both price level and income tax effects. See Lester (1967).

25. Ehrenberg and Goldberg (1977) produced some evidence that local union business

agents in the building trades were rewarded for their performance in raising *wage rates* relative to national union-nonunion differentials in the same trade. Our analysis focuses on the relationship between rent and agent salaries.

24. This also suggests that leaders will be less inclined to favor racial and other discriminatory entrance requirements.

27. In a study of 194 unions covering a declared membership of 17,514,000 individuals, only 16 percent of the unions (15 percent of covered workers) required ratification of collective agreements by the membership. See National Industrial Conference Board, *Handbook of Union Government Structure and Procedures* (1965), p. 51.

28. That level is identical for all in the case of a homogeneous membership and equal to the level of the median voter-member in a heterogeneous world.

29. $\overline{W}(\overline{mH})/P^*$ and $\hat{W}(\overline{mH})/P^*$ are real disposable claims on general purchasing power and may also be expressed in (8.4) in terms of discounted market values of goods that members will consume, (P_0G_0) and $P'_0G'_0)$, respectively. This notation, under certain assumptions, will be used interchangeably with $W(mH)$ at a later point when discussing variations in W.

30. The more senior the card holder, ceteris paribus, the higher is θ.

31. Second order conditions in G_0 and G_1 are:

$$d^2\phi/dG_0^2 = \theta\partial^2\upsilon/\partial G_0^2 + \lambda\alpha\partial^2\rho_m/\partial G_0^2 < 0 \quad (8.7f)$$

$$d^2\phi/dg_j^2 = \theta\partial^2\upsilon/\partial g_j^2 + \lambda\alpha\partial^2\rho_m/\partial g_j^2 < 0 \quad (8.7g)$$

References

Alchian, A. A. 1969. "Corporate Management and Property Rights." In *Economic Policy and the Regulation of Corporate Securities*. Washington D.C.: American Enterprise Institute.

Alchian, A. A., and Demsetz, H. 1972. "Production Information Costs and Economic Organization." *American Economic Review* 62 (December):777–795.

Allison, E. K. 1954. "Financial Analysis of the Local Union." *Industrial Relations* 14, no. 2 (May).

Ashenfelter, O., and Johnson, G. 1969. "Bargaining Theory, Trade Unions and Industrial Strike Activity." *American Economic Review* 59 (March):35–49.

Atherton, W. 1973. *Theory of Union Bargaining Goals.* Princeton, N.J.: Princeton University Press.

Becker, F. H. 1980. "Meany Farewell, Bid to Auto Workers, Teamsters Mark AFL-CIO. Convention." Monthly Labor Review. Vol 103. No. 2. (February). Pp. 58–62.

Belfer, N. 1954. "Trade Union Investment Policies." *Industrial and Labor Relations Review* 6, no. 3 (April).

Berkowitz, M. 1954. "The Economics of Trade Union Organization and Administration." *Industrial and Labor Relations Review* 7 (July):575–592.

Ehrenberg, R., and Goldberg, S. 1977. "Officer Performance and Compensation in Local Building Trade Unions." *Industrial and Labor Relations Review* 30, no. 3 (January):188–196.

Estey, M. 1967. *The Unions: Structure, Development, and Management.* New York: Harcourt, Brace & World.

Estey, M., Taft, P., and Wagner, M. 1964. *Regulating Union Government.* New York: Harper & Row.

Goldstein, G. S., and Pauly, M. V. 1976. "Group Health Insurance as a Local Public Good." In *The Role of Health Insurance in the Health Services Sector*, ed. R. Rosett. New York: National Bureau of Economic Research.

Greene, M. 1964. *The Role of Employee Benefit Structures in Manufacturing Industry.* Oregon: University of Oregon Press.

Jensen, M., and Meckling, W. 1976. "Theory of the Firm: Managerial Behavior, Agency Costs and Ownership Structure." *Journal of Financial Economics* 3 (October).

Lester, R. A. 1967. "Benefits as a Preferred Form of Compensation." *Southern Economic Journal* 33 (April):492–494.

Martin, D. L. 1980. *An Ownership Theory of the Trade Union.* Berkeley and Los Angeles: University of California Press.

Mendelsohn, A. I. 1956. "Fringe Benefits Today and Tomorrow." *Labor Law Journal*, pp. 325–328, 379–384.

National Industrial Conference Board. 1965. *Handbook of Union Government Structure and Procedures.*

Pencavel, J. 1971. "The Demand for Union Services: An Exercise." *Industrial Labor Relations Review*, pp. 180–190.

Perlman, S. 1928. *A Theory of the Labor Movement.* Reissued New York: Kelley, 1949.

Reder, M. 1960. "Job Scarcity and the Nature of Union Power." *Industrial and Labor Relations Review* 13 (April):349–362.

Rice, R. 1966. "Skill, Earnings and the Growth of Wage Supplements." *American Economic Review.*

Ross, A. 1948. *Trade Union Wage Policy.* Berkeley and Los Angeles: University of California Press.

Sayles, L., and Strauss, G. 1967. *The Local Union.* New York: Harcourt Brace & World.

Senate Select Committee on Improper Practices in the Labor Management Field. 1959.

Taft, P. 1956. *The Structure and Government of Labor Unions.* Cambridge, Mass.: Harvard University Press.

Weinstein, P. 1966. "Racketeering and Labor: An Economic Analysis." *Industrial and Labor Review* 14 (April):402–413.

9 THE EMPIRICAL PERFORMANCE OF A MODEL OF TRADE UNION BEHAVIOR

John H. Pencavel

This chapter will report on the progress of an ongoing research program concerned with the evaluation of behavioral models of trade unionism. The ultimate goal of this research is to provide a better understanding of the variations in wage rates and employment in unionized labor markets. A considerable volume of empirical research has documented the existence of an impact on relative wages of trade unions; a small amount of research work on the effect of unionism on employment has been conducted. Yet a convincing and complete explanation for why the wage impact of unionism appears to vary over time or appears to differ across labor markets at a given time is really lacking and will remain so until a plausible and empirically tenable story has been provided about how unions behave. The literature is not wanting in stories, but there is a real poverty in the number of empirical

I am indebted to Michael Lohrer for conscientious and proficient research assistance, to Thomas MaCurdy, Andrew Oswald, and James Rosse for useful discussions during the preparation of this paper, and to a Sloan Foundation grant to the Department of Economics at Stanford University. I owe a special thanks to James Dertouzos, who carefully put together the data used in this chapter and who first proposed the International Typographical Union as a trade union amenable to the sort of analysis described here.

studies that are firmly grounded in these stories. As a consequence, an evaluation today of these models of unionism in terms of their correspondence with observed behavior would depend on only a little more information than was available to Dunlop (1944) when he raised the fundamental issues 37 years ago.

The purpose of this chapter is to address only one of these stories, albeit a very popular one. Although it has been articulated by a number of researchers, it received its most thorough analysis in the work of William Fellner (1947) and Allan Cartter (1959); in recognition of this, I dub this as "the modified Fellner-Cartter model." Fellner and Cartter explicitly portrayed management as conventional profit maximizers, but since I shall not always maintain this hypothesis, I will use the qualifier "modified" with "the Fellner-Cartter model." Reduced to its essentials, this model characterizes the union as maximizing an objective function in which wage rates and employment are arguments and as being constrained by a trade-off between these two variables that either may be interpreted as an employer's conventional labor demand function or may be thought of as the consequence of the employer's resistance to the union's objectives in a bargaining setting. As is made clear in the following section, the solution suggested by this model is likely to be inefficient from the viewpoint of the parties involved (union and management). Whether this represents a defect of the model is an issue that is considered. It should also be noted that the model is silent about the process by which the solution is reached; therefore, without being supplemented with further behavioral hypotheses, it says nothing about the convergence over time of a sequence of offers and counteroffers on the part of union and management. On the other hand, "the modified Fellner-Cartter model" does propose a plausible and determinate solution to union-management bargaining and clearly deserves to be taken seriously as a viable explanation for the determination of wages and employment in unionized labor markets.

The formal resemblance of the Fellner-Cartter model of unionism to the economist's conventional models of the consumer and the firm suggests useful analogies with this literature. Indeed, it will become evident that I draw heavily on the research on estimating systems of consumer demand equations and on fitting the firm's behavioral relationships. My primary purpose is to demonstrate by example that models of unionism can be put to work in a number of different ways and to illustrate this point with data describing the wages and employment of members of the International Typographical Union. This union is remarkable and fascinating, with characteristics that predispose it to a study of the kind undertaken here.

That there is an element of advocacy in this chapter should be made clear. This does not take the particular form of championing the Fellner-Cartter model of unionism whose empirical performance clearly deserves disinterested evaluation, but which has yet to win its spurs. Rather, the advocacy enters by my belaboring the point that models such as the Fellner-Cartter model have operational content and are fully amenable to empirical implementation. Research on trade unionism needs a healthy infusion of a compilation of careful and imaginative empirical studies that are faithful to the institutional underpinnings of the situation and that are firmly grounded in the behavioral models.[1]

The outline of this chapter is first to state the essential features of the modified Fellner-Cartter model of unionism, to indicate precisely what the model does and does not imply. The third section describes the broad characteristics of the American daily newspaper industry, the International Typographical Union, and the data on the ten union locals with which this paper is concerned. In the fourth section, the wage and employment equations suggested by the Fellner-Cartter model are fitted to the annual time-series observations on the ten union locals, and three different strategies are outlined. An assessment of the performance of the model is provided in the concluding section of the paper.

Conceptual Framework

The Modified Fellner-Cartter Model

The union is characterized as behaving as though it possesses an objective function containing as arguments the money wage rate, w; union employment, L; and a vector of variables, Y, taken to be exogenous to the union:

$$U = g(w, L, Y). \tag{9.1}$$

This function is assumed to be smooth, twice differentiable, and strictly concave with positive first partial derivatives in w and L.[2] If the union consisted of a number of different types of workers, then w and L would be vectors. The literature contains a number of candidates for inclusion in Y, such as the price level of commodities consumed by union members, the wage received by a comparison group of workers, the level of unemployment benefits, and some measure of the cost of finding alternative employment.

This objective function is the union leader, who is assumed to take account of the welfare of all "his" members.[3]

The opportunities of the union to achieve its objectives are assumed to be constrained such that, on the boundary of its opportunity set, the union can engineer an increase in the wage rate only at the "price" of a lower level of employment or an increase in employment can be secured only through a lower per-worker wage rate. It is immaterial at the moment whether this opportunity set is viewed as the effective outcome of the employer's resistance to the union's demands in a bargaining setting or as the conventional labor demand function of a wage-taking optimizing firm. In either case, this trade-off between employment and money wages can be represented by a smooth, twice-differentiable function as follows:

$$L = f(w, Z), \tag{9.2}$$

where the notion of a trade-off implies that $\partial f/\partial w$ is negative throughout and where Z is a vector of variables exogenous to both management and the union. Z might include the prices of other inputs in production, the price(s) of output(s), the support the union will receive from other unions in the event of a strike, and so on. The narrative that frequently accompanies this model characterizes the unions as determining the wage rate and then as leaving the employer free to settle employment through the trade-off equation (9.2); no doubt, this characterization represents an appropriate description of the institutional setting in many collective bargaining cases. However, this narrative is by no means necessary: A setting in which the union explicitly places restrictions on employment as well as determines wages is consistent with this model provided these employment restrictions are "purchased" with a lower wage rate and these restrictions are appropriately incorporated in equation (9.2).

The union is assumed to do the best it can given its opportunities, or, more formally, the union selects w and L to maximize its objective function, equation (9.1), subject to the choice of w and L being restricted by equation (9.2). The first-order condition for a maximum is

$$\frac{g_1}{g_2} = -f_w, \tag{9.3}$$

where $g_1 \equiv \partial U/\partial w > 0$, $g_2 \equiv \partial U/\partial L > 0$, and $f_w \equiv \partial f/\partial w < 0$, or the marginal rate of substitution of wages for employment in the union's objective function equals the slope of the trade-off between wages and employment in the opportunity set. The second-order condition involves the second derivatives of the objective function and of the opportunity set.[4] Equations (9.2) and (9.3) may be solved uniquely for w and L as functions of the exogenous variables Y and Z:

$$w = \phi_1(Y, Z), \tag{9.4}$$

$$L = \phi_2(Y, Z). \tag{9.5}$$

When particular functional forms are specified for the objective function (9.1) and for the opportunity set (9.2), then the explicit functional forms for equations (9.4) and (9.5) can often be determined, the parameters of the latter being related to those in equations (9.1) and (9.2).

If these reduced-form equations (9.4) and (9.5) are substituted back into the union's objective function, the maximum value (V) of the objective function is determined as a function of the exogenous variables of the system:

$$V = V(Y, Z). \tag{9.6}$$

Through a straightforward application of the envelope theorem, the following relationships can be established:

$$\frac{\partial V}{\partial Y} = \frac{\partial g}{\partial Y},$$

and

$$\frac{\partial V}{\partial Z} = \frac{\partial g}{\partial L}\frac{\partial f}{\partial Z},$$

or between any two elements of Z, say, Z_i and Z_j:

$$\frac{\partial V/\partial Z_i}{\partial V/\partial Z_j} = \frac{\partial f/\partial Z_i}{\partial f/\partial Z_j}$$

Although the reduced-form equations (9.4) and (9.5) are invariant under positive monotonic transformations of the union's objective function as is the marginal rate of substitution equation (9.3), the indirect objective function (9.6) clearly will not be invariant.

The Qualitative Content of the Model

What are the observable implications of this model of unionism? Without specifying particular expressions for the objective and constraint functions (9.1) and (9.2), what of a qualitative nature is implied for the reduced-form equations (9.4) and (9.5)?[5] The answer is that, at this level of generality, very little is implied, as is evident from the expressions for the partial derivatives of equations (9.4) and (9.5):

$$\frac{\partial w}{\partial Y} = -\Delta^{-1}\left(\frac{\partial^2 U}{\partial w \partial Y} + \frac{\partial f}{\partial w}\frac{\partial^2 U}{\partial L \partial Y}\right); \tag{9.7a}$$

$$\frac{\partial w}{\partial Z} = -\Delta^{-1}\left[\left(\frac{\partial^2 U}{\partial w \partial L} + \frac{\partial f}{\partial w}\frac{\partial^2 U}{\partial L^2}\right)\frac{\partial f}{\partial Z} + \frac{\partial^2 f}{\partial w \partial Z}\frac{\partial U}{\partial L}\right]; \tag{9.7b}$$

$$\frac{\partial L}{\partial Y} = \frac{\partial f}{\partial w}\frac{\partial w}{\partial Y}; \tag{9.8a}$$

and

$$\frac{\partial L}{\partial Z} = \frac{\partial f}{\partial w}\frac{\partial w}{\partial Z} + \frac{\partial f}{\partial Z}, \tag{9.8b}$$

where Δ is the negative determinant defined in note 4. Without any further restrictions on the objective function or on the constraint function, the sign of each of these derivatives is ambiguous. There are, however, restrictions across equations (9.4) and (9.5), as is evident from an examination of equations (9.8a) and (9.8b). Subsequently, it will be useful for equations (9.8a) and (9.8b) to be written in terms of elasticities:

$$\frac{Y}{L}\frac{\partial L}{\partial Y} = \frac{w}{L}\frac{\partial f}{\partial w} \cdot \frac{\partial w}{\partial Y}\frac{Y}{w}; \tag{9.9a}$$

$$\frac{Z}{L}\frac{\partial L}{\partial Z} = \frac{w}{L}\frac{\partial f}{\partial w} \cdot \frac{\partial w}{\partial Z}\frac{Z}{w} + \frac{Z}{L}\frac{\partial f}{\partial Z}. \tag{9.9b}$$

From (9.9a) it is evident that the elasticity of employment with respect to Y must be opposite in sign to the elasticity of wages with respect to Y: An increase in Y shifts the objective function, but leaves the constraint $f(.)$ unchanged so the union responds by moving along the constraint either to a higher wage–lower employment combination or to a lower wage–higher employment combination. Other than this, the model is devoid of qualitative implications. This conclusion results simply from the application of the theorem of conjugate pairs and should occasion little surprise among those familiar with the mechanics of such optimizing models.[6] On the other hand, it is curious that a model with so little qualitative content should have generated such a protracted and heated interchange as that which arose over whether the trade union can usefully be characterized as maximizing anything.[7] There is no unambiguously-signed "utility-constant" effect of an increase in one of the elements of the Z vector until we specify whether the increase in Z increases or decreases the slope of $\partial f/\partial w$.[8] Since neither the constraint nor the objective function is necessarily linear, there are no symmetry conditions in this model.

In fact, most models of union behavior have not been quite as general as this prototype; so let us consider the consequences of imposing more structure on the model. Starting with the trade-off equation (9.2), if we were to assume that the employer faces exogenous prices for the inputs purchased and produces an output that minimizes costs, then equation (9.2) possesses the characteristics of a conventional labor demand function. In this case, Z consists of the (assumed fixed) prices of inputs and the level of output.[9] This labor demand function is increasing with respect to the price of at least one other input, is increasing in output (unless labor is an inferior input, a possibility that subsequently we shall not permit), and is homogenous of degree zero in all input prices. These properties do not help, however, in forming statements about the signs of the reduced-form derivatives (9.7) and (9.8). The sort of qualitative statements that can be made requires far more structure be placed on the model. To illustrate, consider an increase in output and suppose that both the labor demand function (9.2) is strongly separable in w and output and that the union's objective function is strongly separable in wages and employment. Then, on our maintained hypothesis that labor is not an inferior input, this increase in output raises wage rates, but may increase or decrease employment, depending on the slope of the labor demand function.

Now consider supplementing the restrictions on equation (9.2) implied by a cost-minimizing labor demand function with restrictions on the form of the union's objective function. For instance, suppose the union maximizes the total rents from unionization, a maximand considered by Dunlop (1944),

Rosen (1970), and de Menil (1971). If $\bar{w}$ denotes the competitive wage rate, then a rent-maximizing union has as its objective $U = (w - \bar{w})L$. When constrained by a conventional labor demand function, this model yields the unsurprising implication than an exogenous increase in the competitive wage $\bar{w}$ will induce the union to elect a higher w, but, since this change in $\bar{w}$ leaves the labor demand function unaltered, this increase in w can only be achieved by accepting a lower level of employment.[10] Therefore, once more prior structure is grafted onto the relevant functions, the modified Fellner-Cartter model of unionism is by no means empty of qualitative content. The trouble is that, for the most part, empirical work on collective bargaining has not been organized around behavioral models of unionism so that, notwithstanding a large volume of research on the influence of trade unions, the empirical relevance of an objective such as rent maximization for the union cannot be assessed with any pretense at confidence.

Considerations of Efficiency and Information

It should be made clear that the solution described by the modified Fellner-Cartter model is not efficient from the viewpoint of the two parties concerned. The concept of efficiency used here is the familiar one of a situation in which one party's welfare cannot be improved without the other party suffering a loss in its welfare. Thus, if the firm maximizes profits, an efficient contract is one in which equation (9.1) is maximized, subject to a given level of profits for the firm, and the wage-employment contract that results from this sort of behavior is normally different from that implied by the modified Fellner-Cartter model.[11] That is, if the firm maximizes profits, the levels of wages and employment determined by equation (9.3) will not lie on the contract curve and there exists an alternative wage-employment contract which can improve a party's welfare without harming the other's.[12] This is, of course, a well known result, which harks back to Leontief (1946) and Fellner (1947) and to the issue of whether the inefficiency of the Fellner-Cartter labor contract constitutes an objectionable feature of this model. After all, why should contracting parties ever knowingly forego an opportunity to improve their welfare if it does not harm the other party?

The answer presumably is that the parties will not *knowingly* relinquish opportunities to reach the Pareto frontier, but is it appropriate in a collective bargaining setting to presume that sufficient knowledge of opportunities exists? For instance, management may well misperceive the union's utility function and so may make an offer that appears to management to be Pareto superior to the initial contract but that is not judged by the union to be Pareto superior. Indeed, as countless observers of the mechanics of collective bargaining have documented, the very nature of bargaining between management and labor usually involves each party in a series of threats, bluffs, and deceptions that are designed to convey to the other party misleading information on its own utility function. Expressed differently, it is by no means clear that the negotiation process in collective bargaining provides incentives for the parties to reveal their respective valuations, and thus no guarantee that an efficient contract will be reached.[13] Therefore, at this stage of our knowledge on collective bargaining procedures, there seems no powerful reason either to presume that union-management contracts are efficient or that they are not.

Because of the absence of complete information on the part of the union and the employer of its opponent's objective function, the agreement reached by the employer and the union may not be an efficient contract; instead it may well be that described by the modified Fellner-Cartter model. But if the a priori plausibility of this model rests on the absence of complete information, then surely the exposition of the Fellner-Cartter model above is inadequate in that it makes no allowance for uncertainty. In fact, the role of uncertainty in the Fellner-Cartter model seems to be the basis for certain objections that have been leveled against it. Or, at least, this is my interpretation of some of Ross's protests that, under most circumstances, unions dismiss the employment ramifications of their wage policies because the nature of the wage-employment trade-off is liable to shift considerably during the operation of a collective bargaining contract.[14] Now it is certainly the case that the Fellner-Cartter model sketched above presumes complete information about the wage-employment trade-off, but this does not mean that the model cannot be extended to accommodate uncertainty in some form. On the contrary, it should be clear by analogy with other areas of economics that at least certain classes of incomplete information can be grafted onto modes such as the one outlined above and that the broad features of such models resemble those that result from neglecting uncertainty. The particular results from this extension will depend upon the precise manner in which incomplete information enters the model. I postpone to another occasion a full and general treatment of this issue. But one characterization that is in the spirit of Ross's remarks can be indicated here to support my belief that the neglect of uncertainty is not a fatal flaw.

Suppose that the variable (*s*) Z that determines the location of the wage-employment trade-off in equation (9.2) is random with a realized value outside the control of the union. Under these circumstances, the union's problem is to select w to maximize the expected value of the objective function:

$$EU = \int_{Z_1}^{Z_2} g[w, f(w, Z), Y]\psi(Z)dZ,$$

where Z_1, Z_2 indicates the range of Z and $\psi(Z)$ is the probability density function of Z. The first-order condition for the optimal wage rate takes the form:

$$Eg_1 + E(g_2 \cdot f_w) = 0, \tag{9.10}$$

with the second-order condition

$$D = Eg_{11} + 2E(g_{21} \cdot f_w) + E(g_{22} \cdot f_w^2) + E(g_2 \cdot f_{ww}) < 0,$$

and comparative static effects can be evaluated by differentiation of the first-order condition. The similarity of these equations to those derived earlier under certainty is apparent.[15] What is the effect of increased uncertainty on the wage decision? One frequent parameterization of this increase in uncertainty involves replacing Z with

$$\xi(Z - EZ) + EZ,$$

where EZ is the mean of Z and where $\xi > 0$. Then increasing ξ implies a stretching of the distribution of Z around a constant mean so that an increase in ξ is one interpretation of increased uncertainty. Making this substitution for Z defined implicitly in equation (9.10) and then differentiating with respect to ξ yields:

$$\frac{\partial w}{\partial \xi} = -D^{-1}[\text{cov. } (Z, g_{12}f_z + f_w f_z g_{22} + g_2 f_{wz})],$$

where D is the negative definite term required by the satisfaction of the second-order conditions. Clearly, this equation cannot be signed given the general manner in which the model has been set up, but this expression identifies quite clearly the relevant information required.

The point of all this is not that powerful and refutable implications follow from augmenting the Fellner-Cartter model of unionism with some form of uncertainty, for this is clearly not the case. Rather, the essential point is that the theoretical model can be extended to allow for uncertainty, and the fact that the model may be described without allowing for uncertainty, does not imply that it is appropriate *only* when uncertainty is absent. Whether the model is a useful device for understanding wage and employment determination under trade unionism is an empirical question and is a relevant question whether or not the exposition of the theoretical model is couched in terms of complete information.

The Institutional Background and the Data

The data used in the empirical work in the next section consist of annual observations on wages, employment, and other variables describing the membership of the International Typographical Union and the newspaper industry in ten American cities from 1946 to 1965. These data, drawn from various sources published by the ITU and the newspaper industry, were compiled by James Dertouzos (1979) in his seminal investigation of the ITU. Before providing a description of these data, some features of the newspaper industry and the ITU during this period should be outlined.[16]

The Newspaper Industry and the ITU

In the United States, virtually all daily newspapers are designed to meet the interests of the local community. In large cities, the local readership runs into the millions, but, typically, the circulation of the average daily is considerably less.[17] Consequently, an understanding of the variations in the circulation and revenues of daily newspapers can be found in the differences in characteristics of the local community. Circulation is critical to the newspaper, but not because newspaper sales are the most important source of revenue. On the contrary, income from circulation constitutes only 25 percent of the typical daily's total revenue and as little as 10 percent in smaller cities. Most of the daily newspaper's revenue comes from advertising, especially local advertising; hence, the newspaper's concern with circulation is derived from the advertisers' objective of reaching as many people as possible. Since these advertisers have many other avenues to convey their messages—television, radio, billboards, direct mail, magazines—a newspaper operates in a competitive environment even if it is the city's only daily. And, today, owing to the demise of some newspapers and owing to mergers between others, the single daily newspaper city is the norm: The percentage of all cities with daily newspapers in which more than one daily was published fell from almost 40 percent in 1923 to 2 percent in 1978.

In much the same way that the daily newspaper cater to geographically distinct markets, so the structure of the ITU is highly decentralized with collective bargaining taking place at the local level. Although union publications disseminate detailed information about wages and conditions of work in different parts of the country, a national or regional minimum wage has never been established, and there are considerable variations in wage rates and hours of work across cities that have never been satisfactorily accounted for.[18] An indication of the wage rate variation across cities is provided by the data reported in table 9–1. The table provides information on wage rates and standard weekly hours of work in 23 U. S. cities in 1946 and 1965 (the years that will constitute the beginning and end of our estimating period in the next section). In 1946 these workers in Detroit (the highest entry) earned 55 percent more per hour than those in Charlotte (the lowest entry), while in 1965 the percentage difference between the highest (San Francisco) and the lowest (Little Rock) wage per hour is 28 percent. This variation is all the more remarkable when we recognize that the data in table 9–1 describe workers in a narrowly defined occupation, the members of which possess unusually similar characteristics from city to city. Many of the variables commonly employed to account for wage differentials across cities or across regions are being held constant in these data.

The ITU, commonly regarded as one of the most powerful unions of its size in the country, has established considerable control over employment and conditions of work. Thus, the Taft-Hartley Act notwithstanding, the ITU operates a closed shop, whereby every worker in the composing room, including the foreman, is a member of the union. (However, the employer has the right to select the foreman without regard to seniority.) No nonmember of the union is even permitted on the floor of the composing room during production although this rule is seldom enforced. In the popular mind, the ITU is associated with its concern for the employment effects of new technology and with its perennial resistance to new composing methods.[19] Today the very survival of the ITU in its traditional form as an organization of highly skilled workers practicing a craft with a long and prestigious history is threatened by the diffusion of typesetting computers and photographic processes, which have eliminated many of the particular skills once required of printers.[20] These technological changes have markedly disturbed the preeminence of the union in its bargaining with employers. To avoid the modeling complications arising from these drastic technological changes, the research reported in this paper makes use of data from a period during which the production technology was not subject to abrupt changes and during which the bargaining relationship between the ITU and the employers appears to be constant.[21] This period is the twenty years from 1946 to 1965, during which time the ITU clearly held the upper hand in its dealings with employers. The ITU's complete control of the supply of skilled printers and

Table 9-1. Union Wages Rates and Straight-Time Weekly Hours of Work for Hand Compositors at Night Work in the Newspaper Industry

	July 1, 1946		*July 1, 1965*	
	hourly wage rate	*weekly hours*	*hourly wage rate*	*weekly hours*
Birmingham, Ala.	1.620	40.0	3.803	37.5
Boston, Mass.	1.840	37.5	4.018	36.25
Buffalo, N.Y.	1.733	37.5	4.110	36.25
Charlotte, N.C.	1.384	40.0	3.573	37.5
Dallas, Tex.	1.729	35.0	3.878	35.0
Dayton, Ohio	1.666	37.5	3.880	37.5
Des Moines, Iowa	1.710	40.0	4.071	37.5
Detroit, Michigan	2.144	36.3	4.354	36.25
Erie, Pa.	1.580	37.5	3.693	37.5
Indianapolis, Ind.	1.967	37.5	4.027	37.5
Little Rock, Ark.	1.440	36.3	3.480	36.25
Madison, Wisc.	1.512	40.0	3.853	37.5
New Haven, Conn.	1.388	40.0	3.653	37.5
Norfolk, Va.	1.500	40.0	3.680	37.5
Omaha, Nebr.	1.660	40.0	3.928	37.5
Peoria, Ill.	1.595	38.3	3.953	37.5
Phoenix, Ariz.	1.490	37.5	3.733	37.5
Rochester, N.Y.	1.680	37.5	3.986	37.5
St. Louis, Mo.	2.000	36.3	4.360	36.25
San Antonio, Tex.	1.533	37.5	3.547	37.5
San Francisco, Ca.	2.000	37.5	4.452	35.0
South Bend, Ind.	1.543	40.0	3.845	37.5
Tampa, Fla.	1.500	37.5	3.573	37.5
average of all cities	1.930	37.2	4.050	36.5

Note: These data are taken from surveys of the printing industry conducted by the Bureau of Labor Statistics. The figures for July 1946 are published in BLS Bulletin No. 912, and those for July 1965 are published in BLS Bulletin No. 1489. The "average of all cities" entry in the last line is the average over the 75 cities surveyed in 1946 and over the 69 cities surveyed in 1965 and not simply over the 23 cities listed in the table.

the newspapers' vulnerability to an interruption in production meant that the union clearly dominated the bargaining relationship with the employers.[22] Thus, to characterize the course of printers' wages and employment over these years as a mapping out of the union's preferences is a defensible hypothesis.

Other characteristics of the ITU determine the construction of a formal model. First, it is the quintessential democratic union in which a large fraction of the membership participates in well-organized elections and referendums on all sorts of issues, thus effectively reducing the distance between the union leadership and the rank and file that is so characteristic of many other unions.[23] The members of the ITU have always been well educated by the standards of the day, so finding men with the skills needed to undertake the administrative duties of a union has not been difficult.[24] Thus many union members have held some union office at one time or another. Also as a consequence, in the smaller chapels at least, the prerequisites of being an official are few, so that the chairmanship of a local chapel "tends to be regarded as an obligation to be passed around and shared among the chapel members" (Lipset, Trow, and Coleman, 1956, pp. 176–177).

Second, the ITU "from a socioeconomic point of view is as homogeneous as any group of that size could be" (Lipset, Trow, and Coleman, 1956, p. 309). No important skill differentials exist within the union since all workers receive the same basic training. The only differences in contract wage scales in newspapers shops are those between day and night workers. Printers have always felt a considerable pride in their craft and have shared a strong sense of group solidarity, characteristics evident in the membership of the ITU. Perhaps the most important distinction among members is that between regular workers and substitute workers, the latter being printers who have lost their regular jobs or who have recently completed their apprenticeship. Most of the ITU members are regular workers. It is the substitutes who replace absent regular workers and who satisfy the demand for additional workers during periods of peak production (which in newspapers comes each week on Fridays and Saturdays and during the pre-Christmas season). Substitute workers are assisted, however, by union provisions requiring a substitute worker to replace a regular employee once the regular worker has accumulated a certain number of overtime hours.

The consequence of this institutional description of the ITU, therefore, is to provide intuitive support for an objective function such as equation (9.1) that does not differentiate between the interests of the leadership and those of the rank and file. Nor does it seem to be essential to identify divergent interests within the rank and file. The fact that the ITU was clearly the dominant party in the bargaining relationship with newspaper management for the 1946–1965 period helps to justify an interpretation of the movements of wages and employment of these typographers as reflecting the (constrained) objectives of the union. These judgments are all somewhat heroic, of course, and certainly there is ample room for honest disagreement among observers of the institutional setting. However, it is by no means clear that the sort of abstraction involved here is any more demanding of relevant empirical phenomena than are economists' models of the firm or of the family. This is ultimately a judgment that must rest on the correspondence between the central features of the theoretical model and the empirical regularities actually documented. At our present level of knowledge of analytical models of unionism, we are in no position to form that judgment. It is toward correcting our ignorance on these matters that the research reported in this paper is designed.

The Data

Ideally, the data appropriate for a study of this kind should describe the production processes of a particular newspaper; indeed, such data have been obtained for one time series, namely, for Cincinnati.[25] For this city, w is the hourly wage rate for journeyman printers employed by the Cincinnati *Post*, while L is the number of full-time typographical workers in the *Post* composing room. In 1958 the *Post* merged with the Cincinnati *Times-Star*, and the ITU members of the *Times-Star* chapel were absorbed into the *Post* composing room. The major problem with extending the study to other cities is the difficulty of obtaining employment data. Although the *Typographical Journal*, the union's publication, provides data on local union membership, these figures include ITU members employed in commercial (book and job) printing establishments. However, this contamination of the union membership data by commercial printing employment is a serious problem only in large cities that have major book and job establishments so that, if cities such as New York and Chicago with a substantial commercial printing industry are excluded, the correspondence between local union membership and newspaper employment is much closer.[26] Therefore, for the other *nine* cities, the data for L describe the total local union membership. In all nine cities (with the exception of Columbus), there is a single daily newspaper firm. Clearly, a potential for error exists here (more serious perhaps for the large union locals) in the measurement of L, and this should be borne in mind in evaluating the empirical results in the next section.

Average values of wages and employment over the years 1946–1965 for the ten cities are given in table 9–2 along with other characteristics of these cities. The cities range from Fond du Lac, Wisconsin, which over these years had a mean journeyman membership of 41, to Columbus, Ohio, which was almost fifteen times larger. Average money wages ranged from a low of \$2.17 in Dubuque to \$2.94 in Columbus. Information on the trend and cyclical movements over these years of real wages and of employment for

Table 9-2. Mean Values of Variables for Ten Cities Averaged Over the Years 1946-1965

	w^a	w/p^b	L^c	X^d	*1960 Population*
Cincinnati, Ohio[e]	2.88	3.51	172	18.8	503
Augusta, Ga.	2.35	2.96	56	19.5	71
Columbia, S.C.	2.42	2.99	105	23.6	97
Dubuque, Iowa[e]	2.17	2.73	68	9.3	57
Memphis, Tenn.	2.84	3.46	323	42.5	498
Fond du Lac, Wisc.	2.41	2.96	41	7.8	33
Louisville, Ky.	2.89	3.44	397	43.7	391
Elmira, N.Y.	2.63	3.15	120	16.3	47
Columbus, Ohio[e]	2.94	3.58	602	51.0	471
Albany, N.Y.[e]	2.78	3.38	596	30.8	130

[a] w is the average hourly wage scale for journeymen. The data on w are taken from selected issues of the *ITU Bulletin*, while union membership data come from the *Typographical Journal*.

[b] w/p deflates w by the consumer price index.

[c] L denotes average employment at the *Post* for Cincinnati, and it denotes local union membership for the other cities.

[d] The *Post's* average advertising linage (in thousands) in April is given in the column headed X^d, while for the other cities X is total linage sold by all the local daily newspapers. The information on X comes from selected issues of *Editor and Publisher,* a trade magazine. A rough index of potential readership is provided by the numbers on the population (in thousands) of each city in 1960. These population figures are taken from table 30 of the *1960 Census of Population, Vol. 1, Characteristics of the Population, Part 1, U.S. Summary.*

[e] Cities in which a merger took place between newspapers during these years.

each city is conveyed by the simple regression results reported in tables 9–3 and 9–4. As evidenced from these descriptive regressions, there were strong positive trends in both real wages and employment but no discernible business cycle movements in either variable, at least as indicated by the aggregate unemployment rate.[27] The absence of any association with the unemployment rate is, of course, consistent with the belief that unionism tends to insulate labor markets from cyclical movements in economic activity.

To implement the modified Fellner-Cartter model, we need to consider not only the endogenous variables, money wages and employment, in this model of unionism, but also the variables labeled Y and Z that designated exogenous variables in the last section. As far as Y is concerned—that is, the exogenous variables determining the location of the union's objective function—the one clear candidate for consideration here is the consumer

Table 9-3. Descriptive Regressions of the Logarithm of Real Wages, 1946-1965

	Time Trend	*Unemployment Rate*	R^2	*See*
Cincinnati	.0138*	.0037	.87	.035
	(.0015)	(.0081)		
Augusta	.0248*	−.0081	.85	.052
	(.0033)	(.0128)		
Columbia	.0198*	.0078	.90	.042
	(.0020)	(.0098)		
Dubuque	.0184*	.0110	.82	.052
	(.0027)	(.0128)		
Memphis	.0141*	.0036	.88	.033
	(.0015)	(.0076)		
Fond du Lac	.0255*	.0093	.91	.052
	(.0025)	(.0122)		
Louisville	.0180*	.0013	.77	.056
	(.0028)	(.0130)		
Elmira	.0222*	.0098	.93	.038
	(.0018)	(.0090)		
Columbus	.0158*	.0074	.89	.036
	(.0016)	(.0083)		
Albany	.0170*	.0134	.92	.033
	(.0015)	(.0077)		

Note: These are the results from ordinary least squares regressions of the logarithm of real wages on a constant term, on a linear time trend, and on the aggregate unemployment rate. *See* denotes the estimated standard error of the regression. Estimated standard errors are in parentheses. For ease of reading, an asterisk has been placed next to coefficients estimated to be more than 1.96 their standard errors.

price index (p) as a measure of the price level of consumer goods purchased by union workers. Moreover, absence of money illusion (zero homogeneity in w and p) is presumed by deflating the money wage by this price index. The union is involved in producing such a small part of the economy's total output that it neglects any effect of its decisions on the overall price level. Another variable considered in the next section for inclusion in Y is a reference or comparative wage rate that serves as a benchmark for the union, but discussion of this is postponed until later.

Z stood for a vector of variables that determined the constraint between wages and employment as given in equation (9.2). Some of these variables will display most of their variation across cities: Some newspapers,

Table 9-4. Descriptive Regressions of the Logarithm of Employment, 1946-1965

	Time Trend	*Unemployment Rate*	*Merger Dummy*	R^2	*See*
Cincinnati	.0205*	.0210	.329*	.97	.057
	(.0043)	(.0155)	(.058)		
Augusta	.0316*	−.0203		.91	.047
	(.0030)	(.0117)			
Columbia	.0225*	.0026		.93	.038
	(.0018)	(.0088)			
Dubuque	.0237*	.0005	.040	.93	.037
	(.0022)	(.0093)	(.025)		
Memphis	.0291*	.0007		.96	.036
	(.0016)	(.0083)			
Fond du Lac	.0145*	.0038		.56	.083
	(.0039)	(.0194)			
Lousiville	−.0006	.0061		.02	.051
	(.0025)	(.0117)			
Elmira	.0143*	.0233		.64	.079
	(.0038)	(.0189)			
Columbus	.0223*	−.0042	.050*	.95	.029
	(.0014)	(.0066)	(.015)		
Albany	.0083*	.0015	.040	.60	.059
	(.0039)	(.0137)	(.048)		

Note: These are the results from ordinary least squares regressions of the logarithm of employment on a constant term, on a linear time trend, on the aggregate unemployment rate, and (where relevant) on a dummy variable that takes the value of unity after a merger between newspapers takes place. The estimated standard error of the regression is given by *See*. Estimated standard errors are in parentheses. An asterisk has been placed next to coefficients estimated to be more than 1.96 their standard errors.

depending on the availability of other advertising media and on the financial resources the newspaper proprietor can call on, will be more vulnerable to a strike than others. For a single newspaper over time, these Z variables will consist of the prices (or the determinants of the prices) of other inputs to the production process and of the output (or the determinants of the output) to be produced. The nonlabor inputs in the production of newspapers whose movements over time need to be accounted for are newsprint and machinery and equipment; thus, for a single newspaper over time, the variables used to represent Z are as follows:[28]

r_1, the price of newsprint (in hundreds of dollars per short ton) as quoted in national markets;

r_2, the BLS wholesale price index of machinery and equipment;

X, the amount of advertising linage (in thousands) sold annually.

In some estimates, the machinery price index was replaced by a measure of the user cost of capital, but the results were essentially unchanged. This output variable, advertising linage, measures only one dimension (albeit the most important in terms of newspaper revenues) of newspaper output and is not perfectly correlated with other dimensions such as the space devoted to news. Moreover, although many of the primary determinants of output are beyond the control of the newspaper firm (in particular, the size and wealth of a city's population and the number of television channels to which advertisers have access), it would be inappropriate to treat output invariably as exogenous. For these reasons, therefore, and for many of the results reported below, instrumental variable estimates were derived that characterized output as endogenous. These results will be described below, but it is worth mentioning here that nothing of a qualitative nature was affected by the treatment of output as exogenous or endogenous. Finally, in those four cities experiencing newspaper mergers during these years, some allowance for a change in the trade-off equation (9–2) was permitted before and after the merger.

Empirical Results

We turn now to an empirical evaluation of the performance of the modified Fellner-Cartter model of unionism by making use of the data described in the previous section on the newspaper industry and the International Typographical Union. My primary purpose is to illustrate different ways of implementing the model; to this end there are at least three approaches. One approach is to define an objective function of specific form and an employment-wage constraint equation of specific form and then to use the first-order condition (9.3) to solve explicitly for the corresponding reduced-form wage and employment equations. This procedure, described below, was used by Dertouzos and Pencavel (1981). A second approach estimates not the reduced-form wage and employment equations, but the marginal rate of substitution equation (9.3). This requires a specification for the system of indifference curves and for the slope of the employment-wage constraint. This is also illustrated below. The third approach is to fit reduced-form equations (9.4) and (9.5) without first specifying the expressions for the objective function and the employment-wage constraint function and then to impose the approximate restrictions on the derivatives of these reduced-form equations that are implied by the results described earlier. This third procedure is described first.

Approximate Reduced-Form Equations

Our procedure in this section is to work with the reduced-form equations (9.4) and (9.5) by starting with comparatively unrestricted expressions that impose little structure on the data and then by applying increasingly restrictive conditions on the statistical estimation of these equations. The general purpose of this work is to assess the compatibility of the data with the theory outlined earlier in the chapter. This assessment cannot be formed, of course, without first framing maintained hypotheses about functional forms—these may appear exacting to some researchers. That is, there are many alternative ways of forming approximations to reduced-form equations (9.4) and (9.5), and the choice among these different alternatives translates into what can usefully be assumed and what cannot usefully be assumed to be parametric. Since these reduced-form equations combine terms from the union's objective function (9.1) and from the constraint trade-off function (9.2), the assumptions about what to treat as parametric in approximating equations (9.4) and (9.5) are *not* simply equivalent to statements about the underlying production technology.

A natural starting point is with an approximation to the reduced-form equations (9.4) and (9.5) in which the variables are linear in their logarithms and in errors, a specification that can be justified by appealing to Taylor's theorem and collecting remainders in a disturbance term. Using as regressors the consumer price index (p), the price of newsprint (r_1), a wholesale price index of machinery and equipment (r_2), the amount of advertising linage (X), and a dummy variable (D) taking the value of zero before a newspaper merger takes place and of unity after a merger, the expressions for the reduced-form equations (9.4) and (9.5) are as follows:

$$\ln w_t = \beta_0 + \beta_1 \ln p_t + \beta_2 \ln r_{1t} + \beta_3 \ln r_{2t} + \beta_4 \ln X_t + \beta_5 D_t + \varepsilon_{1t}, \tag{9.11a}$$

$$\ln L_t = \gamma_0 + \gamma_1 \ln p_t + \gamma_2 \ln r_{1t} + \gamma_3 \ln r_{2t} + \gamma_4 \ln X_t + \gamma_5 D_t + \varepsilon_{2t}, \tag{9.11b}$$

where ε_{1t} and ε_{2t} are random error terms and where each observation represents the annual average of the variable. In these equations, the reduced-form elasticities are treated as parameters. With respect to the consistency between the data on the wages and employment of typographers and the theory outlined in the second section, the first question we might ask of equations (9.11a) and (9.11b) is whether the effect of an increase in the consumer price index on wage rates is opposite in sign to its effect on employment: that is, whether β_1 is opposite in sign to γ_1. Recall that this is implied by the modified Fellner-Cartter model since a change in p will affect the union's objective function without disturbing the trade-off between wages and employment as given by the constraint equation (9.2).

The city-by-city ordinary least squares estimates of β_1 and γ_1 are listed in table 9–5, and the rest of the estimates are reported in appendix tables 9–A

Table 9-5. Estimates of β_1 and γ_1 in Equations (9.11a) and (9.11b)

	$\hat{\beta}_1$	$\hat{\gamma}_1$
Cincinnati	1.265*	−.853
	(.374)	(.662)
Augusta	.571	−.846
	(.584)	(.768)
Columbia	.703	−.430
	(.376)	(.488)
Dubuque	−.368	.696
	(.322)	(.551)
Memphis	.908*	.150
	(.310)	(.373)
Fond du Lac	.048	−1.580*
	(.599)	(.577)
Louisville	1.518*	−1.607*
	(.422)	(.190)
Elmira	1.524*	−2.543*
	(.566)	(.689)
Columbus	1.220*	.195
	(.321)	(.286)
Albany	.089	1.351
	(.486)	(.730)

Notes: (1) Estimated standard errors are in parentheses. (2) For ease of reading, an asterisk has been placed next to coefficients estimated to be more than 1.96 (in absolute value) their standard errors.

and 9–B.[29] In seven out of the ten cities, β_1 and γ_1 possess opposite signs; in the other three cities, both β_1 and γ_1 are estimated to be positive although for each city at least one of these two coefficients would not be judged by conventional criteria as significantly different from zero. In fact, as equation (9.9a) makes clear, if the modified Fellner-Cartter model is correct, β_1 and γ_1 should not merely be opposite in sign, but their ratio should be equal to the elasticity between employment and wages in the trade off constraint function (9.2). Expressed differently, if the employment-wage elasticity of the constraint function is determined by technological factors that are similar across newspapers that share common production methods or by bargaining characteristics that are similar across cities, then the ratio of γ_1 to β_1 should be approximately the same across cities. Now it seems intuitively implausible to expect these technological and bargaining factors that affect the location of the employment-wage constraint to be the same for newspapers in cities that differed so markedly as Fond du Lac and Memphis, one with a population 15 times the other or one with a newspaper linage 5 times greater than the other.[30] For this reason, I grouped the ten cities into three broad categories of "small" locals, "medium" locals, and "large" locals. The "small" locals, which operated in the smallest cities and whose advertising linage was the smallest consist of Fond du Lac, Dubuque, and Elmira. The "large" locals—Memphis, Louisville, Columbus, and Albany—had the largest advertising linage of these ten cities. The locals in Cincinnati, Augusta, and Columbia, with average annual advertising linage of 18.8, 19.5, and 23.6 (thousands), respectively, are classified as the "medium" locals. This categorization is not incontestable, of course, so to ensure that the following results are not sensitive to this grouping, I experimented with other compositions of the categories. In fact, reclassifying the union locals in this way made no difference to the general sense of the results.

Therefore, classifying these ten union locals into three groups allows equations (9.11a) and (9.11b) to be rewritten as follows:

$$\ln w_{tj} = \beta_{0j} + \beta_{1j} \ln p_t + \beta_{2j} \ln r_{1t} + \beta_{3j} \ln r_{2t} + \beta_{4j} \ln X_{tj} + \beta_{5j} D_{tj} + \varepsilon_{1jt}, \tag{9.12a}$$

$$\ln L_{tj} = \gamma_{0j} + \gamma_{1j} \ln p_t + \gamma_{2j} \ln r_{1t} + \gamma_{3j} \ln r_{2t} + \gamma_{4j} \ln X_{tj} + \gamma_{5j} D_{tj} + \varepsilon_{2jt}, \tag{9.12b}$$

where subscript j identifies the city. The error terms ε_{1jt} and ε_{2jt} are permitted to be contemporaneously correlated and are assumed to be drawn from a multivariate normal distribution. Maximum likelihood procedures were applied to the unrestricted equations (9.12a) and (9.12b), and then increasingly restrictive constraints were imposed on their estimation. The first such constraint is that implied by equation (9.9a); namely, that across cities for a given group of union locals, $\gamma_{1j}/\beta_{1j} = E_{Lw}$, where E_{Lw} is the elasticity of the employment-wage trade-off constraint ($\partial \ln f/\partial \ln w$). Since this constraint involves the coefficients on the consumer price index, I call this "the cost-of-living constraint." The second set of constraints supplements this restriction with the restrictions implied by equation (9.9b) namely,

$$\begin{aligned} \gamma_{2j} &= E_{Lw}\beta_{2j} + E_{Lr_1}, \\ \gamma_{3j} &= E_{Lw}\beta_{3j} + E_{Lr_2}, \\ \gamma_{4j} &= E_{Lw}\beta_{4j} + E_{Lx}, \end{aligned} \tag{9.13}$$

where E_{Li} is the elasticity of employment with respect to the ith argument of the constraint function (9.2). Augmenting the cost-of-living constraint with the constraints in equations (9.13) results in a set of "multiple Fellner-Cartter constraints." Finally, suppose that the employment-wage constraint equation (9.2) is that appropriate for a cost-minimizing employer and, therefore, suppose that it is homogeneous of degree zero in all input prices (w, r_1, and r_2). This homogeneity restriction implies $E_{Lw} + E_{Lr_1} = -E_{Lr_2}$ and augmenting the "multiple Fellner-Cartter constraints" with this homogeneity constraint yields the full set of restrictions.

The consequences of this sequence of maximum likelihood estimations are summarized in table 9–6 where test statistics from the maximized likelihood functions are presented and in table 9–7 where the implied values of the employment-wage and other elasticities of the constraint equation are listed. (Appendix table 9–C presents other information describing the estimation of these equations.) The outcome of the (asymptotically exact) likelihood ratio tests are as follows. The imposition of the cost-of-living constraint cannot be rejected for the "small" union locals and for the "medium" union locals while it is rejected for the "large" locals.[31] For all three groups of unions, however, as is evident from table 9–7, imposing the cost-of-living constraint does imply a negative employment-wage constraint elasticity, which is estimated to be −2.22 for the "small" locals, −.74 for the "medium" locals, and −.68 for the "large" locals. The imposition of the multiple Fellner-Cartter constraints and then, in addition, of the homogeneity restrictions results for all three groups of union locals in an unambiguous rejection of these constraints. The fully restricted estimates (i.e., multiple Fellner-Cartter constraints plus homogeneity) of the constraint elasticities in table 9–7 are

Table 9-6. Summary Statistics from Maximum Likelihood Estimation of Equations (9.12a) and (9.12b)

	"Small" Locals	*"Medium" Locals*	*"Large" Locals*
Unconstrained estimates			
log. of likelihood function	206.8	219.6	327.9
Imposing cost-of-living constraint			
log. of likelihood function	205.9	219.5	319.4
no. of restricted coefficients	2	2	3
calculated chi-squared	1.88	0.32	17.05
critical chi-squared at 5% level	5.99	5.99	7.82
Imposing multiple Fellner-Cartter constraints			
log. of likelihood function	181.2	204.2	288.9
no. of restricted coefficients	8	8	12
calculated chi-squared	51.20	30.96	78.10
critical chi-squared at 5% level	15.51	15.51	21.03
Imposing multiple constraints plus homogeneity			
log. of likelihood function	177.6	193.0	245.8
no. of restricted coefficients	9	9	13
calculated chi-squared	58.36	53.22	164.23
critical chi-squared at 5% level	16.92	16.92	22.36

similar across the three groups of unions being negative between employment and wages (E_{Lw}), negative between employment and the price of newsprint (E_{Lr_1}), and positive between employment and output (E_{Lx}).

These results permit a number of different conclusions, depending on the predilection of the researcher. The judgment most damaging to the theory and yet fully defensible is that the description provided by the Fellner-Cartter model of the wages and employment of typographers in the newspaper industry is false. Once the full set of restrictions of the Fellner-Cartter model is imposed on the estimation of the wage and employment equations, there is no question that they are statistically rejected by them. To deny that this inference is fully legitimate is only a short step from rendering the model incapable of being falsified. Yet while legitimate, this conclusion is also severe. Also fully legitimate is to question the functional-form approximations that constitute the basis of the inferences drawn in this section.[32]

Table 9-7. Maximum Likelihood Estimates of the Elasticities of the Employment-Wage Constraint Equation

	"Small" Locals	*"Medium" Locals*	*"Large" Locals*
Imposing cost-of-living constraint			
E_{Lw}	−2.224*	−.742	−.677*
	(.950)	(.414)	(.232)
Imposing multiple Fellner-Cartter constraints			
E_{Lw}	−.055	.420*	1.874*
	(.108)	(.109)	(.261)
E_{Lr_1}	−.188	−.152	.219
	(.120)	(.087)	(.162)
E_{Lr_2}	.436*	.193*	−.829*
	(.110)	(.090)	(.190)
E_{Lx}	.060	.022	−.278*
	(.060)	(.050)	(.104)
Imposing multiple constraints plus homogeneity			
E_{Lw}	−.273*	−.192*	−.327*
	(.122)	(.084)	(.150)
E_{Lr_1}	−.375*	−.233*	−.084
	(.115)	(.116)	(.145)
E_{Lx}	.155*	.260*	.094
	(.056)	(.038)	(.071)

Notes: (1) Estimated asymptotic standard errors are in parentheses. (2) For ease of reading, an asterisk has been placed next to coefficients estimated to be more than 1.96 (in absolute value) their estimated asymptotic standard errors.

Furthermore, little prior evidence has been adduced to justify the grouping of the union locals and, if indeed each local is more different from the others than our estimating equations have allowed for, then the best strategy at this stage is probably to adopt a city-by-city analysis. This is exactly the approach to be pursued next.

Reduced-Form Estimation of the Stone-Geary Objective Function

In this section we estimate the reduced-form real-wage and employment equations that correspond to particular expressions for the union's objective function (9.1) and for the constraint trade-off equation (9.2). The specified objective function is known in the consumption literature as the Stone-Geary,

$$U\left(\frac{w}{p}, L\right) = \left(\frac{w}{p} - \gamma\right)^{\theta} (L - \delta)^{1-\theta}, \tag{9.14}$$

and has been used in the analysis of union objectives by Dertouzos (1979) and by Dertouzos and Pencavel (1981). Its appeal lies in the fact that it nests popular models of union behavior as special cases and that it can be augmented to accommodate other plausible objectives. For instance, Dunlop's (1944) objective of "maximization of the wage bill for the total membership" (p. 44) implies values for γ and δ of zero and a value for θ of .5. Or the rent maximization hypothesis requires δ to be zero, θ to be .5, and γ to be equal to the competitive wage rate. If γ and δ are interpreted as "reference" or "minimum" values of real wages and employment, then it might be appropriate to specify that these are not parametric constants, but rather are functions of other variables such as the non-union wage rate or lagged employment. The relative importance of wages and employment in the union's objectives is a function of all three parameters, θ, γ, and δ, and cannot be summarized in any one of them. The substitutability of wages for employment in the union's objective function is perhaps best summarized in the Hicks-Allen elasticity of substitution (σ), the expression for which in the Stone-Geary case is as follows:

$$\sigma = 1 - \left[\frac{\gamma(1-\theta)L + \delta\theta\left(\frac{w}{p}\right)}{\left(\frac{w}{p}\right).L}\right] \tag{9.15}$$

Since there is no necessity for γ or δ to be positive (although negative values of these parameters strain their interpretation as "reference" values), the elasticity of substitution for the Stone-Geary may be larger or smaller than unity.

The assumed specification for the employment-wage constraint is the following linear expression:

$$L = \alpha_0 + \alpha_1\left(\frac{w}{r_1}\right) + \alpha_2\left(\frac{r_2}{r_1}\right) + \alpha_3 X + \alpha_4 D, \tag{9.16}$$

which embodies the restriction that employment is homogeneous of degree zero in input prices. The negative trade-off between employment and wage implies α_1 is negative while, if labor is not an inferior input, then $\alpha_3 > 0$. The dichotomous variable, D, takes the value of unity when a newspaper merges with another (for the four cities in which a merger took place over these years); this parameterization is consistent with a merger resulting in a cost function different both in its intercept and in its slope with respect to each of its arguments. This linear-in-the-parameters labor demand function generates tractable estimating equations and yet corresponds to what is known about the production technology in the newspaper industry.[33]

The first-order condition for a maximum of equation (9.14) subject to equation (9.16) is:

$$\theta/(\theta - 1) = [\alpha_1(w - p\gamma)]/[r_1(L - \delta)],$$

which may be solved for the reduced-form real-wage and employment equations as follows:

$$\frac{w}{p} = (1 - \theta)\gamma + \frac{\theta(\delta - \alpha_0)}{\alpha_1}\left(\frac{r_1}{p}\right) - \frac{\theta\alpha_2}{\alpha_1}\left(\frac{r_2}{p}\right) - \frac{\theta\alpha_3}{\alpha_1}\left(\frac{X \cdot r_1}{p}\right) - \frac{\theta\alpha_4}{\alpha_1}\left(\frac{D \cdot r_1}{p}\right), \quad (9.17)$$

$$L = \alpha_0 + \theta(\delta - \alpha_0) + \alpha_1\gamma(1 - \theta)\left(\frac{p}{r_1}\right) + \alpha_2(1 - \theta)\left(\frac{r_2}{r_1}\right) + \alpha_3(1 - \theta)X + \alpha_4(1 - \theta)D. \quad (9.18)$$

These equations are homogeneous of degree zero in p, r_1, and r_2, and they suggest the positive association between firm size (X) and wages that is observed in the newspaper industry.[34] It is straightforward to check that unions with higher values for θ and γ will opt for higher wages and lower employment (other things equal) while unions with higher values of δ select lower wages and greater employment.

Table 9–8 contains maximum likelihood estimates of equations (9.17) and (9.18), on the assumption that the error terms of these equations are drawn from a multivariate normal distribution with mean zero.[35] Of the ten union locals, a well-defined unconstrained maximum to the likelihood function

Table 9-8. Maximum Likelihood Estimates of Equations (9.17) and (9.18)[a]

	θ	γ	δ	α_0	α_1
Cincinnati	.226	2.032	−153.02	217.05	−95.00
	(.085)	(.820)	(262.96)	(122.57)	(51.30)
Columbia	.612	2.239	75.08	−40.95	−92.60
	(.404)	(.825)	(37.97)	(51.29)	(145.65)
Dubuque	.191	1.602	32.612	5.45	−10.98
	(1.224)	(1.016)	(33.399)	(55.44)	(89.14)
Memphis	.256	2.964	232.20	−280.79	−94.04
	(.291)	(.832)	(167.49)	(103.89)	(137.21)
Memphis	.265	2.810[b]	200.89	−282.90	−100.50
	(.242)		(9.82)	(84.58)	(125.26)
Fond du Lac	.938	13.646	82.418	−174.08	−85.42
	(.069)	(8.088)	(9.284)	(177.83)	(79.65)
Fond du Lac	.878	2.280[b]	34.00[b]	−230.52	−105.60
	(.566)			(1108.73)	(561.78)
Columbus	.293	3.442	577.54	−268.84	−121.33
	(.295)	(.734)	(148.93)	(302.96)	(175.16)
Columbus	.359	2.820[b]	468.00[b]	−321.61	−153.55
	(.404)			(398.95)	(273.38)

[a]Estimated asymptotic standard errors are in parentheses.
[b]Constrained parameters.

exists for only six: Cincinnati, Columbia, Dubuque, Memphis, Fond du Lac, and Columbus. For the other four union locals, a maximum could be located for each if the values of certain parameters were constrained. To illustrate, the results in table 9–9 list the maximum likelihood estimates for these four unions under the restriction that $\theta = .5$. The problem is that the system of equations (9.17) and (9.18) is highly nonlinear in the parameters and there are relatively few degrees of freedom with which to estimate the coefficients with much confidence.[36] This is revealed by the poor precision with which these parameters are estimated. Of the six union locals for which an unconstrained maximum was determined, two (Fond du Lac and Columbus) yielded estimates of γ and δ that exceeded the minimum observed values of w/p and L, respectively, for these cities, while for another (Memphis) the estimated value of γ exceeded the minimum real wage observed. The objective function (9.14) is not defined under these circumstances[37];

α_2	α_3	α_4	σ	*DW* *ln(w/p)*	*DW* *lnL*	*log. likeli.*
1.344 (1.441)	3.161 (1.860)	90.59 (18.66)	.757 (.568)	0.47	1.55	−56.69
3.607 (3.743)	4.474 (2.240)		.272 (.318)	1.61	1.94	−24.58
0.628 (1.288)	4.628 (3.076)	.871 (3.553)	.434 (.359)	1.81	1.16	−16.03
9.356 (4.821)	5.302 (1.497)		.202 (.282)	1.07	0.92	−62.28
9.648 (4.638)	5.268 (1.476)		.260 (.045)	1.04	0.94	−62.35
4.517 (4.192)	12.866 (9.239)		−1.170 (.276)	1.85	1.36	−17.00
5.956 (28.656)	13.522 (53.906)		.178 (.033)	1.77	0.71	−30.90
11.860 (9.413)	7.727 (2.108)	30.26 (33.83)	.039 (.217)	1.37	1.90	−67.45
13.282 (13.471)	8.423 (3.194)	36.55 (44.18)	.216 (.004)	1.20	1.91	−70.55

equations (9.17) and (9.18) were therefore reestimated under the constraints that these parameters not exceed the minimum observed values of real wages and employment. The consequences of this constrained estimation for these three cities are also given in table 9–8, where the superscript c denotes restricted coefficients.

Of the three parameters describing the union's objective function, θ, γ, and δ, the "reference" wage parameter (γ) appears to be determined least imprecisely, with its estimated value tending to be lower in such cities as Dubuque with relatively low real wages. (See the descriptive statistics in table 9–2.) Similarly, the estimated values of δ tends to higher for larger union locals. These higher estimated values of γ and δ in larger cities with higher real wages incline one toward an interpretation of these parameters as indicating alternative wage and employment opportunities and toward a characterization in which each union local sets its wage and employment

Table 9-9. Maximum Likelihood Estimates of Equations (9.17) and (9.18)

	θ	γ	δ	α_0	α_1
Augusta	.500[c]	1.017	−17.61	−17.24	−56.55
		(.713)	(51.33)	(31.50)	(19.08)
Louisville	.500[c]	4.137	417.32	296.30	−42.59
		(2.460)	(75.87)	(123.97)	(66.34)
Elmira	.500[c]	2.822	106.17	−150.46	−62.49
		(1.073)	(50.40)	(67.40)	(19.21)
Albany	.500[c]	.046	144.72	359.59	−199.70
		(.880)	(229.13)	(197.65)	(94.92)

[a]Under constraint $\theta = .5$.
[b]Estimated asymptotic standard errors are in parentheses.
[c]Denotes constrained parameters.

goals with reference to these alternatives. On the other hand, these results may be an artifact of the posited functional forms since, in the consumer demand literature on the estimation of the Stone-Geary function, there is a tendency for the estimated values of each of the "subsistence" parameters (γ and δ in this case) to be associated with the observed levels of consumption of each commodity. The estimated values of θ range from a low of .19 for Dubuque to .94 for Fond du Lac. Only for Cincinnati can the hypothesis that θ differs from both zero and unity not be rejected at conventional levels of significance. The relatively poor precision with which these parameters of the union's objective function have been measured is reflected in the estimates given in Table 9.8 of the elasticity of substitution (σ) evaluated at the mean levels of real wages and employment for each union. Those estimates of σ significantly in excess of zero are in each case those estimates that correspond to the constrained fitting of the system of equations. Nevertheless, the fact that each of these objective function parameters is not estimated precisely does not mean that one may appropriately impose the parameter constraints implied by some convenient special cases. In particular, on conventional likelihood ratio tests, the constraints implied by the wage bill maximization hypothesis (that is, $\theta = .5$ and $\gamma = \delta = 0$) are decisively rejected by the data for all of the unions listed in table 9–8.[38]

The point estimates of the parameters of the labor demand function (9.16) are broadly comparable across union locals. In each and every case in tables 9–8 and 9–9, α_1 is negative and, moreover, with the exception of Dubuque,

α_2	α_3	α_4	σ	*DW* *ln(w/p)*	*DW* *lnL*	*log.* *likeli.*
2.248	2.301		.819	1.48	2.34	−20.94
(.292)	(.348)		(.127)			
1.278	2.667		.394	0.91	0.43	−63.74
(1.767)	(3.718)		(.361)			
5.341	3.628		540	0.62	1.16	−55.90
(.873)	(1.837)		(.175)			
10.497	−.081	80.35	.994	1.33	1.40	−79.98
(4.412)	(1.959)	(44.21)	(.117)			

α_1 possesses similar values for different unions. The implied wage elasticities of the demand for labor depend on the values of wages and employment at which they are evaluated and, if they are measured at the mean values for each union, then they range from −.29 for Dubuque to −5.16 for Fond du Lac. In all cases, α_2 is estimated to be positive as is α_3 except for Albany in table 9–9 where it possesses a negative sign (although it is clearly insignificantly different from zero).[39]

How important are these differences across union locals in the estimates of the parameters of the objective function and of the labor demand function constraint for the observed variations in real wages and employment? The numbers given in table 9–10 are designed toward answering this question, they present the values of real wages and employment predicted from the reduced-form equations (9.17) and (9.18) under different sets of assumptions about the values of parameters and the values of the variables. The reduced-form equations (9.17) and (9.18) may be written for union local j as

$$(w/p)_j = F_1(\theta_j,\ \gamma_j,\ \delta_j;\ \alpha_j;\ p,\ r_1,\ r_2,\ D_j,\ X_j),$$
$$L_j = F_2(\theta_j,\ \gamma_j,\ \delta_j;\ \alpha_j;\ p,\ r_1,\ r_2,\ D_j,\ X_j),$$

where α stands for the vector of coefficients in the labor demand function (9.16). Now consider inserting the average values of the exogenous variables for Cincinnati into these equations and also the values of the α parameters

Table 9-10. Using Estimates from table 9-8 to Predict Real Wages and Employment

	column (1) Actual Mean Values		*column (2)* Holding Constraint Equation (9.16) Fixed at Cincinnati's Values and Allowing θ, γ, and δ to Vary Across Locals		*column (3)* Holding θ, γ, and δ Fixed at Cincinnati's Estimates and Letting Constraint (9.16) Vary Across Locals		*column (4)* Holding All parameters Fixed at Values Estimated for Cincinnati and Allowing X to Vary Across Locals	
	real wage	*employment*	*real wage*	*employment*	*real wage*	*employment*	*real wage*	*employment*
Cincinnati	3.51	172	3.50	169	3.50	169	3.50	169
Columbia	2.99	105	3.90	143	3.20	97	3.62	180
Dubuque	2.73	68	2.37	241	8.94	23	3.46	145
Memphis[a]	3.46	323	2.86	209	3.95	294	3.83	227
Fond du Lac[a]	2.96	41	5.19	58	2.88	53	3.44	142
Columbus[a]	3.58	602	1.39	304	4.03	558	3.92	247

[a]For the Memphis, Fond du Lac, and Columbus union locals, the values of the parameters in table 9–8 used in forming these predictions are those corresponding to the restricted estimates.

actually estimated for Cincinnati, but allow the parameters of the union's objective function to vary across the union locals according to their values actually estimated in table 9–8. Then, for each union local, we have an estimate of the levels of real wages and employment that other unions would have selected when faced with Cincinnati's constraints:

$$(\widehat{w/p})_j = F_1(\theta_j,\ \gamma_j,\ \delta_j;\ \bar{\alpha};\ \bar{p},\ \bar{r}_1,\ \bar{r}_2,\ \bar{D},\ \bar{X}),$$
$$\hat{L}_j = F_2(\theta_j,\ \gamma_j,\ \delta_j;\ \bar{\alpha};\ \bar{p},\ \bar{r}_1,\ \bar{r}_2,\ \bar{D},\ \bar{X}),$$

where the bar denotes parameters and variables held constant at their values for Cincinnati. These predicted values of real wages and employment, given in column (2) of table 9–10, indicate, for example, that, if the Columbia local had been faced with Cincinnati's constraints, it would have opted for a higher real wage ($3.90 instead of $3.50) and a lower level of employment (143 instead of 169) than Cincinnati actually selected. The predictions in column (2) indicate that the estimates in table 9–8 of the objective function parameters across different union locals imply a wide range of real wages and employment over cities, a much wider range of real wages and a smaller range of employment than is actually observed. (The observed average values of real wages and employment are given in column (1) of table 9–10.) Since in this conceptual experiment the constraint equation (9.16) is being held fixed, any union local opting for a higher real wage than that chosen by the Cincinnati local must simultaneously experience less employment.

Consider now the implications for real wages and employment of the differences in the constraint (9.16) by holding the objective function parameters θ, γ, and δ constant at their values estimated for Cincinnati and by allowing the α parameters and the average values of the exogenous variables to take on their values for the other union locals. This yields predictions of the real wages and employment implied by the Cincinnati union local's objective function when presented with the constraints faced by other unions:

$$(\widehat{w/p})_j = F_1(\bar{\theta},\ \bar{\gamma},\ \bar{\delta};\ \alpha_j;\ p_j,\ r_{1j},\ r_{2j},\ D_j,\ X_j),$$
$$\hat{L}_j = F_2(\bar{\theta},\ \bar{\gamma},\ \bar{\delta};\ \alpha_j;\ p_j,\ r_{1j},\ r_{2j},\ D_j,\ X_j),$$

where the bar denotes parameters held constant at their values estimated for Cincinnati. These predicted values of real wages and employment are given in column (3) of table 9–10. The entry for Columbia, for example, indicates that, if the Columbia local had Cincinnati's objective function parameters, then when presented with its actual constraint, the Columbia local would have opted for a higher wage ($3.20 instead of $2.99) and a lower employment (97 instead of 105) than it actually selected. With the exception of the predictions for Dubuque, which are essentially the consequence of the unusual set of estimates for the α coefficients for this union local, the range of real wages and employment predicted by this conceptual experiment is comparable with that actually observed.

Finally, the predictions in column (4) are designed toward assessing the impact of firm size on real wages and employment since the existence of an association between firm size on the one hand and real wages and employment on the other hand is well-known in the newspaper industry. Consider holding the objective function parameters (θ, γ, and δ), the labor demand function parameters (α), and the values of the exogenous variables other than output (namely, the variables p, r_1, r_2, and D) constant at their estimated values or their mean levels for Cincinnati. And then allow X to take on its average value for the other union locals. This yields predictions of the real wages and employment implied by the Cincinnati union local's objective function and by its structural labor demand function when presented with different levels of output to produce:

$$(\widehat{w/p})_j = F_1(\bar{\theta}, \bar{\gamma}, \bar{\delta}; \bar{\alpha}; \bar{p}, \bar{r}_1, \bar{r}_2, \bar{D}, X_j),$$
$$\hat{L}_j = F_2(\bar{\theta}, \bar{\gamma}, \bar{\delta}; \bar{\alpha}; \bar{p}, \bar{r}_1, \bar{r}_2, \bar{D}, X_j),$$

where the bar denotes parameters and variables held constant at their Cincinnati values. The output-related real wage and employment predictions are given in column (4) of table 9–10. The mean value of the linage variable that indexes output is 6.5 times greater for Columbus than it is for Fond du Lac, yet the real wage difference implied by this range of output is only 14 percent, ($3.92/$3.44) and the employment difference is 74 percent (247/142). In other words, our results indicate that very much more is at work in producing differences in real wages and employment across these cities than the size of the newspaper firm.

The predictions in table 9–10 make use of the point estimates of the parameters given in table 9–8, but as has been emphasized already and as is evident from inspection of the estimated standard errors in table 9–8, many of these coefficients are not estimated with much precision. A natural issue to consider, therefore, is whether these parameters are sufficiently imprecise to justify a judicious aggregation across union locals. By avoiding a categorization that lumps large unions with small unions (such as grouping Columbus and Columbia) and by not grouping unions whose point estimates in table 9–8 appear quite disparate (such as Fond du Lac and Dubuque), I investigated the consequences of pooling the data across pairs of the six unions whose estimates are reported in table 9–8. The three pairs of unions chosen for analysis are Dubuque with Cincinnati, Fond du Lac with Columbia, and Columbus with Memphis. Of course, this represents only a subset of the 15 possible pairs that can be formed from the six unions in table 9–8, but computational expense requires some prior decision about the particular subset to examine of the total number of feasible combinations. Since a causal inspection of the results suggested that the estimates for the Cincinnati and Dubuque pair resembled those for the Columbus and Memphis pair, I also pooled the data for these four unions.

The information in table 9–11 is relevant to conducting likelihood ratio tests of hypotheses concerning which sets of parameters are insignificantly different from one another across union locals. The notation $\ell(.)$ means the value of the sample log-likelihood function under the parameter constraints (.); thus, for instance, $\ell(0)$ corresponds to no parameter constraints, while $\ell(\theta, \gamma, \delta, \alpha_1, \alpha_2, \alpha_3)$ indicates constraints on all the parameters θ, γ, δ, α_1, α_2, and α_3 across the union locals. According to line 1 of table 9–11, the restrictions of a common employment-wage constraint cannot be rejected at the 1 percent level for any of the three pairs of unions although these restrictions would be rejected for Cincinnati and Dubuque and for Fond du Lac and Columbia at the 5 percent level of significance, and they would also be rejected for the group of four unions at both levels of significance. The next lines inquire into the consequences of imposing restrictions on the objective function parameters. Restricting θ and γ to be the same across unions seems innocuous, but constraints on the δ parameter are less warranted. Perhaps if union locals more similar in size had been combined, the δ parameter restrictions would have appeared less demanding. Line 6 of table 9–11 indicates that restricting all three objective function parameters to be the same cannot be rejected for Cincinnati and Dubuque, but is resoundingly rejected for the other two pairs of unions and for the group of four union locals. For all three pairs of unions, the hypothesis of common objective function parameters and common labor demand function parameters is manifestly inconsistent with the data as they are for the group of four union locals. The conclusion must be that, although some careful and prudent pooling of the union locals may be justified, at the present state of knowledge this is a hazardous procedure and for most purposes the objective functions of these unions are not sufficiently alike to enable us to treat them as a homogenous group.

Table 9-11. Test Statistics for Parameter Constraints Across Union Locals[a]

Line		*Cincinnati and Dubuque*	*Fond du Lac[c] and Columbia*	*Columbus and Memphis*
1	$-2[\ell(0) - \ell(\alpha_1,\alpha_2,\alpha_3)]$[b]	8.97 (3)	8.58 (3)	7.00 (3)
2	$-2[\ell(0) - \ell(\theta)]$	.01 (1)	.00 (1)	.00 (1)
3	$-2[\ell(0) - \ell(\theta,\gamma)]$	.02 (2)	.01 (2)	.70 (2)
4	$-2[\ell(0) - \ell(\theta,\delta)]$	2.88 (2)	3.83 (2)	7.38 (2)
5	$-2[\ell(0) - \ell(\gamma,\delta)]$	6.14 (2)	38.72 (2)	24.36 (2)
6	$-2[\ell(0) - \ell(\theta,\gamma,\delta)]$	7.57 (3)	38.73 (3)	24.92 (3)
7	$-2[\ell(0) - \ell(\theta,\gamma,\delta,\alpha_1,\alpha_2\alpha_3)]$	35.72 (6)	118.10 (6)	72.94 (6)

[a]The number of restricted parameters is given in parantheses following the calculated test statistics.

[b]The notation $\ell(.)$ indicates the value of the sample log-likelihood function under the parameter constraints (.).

[c]The estimates for the pooled Fond du Lac and Columbia sample were fitted throughout under the binding constraint that γ and δ for Fond du Lac not exceed the minimum observed levels of real wages and employment, respectively.

Estimation of the Marginal Rate of Substitution Equation from an Addilog Objective Function

The third empirical procedure applied to the Fellner-Cartter model of unionism is based on the marginal rate of substitution equation (9.3): For a maximum, the union sets the marginal rate of substitution between wages and employment in its objective function equal to the slope of the trade-off between employment and wages in the constraint equation. The advantage of fitting the marginal rate of substitution equation is that it provides information on the union's objective function without having to solve for the wage and employment reduced-form equations, which we have seen from the previous section may prove awkward to estimate. In particular, consider the following expression for the union's objectives:

$$U\left(\frac{w}{p}, L\right) = \mu(1+\lambda)^{-1}\left[\left(\frac{w}{p}\right)^{1+\lambda} - 1\right]$$

$$+ (1-\mu)(1+\eta)^{-1}(L^{1+\eta} - 1)$$

Critical values of Chi-Squared			*Critical values of Chi-Squared*	
5% level	*1% level*	*Cincinnati, Dubuque, Memphis, and Columbus*	*5% level*	*1% level*
7.81	11.35	49.78 (9)	16.92	21.67
3.84	6.34	.66 (3)	7.81	11.34
5.99	9.21	7.74 (6)	12.59	16.81
5.99	9.21	23.18 (6)	12.59	16.81
5.99	9.21	60.34 (6)	12.59	16.81
7.81	11.35	62.16 (9)	16.92	21.67
12.59	16.81	227.04 (18)	28.87	34.81

$$= k + \mu(1 + \lambda)^{-1} \left(\frac{w}{p}\right)^{1+\lambda} + (1 - \mu)(1 + \eta)^{-1} L^{1+\eta}, \tag{9.19}$$

where $k = -[\mu(1 + \lambda)^{-1} + (1 - \mu)(1 + \eta)^{-1}]$ and where the parameters μ, λ, and η satisfy the following restrictions:

$$0 \leq \mu \leq 1;\ \lambda < 0;\ \text{and } \eta < 0. \tag{9.20}$$

This strongly separable function goes by the name of the addilog and specializes to a transformation of the CES function when $\lambda = \eta$ and, a fortiori of the Cobb-Douglas function, when $\lambda = \eta = -1$. Here the maximization of the wage bill would imply $\lambda = \eta = -1$ and $\mu = .5$. The elasticity of substitution (σ) between wages and employment is given by the following expression:

$$\sigma = -\left[\frac{\mu\left(\frac{w}{p}\right)^{1+\lambda} + (1 - \mu)L^{1+\eta}}{\lambda(1 - \mu)L^{1+\eta} + \eta\mu\left(\frac{w}{p}\right)^{1+\lambda}}\right],$$

which collapses to $-1/s$ when $\lambda = \eta = s$. Like the expression for the elasticity of substitution for the Stone-Geary function, equation (9.15), this equation for the elasticity of substitution for the addilog function reveals that the union's preferences for wages vis-à-vis employment cannot be described fully by a single parameter and that the value of the substitution elasticity depends on the particular combination of wages and employment being evaluated.

With this addilog objective function, the natural logarithm of the marginal rate of substitution equation (9.3) is as follows:

$$\lambda \ell n w - \ell n \left(\frac{1-\mu}{\mu} \right) - (1+\lambda) \ell n p - \eta \ell n L = \ell n (-f_w),$$

where, as before, f_w is the (negative) slope of employment-wage constraint, equation (9.2). The empirical implementation of this equation requires an expression for the slope of the employment-wage constraint, and this we have assumed to be $-f_w = e^{\alpha X}/r_1$. This equation is broadly consistent with the labor demand function in the previous section insofar as the slope of the employment-wage trade-off is a function of the price of newsprint (r_1), although in this case this slope is also permitted to depend upon output (X). Note also that, at the moment, the slope of employment-wage constraint maintains the hypothesis of homogeneity of degree minus one in input prices.[40] Therefore, with this specification for the slope of the employment-wage constraint, the marginal rate of substitution equation may be written

$$\ell n \left(\frac{w}{p} \right) = \frac{1}{\lambda} \ell n \left(\frac{1-\mu}{\mu} \right) + \frac{1}{\lambda} \ell n \left(\frac{p}{r_1} \right) + \frac{\eta}{\lambda} \ell n L + \frac{\alpha}{\lambda} X, \tag{9.21}$$

the stochastic form of which may be fitted by nonlinear two-stage least squares (Amemiya, 1974) where ℓnL is treated as endogenous.[41] The resulting estimates of the parameters μ, λ, η, and α and the implied elasticity of substitution σ are contained in table 9–12 for nine of the ten union locals. (The estimates of μ for Columbus were not defined, and so we omit this union from the table.) It is evident that by no means are all the sign restrictions required for concavity of the objective function satisfied: In three out of nine cases, λ is estimated to be positive; in four cases, η is estimated to be positive; and in three cases, the elasticity of substitution (σ) at mean values of real wages and employment for each union is negative (although only for Fond du Lac would this estimate of σ be judged as "significantly"

Table 9-12. Estimates of the Marginal Rate of Substitution Equation (9.21)[a]

	μ^b	λ^c	η^c	α^d	σ^e	See^a	DW^a
Cincinnati	.910	−2.146*	.167	−.045*	.469*	.030	1.32
	(.060)	(.507)	(.141)	(.013)	(.111)		
Augusta	.334*	−.701*	−.304	.008*	1.460*	.047	1.91
	(.126)	(.267)	(.200)	(.004)	(.561)		
Columbia	.0016	−4.407	−3.258	−.014	.228	.028	2.35
	(.0012)	(2.437)	(2.111)	(.020)	(.126)		
Dubuque	.471	−2.906*	−.330	−.134	.346*	.031	1.62
	(.524)	(1.230)	(.605)	(.081)	(.148)		
Memphis	.981	5.978	1.721	.042	−.172	.025	1.88
	(.077)	(4.742)	(1.497)	(.028)	(.131)		
Fond du Lac	.941*	.393	.912	.023	−2.367	.086	1.57
	(.025)	(.116)	(.151)	(.017)	(.653)		
Louisville	.787	2.986	.378	.071	−.373	.049	1.39
	(1.434)	(5.918)	(1.255)	(.135)	(.489)		
Elmira	.086	−.854	−.695	.024*	1.177	.089	0.81
	(.135)	(.485)	(.463)	(.010)	(.670)		
Albany	.006	−3.008	−1.856	−.034	.332	.058	1.42
	(.005)	(3.059)	(1.642)	(.049)	(.339)		

[a]Standard errors are in parentheses, and an asterisk has been placed next to coefficients to indicate approximate significance. The standard error of the regression is given by *See* and the Durbin-Watson Statistic by *DW*.

[b]The asterisk on the μ coefficients denote parameters estimated to be significantly different from both zero and unity at the 5 percent level.

[c]The asterisks on λ and η denote coefficients significantly less than zero at the 5 percent level.

[d]The asterisk on α denotes coefficients significantly different from zero at the 5 percent level.

[e]The asterisk on σ indicates coefficients significantly greater than zero at the 5 percent level.

less than zero). In five cases (Augusta, Columbia, Dubuque, Elmira, and Albany), all sign restrictions (9.20) are satisfied. In these cases, the parameter μ gauging the weight placed on wages relative to employment in the union's objective function is closer to zero than to unity though the standard errors do not permit confident inferences.[42]

It is important to report that a number of variations on this estimation procedure were applied to equation (9.21). First, the output variable (X) was treated as endogenous; the results are listed in appendix table 9–D.[43] Second, equation (9.21) was fitted in first-difference form (year-to-year changes) and allowance was made for a linear time trend in equation (9.22). Third, the constraint that the slope of the employment-wage constraint (f_w) be homogeneous of degree minus unity in input prices was relaxed. Fourth, the objective function parameters were permitted to differ before and after a merger was recorded in these years. In all these cases, the estimates of the parameters of the objective function did not differ in any substantive sense from those reported in table 9–12.

Another line of inquiry took the form of generalizing equation (9.19) by introducing a benchmark (υ) for the real wage variable in the objective function:

$$U\left(\frac{w}{p}, L\right) = k + \mu(1+\lambda)^{-1}\left(\frac{w}{p} - \upsilon\right)^{1+\lambda} + (1-\mu)(1+\eta)^{-1}L^{1+\eta}. \tag{9.22}$$

This modification, which I shall call the "augmented addilog," was induced, in part, by the estimates reported previously of the Stone-Geary function in which the real wage reference parameter (γ) appeared to be the most precisely estimated of all the three objective function parameters. The elasticity of substitution (σ) between wages and employment in the union's objective function for this augmented addilog takes the following form:

$$\sigma = -\left[\frac{\mu\left(\frac{w}{p} - \upsilon\right)^{\lambda}\left(\frac{w}{p}\right) + (1-\mu)L^{1+\eta}}{\lambda(1-\mu)\left(\frac{w}{p} - \upsilon\right)^{-1}\left(\frac{w}{p}\right)L^{1+\eta} + \eta\mu\left(\frac{w}{p} - \upsilon\right)^{\lambda}\left(\frac{w}{p}\right)}\right]$$

Suppose, in addition, that this benchmark value of real wages (υ) is not a fixed constant, but is instead a constant proportion of the real wages of another group of workers, say, $\upsilon = \beta(w^a/p)$. Then the logarithm of the marginal rate of substitution equation may be written:

$$\ell n\left(\frac{w}{p}\right) = \ell n\left\{\beta\left(\frac{w^a}{p}\right) + \exp\left[\frac{1}{\lambda}\ell n\left(\frac{1-\mu}{\mu}\right) + \frac{1}{\lambda}\ell n\left(\frac{p}{r_1}\right) + \frac{\eta}{\lambda}\ell n L + \frac{\alpha}{\lambda}X\right]\right\}, \tag{9.23}$$

whose stochastic form may again be fitted by nonlinear two-stage least squares with employment endogenous.[44] To serve as a comparison wage series (w^a), I used both the average hourly earnings of nonsupervisory workers in the retail trade (who are almost wholly nonunionized) and the average hourly earnings of production workers in the U.S. manufacturing industry. Since these two series move together over the years from 1946 to 1965, operationally there is little material difference between which of the two wage variables is used. The results in table 9–13 correspond to the estimates of equation (9.23) where w^a measures the wage of retail trade workers. These estimates of the augmented addilog are a slight improvement over those in table 9.12 in that a negative estimate of the elasticity of substitution is now obtained just once (for Fond du Lac). However, there is a disturbingly large number of instances in which η is estimated to be positive. In all but two cases, β is insignificantly different from unity (so that the hypothesis that the benchmark level of real wages is equal to w^a/p cannot be rejected in these cases), although clearly a wide range of parameter values is consistent with the estimates.

In an attempt to increase the information available to measure these parameters without at the same time imposing unjustifiable constraints on the coefficients, the six union locals in table 9–12 with positive estimated values of the elasticity of substitution were grouped into three pairs. The pairs (Cincinnati with Dubuque, Columbia with Albany, Augusta with Elmira) were selected on the basis of the similarity of their point estimates in table 9–12. Equations (9.21) and (9.23) were then fitted to each of the three pairs of union locals as well as to all six combined; the resulting estimates are contained in table 9–14. These estimates are more encouraging for the application of the model: The sign restrictions (9.20) on λ and η are not satisfied in only 4 out of 16 cases. For only Cincinnati and Dubuque would the null hypothesis $\beta=0$ not be rejected by conventional criteria; for the other unions, β is not significantly different from unity. Consequently, the unaugmented addilog provides an adequate description of Cincinnati and Dubuque's objective function, while the augmented addilog offers a considerably better fit to the data and more plausible parameter estimates for Columbia and Albany and for Augusta and Elmira. The estimates of the augmented addilog for the pooled six unions in the last row of table 9–14 imply a value for the elasticity of substitution that is significantly greater than zero, but less than unity.

The procedure applied in this section of estimating the marginal rate of substitution function has the advantage of not requiring us to specify the entire employment-wage constraint, but requiring only a specification for its slope in the employment-wage plane. However, the consequence now is that

Table 9-13. Estimates of the Marginal Rate of Substitution Equation(9.23)[a]

	β^b	μ	λ	η	α	σ	*See*	*DW*
Cincinnati	.260*	.904	−2.125*	.210	−.044*	.416*	.031	1.17
	(.361)	(.072)	(.579)	(.184)	(.015)	(.134)		
Augusta	1.146	.561	−.322	.135	.003	1.158*	.038	1.76
	(1.031)	(.336)	(.462)	(.495)	(.008)	(.511)		
Columbia	1.498	.859	−.305	.568	−.011	.562*	.026	1.32
	(.668)	(.379)	(.758)	(.709)	(.008)	(.202)		
Dubuque	.336	.524	−2.163*	−.064	−.101	.372*	.031	1.64
	(.314)	(.425)	(1.075)	(.544)	(.067)	(.150)		
Memphis	1.351	.998	−2.040	1.261	−.027	.173	.021	1.73
	(.660)	(.011)	(4.414)	(1.021)	(.045)	(.234)		
Fond du Lac	1.371	.985	.349	1.172	.009	−.669	.049	1.71
	(.453)	(.028)	(.228)	(.471)	(.037)	(.605)		
Louisville	.862	.989	−1.261	.870	−.025	.464	.033	1.66
	(.213)	(.026)	(1.203)	(.426)	(.027)	(.422)		
Elmira	1.765*	.999	−1.173	4.353	−.440	.060	.036	1.50
	(.109)	(.002)	(10.113)	(43.323)	(4.631)	(.539)		
Columbus	.357	.001	−7.720	−6.439	.018	.108	.029	1.12
	(.526)	(.006)	(15.308)	(13.723)	(.036)	(.192)		

[a]Standard errors are in parentheses, and an asterisk has been placed next to coefficients to indicate approximate significance.

[b]The asterisk on the β coefficients denotes parameters estimated to be significantly different from unity at the 5 percent level. The asterisks on the other parameters follow the description provided beneath table 9–12.

Table 9-14. Estimates of the Marginal Rate of Substitution Equations (9.21) and (9.23)[a]

	β	μ	λ	η	α	σ	See
		.607*	−1.813*	−.175	−.029	.557*	.048
Cincinnati	0[b]	(.130)	(.389)	(.146)	(.014)	(.120)	
and							
Dubuque	.146*	.495*	−1.862*	−.267	−.024	.501*	.048
	(.189)	(.216)	(.451)	(.213)	(.017)	(.141)	
		.986	−6.605	.179	−.145	.151	.060
Columbia	0[b]	(.087)	(9.010)	(.346)	(.215)	(.207)	
and							
Albany	1.141	.257*	−1.134*	−.128*	−.010	.361*	.024
	(.106)	(.043)	(.355)	(.029)	(.008)	(.091)	
		.713*	.459	.288	.030*	−2.211	.175
Augusta	0[b]	(.079)	(.376)	(.134)	(.010)	(1.785)	
and							
Elmira	1.606	.519	−.130	.088	.011	1.018	.046
	(.557)	(.242)	(.490)	(.139)	(.013)	(1.510)	
		.479*	−.869*	−.162*	.005	1.162*	.116
All six	0[b]	(.068)	(.168)	(.056)	(.005)	(.224)	
unions							
together	1.181	.236*	−.723*	−.211*	.007	.525*	.074
	(.137)	(.062)	(.230)	(.083)	(.009)	(.178)	

[a]Standard errors in parentheses and the meaning of the asterisks is explained in the notes to tables 9–12 and 9–13.
[b]Constrained values and corresponds to fitting equation (9.21).

we lack the information to solve for the reduced-form wage and employment equations and to conduct the sort of simulation exercises described in the previous section with the Stone-Geary objective function and with the linear employment-wage constraint. The material in this section that can be compared with that in the previous section concerns the characteristics of the union's objective function. Perhaps the best summary piece of information here is provided by the estimated value of the elasticity of substitution (σ) between wages and employment, a unit-free measure of the curvature of the union's indifference curve. As given in table 9–14, for the augmented addilog objective function and calculated at the observed mean levels of the variables, σ is estimated to be .501 for Cincinnati and Dubuque, .361 for Columbia and Albany, 1.018 for Augusta and Elmira, and .525 for all these six unions combined. These estimates appear to be significantly greater than zero and less than unity for all but the Augusta and Elmira group. By contrast, when the Stone-Geary objective function is fitted to the pairs of union listed in table 9–11, the elasticity of substitution is estimated to be .127 for Cincinnati and Dubuque with an estimated standard error of .028, to be .299 (.056) for Fond du Lac and Columbia, and .589 (.173) for Columbus and Memphis.[45] Without meaning to imply that differences among these union locals can be safely ignored, there appears to be a central tendency for the elasticity of substitution to lie between zero and unity.

Conclusions

This chapter has explored the implications of a popular model of trade unionism, the modified Fellner-Cartter model. Its empirical performance warrants an equivocal assessment. If the ultimate goal is a comprehensive and flawless explanation for the pattern of wages and employment in unionized labor markets, then in its application here to typographers in the newspaper industry the model clearly falls short of this ideal. In too many instances, the parameter estimates have been implausible (such as negative values for the elasticity of substitution between wages and employment in the union's objective function) or the model's qualitative implications have not been satisfied to justify a glowing evaluation of the model's empirical relevance. At the same time, on a sufficient number of occasions, the model has yielded meaningful and useful results to merit its further investigation. In general, these results suggest that the ITU's objectives cannot be associated with wage rates alone or with employment alone or with the wage bill, but that wages and employment enter as arguments of a more general objective function. One important feature of this more general objective function (as indicated by the estimates of the Stone-Geary and augmented addilog functions) is the notion that the union sets its wage rate with references to some benchmark level. The central tendency of our estimates of the elasticity of substitution is a value of .5, which indicates that the ITU's preferences reveal quite restricted opportunities for substituting wages for employment just as Cartter (1959) conjectured.[46] However, a high degree of confidence should not be attached to these point estimates. The problem has been that there are relatively few underlying observations on each union local with which to derive precise estimates of the relevant parameters, while an aggregation over union locals to achieve greater degrees of freedom imposes more homogeneity on the structural relationship than appears justified.

Implementing the Fellner-Cartter model requires, of course, specifications for the behavioral relationships, the union's objective function and the employment-wage constraint (or the first derivatives of both functions). Therefore, an evaluation of the empirical performance of the model tacitly involves jointly appraising both functions. In this respect, the research here gives the appearance of being qualitatively different from analogous work in the literature on estimating systems of consumer demand functions (or systems of input demand functions for the firm) where the researcher presumes complete knowledge of all variables in the budget constraint which is usually written as linearly homogeneous in prices and total expenditures. In fact, these formal differences between the model estimated here and the consumer's budget allocation problem are more apparent than real because the researcher is in truth not fully cognizant of the form of the consumer's budget constraint—which is likely to be nonlinear, if not nonconvex, owing to nonlinear price schedules, nonconstant income tax and welfare benefit rates, differential borrowing and lending rates of interest, and constraints on purchases and sales. These problems in specifying the effective budget constraints of families are receiving greater attention in empirical research in the consumption literature. In so doing, these models bear an increasingly formal resemblance to the Fellner-Cartter model outlined in this chapter, in which components of the constraint function are unknown to the researcher.

The agenda for further research is large. First, the relevance of the model for other unions needs to be determined. Second, the characterization of the model here has ignored several potentially important problems. For instance, job security provisions in union contracts have not been taken into account explicity (although they may be implicitly represented in the employment-wage constraint). The model has been outlined here in an entirely static framework, whereas the union's objective function and the employment-wage constraint surely involve intertemporal substitution possibilities. And only passing attention has been paid to uncertainty. No reason exists why the Fellner-Cartter model cannot be extended to accommodate these factors, but it is work that has yet to be accomplished. Third, other classes of union-management models propose different wage and employment outcomes. The empirical performance of these models also needs to be examined and to be contrasted with the Fellner-Cartter model. The outcome of all this research should be a much better understanding of the pattern of wages, employment, and other characteristics of unionized labor markets. In this event, George Johnson's next survey of trade unionism should be in a position to report a much more favorable assessment of behavioral models of unions than did his previous survey (1975).

Table 9-A. Ordinary Least Squares Estimates of Equation (9.11a)

	β_0	β_2	β_3	β_4	β_5	R^2	DW
Cincinnati	.262	.087	−.025	.260	−.034	.987	1.62
	(1.098)	(.245)	(.212)	(.102)	(.032)		
Augusta	−3.477	.862	.150	−.097		.985	2.11
	(1.979)	(.458)	(.219)	(.132)			
Columbia	−2.038	−.026	.572	.230		.987	1.67
	(1.045)	(.168)	(.206)	(.111)			
Dubuque	−3.573	−.003	.608	.746	−.004	.993	2.10
	(.813)	(.132)	(.147)	(.131)	(.016)		
Memphis	−.296	−.411	.543	.315		.982	1.45
	(.911)	(.199)	(.191)	(.117)			
Fond du Lac	−3.515	−.780	1.698	.380		.977	1.77
	(1.713)	(.284)	(.334)	(.262)			
Louisville	−.732	−.088	.017	.637		.971	1.84
	(1.148)	(.256)	(.294)	(.148)			
Elmira	−.086	−.030	.394	−.086		.983	1.58
	(1.757)	(.324)	(.260)	(.150)			
Columbus	.080	−.384	.588	.129	.044	.984	1.68
	(.950)	(.226)	(.246)	(.139)	(.023)		
Albany	−3.405	.303	.728	−.059	.077	.984	1.58
	(1.463)	(.293)	(.224)	(.131)	(.037)		

Note: Estimated standard errors are in parentheses.

Table 9-B. Ordinary Least Squares Estimates of Equation (9.11b)

	γ_0	γ_2	γ_3	γ_4	γ_5	R^2	DW
Cincinnati	.311	.353	.498	.209	.406	.980	1.64
	(1.944)	(.434)	(.375)	(.181)	(.057)		
Augusta	.064	−.572	1.266	.353		.932	2.69
	(2.606)	(.603)	(.288)	(.174)			
Columbia	1.360	−.300	.847	.308		.929	1.84
	(1.357)	(.218)	(.268)	(.144)			
Dubuque	4.179	−.379	.453	.027	−.004	.931	1.64
	(1.389)	(.225)	(.250)	(.225)	(.027)		
Memphis	3.093	−.312	1.009	−.047		.964	1.26
	(1.094)	(.239)	(.230)	(.141)			
Fond du Lac	−3.598	.863	.659	.007		.877	1.50
	(1.649)	(.273)	(.321)	(.253)			
Louisville	.383	.745	.570	−.208		.905	1.85
	(.516)	(.115)	(.132)	(.067)			
Elmira	−3.948	−.170	2.138	−.101		.892	1.76
	(2.138)	(.395)	(.317)	(.182)			
Columbus	4.538	−.336	.563	.268	.026	.960	2.07
	(.845)	(.201)	(.219)	(.124)	(.020)		
Albany	9.772	−760	.285	−.203	−.023	.729	1.73
	(2.194)	(.439)	(.335)	(.196)	(.055)		

Note: Estimated standard errors are in parentheses.

Table 9-C. Other Summary Statistics from Maximum Likelihood Estimation of Equations (9.12a) and (9.12b)

	"Small" Locals	*"Medium" Locals*	*"Large" Locals*
Mean of ℓnw	.850	.917	1.030
Standard deviation of ℓnw	.263	.244	.212
Mean of ℓnL	4.246	4.629	6.135
Standard deviation of ℓnL	.462	.497	.298
Imposing no constraints			
DW (ℓnw)	1.74	1.81	1.65
DW (ℓnL)	1.64	1.99	1.66
see (ℓnw)	.032	.026	.029
see (ℓnL)	.037	.038	.031
Imposing cost-of-living constraint			
DW (ℓnw)	1.69	1.82	1.47
DW (ℓnL)	1.64	1.95	1.46
see (ℓnw)	.033	.026	.030
see (ℓnL)	.038	.038	.034
Imposing multiple Fellner-Cartter constraints			
DW (ℓnw)	1.13	1.83	.079
DW (ℓnL)	0.65	1.56	1.37
see (ℓnw)	.040	.026	.043
see (ℓnL)	.061	.050	.035
Imposing multiple constraints plus homogeneity			
DW (ℓnw)	0.85	1.60	0.71
DW (ℓnL)	0.57	0.91	0.21
see (ℓnw)	.046	.030	.043
see (ℓnL)	.065	.060	.086

Appendix Table 9-D. Estimates of the Marginal Rate of Substitution Equation (9-21) Treating Output as Endogenous

	μ	λ	η	α	σ	*see*	*DW*
Cincinnati	.891	−2.192	.103	−.041*	.459*	.030	1.15
	(.068)	(.520)	(.144)	(.013)	(.110)		
Augusta	.357*	−.636*	−.264	.009	1.610	.046	1.83
	(.119)	(.311)	(.191)	(.005)	(.794)		
Columbia	.0028	−4.534	−3.130	−.022	.221	.028	2.29
	(.0019)	(2.556)	(2.052)	(.024)	(.125)		
Dubuque	.212	−2.855*	−.660	−.108	.353*	.032	1.56
	(.347)	(1.206)	(.627)	(.072)	(.151)		
Memphis	.999	12.301	4.497	.054	−.085	.025	1.77
	(.008)	(22.841)	(8.764)	(.079)	(.147)		
Fond du Lac	.941*	.499	.909	.040	1.905	.075	1.36
	(.029)	(.143)	(.176)	(.021)	(.520)		
Elmira	.118	−.758	−.602	.024*	1.326	.089	0.88
	(.157)	(.450)	(.408)	(.009)	(.789)		
Albany	.001	−3.670	−1.901	−.046	.273	.056	1.35
	(.007)	(4.516)	(2.047)	(.074)	(.336)		

Note: Estimated standard errors are in parentheses. The meaning of the asterisks is provided in the notes to table 9–12.

Notes

1. The best examples of this sort of work are two recent dissertations: Farber's (1978) of the United Mine Workers and Dertouzos's (1979) of the International Typographical Union.

2. Strict concavity is by no means necessary, but given the assumptions below about the wage-employment constraint, it ensures a unique solution to the constrained maximization problem.

3. The analogy here is with the family whose utility function is constructed from the husband's, wife's, and children's preferences. See Samuelson (1956) and Becker (1974).

4. That is, $g_{11} + 2g_{12}f_w + g_{22}(f_w)^2 + g_2 f_{ww} < 0$.

5. Notwithstanding the large literature on this model of unionism, this question appears to have been raised before in only two papers, those of Oswald (1980) and Dertouzos and Pencavel (1981). There is an obvious formal analogy here with models of consumer demand subject to nonlinear budget constraints, such as Becker and Lewis (1973).

6. See, for instance, Samuelson (1947) pp. 21–39 and Archibald (1965).

7. The sides in this debate were drawn, of course, by Dunlop (1944), who maintained; "An economic theory of a trade union requires that the organization be assumed to maximize (or minimize) something. Although not the only possible objective maximization of the wage bill may be regarded as the standard case" (p. 4) and by Ross (1948), who countered, "Where is the wage policy of unions to be found? It is not to be found in the mechanical application of any maximization principle" (p. 8). The maximizing postulate was only one of the issues separating Dunlop and Ross.

8. The dual problem involves w and L minimizing $L - f(w, Z)$ subject to $U^0 \geq g(w, L, Y)$, which results in "utility-constant" wage and employment equations: $w = h_1(Y, Z, U^0)$ and $L = h_2(Y, Z, U^0)$. It is straightforward to show that $\partial h_1/\partial Z \gtrless 0$ according to $\partial^2 f/(\partial w \cdot \partial Z) \gtrless 0$. Naturally, there are also Slutsky-type decompositions such as:

$$\frac{\partial \phi_1}{\partial Z} = \frac{\partial h_1}{\partial Z} - \Delta^{-1} \frac{\partial f}{\partial Z} \left(\frac{\partial^2 U}{\partial L^2} \frac{\partial f}{\partial w} + \frac{\partial^2 U}{\partial w \partial L} \right),$$

and

$$\frac{\partial \phi_1}{\partial Y} = \frac{\partial h_1}{\partial Y} - \Delta^{-1} \left(\frac{\partial U/\partial Y}{\partial U/\partial L} \right) \left(\frac{\partial^2 U}{\partial w \partial L} + \frac{\partial^2 U}{\partial L^2} \frac{\partial f}{\partial w} \right)$$

9. If the firm maximizes profits, a stronger condition than cost minimization, then the price of output (or the determinants of the product demand function) replaces the level of output in Z. The appropriateness of treating output as exogenous is ultimately a statistical issue and is addressed in the empirical work below.

10. If utility is strictly concave in money and if the union membership (M) is fixed, then rent maximization is qualitatively the same as the maximization of expected per member utility: $(u(w) - u(\bar{w}))L + u(\bar{w})M$. This objective appears in McDonald and Solow (1980), in Oswald (1980), and in Farber (1978), who allows for fringe benefits in addition to wage income and who assumes $u(w)$ is a power function.

11. The first-order condition for an efficient contract is $-g_1/g_2 = L/(dR/dL - w)$, where dR/dL is the firm's marginal revenue product of labor. So, for an efficient contract, employment

is set at a point at which dR/dL falls short of the wage rate, whereas in the Cartter-Fellner model an optimizing firm always equates the marginal revenue product of labor and the wage rate.

12. There is one special case in which the Fellner-Cartter solution does lie on the contract curve and that occurs when (contrary to what has been assumed in the exposition above) the union is concerned with wage rates but not at all with employment. If the union then maximizes the wage rate subject to the employer's labor demand function and subject to losses not being incurred, then the solution is formally equivalent to the labor managed firm as exposited by Ward (1958) and Domar (1966).

13. The explicit analogy here is with the literature on demand revelation procedures in public economics. See Green and Laffont (1977) and Tideman and Tullock (1976).

14. Ross (1948) writes:

> [T]he typical wage bargain (with certain significant exceptions) is necessarily made without consideration of its employment effect . . . " (p. 14); "If the employment effect of the wage bargain is to be the subject of rational calculation, it has to be predictable. There needs to be a reasonable exact relationship between wage rate and volume of employment before the fact, at the time the bargain is made. But this is possible only if other things remain equal. There must be no other and more powerful influences affecting the volume of employment or if there are, then their effects must be predictable. Here, as elsewhere, other things do not remain equal . . . The volume of employment associated with a given wage rate is unpredictable before the fact, and the effect of a given rate upon employment is undecipherable after the fact. The employment effect cannot normally be the subject of rational calculation and prediction at the time the bargain is made, and union officials are normally in no position to assume responsibility for it. [Pp. 79–80]

15. One comparative static result could be mentioned here, namely, the effect of a rightward shift in the distribution of Z. An increase in Z has ambiguous effects on the direction of change of the optimal wage rate under certainty, as is clear from equation (9.7a), so one would not expect to have less ambiguous results by allowing for uncertainty. More important perhaps is that the terms determining the effects on the wage rate of this increase in Z are expected values of the same terms as in the certainty case.

16. The description of the newspaper industry and of the ITU that follows draws heavily on the masterly survey by Rosse and Dertouzos (1978), upon the exhaustive study of Lipset, Trow, and Coleman (1956), and upon the history of the union as told by the ITU (1967).

17. Rosse and Dertouzos (1978) report a mean daily circulation in 1977 of 37,572.

18. For example, in Wachter's (1970) time-series analysis of wages in two-digit manufacturing industries, his preferred equation for the printing industry has only a time trend as a relevant regressor, and he finds no significant role played by the unemployment rate, by price changes, and by movements in the industry's value added. Perhaps even more striking are the results reported by Eckstein and Wilson (1962), where R^2's for wage changes in the printing industry of .01 are recorded, while most other industries generate R^2's greater than .90.

19. In fact, at least up to the mid-1960s, this portrayal of the union is something of a caricature. There have been occasions on which the union has sponsored inventions, and it established its own research and development laboratory and staff in the 1950s. See Kelber and Schlesinger (1967). The more accurate description is that the continuing strength of the ITU during these years is attributable to its *adaptation* to and control of the new technology.

20. The spectacular consequences of this automation for New York's Local 6 of the ITU are documented by Rogers and Friedman (1980).

21. One printer interviewed within the last couple of years by Rogers and Friedman (1980)

made the point with obvious exaggeration: "Mr. Gutenberg would have been at home in the composing room as recently as twenty years ago, but no more" (p. 2).

22. No strikes took place from 1946 to 1965 in any of the union locals analyzed below.

23. "Its members have an income and status which minimizes the disparity between the perspectives and styles of life of workers and union leaders. . . . Side by side with the high average wages earned by journeymen printers is the tendency of the union's political system to operate to keep the income differential between workers and union officers small. Official salaries can be raised only by referendum of the whole membership of the local or international, and the membership persistently refuse to give their officers large or frequent raises. . . . [Union leaders] have very little financial stake in union office, and are that much less inclined to entrench themselves in office to the detriment of the democratic process . . . working printers themselves have very much the sense of meeting their union officers as status equals, with nothing like the deference paid by most semiskilled workers to their white-collared middle-class union officers. Moreover, the union officer's work is not always very attractive to the skilled typographer with pride in his craft" (Lipset, Trow, and Coleman, 1956, pp. 214–215).

24. "In a real sense the printers were the intellectuals of the working class" (Lipset, Trow, and Coleman, 1956, p. 30).

25. The employment data were obtained by James Dertouzos as part of his consulting services for the Cincinnati *Post.*

26. For instance, in Cincinnati, after accounting for the effect of the merger between the *Post* and the *Times-Star* in 1958, the simple correlation between the *Post*'s employment and local ITU membership is .99.

27. The one conspicuous exception is Louisville's employment, which rose from 340 in 1947 to 424 in 1959 and then fell to 362 in 1965.

28. The data on p, r_1, and r_2 are taken from well-known published Bureau of Labor Statistics and Department of Commerce sources. The mean values of these variables over these years are $p = .813$, $r_1 = 1.203$, and $r_2 = 77.485$. The advertising linage data are listed in table 9–2. There are of course, labor inputs to the newspaper production process other than those organized by the ITU, but the work done by pressmen and mailmen for instance, is quite different from that performed by the printers and we may safely posit Leontief technology among these different types of labor input.

29. With the same explanatory variables across equations, the ordinary least squares estimator is fully efficient even in the presence of cross-equation correlation of the disturbances.

30. The relevance of the scale of output for unit costs is documented by Rosse (1970), who finds strong increasing returns to scale for advertising space.

31. Even if the "large" locals are decomposed further and equations (9.12a) and (9.12b) fitted only to the two locals with more than 600 members (Columbus and Albany), the "cost-of-living constraint" is still decisely rejected.

32. If the objective function were addilog as is equation (9.19) below and if the employment-wage constraint equation were linear in the logarithms, then the reduced-form wage and employment equations would be exactly logarithmic.

33. More information on the newspaper production technology is contained in Rosse (1970, 1977). Dertouzos (1979) investigated labor demand functions in which output appeared in quadratic form. The cost function implied by labor demand function (19.16) is:

$$\alpha_0 w + \frac{1}{2}\,\alpha_1 \left(\frac{w^2}{r_1}\right) + \alpha_2 \left(\frac{r_2 w}{r_1}\right) + \alpha_3 X w + \alpha_4 D w + c(r_1, r_2, X, D, r_3),$$

where $c(\cdot)$ is some function independent of w, but dependent upon the prices (r_3) of inputs used in fixed proportions with L. Since our procedure does not require a specification for $c(\cdot)$, our labor demand function is compatible with many different cost functions.

34. See Dertouzos (1979).

35. These estimates are similar to those reported in Dertouzos and Pencavel (1981), whose estimation procedure involved appending stochastic terms to equations (9.17) and (9.16) and assuming that these disturbances are normally distributed. Of course, the stochastic assumptions in this chapter are not equivalent to those made in Dertouzos and Pencavel (1981), although the similarity of the results indicates that the estimates are not sensitive to these two sets of error-term assumptions.

36. For instance, from inspection of equations (9.17) and (9.18), it is evident that, if the intercept, α_0, of the labor demand curve is not well defined, it will be difficult for the data to distinguish α_0 from δ. Or multiply equation (9.17) through by $\alpha_1 p/r_1$ and compare the resulting expression with equation (9.18).

37. This result is by no means uncommon in the fitting of the Stone-Geary system to consumption patterns.

38. The values of the logarithm of the maximized likelihood function under the constraints implied by the wage bill maximand are -82.58 for Cincinnati, -39.09 for Columbia, -25.48 for Dubuque, -85.94 for Memphis, -37.67 for Fond du Lac, and -87.94 for Columbus. The critical value of the chi-squared statistic with three degrees of freedom is 7.81 at the 5 percent level of significance and 11.34 at the 1 percent level of significance.

39. When the system is estimated to allow for output being endogenous, the results are virtually unchanged. To be precise, for Cincinnati, these instrumental variable estimates (with estimated standard errors in parentheses) are as follows: $\theta = .225$ (.080); $\gamma = 2.026$ (.982); $\delta = -157.75$ (315.20); $\alpha_0 = 221.05$ (133.68); $\alpha_1 = -95.30$ (53.79); $\alpha_2 = 1.303$ (1.217); $\alpha_3 = 3.112$ (2.042); and $\alpha_4 = 91.23$ (16.68). The instruments here for newspaper output are U.S. advertising expenditures per household in real dollars, the share of aggregate advertising earned by television, and radio advertising expenditures as a fraction of all advertising expenditures. These advertising data relate to the United States as a whole and clearly are exogenous to an individual union local or newspaper firm.

40. The labor demand function implied by this expression for f_w is $L = \bar{f}(r_1, r_2, X, D) - (w/r_1)e^{\alpha X}$, where $\bar{f}(\cdot)$ is some unspecified function independent of w.

41. The set of exogenous variables consists of X, $\ell n(p/r_1)$, $\ell n r_2$, D, $D.\ \ell n X$, $D.\ \ell n p$, $D.\ \ell n r_1$, and $D.\ \ell n r_2$. A larger set of instruments produced results very similar to those reported.

42. For Cincinnati, replacing the employment series with the union membership series results in the following estimates (with standard errors in parentheses): $\mu = .029$ (.368); $\lambda = -3.172$ (2.304); $\eta = -.903$ (2.230); $\alpha = -.051$ (.037); and $\sigma = .315$ (.229).

43. As before, the instrumental variables, when output is endogenous, are U.S. advertising expenditures per household in real dollars, the share of aggregate advertising expenditures earned by television, and radio advertising expenditures as a fraction of all advertising expenditures. The only substantive difference between the estimates in table 9–12 and those that result from treating output as endogenous obtains for Louisville, whose μ parameter in the latter case was not defined.

44. It should be noted that the stochastic assumptions in fitting equations (9.21) and (9.23) are not mutually consistent: If the disturbance is additive in equation (9.21), then it cannot simply be appended to the right-hand side of equation (9.23). In fact, in estimating the antilogarithm of these equations, similar results were derived to those presented in the text which suggests the parameter estimates are not particularly sensitive to the precise form of these stochastic assumptions.

45. These estimates of the elasticity of substitution correspond to the estimation of the reduced-form wage and employment equations (9.17) and (9.18) under the restriction that the θ, γ, and δ parameters are the same for any pair of unions, but the labor demand parameters (the α's) are completely unrestricted across unions. If the system is estimated requiring only θ and γ to be the same across unions, then σ is .645 (.325) for Cincinnati and Dubuque, .239 (.012) for Fond du Lac and Columbia, and .105 (.181) for Columbus and Memphis.

46. "It would seem most likely, once a union is already enjoying a particular wage-employment combination, that it would take a considerable increase in wages to compensate for a reduction in employment, and it would take a considerable increase in employment to compensate for a wage reduction. This is reasoned to be true because of the internal political pressures the union would be subject to if it openly agreed to either of these reductions" (Cartter, 1959, pp. 89–90).

References

Amemiya, T. 1974. "The Nonlinear Two-Stage Least Squares Estimator." *Journal of Econometrics* 2, no. 2 (July):105–110.

Archibald, G. C. 1965. "The Qualitative Content of Maximizing Models." *Journal of Political Economy* 73, no. 1 (February):27–36.

Becker, G. S. 1974. "A Theory of Social Interactions." *Journal of Political Economy* 82, no. 6 (November/December):1063–1093.

Becker, G. S., and Lewis, H. G. 1973. "On the Interaction between the Quantity and Quality of Children." *Journal of Political Economy* 81, no. 3, part II, "New Economic Approaches to Fertility," March/April, pp. 279–288.

Cartter, A. M. 1959. *Theory of Wages and Employment.* Homewood, Ill.: Irwin.

De Menil, G. 1971. *Bargaining: Monopoly Power Versus Union Power.* Cambridge: MIT Press.

Dertouzos, J. N. 1979. "Union Objectives, Wage Determination, and the International Typographical Union." Unpublished *Ph.D. dissertation*, Stanford University, December.

Dertouzos, J. N., and Pencavel, J. H. 1981. "Wage and Employment Determination under Trade Unionism: The International Typographical Union." *Journal of Political Economy* 89, no. 6 (December):1162–1181.

Domar, E. 1966. "The Soviet Collective Farm as a Producer Cooperative." *American Economic Review* 56, no. 4 (September):734–757.

Dunlop, J. T. 1944. *Wage Determination Under Trade Unions*, New York: Macmillan.

Eckstein, O., and Wilson, T. A. 1962. "Determination of Money Wages in American Industry." *Quarterly Journal of Economics* 76, no. 3 (August):379–414.

Farber, H. S. 1978. "Individual Preferences and Union Wage Determination: The Case of the United Mine Workers." *Journal of Political Economy* 86, no. 5 (October):923–942.

Fellner, W. 1947. "Prices and Wages Under Bilateral Monopoly." *Quarterly Journal of Economics* 61, no. 3 (August):503–532.

Green, J., and Laffont, J. J. 1977. "Characterization of Satisfactory Mechanisms for the Revelation of Preferences for Public Goods." *Econometrica* 45, no. 2 (March):427–438.

International Typographical Union, The Executive Council. 1967. *A Study of the History of the International Typographical Union 1852–1966: Volume II.* Colorado Springs, Colorado.

Johnson, G. E. 1975. "Economic Analysis of Trade Unionism." *American Economic Review, Proceedings* 65, no. 2 (May):23–28.

Kelber, H., and Schlesinger, C. 1967. *Union Printers and Controlled Automation.* New York: Free Press.

Leontief, W. W. 1946. "The Pure Theory of the Guaranteed Annual Wage Contract." *Journal of Political Economy* 54, no. 1 (February): 76–9.

Lipset, S. M., Trow, M. A., and Coleman, J. S. 1956. *Union Democracy: The Internal Politics of the International Typographical Union.* Glencoe, Ill.: Free Press.

McDonald, I. M., and Solow, R. M. 1981. "Wage Bargaining and Employment," *American Economic Review* 71 (December):896–908.

Oswald, A. J. 1980. "The Microeconomic Theory of the Trade Union." Oxford Institute of Economics and Statistics, unpublished *Mimeo*, May.

Rogers, T. F., and Friedman, N. S. 1980. *Printers Face Automation.* Lexington, Mass.: D.C. Heath.

Rosen, S. 1970. "Unionism and the Occupational Wage Structure in the United States." *International Economic Review* 11, no. 2 (June):269–286.

Ross, A. M. 1948. *Trade Union Wage Policy*. Berkeley: University of California Press.

Rosse, J. N. 1970. "Estimating Cost Function Parameters Without Using Cost Data: Illustrated Methodology." *Econometrica* 38, no. 2 (March):256–279.

______. 1977. "The Daily Newspaper Firm: A 24 Equation Reduced Form Model." *Studies in Industry Economics*, no. 76, Department of Economics, Stanford University, January.

______. 1978. "The Evolution of One Newspaper Cities." *Studies in Industry Economics*, no. 95, Department of Economics, Stanford University, December.

Rosse, J. N., and Dertouzos, J. N. 1978. "Economic Issues in Mass Communication Industries." Prepared for Federal Trade Commission, December 14–15, *Studies in Industry Economics*, no. 99, Department of Economics, Stanford University.

Samuelson, P. A. 1947, *Foundations of Economic Analysis,* Harvard University Press.

Samuelson, P. A. 1956. "Social Indifference Curves." *Quarterly Journal of Economics* 70, no. 1 (February):1–22.

Tideman, T. N., and Tullock, G. 1976. "A New and Superior Process for Making Social Choices." *Journal of Political Economy* 84, no. 6 (December):1145–1160.

Wachter, M. L. 1970. "Relative Wage Equations for United States Manufacturing Industries 1947–1967." *Review of Economics and Statistics* 52, no. 4 (November):405–410.

Ward, B. 1958. "The Firm in Illyria: Market Syndicalism." *American Economic Review* 48, no. 4 (September): 566–589.

10 THE DETERMINANTS OF UNION STAFF SALARIES: *A New Meaning to Business Unionism*

Bernard Lentz

In the past few years an increasing range of neoclassical labor economists have attempted to model and estimate the behavioral implications of unions. We have seen a burgeoning of new theories of the union based on advances in other fields of economics, e.g., the property rights approach of Martin (1980) or the public goods—collective voice perspective, most recently, of Duncan and Stafford (1980). Similarly, the empirical work, particularly of Freeman, Brown, and Medoff, has raised some interesting issues on the theoretical plane. However, even if Freeman and Medoff (1980) can confidently title their book *What Do Unions Do*? we are still left with some burning issues of *why and how* unions do it.

Martin's (1980) recent answer to this quest for a union objective function and its constraints is that there is no unique objective function due to the attentuated property rights of union members in the asset called "union monopoly rents." Indeed, while the public good–collective voice theorists have tended to hypothesize median-voter, democratic, objective functions, a more sophisticated reading of the public-choice literature would show the restrictive conditions for this result are not met by unions.

Thus, one could readily conclude that there is very little consistency or regularity in the economic behavior of unions. Interestingly enough, very few attempts have been made to analyze the resource allocation behavior of unions per se, as opposed to the allocation of labor by unionized firms and by unionized workers. It is as though we were trying to estimate a production function for a firm by observing the resource allocation of its customers. Indeed, property rights theorists of the union must maintain a tenuous position, inasmuch as the property rights of union members are so attenuated as to allow great scope for union "managerial discretion," yet this same leadership has itself attenuated control over union resources.

Otherwise, union leaders with unattenuated property rights over union "assets," whether these be union jobs or pension and welfare funds, will be analyzable as owner-operators or self-employed entrepreneurs. As several authors have shown, as long as these self-employed, residual claimant, union leaders can hire managerial labor to supplant their own, they will maximize their utility by maximizing the present value of the future stream of profits, i.e., the value of the firm.

As economists have widely accepted since Friedman's (1953) *Essays in Positive Economics*, whether unions meet all the assumptions of any particular model is in theory unimportant, but only that they act *as if* they meet those assumptions. Thus it is the prediction powers and defeasibility of a model that are important, as well as its generality, that make it useful for understanding phenomena.[1] On the grounds of positive proof for Martin's property rights approach, Martin himself produces mainly the hypotheses to be tested. However, a property rights model put forward and tested by Bennett and Johnson (1980) gave weak confirmation or refutation of several of their specific hypotheses relating to the impact of right-to-work laws on member property rights and the allocation of union resources. A similar attempt to test an eclectic public goods model made by Ehrenberg and Goldberg (1977) showed little responsiveness of building trades business agents' salaries to measures of performance *as viewed from the rank-and-file member's perspective.*

The present work started out to assess whether there might be some old-fashioned regularities in the behavior of unions as allocators of resources, not, as suggested earlier, to assess the allocation of unionized labor by management, unionized workers, and unions. Of course, some attempts have been made to grasp the economics of the supply of union services. An early and oft-cited attempt is Berkowitz's (1954) somewhat straightforward application of the theory of the firm to unions. Berkowitz, however, vacillated on what he regarded as the product being produced by unions and fell short of any empirical tests of his hypotheses, in all probability due to insufficient data.[2] Hopefully, the empirical evidence presented below will shed some light on certain of Berkowitz's conjectures.

Rather than look at supply curves per se, the approach taken here is a quite traditional one that examines factor utilization by unions. In particular, an attempt is made to estimate the demand for an input, union staff, and officers, much as Arrow et al. (1961) investigated production functions and, hence, supply in their seminal empirical work on the CES. Any such empirical inquiry must naturally deal with the natures of the product, inputs, demand, etc., as well as industry organization, and shed some light on these topics as well. It is to these considerations that we turn to in the next section. The third section presents the explicit empirical model and the estimates of that model, while the last section concludes the paper with some reflections on modeling union behavior and its interaction with unionized workers and management.

Descriptive Model

As suggested earlier, Berkowitz (1954) fell short of his object "to look at the trade union from yet another vantage point: as a seller not of labor power, but of memberships in the organization" (p. 575). On the other hand, the more recent empirical works of Pencavel (1971), Moore and Newman (1975), Lumsden and Petersen (1975) and the international comparisons of Bain and Elsheikh (1976) have apparently had some success in modeling the *demand* for union services based on demand for union membership as being independent of the complex range of services that preoccupied Berkowitz. The assumption here will indeed be that the product sold by unions is union membership, but not in the theoretical vein of Block and Saks's (1980) bureaucratic model of new union organizing as an attempt to maximize the size of the union. Rather, it will be assumed that unions act as though they are maximizing profits from the sale of these memberships.

In this vein, local unions are viewed as "plants" of these union "firms," and the output of concern is union memberships and the revenues they bring. Unlike the simplistic output/memberships maximization models mentioned above, we have something more old-fashioned as a maximand, something akin to profits or value of the union "firm."

Concerning the demand by workers for this good, it seems apparent that, under present law, at least a majority of workers at some point in time must have obtained benefits outweighing dues, initiation fees, and other costs of unionization. As Lewis (1959) argued, these benefits may be of a nonmonopoly sort, but overwhelming empirical evidence suggests a positive union wage effect.

While more will be said on this subject in the final section of this paper, the approach taken here is comparable to that of other cross-section studies of the demand for unionism, notably Moore and Newman (1975) and Lumsden and Petersen (1975). What is perhaps most noteworthy in this approach and that of Pencavel (1971) is that they essentially regard joining a union as purchasing an array of goods, some of which may be investment goods or assets, but which can be fruitfully explained or predicted by assuming that one membership equals one standard unit of union services. Since membership is the source of dues revenue for union leaders, this comes out to be a convenient demand concept on the other side of the market from the supply of union services considered above. On the other hand, estimates discussed in the next section will attempt to control for "product quality variations" in the protection of workers' rights under contracts and the labor law.

On a more technical plane, the nature of the production function for union services is one about which some hypotheses certainly have been implicitly put forward. Berkowitz (1954, p. 586) draws average variable costs as horizontal, but Segal (1964) argues there are economies of scale in organizing. The recent public goods–collective voice literature would certainly lead one to sustain the latter position. Thus a key aspect of any estimation of the production function for union services is to allow for economies of scale in the assumed specification and interpretation of econometric estimates thereof.

Further, causal empiricism on the production methods of unions suggests a rather low elasticity of substitution between capital and labor. Grievance processing, contract negotiation, and organizing, while they may involve offices, typewriters, and computers, are essentially service activities rendered by labor. Thus, one must specify a production function such as the CES, which allows for a nonunitary elasticity of substitution.

In the empirical analysis of the following section, it will be assumed that the supply of union staff is some function of the observed relative salary these staffers earn, a view that probably accords well with the high turnover rates observed by Applebaum (1966) and Applebaum and Blaine (1975). However, Edelstein and Warner (1976, table 5.3) found that higher salaries of national union officials other than the president correlated negatively and significantly with challenges to the national union presidency. This finding implies that a sharing of the proceeds of residual maximization may increase the probability of retention of residual claimant status. Thus, salaries need not be "competitive" but may indeed be choice variables of the union president.

In summary, the model of a union's demand for staff that will be tested in the next section is one based on ownership by the international president of the residual between revenues received from union members and the costs of "producing" those memberships. The relevant output measure is thus union memberships, and the price received is the dues, initiation fees, etc. Workers demand memberships for either monopoly rent *or* collective voice reasons, but each will be assumed to receive an equal share of "union services" per membership, as several studies of the demand for union services have shown to be plausible. The structure of market and union "firm" demand is an open question, and alternative models of price determination will be tested, ranging from the perfectly competitive firm to the monopolist. The production of union memberships would appear to exhibit a low elasticity of substitution between capital and labor, while there are some questions about the existence of economies of scale in this production process. Finally, unions are not assumed to act as price takers in the market for their personnel.

Mathematical Model and Empirical Tests

The explicit construction of the descriptive model of the last section will proceed very directly with but brief references to the hypotheses drawn from the prior discussion. After a presentation of this mathematical model, its optimum conditions and econometric specification, an analysis of the data sources and the empirical estimation of the parameters of the model will be presented.

The basic CES production function is presented in equation (10.1):

$$q = [\alpha(E_L L)^\rho + (1 - \alpha)(E_K K)^\rho]^{v/\rho}, \qquad (10.1)$$

where:

q = output of union memberships;

K = physical capital of the union;

L = labor input of union staff;

$\hat{v}$ = (dis) economies of scale parameter;

ρ = parameter determining elasticity of substitution;

$\sigma = 1/(1 - \rho)$;

α = factor share distribution parameter;

E_L = efficiency of labor parameter;

E_K = efficiency of capital parameter.

In some estimates presented below, an attempt will be made to assess whether quality of union membership has any impact on the demand for union staff—i.e., $q = q_1 q_2$, where q_1 is a quality of membership-services variable, e.g., relative union member wages, and q_2 is the union membership variable.

With regard to the revenues produced by marketing this membership output, the most simple market structure is that of the price-taking firm, i.e.,

$$P = P^o. \tag{10.2}$$

Equation (10.2) thus implies that each local union must, because of competition from other local unions, sell its memberships at the prevailing market level of dues, initiation fees, etc., a price taken as being exogenous to the demand for union staff. On the other hand, the statewide observations that will be used to test the theory may be generated by a market interaction of supply of union memberships and demand thereof. Thus the demand function in equation (10.3) may be relevant to an empirical estimation of the demand for union staff:

$$P = P(Q, \bar{X}). \tag{10.3}$$

Where market output of union memberships, Q affects market price as well as such traditional variables as income and tastes, represented by a vector, $\bar{X}$. Similarly, in the monopoly structure of the market for union memberships, it is firm output, q, that is the relevant market output for price determination. For ease of estimation, it will generally be assumed that the demand for union memberships is of the form given by equation (10.4), at least in the range of observed relations:

$$P = Q^{-\gamma} \bar{X}^{\psi}. \tag{10.4}$$

Since our data are based upon statewide averages, Q in equation (10.4) may represent an average over either monopoly or competitive union firms. Thus the endogenous price variable will usefully be omitted and replaced by an endogenous quantity demand relation. Given that union leaders seek not only dues revenues but also unpaid strike labor from members, and given that the true cost of union membership is imperfectly measured by dues, fees, etc., as shown in Lentz (1980), the quantity of union membership demand may better show the relevant costs and benefits, as Becker (1959) showed.

Finally, as argued at the end of the last section, the supply of union staff will be assumed to be a function of their observed relative wage, i.e.,

$$L = kW_S^{\delta} W_o^{\beta}, \tag{10.5}$$

where W_S is the observed staff wage and W_o is some observed opportunity wage; $\delta > 0$, $\beta < 0$, $k > 0$ are parameters of the supply of union staff. Again, as argued in the previous paragraph, statewide data may reflect market phenomena even if individual unions have no market power in either their membership market or their staff labor market. Similarly, the "up-through-the-ranks" supply channel seems to imply substantial transfer costs of switching into or out of union staff positions.

Maximizing residual income (10.6) with respect to W_S and L,

$$PQ = W_S L - r\bar{K}, \tag{10.6}$$

and given the production function (10.1), the demand for memberships (10.2), and the supply of staff (10.5) yields the first-order condition, expressed in logarithmic form, given in (10.7):

$$\ln W_S = \ln C + (\rho - 1)\ln L + (1 - \rho/v)\ln q + \ln P_o \tag{10.7}$$

where $C = v\alpha E_L^{\rho}(1 + 1/\delta)$. If, on the other hand, union staffing observations are generated by (10.1), (10.4), and (10.5) in either the competitive or monopoly market structure for union membership, then residual maximization yields the logarithmic form of the first-order conditions:

$$\ln W_S = \ln C + (\rho - 1)\ln L + (1 - \rho/v - \gamma)\ln Q \tag{10.8}$$

where Q is monopoly market–firm output of union memberships.

While the above demand for union staff relations expressed in (10.7) and (10.8) present the most general aspects of the descriptive model of the last section, they do not in all cases allow identification of the parameters of interest with respect to the hypotheses set forth above. Thus, alternative specifications, in which additional restrictions are imposed, will be tested below, e.g., assuming that economies of scale do not exist in order to obtain information on the elasticity of the demand for union membership.

For example, if we directly estimate equation (10.8) by

$$\ln W_{S_i} = \hat{\alpha} + \hat{\beta}_L \ln L_i + \beta_Q \ln Q_i + \varepsilon_i, \tag{10.9}$$

ρ may be estimated by $\hat{\beta}_L + 1$, but the economies of scale parameter, ν, and the elasticity of demand parameter, δ, are related to the estimated coefficients as shown in equation (10.10):

$$\delta = \hat{\beta}_Q + (\hat{\beta}_L + 1)/v \mp 1. \qquad (10.10)$$

If we make the most general assumption about the demand for union memberships, then $\delta \geq 0$ in order that the demand curve is downward-sloping or at most in the competitive firm, horizontal. If, further, $\hat{\beta}_Q < 1$, then we may infer a lower bound on economies of scale, $(\hat{\beta}_L + 1)/(1 - \hat{\beta}_Q) < v$. However if $\hat{\beta}_Q > 1$, the inequality is reversed and we have some idea about an upper bound on ν. In summary, restrictions of the assumed production and demand relations may help to obtain information on other parameters and, of course, appropriate F tests of the restrictions can be made in the case of ordinary (but, unfortunately, not two-stage) least square.

Similarly, the specific functional forms of equations (10.1)–(10.5) will not invariably be imposed on the econometric estimation in order to allow for economic relations that theory suggests but that equations (10.1)–(10.5) may eliminate. For example, the specific form of the labor supply function in equation (10.5) implies that the opportunity wage W_o need not enter an econometric estimation of equation (10.7) or (10.8). In the empirics discussed below, however, opportunity wages will be allowed to enter the estimation of the determinants of the wages of union staff.

Finally, instead of the usual CES estimation with average product, Q/L, being the dependent variable and with wage, W, being the independent variable, the estimates presented below will have the wage W_S as the dependent variable as expressed in (10.7) and (10.8). Not only is this done in order to accord with the "internal labor market" for union staff implied by Rees (1977) and Strauss (1977), but also to be comparable to the estimates of Ehrenberg and Goldberg (1975), which attempted to relate compensation as a dependent variable to various performance measures. Similarly, given the property rights perspective taken here, estimates with compensation as the dependent variables are more readily compared with the union member property rights perspective of Bennett and Johnson (1980). In general, then, the specification estimated will be a logarithmic specification of the wage of union staff, W_S, as a linear function of the logarithms of various endogenous output, staff input, and price variables, as well as exogenous opportunity wages.

An original aspect of this chapter is its use of U.S. government published data that have not heretofore been used by other students of trade unions—e.g., Bennett and Johnson (1980), Ehrenberg and Goldberg (1975),

Applebaum and Blaine (1975), who have all resorted to small samples of the union financial reports (LM–2 forms). Data by state and by level of union organization (national, intermediate body, and local) are in fact given for the nearly 50,000 unions in *Union Financial Statistics 1960–1970* and in similar titles published by the Office of Labor-Management and Welfare Pension Reports (1971).[3] This is done because the reporting requirements detailed in *Guide to Reporting Your Union Finances* (1960, p. 19) may spread the "disbursements to officers and employees" paid to a given union official over the various levels of a union's organizational reports and make analysis of local reports erroneous.

While the empirical work discussed here will make use of the aforementioned *Union Financial Statistics*, based on LM–2 reports, it diverges from prior studies by aggregating across all levels of unions in these data to take account of the role of the national and its intermediate bodies in the compensation of union officers and in the production of "union services." More importantly, a separate data base on union staff salaries is used based on the U.S. Department of Commerce publication, *County Business Patterns*, which lists first-quarter employment and payrolls for "Labor Organizations," S.I.C. 863. Now, it might be argued that union officers have a strong interest in understating their compensation on LM–2 forms; it is less obvious that they wish to hide income that makes them eligible for higher social security benefits, since OASDHI coverage is the basis of the *County Business Patterns* data. These data exclude union officers who are "unpaid" but receive reimbursements, etc., although this fact is apparently of no great empirical importance, as will be discussed below. Thus, econometric estimate of the determinants of "total compensation" as taken from LM–2 reports will be compared and contrasted with "salary" determinants derived from *County Business Patterns*. It might also be noted that the "Labor Organization" category will allow inclusion of paid officers and employees of smaller labor unions that need not file LM–2 reports, as well as those large and growing labor organizations that are not covered by Landrum-Griffin's reporting requirements, especially public employee labor organizations. Finally, a variable that accounts for the different scope of coverage by OASDHI and the Landrum-Griffin reporting requirements will be explicitly entered in the regression analysis that follows.

The "price" variable used here is also taken from the LM–2 reports on receipts of labor organizations. While it has been argued, even in the *Statistical Abstract of the United States* (1973, p. 251), that aggregating across levels of unions may entail double counting of receipts, it is equally true that this duplication occurs on both sides of the income statement, particularly of local unions: Locals pay per capita assessments to their internationals, but they also receive funds back from the internationals. Thus, empirical estimates will be discussed that attempted to "net-out" affiliation payments as constituting the major double counting problem, although these proved to be statistically inferior to a simple summation of receipts across levels of union organization.

Another crucial variable in the following estimation is union membership, the output measure *Q*. The source used here is that reported in the various *Directory of National and International Labor Unions in the United States* or comparable titles. While there may be problems with accurate data on local membership, as suggested in the citation from Bennett and Johnson (1980), the reports that the Department of Labor solicits come, for the most part, from the international unions, with some estimation of the distribution of union membership by state being done by the Bureau of Labor Statistics for those unions not reporting such a distribution. However, in the vein of a model of international union presidential ownership, these figures held by the international are the ones of relevance to decision making by the president of the "firm." Hopefully, any shirking or slack at lower levels with respect to accurate measurement of membership will have a random influence on allocation decisions presumed to emanate from the (inter) national union.

Finally, with respect to variables that will regularly enter the regressions on union staff determination, the opportunity wage of union staff is most often taken to be the average weekly earnings in manufacturing in a state. While this measure is by no means ideal, it appears to perform as well as union wage estimates by state for the subset of states and occupations listed in the BLS union wage surveys reported for metropolitan areas in the *Handbooks of Labor Statistics*. This is equally true of its performance compared to that of the average monthly earnings of employees of "Business Associations" (SIC 861), organizations that would seemingly be closely related to unions in terms of the skill mix of their staffs. The key variables to estimation of the determinants of union staff salaries are presented in table 10–1 with their definitions and sources as well as the variables in the model they are intended to measure.

Of course, several further variables are mentioned below that will enter the reduced-form estimates of endogenous, included variables in the first stage of two-stage least squares regressions explaining union staff salaries. Most of these have come from the aforementioned studies of the demand for union "services": percentage of a state's black employment, percent female, right-to-work laws, etc., which are intended to measure tastes for unionism. One variable of interest and novelty is the ratio of private employment agencies' (SIC 741) level of employment to total employment in each state, a variable intended to capture the demand for labor market "intermediation" between

Table 10-1. Definitions of Key Variables[a]

Symbol in Model	*Variable Label*	*Variable Definition (Source of Data)*[b]
W_S	LSAL	First quarter monthly payroll per employee of labor unions and similar organizations. (Source: *County Business Patterns*)
W_S	LCOMP	Disbursements to officers and employees + loans to same per employee of labor organizations. (Source: Union Financial Statistics: *County Business Patterns*)
L	LSTAFF	Number of employees on payrolls of labor organizations during first quarter. (Source: *County Business Patterns*)
Q	LMEM	Union membership. (Source: *Statistical Abstract*)
Q/L	LMEMPW	Union members per union staff employee. (Source: See above)
P	LALREC	Receipts of labor unions per union member, summation over local, intermediate, and national unions. (Source: Union Financial Statistics; *Statistical Abstract*)
P	LNETREC	LALREC-Affiliation payments per union member. (Source: See above)
W_0	LAVWAG	Average weekly earnings of employees in manufacturing. (Source: *Statistical Abstract*)
—	COVER	Ratio of number of labor organizations covered by OASH*DI* to number of unions reporting under Landrum-Griffin (LMRDA). (Source: *County Business Patterns*; Union Financial Statistics).

[a]*L* (variable name) = natural logarithm of variable.
[b]All data are statewide averages or totals.

employers and potential employees. Not only has this intermediation role frequently been attributed to craft unions and their hiring halls, but also the "need" for such intermediation shows a higher cost of job search and labor mobility by individual workers. This, in turn, directly relates to the exit-voice explanations of unionism given by Freeman (1976). Finally, a variable measuring organized opposition to unions is intended to capture the frequent assertion, originally put forward by Perlman (1927), that the level of unionism in the United States is as low as it is due to the "resistance power" of American business. The measure of this "resistance power used here is the ratio of business association employment to total employment in each state."

Several measures of the "quality of union services" were explicitly entered in some of the regressions in an attempt to assess whether any objectively measurable "performance measures," to use Ehrenberg and Goldberg's (1975) terminology, had a significant influence on union staff salaries. Closest to these authors' methodology were variables measuring the union wage differential in selected occupations on which the BLS regularly collects data, building trades, and local truckings. If the sort of pattern bargaining described by Eckstein and Wilson (1962) or the "orbits of coercive comparison" of Ross (1957) exist among unions in the same geographic area, then these occupational differentials should be good proxies for the benefits of unionization. However, the work by Miller, Zeller, and Miller (1965) points to grievance processing as the most important basis on which union members evaluate the performance of their unions. Although data on grievance processing are unavailable, two closely related measures of grievance activity have been used: "arbitration cases per union member and unfair labor practice cases per member. The arbitration measure is, of course, the furthest extent to which a union may pursue a member's rights under an existing collective bargaining agreement. The unfair practice measure is justified largely by the pre-Collyer doctrine (194 NLRB 837) practice of unions' filing an unfair labor practice charge simultaneously with the filing of a grievance as a means of causing greater costs to the employer's alleged contract violation. Furthermore, employer charges against unions must certainly be regarded as union attempts to increase member bargaining power though such (illegal) measures as secondary boycotts and hot-cargo contract clauses.

The variables entering the reduced-form estimates of the endogenous right-hand-side variable, which determine union staff salaries, are labeled and defined in the upper portion of table 10–2. The union services "quality" measures are treated likewise in the lower portion of this same table.

The observations on all of these variables are statewide averages or totals take for the years 1960, 1966, and 1970. In all three years, data for the state of Maryland are omitted because its union membership is combined with that of the District of Columbia, which in turn contains the AFL-CIO headquarters as well as the national headquarters of 53 unions, a clearly unrepresentative case of union "plants" in operation. However, excluding Maryland and the District of Columbia entails excluding only 4.2 percent of the nearly 139,000 union staff employed in 1970. Due to there being no data for some variables in 1960 and 1966 for the states of Alaska and Hawaii, these two states were excluded from the subsamples for these two years,

Table 10-2. Definitions of Exogenous and Quality Variables

Variable Label	*Variable Definition (Source of Data)*
FEM	Female proportion of employment. (Source: *Census of Population*)
BLK	Black population of employment. (Source: *Census of Population*)
RTWL	Dummy variable for state right-to-work law, (1 = state has a right-to-work law, 0 = state doesn't have right-to-work law). (Source: *Directory of National and International Labor Unions*)
BADMKT	Employees of private employment agencies per total employed persons. (Source: *County Business Patterns; Census of Population*)
OPPOSE	Employees of business associations per total employed persons (Source: *County Business Patterns; Census of Population*)
RENTB	Ratio of union wages in building trades occupations in the most populous metropolitan area to average hourly earnings in manufacturing. (Source: *Handbook of Labor Statistics*)
RENTT	Ratio of union wages in local trucking occupations in the most populous metropolitan area to average hourly earnings in manufacturing. (Source: *Handbook of Labor Statistics*)
LULPPM	Natural logarithm of unfair labor practice cases per union member. (Source: *National Labor Relations Board Annual Report; Statistics and Abstract*)
LARBPM	Natural logarithm of arbitration cases per union member (Source: *Federal Mediation and Conciliation Service Annual Report; Statistical Abstract*).

although they were included in the 1970 statistical analysis. Thus results will be reported below on a sample of 47 states in 1960, an equal number in 1966, and 49 states in 1970, as well as a pooled sample of 143 observations.

Due to the large number of alternative hypotheses and restrictions on coefficients, which will be helpful in deriving information on the production of union memberships, many hypotheses will be tested on the cross-sectional subsamples and the results from these later used as restriction in other cross-sectional samples. While a brief discussion of ordinary least squares estimates will be given, due to their properties being better known, the bulk of the statistical evidence presented will be two-stage least squares estimates. This, of course, implies that all standard errors of coefficients and hence t-statistics are only asymptotically unbiased and that R^2 is bounded not by 0 and 1 but rather by $-\infty$ and 1. Finally, since the quality of data varies

Table 10-3. Ordinary Least Squares Estimates of the Determinants of Union Staff Salaries

Equation Number	*Dependent Variable*				*Independent*
	W_s *(years)*	*LMEMPW (Q/L)*	*LMEM (Q)*	*LUE (L)*	*LALREC (P)*
(10.1)	LCOMP	.831	—	—	.980
	(1960)	(.076)			(.065)
(10.2)	LCOMP	.941	—	—	.704
	(1966)	(.227)			(.095)
(10.3)	LCOMP	.848	—	—	.590
	(1970)	(.220)			(.102)
(10.4)	LCOMP	.740	—	—	.730
	(POOLED)	(.084)			(.053)
(10.5)	LSAL	—	1.058	−1.056	.369
	(1970)		(.159)	(.163)	(.076)
(10.6)	LSAL	1.037	—	—	.373
	(1970)	(.130)			(.062)

Note: Standard errors of coefficients in parentheses.

among the cross-sectional subsamples, different emphases should be placed on the interpretation of the various coefficients across these subsamples. For example, data taken from the Census of Population had to be interpolated between 1960 and 1970 in order to create these same variables for the 1966 subsample. The other major adjustment necessary was to create the 1966 and 1970 LCOMP variables based on the 1960 ratio of total disbursements to officers and employees to union staff payroll. However, when this adjustment factor, WAGEPR, was entered as an explanatory variable in the 1966 and 1970 subsamples using payroll per employee as the dependent wage variable, it did not attain statistical significance, as may be seen in equation (10.16) of table 10–3.

While the specific coefficients in table 10–3 must be interpreted with caution because of simultaneous equation bias, it seems hard to reconcile the relatively high R^2 and *t*-statistics with the following comment from Bennett and Johnson (1980):

> As Alchian and Demsetz (1972, p. 779) observed, "if the economic organization meters poorly, with rewards and productivity loosely correlated, then productivity will be smaller; but if the economic organization meters well productivity will be

Variables				
LAVWAG (W_0)	*Other Variables*	*CONSTANT*	R^2 *(F-test)*	*S.E.E.* *(N)*
.068		−.282	.869	.134
(.138)		(.576)	(94.94)	(47)
.383		+.067	.684	.235
(.259)		(1.287)	(31.07)	(47)
.328		1.090	.585	.261
(.309)		(1.259)	(21.14)	(49)
.232		1.099	.7145	.220
(.110)		(.541)	(115.95)	(143)
.679		−5.149	.6869	.187
(.221)		(1.478)	(24.13)	(49)
.211	+.122 WAGEPR + .011 COVER	−1.757	.8030	.150
(.200)	(.120) (.003)	(1.382)	(35.05)	(49)

greater." The phenomenon that Alchian and Demsetz referred to as "shirking" will be present in the local union. [P. 11]

Of course, the multiple correlation here between union staff salaries (rewards) and productivity (revenues from union membership) is based on a theory of (inter) national union president's ownership of the union, not ownership by rank-and-file members as is the basis of Bennett and Johnson as well as Martin (1980). The ordinary least squares (OLS) statistical results in table 10–3 compare quite favorably to Bennett and Johnson's low *t*s and R^2 in their regression on the percentage of union receipts of officers' and employees' compensations, Ehrenberg and Goldberg's (1975) results on business agent salaries and the goals of union members, and even with the CES-type estimates for two-digit manufacturing industries across the states done by Liu and Hildebrand (1965).

However, whereas the results in table 10–3 are at first glance quite reassuring concerning the verbal and mathematical models presented here, the probable existence and direction of simultaneous equations biases lead us to reject the parameter values implied by these estimates. The foremost problem in this regard is the values of the elasticity of substitution, σ, implied

Table 10-4. Two-Stage Least Squares Estimates of the Determinants Union Staff Salaries[a]

Equation Number	*Dependent Variable*		*Independent*	
EQUATION NUMBER	*DEPENDENT VARIABLE (W_s) (Years)*	*LMEMPW (Q/L)*	*LMEM (Q)*	*LUE (L)*
(10.1)	LCOMP	1.115	—	—
	(1960)	(.228)		
(10.2)	LCOMP		.992	–
	(1960)		(.282)	(.282)
(10.3)	LCOMP	1.247	—	—
	(1960)	(.203)		
(10.4)	LCOMP	1.310	—	—
	(POOLED)	(.610)		
(10.5)	LCOMP	—	1.435	−1.396
	(POOLED)		(.544)	(.544)
(10.6)	LSAL	—	1.365	−1.266
	(POOLED)		(.476)	(.476)
(10.7)	LCOMP	1.235	.083	—
	(1970)	(.690)	(.071)	
(10.8)	LSAL	1.595	.062	—
	(1970)	(.435)	(.044)	
(10.9)	LCOMP	1.250	—	—
	(POOLED)	(.621)		
(10.10)	LCOMP	1.701	—	—
	(1966)	(.902)		

[a]All standard errors are in parentheses below coefficients.
[b]*F*-test, and R^2 are only asymptotically valid.

by the coefficients in the LMEMPW, LMEM, and LUE columns of table 10.3, according to which σ lies betwen 95 and 1.35. This latter figure lies outside the range of the Liu-Hildebrand estimates of σ for U.S. manufacturing and is in all probability an upwardly biased estimate of the ease of substituting capital for labor in union membership production.

Thus, table 10–4 presents the results of two-stage least squares (2SLS) estimations of the parameters of the determinants of union staff salaries, where output, LMEM, staff input, LUE and price of output, LALREC, are simultaneously determined with the salaries of union staff. Alternative 2SLS

Variable					
LALREC *(P)*	*LAVWAG* *(W_0)*	*COVER*	*CONSTANT*	*R^2* *(F-TEST)*	*S.E.E.* *(N)*
1.119	.044		−2.654	.8265	.154
(.123)	(.206)		(2.481)	(68.29)	(47)
1.414	−.395		−2.423	.7233	.197
(.399)	(.481)		(2.631)	(27.44)	(47)
1.218	—		−3.388	.7762	.173
(.121)			(1.502)	(76.30)	(47)
.732	.509		−5.959	.6089	.258
(.378)	(.591)		(6.099)	(72.13)	(143)
—	1.549		−5.732	.6124	.266
	(.308)		(5.827)	(54.376)	(143)
—	1.351		−3.879	.4808	.254
	(.270)		(2.915)	(42.92)	(143)
—	1.231	.0003	−18.055	.1667	.374
	(.451)	(.0071)	(9.214)	(2.20)	(49)
—	.839	.011	7.150	.4926	.238
	(.795)	(.005)	(3.393)	(10.68)	(49)
.869	.406	−.005	−5.667	.6100	.258
(.453)	(.621)	(.008)	(6.135)	(51.18)	(143)
.475	.612	—	−1.169	.6311	.252
(.573)	(.881)		(4.909)	(25.17)	(47)

estimates are also presented where output per worker, or union memberships per staff worker, LMEMPW, is jointly determined with salary.

The most heartening improvement of 2SLS over OLS may be seen in the estimated coefficients on LMEM, LUE, and LMEMPW, where the estimated values of $\sigma = {}^1/(1-\rho) = {}^1/-\hat{\beta}_{\text{LUE}} = 1/\hat{\beta}_{\text{LMEMPW}}$ range from a high of 1.004 down to .588. While these values are much more plausible, since it seems unlikely that capital is a close substitute in the production of union memberships, they are perhaps still too high due to our use of number of union staff workers, not hours of staff labor input. If union staff or, more probably, paid local union officials work part-time, then there would appear to be a more fixed input appearance to membership production than if we could observe hours variation in this labor input. Using the LMEMPW variable to estimate ρ and hence σ, there appears to be quite little variation over time in substitution possibilities and indeed a fairly narrow range of the estimated values of σ, $.588 - .897$.

The evidence on economies of scale in the production of union memberships is somewhat mixed, but the estimates in table 10–4 certainly imply no tremendous economies of scale. For equations (10.2), (10.5), and (10.6), recall that if the demand for union memberships is downward sloping (as all economists would assuredly believe it to be), the economies of scale parameter v may be bounded by $(\hat{\beta}_{LUE} + 1)/(1 - \hat{\beta}_{LMEM})$. If, in turn, $(\hat{\beta}_{LUE}) > 1$, this is an upper bound; otherwise, as in equation (10.2) of table 10–4, it is a lower bound. The two values of v implied by equations (10.5) and (10.6) the pooled cross-sections results, are respectively .910 and .729, whereas the range of results not reported in table 10–4 for the individual cross sections on LCOMP, the broad salary measure, is from .774 to .910. These results compare quite closely with those obtained by a different specification in equations (10.7) and (10.8) where the "scale factor," LMEM, is entered along with the substitution variable LMEMPW. Again, if $\delta \geq 0$, and $\hat{\rho} < 0$ implying $\sigma < 1$, equations (10.7) and (10.8) imply lower bounds on $v > (1 - \hat{\beta}_{LMEMPW})/(\hat{\beta}_{LMEMPW})$, or respectively $v \geq .736$ and $v \geq .906$. Finally, separate estimates using the method described in Kmenta (1967) give values of v not significantly different from 1 and $\sigma = .858$. Thus, in much of the remaining discussion, estimates using the coefficient on output per worker, LMEMPW, will be the bases for inferences about the elasticity of factor substitution.

The apparent absence of economies of scale in the production of union memberships has two possible explanations. First, authors such as Segal (1964) suggest that economies of scale may exist in the *initial* organization of plants, but that large organizations produce proportionately more grievances to process, which are taken all the way to arbitration, as recently found by Gandz (1979). Thus, in the sample period 1960–70 used here, when new union organizing in the United States was quite slow, the maintenance and servicing of current memberships may readily have exhibited no economies of scale. Second, as suggested in the last section, there may be higher salaries of union staff as a union grows in size in order that an international president insulate himself from electoral challenge, as discussed in Edelstein and Warner (1976, pp. 319–335). This, in turn, implies a certain amount of diseconomies of scale as far as cost curves would be measured, but also the sorts of positive coefficients on LMEM seen in equations (10.7) and (10.8). On the whole, to repeat the conclusion reached above, these effects are not of any great proportional influence.

If one accepts the lowest inferred value on the diseconomies of scale parameter, v, and applies this figure to the coefficients in equations (10.5) and (10.6), the pooled sample estimates on both measures of union staff pay, one may infer values of the elasticity of the demand for union membership to be at least 6.18 or above. However, the closeness of the coefficients on LMEM and LUE in these two equations, as well as comparable but unreported esimtates for each of the sample year cross sections, implies that the data considered here emanate from a seemingly competitive environment and/or one in which market demand is quite elastic with respect to the explicit and implicit costs of unionization. Thus, it seems that Berkowitz (1954) was correct in arguing, "Unions are selling a service in a competitive world" (p. 584). If this is true, it is perhaps not surprising that union leaders have traditionally not pushed for the sorts of union dues and initiation fees that Becker (1959) thought union monopoly wages warranted. On the other hand, it is these other costs of unionization that Becker neglected, especially pay lost to strikes and particularly recognition strikes, and low job security early in a union member's career, as shown in Lentz (1980).

If it mav be conditionallv accepted that our data base is an average across firms in a fairly competitive market, it becomes interesting to consider the estimates in table 10–4, where the price variable, LALREC, is explicitly entered in the regression equations. In the estimates of table 10–3, where LALREC was taken to be exogenous, several of the estimated coefficients implied that union staff salaries had an elasticity with respect to the "price" of memberships that was significantly less than 1, something that is highly improbable. When, however, LALREC is viewed as being determined in a market for union membership, as is true when it is an endogenous variable throughout table 10–4, one finds that the elasticity of union staff total compensation with respect to receipts from union membership is not significantly different from 1. The fact that the coefficients on the price variable, LALREC, in the two pooled sample equations (10.4) and (10.9) is still less than 1 still suggests that one should not neglect the insurance and pension benefits of officers and staff, as Bennett and Johnson (1980) did. Obviously, the dependent variable, LSAL, as shown by equations (10.5) and (10.6) of table 10–4, does not capture the full range of employee compensation. But, to try to disentangle officer and staff benefits from member benefits is beyond the limits of the data available.

With respect to the opportunity wage variable, LAVWAG, one must note that it never attains statistical significance when the price variable, LALREC, is also entered in the regression equations on total compensation

Table 10-5. Estimates Impact of Union Membership "Quality" on Compensation of Union Staff

Quality Variable	*Sample Year (S)*	*Estimation Technique*	*Estimated Coefficient*	*t-Statistic*[a]
ULPPM	1960	OLS	.056	1.65
"	"	2SLS	−.071	.11[a]
"	1966	OLS	.082	1.19
"	"	2SLS	.202	.40[a]
"	*1970*	*OLS*	*.064*	.70
"	"	2SLS	−.001	.01[a]
"	POOLED	OLS	.066	1.94
"	"	2SLS	.083	.98[a]
RENTB	1970	OLS	.516	1.40
"	"	2SLS	.367	.32[a]
RENTT	"	OLS	.180	.36
"	"	2SLS	−.140	−.72[a]
LARBPM	"	OLS	.020	.85
"	"	2SLS	.159	1.33[a]

[a]For 2SLS estimates, *t*-statistics are only asymptotically valid.

of union staff. This seems to sustain the mathematical model presented earlier in this section, though it could be a result of an incorrect choice of an "opportunity wage" for union staff. On the other hand, estimates using the average first-quarter payroll per employee of business associations rather than the average weekly earnings in manufacturing (LAVWAG) proved to be no better; e.g., the coefficients of this variable in 2SLS estimates for 1960 similar to equation (10.1) of table 10–4 was −.07 with a standard error of .10. When, however, LALREC is not explicitly entered in the regression equation as in equations (10.5) and (10.8) LAVWAG attains statistical significance. Comparing, then, equations (10.1) and (10.3) of table 10–5, one notes that the R^2 is increased and the standard error is decreased when LAVWAG is entered in the estimation along with LALREC. Thus, this specification appears, albeit asymptotically, to be superior, although it may tend to increase standard errors and hence imprecision of estimates on LALREC.

Finally, the COVER variable measuring the difference in sample coverage between employment and payroll data, on the one hand, and the disbursements to officers and employees, on the other hand, appears in equations (10.7) and (10.9) have no discernible impact on the determinants of union staff total compensation. Comparing equation (10.9) with equation (10.6) one finds that neither individual coefficients nor overall (asymptotic) significance is affected by its inclusion or exclusion. However, it should be noted that COVER enters significantly in the LSAL equation (10-8) where, again, the dependent variable is salary subject to OASDHI only. Thus, it appears that the *County Business Patterns* employment figure is a good measure of the number of those union staff and officers who receive the total disbursements reported under Landrum-Griffin, but, as perhaps expected, the salary figure derived from these payroll statistics is an inadequate measure of the economist's notion of union staff "wages."

Table 10–5 presents only the coefficients and *t*-statistics on the various *member-defined* union membership "quality" variables. Whether it be processing grievances to arbitration (LARBPM), filing unfair labor practices against employers (LULPPM), or garnering union wage differentials (RENTB and RENTT), it appears that member-defined quality variables have little statistical significance in the compensation of union staff and officers. Of course, these results correspond quite closely with the unsuccessful statistical tests of Ehrenberg and Goldberg (1975) and Bennett and Johnson (1980) who all argued for a model of union staff compensation based on member goals. To repeat, the model proposed here argues that these variables should certainly be of secondary importance only to an international union president seeking to maximize the residual between fees from members and costs of obtaining and retaining them. Indeed, though not reported in table 10–4 and 10–5, the inclusion of these quality variables did not substantially alter the coefficients on the other membership "profit" maximizing variables. It should, however, be pointed out that the vast majority of the coefficients in table 10–5 are positive in sign, and one would expect that international union presidents would realize that union memberships are "produced" by serving the interest of the memberships, just as a retailer recognizes that after-sale servicing by employees may be profitable.

To summarize the empirical results of this section, it seems fair to say that union memberships are produced under a "technology" or internal union organization which exhibits low substitution possibilities for capital and labor and limited economies or diseconomies of scale in the production and retention of union members. It further seems justified to conclude that the market for union memberships is competitive and exhibits a quite elastic demand on the part of members and potential members. The empirical estimates presented here clearly reveal that, while unions may be competitive in the memberships "product" market, they do not behave as price takers in the labor market for their staff.

Finally, and perhaps most importantly for the central perspective of this work, as opposed to the current property rights–collective voice explanations of unionism, the model proposed and tested in this section is one that gives a cogent and cohesive economic explanation of unionism, without any free rider latent group problems, based upon international union presidents being viewed as enterpreneurs and residual claimants of the union organization.

Conclusions and Implications

The empirical results of the last section seem to imply that it is not unfounded to consider unions as economic entities "owned" or motivated by their international union presidents. This president's behavior was modeled as one of maximizing the revenues minus cost, or "profits," from union memberships "produced" by the field staff and local union staff and officers. This "top-down" perspective on the behavior of unions is not new to labor economics and labor relations—e.g., Berkowitz (1954) discussion and Taft's (1956) noting many of the near kingdoms of union presidents—but it is one that is also an extension of the some of the very new and very different theories of unions, especially that of Martin (1980). As argued above, the "bottom-up" theories of unions, ranging from Martin's (1980) to the collective voice discussions of Freeman (1976) and his disciples, lack a coherent explanation of why unions began and survive, as was also argued by Olson (1971). The model presented here of the international union president as entrepreneur overcomes many of the lacunas in these and other theories, e.g., Henry Simon's (1948) prediction that democratic unions would quickly march up the demand curve for labor and have only one member.

The empirical testing put forward here, however, has been only in terms of the allocation of resources actually purchased on the market by unions or purchasing power that they may exercise in markets. On the other hand, most prior theories of union goals and empirics on their behavior have stressed the compensation and allocation of union labor, something that comes about as a result of the interaction between unions, members/workers, and plant managers. As is true of the classic identification problem in econometrics, we don't know whether the empirical results discussed in Freeman and Medoff (1980) are generated by unions acting as price takers in varying environments or are generated by other functions, such as the interaction between the demand for union memberships and the supply thereof by union organizations.

Given the perspective put forward here, it is possible to make some further predictions about how union international presidents would proceed in their attempts to maximize residual revenues by their actions in collective bargaining. First, it is clear that no one will pay something for nothing, so union presidents will seek to provide either monopoly union wages or the public goods so often discussed by the collective voice theorists. If union presidents can obtain these through their National Labor Relations Act powers, then they may sell them in exchange for dues, fees, and strike activity from members. In light of the present theory, it is surprising that Lloyd Reynolds (1978) could ask the question, "Why has the overall (wage) impact of unionism apparently been rather moderate?" (p. 508) and in the same book state the following, "Trading between cost and noncost items is also possible as indicated by the union official who said, 'Every year I sell the union shop for a nickel'" (p. 422). Indeed, the reasonableness of union leadership is readily expected if excessive wage settlements would harm memberships, as Kochin (1977) argued was the motivation behind, and Mills (1980) showed was the effect of, the Construction Industry Stabilization Board. In summary, we would anticipate union presidents to negotiate improvements in "benefits" in exchange for dues, etc., but to contain these so as not to reduce revenues from union memberships either from marching up the demand curves (or value of average product) of union labor or from setting too low an incentive to maintain membership. Thus, Block and Saks (1980) bureaucratic objective function, i.e., maximization of membership, as well as Martin's (1980) discussion in the same vein both seem to err by implying that there is little role for a positive union wage differential in maximizing membership as well as by failing to see that obtaining more members has a cost to the union organization. If the estimates in the last section are to the taken literally, the diseconomies of scale inherent in membership production imply that there is an optimal scale of union even if, as it appears from these same estimates, there is a competitive product market. For example, in the context of a human capital model of unionization such as that provided in Lentz (1980), it can be shown that union initiation fees may not be "too low" as suggested by Becker (1959), and periodic dues payments and seniority practices of unions maximize the net present value of revenues acrruing to the union organization.

Indeed, while Martin (1980) argues that attenuated membership property rights should lead to a "more, more, more NOW!" bargaining stance, seniority privileges in pay and employment seem to correspond much more to leadership objectives and constraints.

Again, one need not invoke purely selfish (in the commonsense usage) motives to a union leader's managing the union in an efficient manner. A union president may have the most idealistic visions of members' losing their "chains of wage slavery", but as Lloyd Reynolds (1978) argues, "He becomes convinced after a few years that he can run the union better than anyone else, and in many cases he is right" (p. 374). At the height of incongruity in this context is George Strauss's (1977) characterization of David Dubinsky, former president of the ILGWU and one of the founding fathers of the CIO, as having reacted "with all the ferocity of the most antediluvian employer to the creation of a union among his union staff" (p. 228). Indeed, one might assert that Dubinsky was acting as if he owned the ILGWU.

While the argument presented here implies a "value of the union" or "profit" maximization and attendant efficiency in the allocation of union staff, whether this has welfare and hence public policy implication is still quite open to question. If unions receive their dues for providing public goods that otherwise would not have been provided, as Freeman and others assert, then vesting ownership rights in an entrepreneur-union president may possibly, as Hirshleifer (1976, pp. 455–457) has shown, produce a Pareto-optimum solution. If, however, unions produce basically monopoly rents, the story becomes more cloudy as to whether a Martin (1980) model union of attenuated owners produces less deadweight loss than does the union president ownership model presented here. This is mainly so because the Martin-type union could readily by seen to have a much shorter probable existence given the shortening of its time horizon due to property rights attenuation. On the other hand, the union president will more rationally exploit his monopoly powers and not "kill the goose that lays the golden eggs."

Further international comparisons seem highly warranted given the reliance here on U.S. labor law, history, and ideology, as well as the data used for this study. However, Taft (1956) appraises the apparent de facto property rights of union presidents as follows, "This extraordinary (SIC) slow rate of change among leaders seems to be a general law in trade union organization throughout the world" (p. 36). However, Edelstein and Warner (1976, pp. 15–16) maintain that the formal union constitutional powers of national presidents differ widely between the United States and Great Britain. Similarly, in France and in many other countries of Western Europe, according to Kassalow (1980), unions receive revenues and/or resources directly from governments regardless of their relative membership size. In such a case, as Rosa (1980) has implicitly argued, a model based on maximization of residual revenues from union membership is inappropriate. However, this need not imply that these unions act willy-nilly in their allocation of resources, as long as union leaders still have strong ownership rights, as Taft (1956) contends.[5]

It must be recognized that the new perspectives on unions and union economic behavior, particularly Martin (1980) and Freeman (1976), have greatly stimulated this and other recent studies of unionism. However, what these "grass roots" or "bottom-up" theories of union behavior fail to do is to take account of what might be called the "corporate structure" of unions. While Martin (1980) emphasizes participation of members in union decision making, surely this is of little importance at the national union level, as well documented by Edelstein and Warner (1976). Indeed, this grass roots–local union democracy may be a monitoring device contrived by national union presidents, for in a large national union it is quite helpful to have competitive markets for local union leadership–staff. That this produces monitoring is perhaps shown by the data of Applebaum and Blaine (1975) on local leader turnover and by experience under Landrum-Griffin cited above on prosecutions for mishandling of union funds.

In conclusion, recent theories of unionism and its impacts have yet to provide a plausible explanation of how the public goods and free-rider problems of unions can be solved in order that unions might originally come into being or persist in the face of the organization-dissipating forces inherent in the analyses of most recent theories. As suggested in the second section, the theory put forward here is one that meets the test of the survival of business unionism over the other type of unionism described by Hoxie (1921) and implicitly elaborated by recent work of Freeman (1976). The new meaning of "business unionism" is, contrary to Hoxie's notion that unions emerge out of "group psychology," that every business needs an entrepreneur residual claimant to make it operate with sufficient efficiency in order that it may survive economically.

Notes

1. However, this positivist approach leaves something to be desired when we come to talk about policy intervention with agents who think they are doing something other than what economists assume them to be doing.

2. Berkowitz switches back and forth between discussing memberships as the output produced and units of service. The empirical estimates attempted to control for quality measures but found them to be insignificant.

3. In defense of Bennett and Johnson and other authors, it should be noted that I inquired in 1978 whether this office had any published data and received a negative answer. Subsequent bibliographic investigation revealed the statistical bulletins mentioned in the text but the item for 1970 had to be obtained on interlibrary loan from the U.S. Department of Labor.

4. Empirical work currently under way concerning French data somewhat comparable to tha used here is the subject of a forthcoming paper by the author.

References

Applebaum, L. 1966. "Officer Turnover and Salary in Local Unions." *Industria and Labor Relations Review* 19, no. 2 (January):224–230.

Applebaum, L., and Blaine, H. R. 1975. "Compensation and Turnover of Unio Officers." *Industrial Relations* 14, no. 2 (May):156–157.

Arrow, K. J., et al. 1961. "Capital-Labor Substitution and Economic Efficiency. *Review of Economics and Statistics* 63:225–250.

Ashenfelter, O., and Johnson, G. E. 1969. "Bargaining Theory, Trade Unions, an Industrial Strike Activity." *American Economic Review* 59 (March):35–49.

Bain, G. S., and Elsheikh, F. 1976. *Union Growth and the Business Cycle.* Oxfor Blackwell.

Becker, E. H. 1980. "Meany Farewell, Bid to Auto Workers, Teamsters Mark AFI CIO Convention." *Monthly Labor Review* 103, no. 2 (February):58–62.

Becker, G. S. 1959. "Union Restrictions on Entry." In *The Public Stake in Unio Power,* ed. P. D. Bradley. Charlottesville: University of Virginia Press.

Bennett, J. T., and Johnson, M. H. 1980. "The Impact of Right to Work Laws on th Economic Behavior of Local Unions. A Property Rights Perspective." *Journal Labor Research*, no. 1 (Spring):1–27.

Berkowitz, M. 1954. "The Economics of Trade Union Organization and Administr tion." *Industrial and Labor Relations Review* 7, no. 4 (July):537–549.

Block, R. N., and Saks, D. H. 1980. "Union Decision-Making and the Supply Union Representation: A Preliminary Analysis. *Industrial Relations Resear Association*, pp. 218–225.

Duncan, G. J., and Stafford, F. P. 1980. "Do Union Members Receive Compe sating Wage Differentials?" *American Economic Review* 70 (June):355–371.

Eckstein, O., and Wilson, T. A. 1962. "The Determinants of Money Wages American Industry." *Quarterly Journal of Economics* 85, no. 3 (August):37 414.

Edelstein, J. D., and Warner, M. 1976. *Comparative Union Democracy: Oppositi and Democracy in British and American Unions.* New York: Random House.

Federal Mediation and Conciliation Service. 1960. *Thirteenth Annual Repo* Washington: U.S. Government Printing Office.

______. 1966. *Nineteenth Annual Report.* Washington: U.S. Government Printi Office.

______. 1970. *Twenty-Third Annual Report.* Washington: U.S. Governme Printing Office.

Freeman, R. B. 1976. "Individual Labor Mobility and Union Voice in the Lab Market." *American Economic Review* 66, no. 2 (May): 361–368.

Freeman, R. B., and Medoff, J. L. *What Do Unions Do?* forthcoming.

Friedman, M. 1953. *Essays in Positive Economics*. Chicago: University of Chicago Press.

Gandz, J. 1979. "Employee Grievances: Incidence and Patterns of Revolution." In *Industrial Relations Research Association Series, Proceedings of the Thirty-First Annual Meeting*, ed. D. Barbara. Madison: Industrial Relations Research Association, pp. 167–269.

Hirshleifer, J. 1976. *Price Theory and Applications*. Englewood Cliffs, N.J.: Prentice Hall.

Hoxie, R. J. 1921. *Trade Unionism in the United States*. New York: D. Appleton.

Kassalow, E. M. 1980. "The Closed and Union Stop in Western Europe, and American Perspective." *Journal of Labor Research* I, no. 7 (Fall):323–339.

Kmenta, J. 1967. "On Estimation of the CES Production Function." *International Economic Review* 8, no. 2 (June):180–189.

Kochin, L. 1977. "The Social Cost of Union Monopoly." *Department of Economics, University of Washington* (unpublished).

Lawler, E. E., III, and Levin, E. 1968. "Union Officers Perceptions of Member's Pay Preferences." *Industrial and Labor Relations Review* 21, no. 4 (July):509–517.

Lazear, E. P. 1979. "Why Is There Mandatory Retirement?" *Journal of Political Economy* 87, no. 6 (December):1261–1284.

Lentz, B. 1980. "The Benefits of Union Membership and the Decision to Join a Union." *Journal of Labor Research* 1, no. 2 (Fall):377–407.

Levinson, H. M. 1980. "Trucking." In *Collective Bargaining Contemporary American Experience*, ed. G. M. Somers. Madison: Industrial Relations Research Association.

Lewis, H. G. 1959. "Competitive and Monopoly Unionism." In *The Public Stake in Union Power*, ed. P. D. Bradley. Charlottesville: University of Virginia Press.

Liu, T. C., and Hildebrand, G. H. 1965. *Manufacturing Production Functions in the United States 1957*. Ithaca: Cornell University Press.

Lumsden, K., and Peterson, C. 1975. "The Effect of Right-to-Work Laws on Unionization in the United States." *Journal of Political Economy* 83, no. 6 (December):1237–1248.

Martin, D. L. 1980. *An Ownership Theory of the Trade Union*. Berkeley: University of California Press.

Miernyk, W. H. 1980. "Coal." In G. H. Somers, ed., *Collective Bargaining*, pp. 1–48.

Miller, R. W., Zeller, F. A., and Miller, G. W. 1965. *The Practice of Local Union Leadership*. Columbus, Ohio: Ohio State University Press.

Mills, D. Q. 1980. "Construction." In G. M. Somers, *Collective Bargaining*, pp. 49–98.

Modigliani, F., and Miller, M. H. "The Cost of Capital, Corporate Finance, and the Theory of Investment." *American Economic Review* 48, June 1958. pp 261–297.

Moore, W. J., and Newman, R. P. 1975. "On the Prospects of American Trade Union Growth: A Cross-Section Analysis." *Review of Economics and Statistics* 57, no. 4 (November):435–445.

Olson, M. 1971. *The Logic of Collective Action*. Cambridge: Harvard University Press.

Pencavel, J. 1971. "The Demand for Union Services: An Exercise." *Industrial and Labor Relations Review* 25, no. 7 (January):180–190.

Rees, A. 1977. *The Economics of Trade Unions*. Chicago: The University of Chicago.

Reynolds, L. G. 1978. *Labor Economics and Labor Relations*. Englewood Cliffs, N.J.: Prentice-Hall.

Rosa, J. J. 1980. "Théorie de la firme syndicale." *Vie et Sciences Economiques*, no. 86 (July):1–22.

Segal, M. 1964. "The Relation Between Union Wage Impact and Market Structure." *Quarterly Journal of Economics* 77, no. 1 (February):94–114.

Seidman, J., et al. 1958. *The Worker Views His Union*. Chicago: University of Chicago Press.

Simkin, W. E. 1968. "Refusal to Ratify Contracts." *Industrial and Labor Relations Review* 21, no. 4 (July):518–540.

Simons, H. 1948. "Some Reflections on Syndicalism." In *Economic Policy for a Free Society*. Chicago: University of Chicago Press.

Somers, G. G., ed. 1980. *Collective Bargaining: the Contemporary American Experience*. Madison: Industrial Relations Research Association.

Stieber, J. 1980. "Steel." In G. G. Somers, *Collective Bargaining*, pp. 151–208.

Strauss, G. 1977. "Union Government in the U.S.: Research Past and Future." *Industrial Relations* 16, no. 2 (May):216–242.

Taft, P. 1956. *The Structure and Government of Labor Unions*. Cambridge: Harvard University Press.

Troy, L. 1975. "American Unions and Their Wealth." *Industrial Relations* 14, no. 2 (May):134–144.

U.S. Department of Commerce. 1970. Bureau of Census, *Census of Population*. Washington: U.S. Government Printing Office.

______. 1959. Bureau of Census, *County Business Patterns*. Washington: U.S. Government Printing Office.

______. 1966. Bureau of Census, *County Business Patterns*. Washington: U.S. Government Printing Office.

______. 1970. Bureau of Census, *County Business Patterns*. Washington: U.S. Government Printing Office.

______. 1973. Bureau of Census, *Statistical Abstract of the United States*. Washington: U.S. Government Printing Office.

U.S. Bureau of Labor Management Reports. 1960. *Guide for Reporting Your Union Finances*. Washington: Department of Labor.

U.S. Bureau of Labor Statistics. 1970. *Selected Earnings and Demographic Characteristics of Union Members*. Report 417.

_____. 1972. *Directory of National and International Unions in the United States*. Bulletin 1750. Washington: U.S. Government Printing Office.

A Comment on Lentz, by Jean-Francois Hennart

In this paper, Lentz assumes that American union managers behave as though they owned their unions and that they must therefore strive to maximize the difference between membership receipts and the cost of generating that membership. Membership receipts consist of dues and initiation fees, while the cost of "producing" membership is that of creating monopoly rents and of providing such individual services as grievance processing, seniority, and social activities.

In a longer version of this paper, Lentz supports his assumption by a variety of empirical evidence that shows that (1) international union presidents control both the financial assets of individual unions and their exclusive bargaining rights; (2) they have strong property rights in union "profits," enjoying both long tenures and the ability to transfer their right to tenure to a chosen successor; (3) they can use "profits" earned by the union either as personal consumption or to further their goals, free from constraints from the membership.

If international union presidents can appropriate the difference between receipts from the sale of union services and costs of supplying these services, then they will maximize their utility by maximizing the present value of the future stream of union profits. International union presidents should then hire and pay their employees so as to maximize residual, given the production function for union services, the demand for union membership, and the supply of union staff. Union staff salaries should therefore depend on staff productivity and on the price of output. Lentz specifies both an ordinary least squares and a simultaneous two-stage least squares model in which output, labor inputs, and the price of outputs are simultaneously determined with union staff salaries. The model explains between 49 percent and 82 percent of the variance in staff wages.

One of the implications of Lentz's model is that the productivity of union employees is not a function of the quantity and quality of the services they perform, but of their ability to increase the difference between dues receipts and the cost of supplying services. As hypothesized, Lentz finds that output quality variables, such as wage differentials, arbitration cases presented per union member, and unfair labor practices filed per union member, had no statistically significant influence on the compensation of union staff and officers.

Lentz draws from his model some interesting implications. First, union leaders will strike a balance between increases in wage and nonwage benefits and membership gains. They will not maximize wage gains, and thus march up the demand curve for labor, nor will they maximize membership, and dilute wage gains and the incentive to unionize. Second, the model explains why unions have found periodic dues payments coupled with seniority preferable to high initiation fees. Lastly, Lentz's model explains why, in spite of the formidable freerider problem emphasized by Olson (1965), large industrial unions have come into being. The Lentz hypothesis is consistent with the crucial role played by a small number of individuals in the creation of encompassing trade unions.

The model presented by Lentz is interesting and stimulating, but the robustness of its conclusions is reduced by some data weaknesses. Union membership data are notoriously unreliable. Lentz argues that the reporting of inaccurate membership figures by local unions to the international will have no impact on the results, since international union presidents will base their allocative decisions on the reported figures. But it is possible that international unions have two separate sets of figures, one for external consumption and the other for internal allocative decisions.

Both the LCOMP and the LSAL variables also have major weaknesses. The LSAL variable uses County Business Patterns data. This data source provides a head count of union staff, but does not distinguish between full and part-time employees. Neither LSAL nor LCOMP includes union labor directly paid by the firm. This is a grave omission, since 40 percent of all union contracts in the United States allow employer-paid time off for union business. Lentz's results are probably biased, although it is difficult to guess in what direction.

If Lentz's model seems to describe reasonably well American unions, French unions exhibit characteristics that are closer to the Martin (1980) model. Although much more research is needed on this point, it appears that French union leaders do not have the property rights enjoyed by their American counterparts.[1] Val Lorwin (1966) thus notes:

> There are no one-man unions in France. There are unions run by small cliques; there are unions run essentially by a political party. But there is no important union identified as that of a single leader, controlling it through a personal machine. No one speaks of "Dupont's union" or "Durands union . . . " Whatever their real power or way of living, union officials receive modest pay and need frequent mandates from their membership. [P. 196]

There are two main reasons for this situation. First, the potential gains from union membership are lower, and the unionization costs higher, than in the United States. Second, competition between unions and within unions severely restricts the property rights of union leaders.

The benefits to be gained from joining a union (and therefore the possible level of dues) are much lower in France than in the United States because

French unions do not have a monopoly of representation. A worker may decide to be represented for collective bargaining by any of the five representative unions, or by autonomous unions, if they are deemed to be representative at his plant. In marked contrast to the United States, where the law forbids an individual represented by a union from bargaining with the employer for better or different terms than those mentioned in the collective agreement, French workers are free to negotiate better terms for themselves. French unions do not therefore hold exclusive bargaining rights.

The scope of collective bargaining is also much more limited in France, because many of the fringe benefits obtained by collective bargaining in the United States (such as paid vacations and leave, severance pay, unemployment and retirement benefits, health insurance, job safety and health, and overtime pay) are granted by law to all French workers. Moreover, French unions have no exclusive control on the main source of bargaining power, the right to strike. In France, the right to strike is an individual right, not a union right. Employees may thus strike even during the life of a collective agreement.

Furthermore, unions in France do not provide some of the private goods supplied by their American counterparts. For example, unions do not have exclusive control of the grievance procedure. Ship stewards (delegués du personnel) are elected by the whole work force, and a substantial number of them are not union members. Individual grievances can also be presented to the government labor inspector, or to the local labor court (conseil de prud'hommes). In contrast to the United States, unions do not guarantee seniority rights in France: The order of layoffs is fixed in part by law, and in part is left to the employer.

If the benefits of union membership are lower in France, the cost of collecting dues are markedly higher. That no union or closed shops exist in France makes the sale of union cards much more difficult. The law also forbids checking off dues. Since the potential value of union services is much lower, and the cost of selling these services higher, than in the United States, the potential profits to be made by supplying union services are likely to be lower. Thus, the incentive of union leaders to obtain exclusive property rights in the residual should be reduced.

The presence of competing unions limits also the property rights enjoyed by the union hierarchy. In France, switching unions is very easy. A union leader who increases dues without a compensating increase in benefits, or who decreases benefits without lowering dues, is likely to lose many dues-paying members. As a result, French unions have experienced wide swings in membership. Membership in the Confédération Générale du Travail (CGT),

France's largest union, is today only one-fourth of what it was in 1945–1947.

Moreover, internal competition seems stronger in French unions, leading to occasional splits, such as the secessions of Force Ouvrière and the Fédération de L'Education Nationale from the CGT in 1947, and the split of the Confédération Française Démocratique du Travail from the Confédération Française des Travailleurs Chrétiens in 1966. Unlike in the United States, seceding unions are entitled to a share of union assets. Thus, internal threats to withdraw and competition between unions and between union and nonunion candidates reduce greatly the opportunity of top-level union managers to appropriate union profits. These factors probably explain why union leaders have increasingly turned to the government for direct subsidies.

The preceding considerations argue that French unions should show some of the characteristics pointed out by Martin. Martin predicted that, if union members have attenuated property rights, union policies will display a higher rate of time discount than in a Lentz-type union, where union leaders have full property rights in the residual. In a Martin-type union, "rents not claimed in the present are not secure if left to the future, because there is no way to capitalize future streams of earnings into present transfer prices. This suggests that members should risk the diversion of current rents to investments for the purposes of producing future rents" (Martin, 1980, p. 95).

Union members will therefore have an incentive to maximize short-term gains. They will find it in their interest to resist dues increases and to deplete strike funds in order to gain immediate advantages. The rank and file will also push for "unreasonable demands" that threaten the long-run survival of the firm or the industry (Martin, 1980, p. 89).

The ability of managers to appropriate the residual will consequently hinge on their control of the strike weapon. Managers in a Lentz-type union will therefore exercise tight control over strike and strike funds. As Martin points out, strikes in most American unions are subject to authorization by the executive board of the national or international union. International unions manage the strike fund and will withhold such funds from any local starting an unauthorized strike.

In France, fédérations and confédérations seem to have been unable to control local union bargaining and strikes. Rank-and-file participation in collective bargaining is common and acceptance or rejection of settlements is usually left to a vote by the local membership. Union constitutions grant to local unions the right to start strikes, their only obligation being to inform the federation. Many authors have noted the absence of central coordination in the major strike waves that have been characteristic of French labor relations. Shorter and Tilly (1974) thus note that in 1936 and 1968 the strikers "were mobilized by local unions taking command at the outset, but in disregard of and in opposition to the wishes of the national federations and confederations" (p. 141). As predicted by Martin, in France, rank-and-file autonomy in calling strikes and setting demands has resulted in low dues and in a pattern of frequent, ineffective strikes.

Dues in French unions are very low and are irregularly paid. Textile workers who are members of the CGT textile federation will pay in monthly dues one-fifth of the amount paid by their Swedish counterparts. In spite of compulsory financing by employers (in the form of time credits for union members elected to various representative positions) and of government subsidies for training, French unions are poor in assets and in personnel.

The democratic nature of French unions has also made it difficult to invest in strike funds. The CFDT is the only union with a strike fund, and this fund is centrally controlled. Decentralized decision making, coupled with the absence of strike benefits, has led to frequent, short, and generally ineffective strikes. Over the 1969–1977 period, strikes lasted an average of 1.81 days, compared to 16.28 days for the United States.

The interesting hypothesis presented by Martin thus seems to be verified in the French case, whereas there is some evidence that American unions are closer to the Lentz model. Although the preceding observations are highly tentative, they show how fruitful the property rights approach to trade unions can be in explaining international differences in their structure and behavior.

Note

1. The following views were developed jointly with Bernard Lentz.

References

Lorwin, V. 1966. *The French Labor Movement.* Cambridge, Mass.: Harvard University Press.

Martin, D. 1980. "Unions as Nonproprietary Institutions." In *The Economics of Nonproprietary Institutions,* ed. K. Clarkson and D. Martin. *Research in Law and Economics,* Supplement 1. Greenwich, Conn.: JAI Press.

Olson, M. 1965. *The Logic of Collective Action.* Cambridge, Mass.: Harvard University Press.
Shorter, E., and Tilly, C. 1974. *Strikes in France 1830–1968.* London: Cambridge University Press.

III PERSPECTIVES FOR RESEARCH

11 UNIONS: ECONOMIC PERFORMANCE AND LABOR MARKET STRUCTURE

Peter B. Doeringer

This chapter takes as its point of departure two themes in trade union research, one originating in the 1940s and 1950s and the other in the early 1960s. The former centered on the role of economic considerations and trade union politics in the formulation of union wage policy (Dunlop, 1944; Ross, 1948). The latter addressed the question of how best to understand the economic impact of the unions (Lewis, 1963).

The discussion of union wage policy offered the proposition that unions confront an inescapable wage-employment trade-off embodied in the demand curve for labor for the firm, occupation, or industry. Wages could be increased above their competitive level, but only at the expense of jobs in the long term. Thus, as part of their bargaining policy, unions must determine the balance between wage and employment effects. The balance chosen, however, depends on a variety of factors: the overall state of the economy, the preferences of union members, the bargaining goals of employers, bargains struck elsewhere, and the like.

The bulk of the research done on union economic policy has concentrated on measuring one variable in this trade-off: the extent to which union wages have been shifted relative to those of nonunion labor. The choice of the relative wage as the principal focus of study has occurred partly through the belief that unions themselves are most concerned with raising wages, partly because there is little evidence of unions' shifting the functional distribution of income between capital and labor, and partly because wages are the most readily observed and obvious variable for economists to study. More recently, there have been attempts to get at a larger set of relative economic effects—fringe benefits, turnover, seniority, and the like—but these have been conducted mainly in the spirit of the earlier wage studies (Freeman, 1980, 1978c, 1978d).

Studies of union wage effects have been criticized for analyzing the economic impact of unions in an unnecessarily limited way. Unions are assumed to leave labor markets unchanged except for wage or other related effects. Measurements of union effects made under such assumptions do not allow for the possibility of more dynamic considerations. As Dunlop (1962) noted in an earlier critique of such studies:

> All we know about collective bargaining suggests that the most important effects involve fundamental changes in an enterprise and its surrounding product and labor markets. It is really not possible to leave the enterprise and its markets alone, introduce a union, and then see what happens to the wage structure. The introduction of unionism typically involves a wholesale transformation. [P. 343]

The debate over how best to measure and analyze union economic impacts raises the larger question of the significance of unions as labor market institutions. Those who study the impact of unions on relative wages tend to emphasize the tension between market competition and unions and to equate unions with the exercise of monopoly power and with the distortion of the labor market.

Alternatively, many view unions as both economic and social institutions firmly embedded in the large fabric of a constantly changing and evolving society. Unions belong to a class of institutions—families, firms, unions, schools, and the like—having decision-making characteristics distinct from those of the individuals who belong to them. Just as families make decisions regarding labor supply that differ from those that would be made by the same individuals if they were unrelated, groups of individuals within a union may make different decisions about wages collectively than they would individually. According to this broader view, the existence of unions is not simply a matter of economic costs and benefits. Unions may be concerned with the distribution as well as the level of economic benefits achieved through bargaining, their economic policies may induce a wide range of adjustments and innovations at the work place, and they may devise economic policies to alter the market context within which they bargain.

In this chapter, an attempt is made to interpret the economic behavior of trade unions in a more complex and dynamic fashion than is found in many studies of the economic impact of unions. An examination of a broad spectrum of research relating to union economic policies demonstrates the variety of ways in which unions and markets interact. The examples used draw heavily on the United States experience, but parallels with other advanced market economies are used when appropriate. In the first section, various modes of union economic behavior are described. The second section addresses the issue of relative union effects upon the wage-employment relationship and also examines more macro issues of economic performance. The third section discusses questions of inequality, equity, and labor market structure. The chapter then concludes with a discussion of unions, markets, and public policy.

Union Economic Strategies

Studies focusing on wage effects and various trade-offs against wage increases are consistent with the traditional adversary model of unionization. Power and bargaining skill are thought to determine the distribution of economic outcomes within a range set by competitive constraints. The range in which bargaining can occur is inversely related to the degree of product and labor market competition. Where oligopoly power permits discretion over prices and output, and where nonunion product or labor market competition can be limited, opportunity exists for unions to influence wages.

Unions, however, can develop policies toward market variables other than wages. Where unions can encourage the reorganization of labor markets or production processes, resource utilization can be improved and the range for bargaining increased. There are also possibilities for expanding the resource pool from which economic benefits can be paid by using public policy to shift the demand for labor in particular sectors, as in the case of production subsidies and import restrictions. These examples illustrate that unions may not always operate in a conflict-based, zero-sum bargaining mode. Instead, there may be occasions when unions, and employers, engage in activities that alter sectoral markets.

To understand more generally how unions relate to the markets within which they operate, it is useful to define three distinct modes of union behavior: "conflict" unionism, "transaction" unionism, and "regulatory" unionism. Conflict unionism corresponds to the conventional view of labor-management relations. Workers seek to extract economic benefits from employers through the threat of economic sanctions, and bargaining power arises through the ability to disrupt production by withdrawing labor: situations in which employers cannot find suitably skilled replacement workers, in which strike sanctions are reinforced by boycotts of various types, in which the product demand is inelastic and expanding, in which labor is a small fraction of production costs, and so forth (Ulman, 1955; Segal, 1969).

Transaction unionism arises in industries in which employment is casual and on-the-job training needs are substantial. The construction industry is typical of such an industry. The instability of employment by craft on different job sites and the atomism of employers create the need for labor market information systems that can quickly match workers and jobs.[1] Such systems must not only provide job information, they must also certify the quality of workers referred to short-duration jobs. Similarly, meeting the skill needs of an industry such as construction requires the systematic rotation of trainees among different types of work situations so that continuity and breadth of training can be provided on the job. The placement, training, and quality control functions in this market are thus closely intertwined with employment and production.

Such improvements in labor market functions could be provided by any number of institutions—unions, government agencies, or by employers—but there are substantial economies of scale, so that no more than one such institution is needed for any labor market area. Historically, in the United States, unions have played this role. Early craft unions gradually organized labor market information and training systems for their members. During this formative period, unions did not bargain with employers, but sought to enforce union-determined wage minima. Since the union scale could be undermined by competition, the unions tried to adjust supply relative to demand in order to maintain the union scale through market mechanisms. An unfavorable political climate for collective bargaining made strikes a costly instrument for controlling labor supply, so unions sought instead to use labor market information to allocate workers to higher wage markets and to limit training so as to avoid depressing the long-term earnings of incumbents.[2]

Unlike bargaining or transaction unionism, regulatory unionism seeks to shift market constraints through political action. Craft unions in the United States, for example, found that while their ability to control labor market information and apprenticeship training allowed them to raise the pay of unionized labor, at some point the wage-employment trade-off placed a limit on these gains. Similarly, industrial unions discovered that once they had organized all the major producers in their market in order to "take wages o of competition," their ability to raise union wages was ultimately limited by this same tradeoff. This in turn encouraged the political organization, locally or nationally, necessary to relieve market constraints through protective legislation and policies to subsidize or otherwise expand output.

These three modes of union behavior are not mutually exclusive and are often complementary. Unions can and do develop economic strategies that blend conflict or transaction unionism with economic policies directed toward relieving market constraints. Union wage policies, therefore, cannot easily be seperated from other economic policies of unions.

Union Effects on Wages and Employment

Relative Wages

A dominant theme in union research stretching back to the 1920s has been the effect of collective bargaining on relative wages. The pioneering work done at the University of Chicago has proved remarkably robust in the light of more recent and sophisticated econometric research. Unions have been shown to have a persistent effect, averaging between 10 and 15 percent on relative wages (Lewis, 1963). Studies using data on the earnings of individual workers, and controlling for other influences on wages, yield a wider range of estimated union effects, depending on the data source and control variables used. The basic findings, however, have not been altered (i.e., Johnson and Youmans, 1971; Rosen, 1970; Weiss, 1966). Several decades of research have revealed little evidence of systematic changes in union effects over time, although the measured effect of unionization is lessened in periods of high employment and increased during recessions.[3]

While these studies confirm the positive effect of unions on relative wages, they suffer from a number of well-known methodological problems. The most conceptually important are those related to "spillover" effects and to the difficulty in separating oligopoly business behavior from union behavior. "Spillover" effects, whereby union bargaining influences wages in nonunion employment, sometimes occur through informal emulation of union settlements by nonunion employers, and sometimes it is formally embodied in legislative or regulatory arrangements for "extending" the union wage.[4]

The oligopoly problem arises because the pattern of union organization in the United States is concentrated in heavy industry and in transportation, as well as in the skilled trades. There is, therefore, a high correlation between unionization, industrial concentration, and plant size, and union effects become intertwined with oligopolistic product and factor markets.

Employer Adjustments to Union Wage Effects

Taking as an established fact that unions do raise relative wages, even if the measurement of this effect is muddied by other intervening considerations, it is important to explore how markets adapt to this changed price of labor. These adaptations are best understood by tracing through adjustments within the internal labor market of the firm.

One obvious possibility is that an increase in the relative pay of union workers will induce employers to reduce their demand for union labor through factor substitutions. Moreover, if pay increases are translated into higher prices or if labor incomes rise, then a complicated set of price and income effects come into play, which are also likely to shift the derived demand for labor from unionized to nonunion sectors.

Because such employment adjustments are not likely to occur instantaneously, and because union pay increases are staggered over time, no series of discrete natural experiments, comparable to those available in studies of minimum wages, is available for directly judging the employment effects of unionization. Similarly, econometric estimates of labor demand functions, which might provide an indirect means of estimating these employment effects, generally rely on such aggregated data that they do not provide reliable insights.[5]

Indirect evidence, however, supports the presence of such employment effects in the widespread presence of union policies to limit or defer employment reductions. In the United States and Canada, for example, almost all collective agreements contain provisions governing layoffs. In some industries, such as the steel and the autos, there are also financial penalties to layoffs in the form of supplemental unemployment benefits. In great Britain, and in many Continental countries, legislation governs redundancy pay and laws limiting or delaying layoffs are common.

Informal arrangements at the work place may also be used to deter layoffs. The threat of local job actions to discourage layoffs is frequently mentioned in the British industrial relations literature and examples of similar practices can be found on the Continent. The literature on "featherbedding" and make-work practices can also be interpreted as a form of employment protection.

While employment adjustments are the most obvious reaction to union wage policies, increases in relative pay can also be offset through adjustments in the *quality* of labor hired. If unions raise pay, employers can then recruit from a more highly qualified pool of labor. New hires can thus be of higher "quality" than incumbents when union pay increases are first adopted. Over time, as incumbents are replaced, the average quality of the enterprise's labor force will rise (Ashenfelter and Johnson, 1972). This effect on the hiring process and labor quality can also reduce the firm's labor recruitment and training costs, thereby further offsetting the effect of wage increases on production costs.

A final set of adjustments at the level of the enterprise involves transformations of the production process. As mentioned earlier, the conventional economics of factor substitution postulates labor-saving adjustments if wages are increased by unionization. While the literature on capital budgeting does not give strong support to the idea that wage increases in the range usually associated with unionization would provide a market stimulus to investment or to technological change, it is possible that production throughout the economy could shift from less-capital-intensive firms to more-capital-intensive firms as a result of such wage increases. (Doeringer and Piore, 1971, Ch. 6; Dean, 1951).

A second possibility is that the presence of a union will stimulate more rational and productive use of labor resources. One way of increasing labor productivity is through "speedups" or other devices to increase work effort, but such attempts are commonly resisted by unions through collective bargaining or grievance procedures (Slichter, Levernash, and Healy, 1960). The economic literature on managerial behavior, however, suggests that there are often opportunities within firms for removing slack and inefficiency (Marris, 1964; Leibernstein, 1966). Studies of management responses to unionization support the conclusion that collective bargaining leads to a reduction in such inefficiency through more rational utilization of employees (Slichter, Livernash, and Healy, 1960, Chs. 2 and 31). While empirical studies of the relationship between unionization and productivity are rare, positive union effects have been documented.[6]

Productivity can also be improved through enterprise training programs. Current estimates suggest that employers in the United States provide around $50 billion in training annually.[7] Most of this training is provided by companies that are unionized or that operate under personnel policies comparable to those in the unionized sector.

Economic Performance

The micro studies of union effects on pay, and of employer adjustments to such pay effects, have implications for the overall performance of the economy. Do unions adversely affect economic performace by raising wages and preventing the efficient utilization of labor, and does collective bargaining destabilize the economy by causing unemployment or inflation? Or, do unions contribute to productive efficiency by encouraging more rational utilization of labor, do they provide a vehicle for expressing worker preferences and improving job satisfaction, and does collective bargaining provide a means of reducing industrial conflict? Since unions also engage in political activity, do they serve as mechanisms for securing worker support for national economic goals or as a force for disrupting of the flow of economic activity?

The first set of questions flows naturally from the traditional themes in the economic analysis of unions. Shifts in relative wages induced by unionization imply a deviation from competitive wage-setting norms and are likely to lead to further distortions in employment, output, and prices. If unions are successful in further constraining labor market behavior of employers, thereby reducing the options for adjustment to union wages, then even greater inefficiency must result.

The second set of questions is derived from a view of markets in which competition is less than perfect, even without unions, and in which industrial relations arrangements are concerned with social as well as economic outcomes. This view implies the widespread presence of economic power, the possibility that workers are motivated by a broader range of concerns than individual economic maximization, and that the performance of unions should be judged by social, as well as economic, standards.

There has been little systematic research on unions and national economic performance. One notable exception is a study of British industrial relations that paid particular attention to productivity issues (Ulman, 1968). It found that the structure of unions and the nature of bargaining relationships in Britain tended to inhibit productivity but that the capability and organization of management was an equally important factor. Attempts to implement a national policy of "productivity bargaining," in Britain, however, showed that the bargaining process could be used to improve economic performance. Another piece of evidence on this issue comes from Germany, where there was a concern that policies favoring codetermination in industry might lead to an accumulation of unworkable constraints on management. Studies of business productivity under various codetermination schemes, however, do not support this concern (Hartmann and Conrad, 1981, pp. 217–244).

The effect of unions on economic performance has also been examined in the context of inflation. Studies of unions and wage inflation have been plagued by difficulties in identifying stable aggregate wage relationships needed to provide a baseline against which to judge union impact. some studies have searched for evidence of union-induced linkages among pay settlements in different sectors. In general, there is evidence to indicate that unions contribute to inflation at some stages of the business cycle and restrain pay at other stages (Mitchell, 1980). Long-term and stable wage interdependencies among firms or sectors, however, have proved somewhat elusive (Flanagan, 1976; Eckstein and Wilson, 1960; Knowles and Robinson, 1962).

The role of unions in incomes policies has received considerable attention. The conventional wisdom holds that incomes policies inevitably collapse so that any effect is bound to be short-lived. But even policies that are able to defer, smooth out, or otherwise affect the timing of settlements can play a constructive role in economic management.

There is some evidence that the effectiveness and durability of incomes and wage restraint policy depend on the active cooperation of unions, independent of the sources of inflationary pressures, and that some industrial relations systems may be more suited to producing wage restraint than others (e.g., Ulman and Flanagan, 1971). While generalizations are difficult, several factors seem to contribute to the effectiveness of unions in national wage policy. If there are strong connections between the unions and the ruling political party, then greater rank-and-file support for restraint can be mustered and a greater range of public-private economic trade-offs may be available to support the pay restraint. Strong plant or local unions seem to be important to the implementation of wage policy and to the avoidance of wage drift. Finally, where labor and management are actively involved in fashioning compensation packages and in charting their course over time, wage restraint policies are likely to be more effective than if they are devised and implemented solely by the government.

While union political positions on legislation affecting economic performance have been well documented in a number of countries, there is little solid information on either organized labor's contribution to the passage of such legislation or its ultimate impact on the economy. With the possible exception of work-place health and safety legislation, political support for sectoral legislation generally has a broader political base than trade union members, making it difficult to assess the independent political influence of organized labor. Attempts to find a quantitative relationship between national economic performance and the electoral importance of organized labor have been limited, but there are indications that national strike activity may be inhibited under social democratic governments (Hibbs, 1978).

Unions, Inequality, and Labor Market Structure

Inequality

As economic institutions, unions must inevitably affect the distribution of income. Conflict unionism seeks to raise union wages relative to other wages and redistribute income from capital to labor; regulatory unionism implies the redistribution of income among productive sectors; positive or negative contributions to economic performance also have distributive implications.

Many of these effects on income distribution are a byproduct of policies aimed at improving the economic benefits of union members. In most countries, however, there are also deliberate union policies targeted at reducing inequality. Examples are found in legislation aimed at raising the incomes of the low paid, in bargaining policies designed to narrow the occupational wage structure (vertical equity), and in attempts to reduce inequality within occupations or job classifications (horizontal equity). Union policies toward rage regulation by government may reduce inequality by raising national wage minima and by extending union pay scales to the nonunion sector. While the effects of unions on overall economic performance have not been well documented, it would appear that policies that contribute to growth and full employment both diminish the relative impact of unions on wages and also improve the earnings of the least well-paid workers. To the extent that union participation in stabilization policies is successful, inequality is likely to be reduced, whereas when unions detract from economic performance, inequality may increase.

Anecdotal evidence from the United States suggests that unions have played a role in promoting both vertical and horizontal wage equity (Slichter, Livernash, and Healy, 1980, Chs. 2, 23–26, and 31; Freeman, 1978a). The earliest unions in the United States negotiated wage minima designed to place a floor under wages in craft occupations, and this tradition was carried forward in the early stages of industrial unionism. Subsequently, unions have sought to standardize and equalize pay within occupations and job classifications and have also tried to extend the use of seniority as a factor controlling movement between job classifications to standardize earnings among workers of equivalent experience within seniority districts.

Industrial unions regularly confront the issue of vertical equity because they negotiate pay schedules for a wide range of skill levels. During the late 1940s and early 1950s in the United States, many of the largest industrial unions negotiated equal absolute pay increases for their members, which had the effect of narrowing relative pay differences by skill. After the late 1950s, however, skill margins were maintained or widened as a matter of deliberate union policy. This conflict between skilled and semiskilled workers is a recurring phenomenon in many countries where industrial unionism is prevalent. More generally, comparisons of wage structures among countries with advanced market economies show considerable similarity in the structure of pay by industry, but much more variation in the pay structure by occupation and job classification (Brown, 1977; Rosen, 1970; and OECD, 1965). It is tempting to attribute these variations in occupational wage structure among countries with similar economies to the distinctive features of their national industrial relations systems.

Attempts to promote vertical equity by raising the pay of the poorest workers has met with only limited success. In the United States, periodic increases in the minimum wage have temporarily raised the wages of the least well-paid relative to average hourly earnings, but over several years the differential is usually reestablished (e.g., Kosters and Welch, 1972; Mincer, 1976). In Sweden, the solidaristic wage policy is periodically threatened by wage drift (Korpi, 1981). In England, the wage boards tend to follow more general trends in the economy (Pollard, 1969). In addition, the effect is that most minimum wages are often modified by limitations on eligibility and coverage.

While comprehensive assessments of the net effects of union influences on inequality are not available, one study did analyze the direct effects of unions on the distribution of earnings (Freeman, 1978b). It found that unions in the United States have on balance reduced inequality slightly, principally by equalizing earnings among individuals.

Equity

Closely related to earnings inequality is the more general question of equity at the work place. Most countries provide some form of legal redress for unfair or unequal treatment at the work place. The methods vary from country to country, but typically include only a narrow range of issues such as discharges, discrimination, or unequal maintenance of labor standards. In the United States and Canada, however, collective bargaining provides for a much wider range of protections against unequal treatment, through detailed agreements governing wages and working conditions and through grievance procedures designed to ensure equitable application of agreements.

This concern with equity also spills over into nonunion enterprises for many of the same reasons that union wage spillovers are observed. Employers recognize that workers are deeply concerned with equitable treatment and that this concern affects their job satisfaction, commitment, and productivity. Therefore, many of the most progressive nonunion companies seek to emulate the standards of equity that have been developed in the union context.[8]

Labor Market Segmentation

There is a growing awareness in advanced market economies of another dimension of inequality, a phenomenon known as labor market segmentation.

Briefly, the segmentation thesis argues that the labor market can be understood to be divided into different sectors in which the pay, working conditions, career earnings prospects, and rules of market behavior are substantially different. While the number, boundaries, and internal organization of these different labor market segments vary among countries, and are matters of considerable debate even within countries, it is agreed that market competition does not apply with equal force in all parts of the labor market. In those work places and sectors that are sheltered from competition (the "primary" labor market), workers receive economic benefits exceeding those that would apply in the more competitive sectors of the economy (the "secondary" labor market) (Doeringer and Piore, 1971; Doeringer, 1974; and Cain, 1976).

In Italy, labor market "dualism" is both a regional distinction between the industrial north and the underdeveloped south and a distinction between the core of large industrial firms and the periphery of small subcontractors and the cottage industry (Giugni, 1981). In Japan, dualism is also defined by the size of enterprises. The large industrial firms provide relatively good pay and career prospects, sharply stratified by educational level (Sumiya, 1981). In the United States and Great Britain, labor market dualism shares many features with Italy and Japan, but is also intertwined with labor market segregation by race and sex (Doeringer and Piore, 1971; Bosanquet and Doeringer, 1973).

Unionism and labor market segmentation are related phenomena. This relationship is partly a statistical one—those employment situations that are defined as advantageous or primary are more likely to be unionized or to be affected by union spillovers than are those that are unattractive or secondary. To what extent does this correlation reflect some positive contribution by unions, and to what extent it is a function of other factors?

Where enterprises are large and production concentrated, employment is likely to be sheltered from the full effects of market competition, and the combination of shelters and market power permit unions to raise wages above competitive levels. It is, however, the process of enterprise adjustments to union wages that contributes to labor market segmentation. In sectors where unions raise relative wages, employment becomes more attractive than that available in competitive sectors. One result is that the supply of labor exceeds the demand, and nonprice rationing therefore must be used to fill jobs. Where rationing occurs, employers may seek to hire more qualified workers by raising hiring standards, or they may apply other criteria such as race or sex in selecting among workers. Rationing of this kind can therefore make it more difficult for less well-educated workers, and those facing prejudice, to obtain employment in the unionized sector.

It has also been argued that in many parts of the unionized sector there are greater opportunities for training than in the nonunion sector. Partly, this stems from apprenticeship training offered by some craft unions, but in industrial situations there also appears to be substantial on-the-job training. Because of advantageous pay and because of "enterprise specific" on-the-job training, voluntary turnover is relatively lower in unionized sectors and unions seek to restrict layoffs (Freeman, 1978c).

Limitations on layoffs and opportunities for training reinforce the attractiveness of union sector work and further accentuate excess labor supply. They also encourage employers to hire workers who will be quick to learn, are highly motivated, and are compatible with social relations at the work place. One consequence of these adjustments is that labor becomes more of a "fixed" factor of production, a conclusion consistent with the distinctions in pay, turnover, continuity of employment, and educational differences between the primary and secondary labor market sectors (Oi, 1962).

Because of spillover effects between union and nonunion employers, it is difficult to determine the extent to which unionization has independently led to these results. Nevertheless, it is possible to reach some judgments by observing the behavior of unions in those situations where unionization has managed to gain a foothold in competitive, low-wage industries.

There are few examples of successful union organization of low-paid employment. Such employment does not provide fertile ground for transaction unionism, and the competitive nature of product and labor markets in low-paid sectors provides little room for payoffs to conflict unionism. Therefore, most union efforts directed at improving economic conditions in low-paid work have relied on government to establish minimum pay and other labor standards. While such activities are often pursued on grounds of social justice, they also have the effect of protecting lower-paid, unionized employment from competition from nonunion employers.

Unions in the United States have been able to organize in low-paid sectors only by finding mechanisms for regulating competition. In apparel, restaurants, hotels, and agricultural work, unions have relied on secondary boycotts to organize the entire market and to prevent the entry of nonunion competition (Doeringer, 1973). In the case of East Coast longshoring and building service, organized crime played a role in spreading union organization and discouraging nonunion competition (Hutchinson, 1970). In construction, longshoring, and trucking, localized labor market control has been important.

Once established, unions in competitive industries have turned to regulatory unionism to protect the union rate and to relieve competitive constraints on bargaining. Apparel unions have pressed for import restrictions, longshoring unions have encouraged the subsidization of U.S. port facilities, building service unions have encouraged policies that have increased the ability of landlords to pay.

At the work place, unions have tried to stabilize employment and to create internal promotion opportunities similar to those in the primary sector. Their ability to make gains in these areas, however, is constrained by the dead-end nature of the job structure, by jurisdictions of other unions, and by cost constriants that political action has been unable to relieve.

Unionization thus seems to flourish in situations where product and labor market competition can be most readily controlled; where labor market processes of wage determination, allocation, and training can be internalized; and where the prospects for shifting competitive constraints through regulation are greatest. More generally, unions appear to seek to capitalize on the existing potential for wage, employment, and equity gains available with the firm or industry and to extend this potential through political action whenever possible.

Unions, Markets, and Public Policy

The preceding discussion of union economic policies has drawn heavily on the experience of American trade unions with their unusually strong emphasis on business unionism. The issues raised, however, are widely applicable to the study of unions in market economies. In such economies, no trade union movement remains aloof from politics and even the most political trade unions are significantly concerned with the economic well-being of their members.

Unions and Markets

Three types of union behavior in labor markets have been identified: transaction unionism, conflict unionism, and regulatory unionism. Each type of union behavior illustrates a particular set of union-market relationships, and each has different implications for market performance and for inequality.

Transaction unionism represents the union equivalent of the firm as an institution for facilitating resource allocation. Such unionism aids market operation by efficiently organizing information and training. Conflict unionism involves bargaining with employers over the distribution of profits and the extent to which wages and employment will depart from competitive levels. Regulatory unionism operates on labor markets through political processes aimed at directly altering wages and working conditions and at shifting the derived demand for union labor through labor and product market protectifon and through subsidies. Regulatory unionism may also involve collaboration with government in the achievement of national economic goals, particularly in the area of stabilization policies.

These different types of union behavior take root in markedly different types of markets. Transaction unionism can arise in competitive markets where the small size and instability of employers makes them ill-suited to capture scale economies in information and training and where the casual nature of work creates special training and information needs.

Conflict unionism depends on the presence of labor and product market power. Where competition among firms is strong, conflict unionism cannot obtain economic benefits for its members unless all competitors are organized and barriers are raised to keep nonunion production out of the market. Regulatory unionism can operate in all types of markets, its goal is to shift competitive constraints through political action so as to raise the ability to pay of employers and to relieve wage-employment trade-offs.

Economic Performance, Inequality, and Labor Market Structure

Each of these modes of union behavior has implications for economic performance, inequality, and economic structure. Transaction unionism improves economic performance and can raise the income of workers benefiting from improved labor market operation. Conflict unionism raises the income of union workers relative to nonunion workers. To the extent that these increases result in economic dislocations beyond the transfer of excess profits from capital to labor, they will impair static economic performance. There may also be dynamic effects of conflict unionism, however, which can promote rationalization of work methods, improved resource management, and increased productivity at the work place. Regulatory unionism seeks to alter market relationships by fostering political shelters for workers and firms. These protections usually inhibit market performance.

Union policies increase inequality by creating pay premiums for union work. At the same time, unions promote horizontal wage equality among workers. Moreover, unions traditionally support national policies to raise the minimum pay of low-wage workers and to promote economic growth. Both these policies tend to narrow the earnings distribution.

Union wage policies also set in motion adjustments by employers that reinforce tendencies toward labor market segmentation. Labor market dualism, for example, is not caused by unions, but union policies do serve to strengthen the advantages of primary sector employment.

Relationships to Union Structure

Issues of inequality, labor markct structure, and equity are also related to union structure. For example, industrial unionism is more likely to narrow interoccupational inequality than is craft unionism and is also more likely to promote lifetime career mobility. Craft unionism, however, is a more likely vehicle for taking advantage of transaction opportunities in the labor market.

Union movements with strong locals are necessary to provide the training and information services of transaction unionism. Strong locals are also necessary for maintaining equity at the work place and for influencing internal career structures within enterprises.

National unions have the advantage over locally oriented unions in influencing national programs to improve economic performance. Where these programs seek to improve worker productivity, however, a local union structure is also needed to implement national policies at the work place level. National unions are more adept at regulatory unionism when national and international markets and involved, whereas local unions can regulate local markets more effectively.

The type of union structure most suitable for conflict varies considerably. Because employer organization can parallel union organization in bargaining, it is not certain whether differences in union structure can significantly alter the balance of bargaining power in the long term.

The structure of unions in the United States and Canada, with its emphasis on strong local and weaker national unions in craft areas and more balanced strength between local and national industrial unions, is well suited to all three modes of union behavior. Since many crafts operate in local markets, transaction, conflict, and regulatory unionism require strong local union organization. In industrial unions, locals provide the organizational strength for conducting strikes and for implementing horizontal equity at the work place. National unions can negotiate framework economic agreements in concentrated industries and lobby nationally for regulatory policies to benefit their members. The relative weakness of national union federations, however, does not encourage coordination of regulatory policies among national unions operating in different sectors. It also makes it more difficult to design and implement national programs for improving economic performance.

The situation with respect to continental European unions would appear to be very different. These unions have their roots, not in local plants and local labor markets, but in national political movements. In some countries, the craft and industrial union distinction is useful, but there are also general unions. Also important are political distinctions among Communist, Socialist, and Christian Democratic unions. Moreover, in many countries, the formal union movement has virtually no work-place organization, and many of these issues determined by bargaining in the United States and Canada, and to some degree Great Britain, are determined through law and regulation on the Continent.

While the origins and pattern of trade union behavior in these countries differ markedly, the categories of union behavior are still useful. In Continental countries, the union organization is much better suited to establishing limited framework agreements through conflict bargaining and to pursuing worker goals through regulatory unionism. As a result, wages and working conditions are governed as much by the exercise of political power through government as by conflict bargaining. Even in the Swedish case, where national bargaining occurs with little governmental intervention, the bargaining relationships between the parties are much more characteristic of governmental regulatory processes than private collective bargaining as it is known in the United States.

Transaction unionism is also relatively weak on the Continent because it requires a locally oriented union structure that has been absent in most European countries. As a result, other labor market institutions such as state employment services and employer associations have taken on economic responsibilities held by some craft unions in America.

Economic Management in a Unionized Economy

Having reviewed a number of themes relating to the economic behavior of unions, what conclusions can be drawn about their overall impact on the economy? As economic institutions, they seem to be successful in delivering modest benefits to their members through a variety of market and political types of activity. At the same time, they build into microeconomic markets wage distortions and constraints on markets adjustments, which appear potentially disruptive of market efficiency. Studies of union economic impacts that focus on measuring these effects inevitably lead to the conclusion that unions make a negative contribution to economic performance.

The recent attempts to measure the contribution of unionization to enhancing productivity and to show that unions can reduce inequality help to offset this negative characterization of how unions affect the economy. Nevertheless, these studies also tend to confirm the disruptive economic qualities of unions at the work place by identifying certain positive results that are derived from union-inspired distortions in wages and employment. On balance, the positive contribution of unions should be interpreted as a fortuitous occurrence, not as an inevitable consequence of unionization.

This emphasis on the distorting effects of unions needs to be placed in some perspective, however. For example, the average impact of unions on relative wages of 10 to 15 percent is not large. Moreover, when these wage effects are adjusted for the relationship between wages and unit production costs in unionized sectors, for compensating staffing practices by employers, and for the extent of union coverage in the economy, the dead-weight economic loss attributable to unions is likely to be trivial in comparison to the estimated effect of market power exercised by business.[9] If further allowances are then made for the possible contributions that unions make to efficiency and productivity, it seems reasonable to conclude that the traditional studies of microeconomic impacts of unions have analyzed a problem of little normative significance. Even though the case can be made that union wage policies have not been a major factor in distorting economic performance, there are other facets of union policy that may have been more significant.

Where there are local unions or similar organizations at the work place, for example, they may have played an important role in shaping the design and operation of internal labor markets. Increasingly, there is evidence that the internalization of labor market functions within the enterprise has a substantial bearing on the ability of the economy to meet the skill needs of growth and economic change in a flexible way while meeting many of the concerns of the labor force for equitable economic relationships (Doeringer and Piore, 1971; Wachter and Williamson, 1977). How these internal labor markets are formed, their pervasiveness in the economy, and the nature of barriers to employment within such markets appear to be critical factors affecting both efficiency and inequality in modern economies.

Even more important is the political role of trade unions in stabilization and growth policy. Unemployment, inflation, growth and inequality are the key economic concerns of advanced market economies. Policies to improve the trade-off among these concerns have been a key goal since World War II and have become increasingly elusive in recent years. Unions can be a force either for improving or for inhibiting the accomplishment of this goal.

Unions that engage in special-interest political activities may benefit their members but at the expense of economic performance in the large society. Unions that participate in stabilization policy and that seek to promote economic growth can improve the economic well-being of their members while aiding overall economic performance. The question for public policy, therefore, is how to shift the balance of regulatory unionism away from special-interest considerations and toward the interests of society at large.

While the use of regulatory power to relieve competitive constraints will always be a temptation for trade unions, the incentives for such action are greatest in economies where unemployment is high and growth rates low. This often creates a perverse situation where aggregate economic policies designed to control inflation create an environment that encourages protective responses by unions. These protections become difficult to reverse when policy becomes more expansionist. Similarly, when controlling inflation and stimulating growth are goals of national policy, there is often a tendency to strip away protective legislation in which unions have invested without laying the institutional foundation for unions to participate in the design and implementation of noninflationary growth policy. Only as a last resort do governments typically turn to unions and incomes policy as an alternative to restrictive monetary and fiscal policies to control inflation. In such times of economic crisis, it is usually too late for more than cosmetic and temporary solutions.

Few countries have sought to reform their labor legislation or to design their economic institutions so as to integrate better public and private economic interests within framework which could facilitate economic management.[10] Nor has there been much serious attention paid to how such institutions interact with their economic and political environment.

The lessons from repeated experiments with incomes policies emphasize the need to involve unions in the design and implementation of a broad spectrum of national economic policies. They also highlight the importance of building a foundation of institutional strength and institutional relationships—nationally, by industry sector, and locally—needed to deal with matters of economic policy and management in advance of economic crises. With the possible exception of Sweden, most governments have separated their industrial relations policy from their economic policy, with the result that these two sets of policy have often moved in contradictory directions. The former has typically sought to deal with union structure and industrial conflict; the latter has relied on monetary and fiscal policies. Yet, problems in one policy sphere have often aggravated those in the other sphere. The blending of these two branches of policy in the occasional "social contract" has too often been the result of political expediency than of an understanding of the potential role of organized labor in improving economic performance.

This imbalance in approaches to economic policy is mirrored in the pattern of research on the economics of trade unions (Dunlop, 1977). The American fascination with relative wage effects and the European concern with the politics of conflict have consumed a disporportionate share of research attention. In the process, there has been a serious neglect of research on how industrial relations relate to economic performance and the distribution of economic well-being. This imbalance must be redressed if research is to provide a better guide in the future for synchronizing trade union economic policies with those of business and government.

Notes

1. For a discussion of the construction industry labor market, see Daniel Quinn Mills (1972) and Peter B. Doeringer and Michael J. Piore (1971).
2. For a historical discussion of union policies toward labor supply and strikes, see Lloyd Ulman (1966).
3. See Lewis (1963). There has been some speculation that the overall union effect may have widened during the 1970s (see Orley Ashenfelter, 1978), but more precisely specified econometric analysis indicates that this finding is related to cyclical developments in the U.S. economy. See William J. Moore and John Raisian (1981).
4. For a study of the extension of union wages in France, see Yves Delamotte (1973). On spillovers more generally, see John T. Dunlop (1957), Timothy McGuire and Leonard Rapping (1966).
5. One study did test for substitution elasticities and found that the demand for production labor was relatively more inelastic in unionized employment. See Freeman and Medoff, *Review of Economics and Statistics* Vol. 64(2) May 1987 pp. 220/233 and Daniel S. Hammermesh (1976).
6. For a report of this work, see Richard B. Freeman and James L. Medoff (1979).
7. For a review of employer training investments, see Ernst W. Stromsdorfer (1981).
8. For a discussion of nonunion personnel practices, see Fred K. Foulkes (1980).
9. For a discussion of estimates of monopoly loss, See F. M. Sherer (1980, ch. 17). Raising the relative pay of union workers by 10 to 15 percent is not likely to be translated into substantial product market distortions.

10. Some related work in this area has been done in Europe. See, for example, Michele Salvati and Giorgio Brosio (1979) and Andrew Martin (1980). For a discussion of national differences in attitudes towards unions, see Everett M. Kassalow (1978, p. 120).

References

Ashenfelter, O. 1978. "Union Relative Wage Effects: New Evidence and a Survey of their Implications for Wage Inflation." In *Econometric Contributions to Public Policy,* ed. R. Stone and W. Peterson. New York: MacMillan Press.

Ashenfelter, O., and Johnson, G. E. 1972. "Unionism, Relative Wages, and Labor Quality in U.S. Manufacturing Industries." *International Labor Review,* 13, (October): 488–508.

Bosanquet, N., and Doeringer, P. B. 1973. "Is There a Dual Labor Market in Great Britain." *Economic Journal* 83.

Brown, H. P. 1977. *The Inequality of Pay.* Oxford: Oxford University Press.

Cain, G. G. 1976. "The Challenge of Segmented Labor Market Theories to Orthodox Theory: A Survey," *Journal of Economic Literature* 10 (December): 1215–1257.

Dean, J. 1951. *Capital Budgeting.* New York: Columbia University Press.

Delamotte, Y. 1973. "Recent Collective Bargaining Trends in France." In ILO, *Collective Bargaining in Industrialized Market Economies.* Geneva: ILO.

Doeringer, P. B. 1973. "Explorations in Low Pay, Collective Bargaining, and Economic Mobility." Report to the Office of Research and Demonstration, U.S. Department of Labor, mimeo, August.

______. 1974. "Low Pay, Labor Market Dualism, and Industrial Relations Systems." In *Wage Determination,* ed. Derek Robinson. Paris: OECD.

Doeringer, P. B., and Piore, M. J. 1971. *Internal Labor Markets and Manpower Analysis.* Lexington: D.C. Heath.

Dunlop, J. T. 1944. *Wage Determination Under Trade Unions.* New York: MacMillan.

______. 1957. "The Task of Contemporary Wage Theory." In *The Theory of Wage Determination,* ed. John T. Dunlop. New York: St. Martin's Press.

______. 1962. "Comment" in National Bureau of Economic Research. *Aspects of Labor Economics.* Princeton: Princeton University Press.

______. 1977. "Policy Decisions and Research in Economics and Industrial Relations." *Industrial and Labor Relations Review* 30 (April), 275–282.

Eckstein, O., and Wilson, T. A. 1960. "The Determination of Money Wages in the American Economy." *Quarterly Journal of Economics* 74, pp. 296–317.

Flanagan, R. J. 1976. "Wage Interdependence in Unionized Labor Markets." *Brookings Papers on Economic Activity* 3.

Foulkes, F. K. 1980. *Personnel Policies in Large Nonunion Companies.* Englewood Cliffs, N.J.: Prentice-Hall.

Freeman, R. B. 1978a. "Job Satisfaction as an Economic Variable." *American Economic Review* 68 (May): 135–141.

______. 1978b. "Unionism and the Dispersion of Wages." *NBER Paper* 248 (June).

______. 1978c. "A Fixed-Effect Logit Model of the Impact of Unionism on Quits". *NBER Working Paper* 280 (September).

______. 1978d. "The Effect of Trade Unions on Fringe Benefits." *NBER Working Paper* 292 (October).

______. 1980. "The Exit-Voice Trade-off in the Labor Market: Unionism, Job Tenure, Quits, and Separations." *Quarterly Journal of Economics* 94, no. 4 (June): 643–673.

Freeman, R. B., and Medoff, J. L. 1979. "The Two Faces of Unionism." *Public Interest* (Fall).

______. 1982. "Substitution Between Production Labor and Other Inputs in Unionized and Nonunionized Manufacturing." *Review of Economics and Statistics,* 64 (May) 220–233.

Giugni, G. 1981. "The Italian System of Industrial Relations." in *Industrial Relations in International Perspective,* ed. P. B. Doeringer. London: MacMillan.

Hammermesh, D. S. 1976. "Econometric Studies of Labor Demand and Their Application to Policy Analysis." *Journal of Human Resources* 11 (Fall): 502–525.

Hartmann, H., and Conrad, W. 1981. "Industrial Relations in Western Germany." in *Industrial Relations in International Perspective,* ed. P. B. Doeringer. London: MacMillan.

Hibbs, D. A., Jr. 1978 "On the Political Economy of Long-Run Trends in Strike Activity." *British Journal of Political Science* (April).

Hutchinson, J. 1979. *The Imperfect Union.* New York: E. P. Dutton.

Johnson, G. E., and Youmans, K. 1971. "Union Relative Wage Effects." *Industrial and Labor Relations Review* 24 (January): 171–179.

Kassalow, E. M. 1978. "Industrial Conflict and Consensus in the United States and Western Europe: A Comparative Analysis." In Industrial Relations Research Association, *Proceedings of the Thirtieth Annual Winter Meeting.* Wisconsin: IRRA.

Knowles, K. G. J. C., and Robinson, D. 1962. "Wage Rounds and Wage Policy." *Bulletin of the Oxford University Institute of Economics and Statistics* 24.

Korpi, W. 1981. "Sweden: Conflict, Power, and Politics in Industrial Relations." *Industrial Relations in International Perspective,* ed. P. B. Doeringer. London: MacMillan.

Kosters, M., and Welch, F. 1972. "The Effects of Minimum Wages on the Distribution of Changes in Aggregate Employment." *American Economic Review* 72 (June): 323–332.

Leibenstein, H. 1966. "Allocative Efficiency Versus X-Efficiency." *American Economic Review* pp. 392–415.

Lewis, H. G. 1963. *Unionism and Relative Wages in the United States: An Empirical Inquiry.* Chicago: University of Chicago Press.

Marris, R. 1964. *An Economic Theory of Managerial Capitalism*. New York: Free Press of Glencoe.

Martin, A. 1980. "Distributive Conflict, Inflation and Investment: The Swedish Case." Brookings Institution, mimeo, March.

———. 1982. "Substitution Between Production Labor and Other Inputs in Unionized and Nonunionized Manufacturing." *Review of Economics and Statistics, 64 (May) 220–233.*

McGuire, T., and Rapping, L. 1966. "Interindustry Wage Change Dispersion and the Spillover Hypothesis." *American Economic Review* 50 (June): 493–501.

Mincer, J. 1976. "The Unemployment Effects of Minimum Wages." *Journal of Political Economy* 84 (August) S87–S104.

Mitchell, D. J. B. 1980. *Unions, Wages and Inflation.* Washington: Brookings Institution.

Moore, W. J., and Raisian, J. 1981. "A Time Series Analysis of the Growth and Determinants of Union/Nonunion Relative Wage Effects 1967–1977." U.S. Department of labor, *Bureau of Labor Statistics Working Paper 115,* April.

OECD. 1965. *Wages and Labor Mobility.* Paris: OECD.

Oi, W. Y. 1962. "Labor as a Quasi-Fixed Factor." *Journal of Political Economy,* 70 (December): 538–555.

Pollard, S. 1969. The Development of the British Economy, 1914–1947. London: Edward Arnold.

Quinn, M. D. 1972. *Industrial Relations and Manpower in Construction.* Cambridge: MIT Press.

Rosen, S. 1970. "Unionism and the Occupational Wage Structure in U.S." *International Economic Review* 11 (June): 269–286.

Ross, A. M. 1948. *Trade Union Wage Policy.* Berkeley: University of California Press.

Salvati, M., and Brosio, G. 1979. "The Rise of Market Politics: Industrial Relations in the Seventies." *Daedalus* 108 (Spring): 43–59.

Segal, M. 1969. "The Relationship between Union Wage Impact and Labor Market Structure." *Quarterly Journal of Economics* 78: 94–114.

Sherer, F. M. 1980. *Industrial Market Structure and Economic Performance,* 2nd Edition. Chicago: Rand McNally College Publishing.

Slichter, S. H., Livernash, E. R., and Healy, J. J. 1960. *The Impact of Collective Bargaining on Management.* Washington: The Brookings Institution.

Sumiya, M. 1981. "The Japanese System of Industrial Relations." In *Industrial Relations in International Perspective,* ed. P. B. Doeringer. London: MacMillan.

Stromsdorfer, E. W. 1981. "Training in Industry." In *Work-place Perspectives on Education and Training,* ed. P. B. Doeringer. Boston: Martinus Nijhoff Publishing.

Ulman, L. 1955. "Marshall and Friedman on Union Strength." *Review of Economics and Statictics.*

———. 1966. *The Rise of the National Trade Union.* Cambridge: Harvard University Press.

———. 1968. "Collective Bargaining and Industrial Efficiency." In *Britain's Economic Prospects,* ed. R. E. Caves. London: George Allen and Unwin.

Ulman, L., and Flanagan, R. J. 1971. *Wage Restraint: A Study of Incomes Policy in Western Europe.* Berkeley and Los Angeles: University of California Press.

Wachter, M. L., and Williamson, O. E. 1977. "Obligation Markets and the Mechanics of Inflation." *Bell Journal of Economics* (Autumn): 549–571.

Weiss, L. 1966. "Concentration and Labor Earnings." *American Economic Review,* 56: 96–117.

12 UNION MEMBERSHIP AND UNION MANAGEMENT: A Research Agenda for the 80s

Leo Troy and Neil Sheflin

Introduction

There has been an extraordinary resurgence of interest in the economics of trade unions, especially when one considers that, as recently as 1975, George Johnson concluded that the field was not one of economics "growth industries." Since his pronouncement, published research has increased greatly, a new journal devoted exclusively to this area—*the Journal of Labor Research*—has been established and is prospering, and, now, an international conference focusing on the economics of labor unions is underway.

Nevertheless, important gaps remain in our understanding of union structure, management, and impact. Information is incomplete on such basic matters as the size, penetration, and distribution of unions; trends in the geographic and structural distribution of membership over the past two decades; the magnitude and management of union finances; and union planning and managerial practices.

In this chapter, we explore future research areas in two aspects of the economics of trade unions: union membership and union management. We examine some of the difficulties with the concept of union membership and indicate shortcomings of current figures and then suggest future work to remedy them. Desirable analyses of trends in unionism are proposed, including examination of changes in the geographic distribution of membership and in its distribution within and between various unions and levels of union organization.

As for union management, despite the oft-used sobriquet of "business-unionism" in describing the organized labor movement in America, there has been, paradoxically, little analysis of unions as managerial organizations. Yet, American unions clearly are "big business," with gross assets approaching $5 billion, billions more in pension and other benefit funds over which unions have substantial or unilateral control, and an enormous "customer" base of over 20 million members and millions more whom they represent. Clearly, the performance of unions has important implications for the services provided to union members, to those whom they represent, for the economy, and indeed, for the future of the institution of unionism. Future research on union goals, structure, planning, and finances is proposed, with the focus of such studies on unions as managerial organizations.

Union Membership

A prerequisite for the description and analysis of trade unions is data on their membership and its composition. Such information provides the basis for assessing organized labor's strength, vitality, and impact on political and social affairs. Knowledge of union membership is needed to examine geographic, industrial, occupational, and demographic developments, to study changes in the distribution of strength among specific unions and the various levels of unions—locals, intermediates, and international organizations. Forecasts of union growth depend upon a data base as well. Statistical studies of the determinants of union membership, new organizing, NLRB certification and decertification, election outcomes, union impacts on relative wages, inflation and productivity, and the effect of right-to-work and other social legislation require accurate, often disaggregated data on union membership and its composition.

Despite the requirements and a wide recognition of unionism as a significant economic and social factor, reliable and comprehensive data on American union membership do not exist. It would be surprising if the weaknesses and limitations of existing sources have not affected our views of the size and distribution of union membership and distorted statistical estimates of their economic impacts.

Measuring Union Membership

As with other social statistics, measures of unionism are invented, not discovered. Clearly, the determination of the proper measure of the dimensions and influence of organized labor depends on the purposes to which it is to be put. It is common to use as such a measure the unionized percentage of the civilian labor force, or of nonagricultural employment. As obvious as these measures of unionism appear, they conceal a host of ambiguities.

Looking first at total membership, both as an absolute measure or as the numerator in the extent of organization, many questions arise. Should this figure include inactive, retired, part-time, dual or partial (apprentice), or unemployed members, or only reflect full, dues-paying membership? Should the figure reflect average annual membership or membership at a point in time? And should Canadian or other foreign membership in U.S. unions be included? What about members of employee associations, once referred to as "near-unions" by John Dunlop? Does one wish to include their membership as well?

In determining the extent of organization, the coverage of the denominator should be comparable to the membership coverage. For example, if the base is to be civilian labor force—employed and unemployed—then one would wish the membership definition also to include unemployed members. If, alternatively, the base is nonagricultural employment, unemployed members should not be included (Thieblot, 1978). Other bases for measuring the membership ratio are possible as well. For example, the working-age population or some suitably defined measure of the "potentially unionizable" population might and indeed has been used (Bain and Elsheikh, 1975).

Beyond the aggregate figures on the size and extent of membership (however defined), geographic, industrial, occupational, and demographic breakdowns are important elements in assessing and explaining union trends and developments. Measures of membership of individual local unions and intermediate organizations round out the statistics of union size and strength.

The 80s seem a suitable time for a renewed discussion of the appropriate measures of union size and strength. While the recent decline in the extent of organization and the slow growth in total membership are not disputed, there is disagreement over their implications for union influence (Dunlop, 1980).

Data Sources

The most widely cited aggregate membership figures are those of the Bureau of Labor Statistics, U.S. Department of Labor. They are developed from a biennial survey of some 200 international labor organizations and include AFL-CIO affiliates, independent national and international unions, and employee associations (see the *Directory of National Unions and Employee Associations*). The figures reprinted in the directory are voluntarily, self-reported estimates of "annual average dues-paying membership" for each of two years, only one of which is reported. Estimates for nonreporting organizations are developed from other sources, including the AFL-CIO's biennial convention reports. Union-supplied estimates of the industrial, state and foreign, sex and occupational breakdowns, are provided as well.

The BLS "guesstimates" have long been subject to substantial criticisms (Freeman and Medoff, 1979). It has been estimated that the BLS figures overstate total membership anywhere from 10 to 40 percent (Troy, 1965; Thieblot, 1978; and Ginsburg, 1970). And, the figures reported to the BLS often remain, improbably, unchanged year after year. There is no reason to believe that there are both secular and cyclical changes in the bias, reflecting unions' aversions to reporting declines in membership.

There are other definitional problems resulting from differing practices among unions in reporting unemployed, part-time, inactive, and retired members (although the BLS asks the number, if any, of retired members included in the count). Even more serious is the treatment of Canadian members of U.S. unions, also self-reported. Canadian members are included in the individual union figures, although substracted from the U.S. figures—a practice even more suspect, given the additional uncertainties associated with the Canadian figures.

Beyond these difficulties, the industrial and geographic breakdowns provided by the unions are often missing, incomplete, and, generally, rough estimates. And, while the BLS data provides some basis for examining and comparing membership patterns and trends in individual international unions, these figures, as noted, included Canadian members. The BLS data provide no basis whatever for comparing local and intermediate union membership.

There are two alternative, although unfortunately no longer current, sources of data available. The first was developed at the National Bureau of Economic Research (NBER) by Leo Troy (1965). Using reported dues receipts, Troy obtained estimates of the annual dues-paying membership of every U.S. international union between 1935 and 1962. In 1969, Troy extended and expanded this series, using the uniform financial reports required of all (private sector) union under the Labor-Management Reporting and Disclosure (Landrum-Griffin) Act and various executive orders. Annual membership estimates for each of the roughly 50,000 local, intermediate, and national unions in the United States between 1962 and 1969 were derived, providing a continuous, consistent source of membership for every international union back to 1935, and disaggregated estimates for 1962–1969.

The series thus obtained does suffer from some conceptual problems resulting from the use of the "average" dues rate, and the treatment of part-time, apprentice, and retired or inactive members who pay lower rates. Nonetheless, the figures are generally viewed as more reliable (and are significantly lower) than those of the BLS. They are conceptually more appealing since they correspond more closely to "potential membership" and provide considerably more geographic and union-specific detail. Indeed, the data allow examination of individual local, intermediate, or national unions, on a city, county, SMSA or state basis. Unfortunately, no industrial detail is provided, and the published series ends in 1969, although as discussed below, work is currently underway on updating and continuing this data base.

Since 1973 (and sporadically prior to this), the May Current Population Survey of Households, conducted by the U.S. Bureau of the Census and commissioned by the BLS, has included questions on union membership, thus providing a "micro" source of data with considerable demographic and economic detail. Despite problems resulting from some lack of clarity about inclusion of employee association membership, and the CPS' reference to full-time workers at a single point in time (the survey date), this data is clearly a rich source that has seen relatively little use (Freeman and Medoff, 1979). The data are not union-specific, but they do provide considerable industrial and geographic detail, including state groups and large SMSAs. Another source of micro-information is the Michigan Panel Study of Income Dynamics. Tracking 5,000 families for more than nine years, the survey includes questions on union membership, employment, and demographic characteristics of respondents.

As noted at the outset, current, consistent data on American unionism do not exist, and the development of such information should be an important element of future research. The estimation and maintenance of membership figures derived from dues or per capita receipts is, we believe, the correct approach to providing such information. Work underway by Leo Troy and Neil Sheflin with funding from the National Science Foundation and the Fund for the Advancement of the Public Trust will update the NBER union-specific data and provide a unique and valuable empirical base for further research. It will provide, for the first time, a continuous, consistent, reliable record of membership for every local, intermediate, and international union in the country over the last two decades, with figures on international organizations extending back to the beginning of the century.

While the resulting estimates are conceptually and practically superior to those of the BLS, some unresolved issues remain. For one, Canadian members of the international unions cause a problem in determining net U.S. membership. The financial reports of the Labor Management Services Administration (LMSA) do not separate dues receipts into Canadian and U.S. components. Thus, it is impossible to develop independent estimates of the membership of each from these reports. Use of the Canadian membership estimates reported to the BLS to derive the net U.S. total weakens the reliability of this figure. It appears that one can develop Canadian estimates from reports of some of the larger unions, such as the auto workers and the steel workers, but this only partially solves the problem. A relatively minor revision of the LMSA financial reporting form might help resolve this issue.

Another set of related issues requiring further investigation is the membership of both public sector unions and employee associations. The problems noted in the BLS figures are even more severe for each of these groups. Furthermore, a solution is less readily available since these organizations have not generally been required to file financial reports to the LMSA. Reliable estimates of membership of these groups are most desirable, for it is the reported strong growth in public sector unionism that has partially offset the stagnation in organized labor observed over the past several decades. Employee associations have been an important element in this growth. Indeed, the second largest union in the United States today is not the auto workers or steel workers, but rather an employee association—the National Education Association—with a membership of 1.6 million.

Future research should be directed toward the development of financially based estimates of the membership of these unions. Such estimates would be derived from financial reports (form 990) filed with the U.S. Treasury Department, Internal Revenue Service, as nonprofit organizations. Using computer transcriptions of these returns, available from the IRS, it should be possible to develop the first objective estimates of the dues-paying membership of public employee unions.

Two other possibilities for improving membership statistics should be pursued in the '80s. The first involves the CPS. There seems to be no insurmountable barrier to expanding the inclusion of the membership question from a single month, to several, perhaps even all, months. The resulting estimates should be made more widely available and could, perhaps, provide the basis of alternative "official" membership estimates. It may also be desirable to apply the CPS industrial and occupational percentages on a state or SMSA basis to the Troy-Sheflin series under development, to result in cross-sectional and occupation estimates of membership by industry.

Improved membership statistics could also be derived from changes in the LMSA reporting practices and forms. Currently, the reported dues or per capita tax rates are, in too many cases, missing or clearly inaccurate. Requiring unions to report current, accurate figures would allow the derivation of membership without recourse to external sources of dues information. Requiring separate reporting of Canadian dues from only 150 or so unions would resolve the issue of separating Canadian and U.S. members. The possibility of requiring reporting of active, dues-paying members on the LMSA forms would be a rather direct way of obtaining more reliable estimates than the BLS currently produces. These would be annual and include every union required to file financial reports.

Analyses of Membership

Improved membership data will provide the basis for improved and expanded examination and analysis of changing patterns and trends in organized labor. The data under development by Troy and Sheflin should allow a more accurate assessment of the extent of the decline in unionization over the past two decades. It will provide the first accurate look at geographic trends in membership over this period, at the state, SMSA, and county levels. The effects on unions of the shift of industry and employment to the Sunbelt, the growing service orientation of the economy, and right-to-work and other legislation may become clearer. More analyses of the relative distribution of membership both within and between unions, and study of the growth and decline of individual unions in response to changes in their economic environment and technical changes, should also be included in the list of future research areas. Both the CPS and the Michigan data should, and almost certainly will, lead to increased examination of the characteristics of union members and comparable nonmembers, and further monitoring of changes in the extent of unionism.

Beyond these descriptive studies, we believe the '80s should continue to see more analytical and statistical studies of the determinants of union growth, the membership decision, and other related areas. On the aggregate level, the Troy-Sheflin data will allow reexamination of the adequacy of business-cycle-oriented models of union growth (Ashenfelter and Pencavel,

1969; and Bain and Elsheikh, 1975). These data will allow more reliable and disaggregated cross-sectional studies of structural determinants of membership and of the effects of right-to-work legislation using "population" rather than sample data. We expect to see more use made of the micro sources—the CPS and Michigan data—to examine the determinants of the decision to join or leave unions, thus shedding light on the causes of the decline in unionization.

Finally, we believe that future analyses of the behavior of unions may profit from viewing them, at least partially, as "businesses" and examining their managerial performance and its role in their successes and failures. While Freeman and Medoff (1979) attribute 60 percent of the decline in unionization to demographic and employment changes, 40 percent remains to be explained. At least some of the answers may lie in the unions themselves, that is, in how they are managed.

Union Management

Interest in the organization and administration of unions has been rather limited during the past two decades. Yet, there have been dramatic changes in both unions and their environment since the '40s and '50s, when much of the descriptive literature on their structure and governance was developed. Since the policies, organization, and practices of unions have important consequences for their growth and for collective bargaining and labor relations, an important element of the research agenda for the '80s must be updating and extention of our knowledge in this area (Dunlop, 1980; and Kochan, 1980a).

In addition, examination of the goals, structure, planning, and finances of unions from a managerial perspective, treating them (at least partially) as economic entities, may yield important insights into causes of the decline in unionization, certification victories, and new organizing, as well as other aspects of their activities (Berkowitz, 1954).

Goals and Objective

George Johnson (1975) observed that there is no consensus on the goals of union activity. This ignorance may extend to the unions themselves. Case studies reported by Malcolm Salter (1975) suggest that some unions lack clear long-run objectives and goals, thus limiting their ability to undertake strategic planning and to allocate their resources optimally. Furthermore,

Richard Block (1979) noted that there may have been a misperception of the objectives of mature unions. He suggests that unions may now be more concerned with providing services to enrolled members than with new organizing, a notion that finds qualified support in his empirical work.

It is clear that our knowledge of the goals and objectives of unions at all levels is deficient. This lack has constrained our ability to understand and evaluate union actions in diverse areas and has limited behavioral studies. There are several directions that, if pursued, should serve to expand our knowledge in this area. A survey of union policies and practices, similar in some ways to the Conference Board's survey of corporate labor relations policy, could provide a great deal of information on many aspects of unions, including more understanding of their goals and objectives (Dunlop, 1980; Kochan, 1980b). While we are cautious about union response to such a survey, the benefits to researchers, policy makers, management, and the unions themselves, warrant the effort. Careful case studies of local and international unions would also improve our understanding of unions' goals and objectives and allow comparisons between unions, and at the different level of organization (Salter, 1975).

Statistical studies, such as Block's employing as working hypotheses the framework of unions as profit-oriented if not profit-maximizing organizations may generate interesting implications, the testing of which will indicate the usefulness of such hypotheses (Berkowitz, 1954). Similarly, Donald Martin's (1980) approach based on ownership characteristics associated with labor organizations bears further examination and empirical testing.

Structure

The structure of organized labor—the degree of centralization of function, finance, and power between local and international unions, between the internationals and the AFL-CIO, and among the internationals—is another topic overdue for careful examination. A long-run trend toward increasing centralization of power within the national and international unions, reflecting changes in product markets and corporate management, and the need for more sophisticated union management has often been cited (Estey, 1981). On the other hand, the strong position of locals vis-a-vis the international remains. Historically, this feature has been a distinctive one of American unions, with important implications for collective bargaining. The environment of the '80s may indeed push toward decentralization, as unions find it necessary to deal with a greater number of noneconomic bargaining issues, to organize smaller employer units associated with the service-oriented economy, and to attract white-collar and professional employees concerned with image, independence, and individuality.

Merger activity, at the highest level during 1978–79 in a decade, is another area in which a managerial perspective might provide useful insights. Unions argue that mergers provide increased bargaining power, more services to members, a basis for more successful organizing, and improved union finances. Case studies, as pursued by the IRRU Britain (see Bain, 1980, p. 53) evaluating the causes and the consequences of union mergers, should expand our understanding of the dynamics and impacts of such activity. Evaluating union mergers with the same perspective and yardstick used in examining corporate mergers may also provide additional insight.

The distribution of membership, decision making, and financial power between locals and internationals, examination of the relative fortunes of various international unions, and the evolving relationship between the internationals and the AFL-CIO are each important topics for further examination. The Troy-Sheflin membership data currently being developed should, in conjunction with the computerized financial reports from the LMSA, provide an important empirical base for some of this work. These sources should also provide the basis for a current and extended look at the characteristics of local unions (see USDL, 1969).

Management and Planning

An interesting speculation, as we noted earlier, is whether some of the decline in union pentration in the United States might be due to managerial weaknesses in organized labor. Perhaps failures in marketing research and marketing strategy, in planning and general management, or poor financial management might have contributed to the hard times unions seem to have fallen on. It is most difficult to evaluate this possibility since, as noted, few attempts have been made to study unions as economic entities, entities selling membership and incurring costs of organization and administration (Berkowitz, 1954).

While a "managerial revolution" is underway (Raskin, 1980), the complete professionalization of union management has yet to occur (Estey, 1981). Indeed, Malcolm Salter (1975) observed that, not surprisingly, many union leaders were strong in political and leadership, rather than management, skills, resulting in an inability to plan strategically. Salter notes other managerial failures within the unions he examined in the late 1960s and early 1970s including a lack of knowledge of their "market" and of finances, a lack of trust within the organization, and a lack of belief in the concept of accountability and techniques of internal audit and control (Salter, 1975, pp. 14–19).

Future research should explore the nature of union management and planning—on the local, intermediate, and international levels and by the AFL-CIO. Questions on the decision-making process, the degree of professionalization and career paths of staff, compensation policies, and union management institutions and functions should be examined. The survey of unions, suggested earlier, could fill in many gaps in these areas, although the most fruitful approach would involve careful case studies (Salter, 1975; Bain, 1980).

Finances

The consolidated assets of reporting American unions totaled about $4 billion in 1976, with their net assets exceeding $3.3 billion. Income was close to $3 billion, with slightly less expended (Sheflin and Troy, 1980). The very magnitude of the sums involved, the importance of finances both as a measure of union "success" and as a basis for union organizing, and administrative, bargaining, strike, and political activities—all would suggest that this topic should be of great interest.

It is therefore surprising that so little has been done on the subject in light of the rich sources of data available. Financial data for virtually every private sector and many public sector unions reporting under the Landrum-Griffin Act and executive orders have been collected and, with some exception, transcribed into a machine readable form on magnetic tape since 1962. Supplemented by financial information on public sector unions available on the IRS tapes containing nonprofit organization financial reports (form 990), there exists a rather extraordinary source of data on the finances of virtually every union in the country for the past two decades.

The 1980s should clearly see more study of union finances. Work in progress by Troy and Sheflin examines consolidated balance sheets and income statements at the aggregate level, separately for local, intermediate, and international organizations, and by various geographic breakdowns. Such analyses can increase our understanding of union financial and portfolio management practices, and union's ability to finance new organization, strikes, and political activities. Further work could be directed toward examination of the flow of funds of unions, the analysis of financial aspects of mergers, and the incorporation of financial data in micro studies of union organizing and the effects of right-to-work legislation.

Conclusion

With so broad and varied a subject, an agenda for future research on the economics of trade unions should be wide-ranging. We have limited our concern, however, to aspects of membership and management of unions, suggesting further work in three areas: development of improved membership data; increased analysis of changes and trends in the geographic and industrial distribution of membership and of changes in the membership of individual unions and the various levels of union organization; and renewed study of the management, planning, and finances of American unions.

Specifically, estimates of membership for all unions in the United States between 1962 and 1979 can and should be derived from the LMSA financial reports, supplemented by IRS 990 reports for public-sector organizations. Studies describing changes in the distribution of membership over the past two decades, and examining the causes and consequences of such changes should be undertaken. Finally, the management of unions should be examined through case studies, surveys of union administrators, and, in the financial sphere, through analyses of the financial reports of the LMSA.

Such studies, as we've suggested, will provide some insight into the prospects for American unionism in the '80s. In light of the decline in the extent of organization over the past three decades, and the stagnation in total membership growth since the late '70s, it is tempting to speculate that this outlook is poor. It is, however, well to be reminded of Slichter's prediction in 1949 that, as a result of the growing strength of unions, America was being transformed into a laboristic, rather than a capitalistic, society. A mere four years later, the long decline in American unionization began.

References

Ashenfelter, O., and Pencavel, J. 1969. "American Trade Union Growth: 1960–1960s." *Quarterly Journal of Economics* 83 (August): 434–448.

Bain, G. 1980. *Industrial Relations Research Unit, The First Ten Years, 1970–1980.* Coventry: University of Warwick.

Bain, G., and Elsheikh, F. 1975. *Union Growth and the Business Cycle: An Econometric Analysis.* Oxford: Blackwell.

Barbush, J. 1979. "American Labor Unions in the 80s: Reading the Signs." *IRRA Proceedings 32nd Annual Meetings,* March.

Berkowitz, M. 1954. "The Economics of Trade Union Organization and Administration." *Industrial and Labor Relations Review* 7 (July): 575–592.

Block, R. N. 1979. "A Theory of the Supply of Union Representation and the Allocation of Union Resources," *mimeo*, December.

Dunlop, J. 1980. "The Changing Character of Labor Markets." In *The American Economy in Transition*, ed. Martin Feldstein. Chicago: University of Chicago Press.

Estey, M. 1981. *The Unions, Structure, Development, and Management,* third ed. New York: Harcourt, Brace and World.

Freeman, A. 1979. "Managing Labor Relations." Report 765. New York: The Conference Board.

Freeman, R. 1980. "The Evolution of the American Labor Market , 1945–80." In *The American Economy in Transition,* ed. Martin Feldstein.. Chicago: University of Chicago Press.

Freeman, R., and Medoff, J. L. 1979. "New Estimates of Private Sector Unionism in the United States." *Industrial and Labor Relations Review* 32, no. 2 (January): 143–174.

Ginsburg, W. L. 1970. "Union Growth, Government and Structure." *A Review of Industrial Relations Research, Vol. 1.* Industrial Relations Research Association, pp. 207–260.

Janus, C. J. 1978. "Union Mergers in the 1970s: A Look at the Reasons and Results." *Monthly Labor Review* (October): 13–23.

Johnson, G. E. 1975. "Economic Analysis of Trade Unionism." *American Economic Review Proceedings* 64 (May): 23–28.

Kochan, T. A. 1980a. *Labor Management Relations Priorities for the 1980s.* Washington: U.S. Department of Labor.

______. 1980b. "Industrial Relations Research: An Agenda for the 1980s." *Monthly Labor Review,* September, pp. 20–25.

Martin, D. L. 1980. *An Ownership Theory of the Trade Union.* Berkeley: University of California Press.

Moore, W. J., and Newman, R. J. 1975. "On the Prospects for American Trade Union Growth: A Cross-Section Analysis." *Review of Economics and Statistics,* November, pp. 435–445.

Raskin, A. H. 1980. "After Meany." *New Yorker,* August 25, pp. 36–76.

Salter, M. S. 1975. "Should Unions Practice Strategic Planning?" *Mimeo,* August.

Sheflin, N., and Troy, L. 1980. "Finances of American Unions in the Seventies." *Working Paper 80.2.* Rutgers University.

Stafford, F. P., and Duncan, G. J. 1980. "Do Union Members Receive Compensating Wage Differentials?" *American Economics Review* 70 (June): 355–371.

Thieblot, A. J., Jr. 1978. "An Analysis of Data on Union Membership." *Working Paper 38,* October, Center for the Study of American Business.

Troy, L. 1976. *Trade Union Membership 1897–1962.* New York: National Bureau of Economic Research.

______. 1969. "Trade Union Growth in a Changing Economy." *Monthly Labor Review,* September.

U.S. Department of Labor, Bureau of Labor Statistics. 1980. *Directory of National Unions and Employee Associations.* Bulletin. Washington: U.S. Government Printing Office.

U.S. Department of Labor. 1969. *Financial and Administrative Characteristics of Large Local Unions.* Washington: Labor Management Services Administration.

Contributing Authors

John T. Addison, Professor of Economics, University of South Carolina; Visiting Fellow, Australian National University.

John Burton, Research Fellow, Institute of Economic Affairs, London, U.K.

Peter Doeringer, Institute for Employment Policy, Boston University, Boston, Massachusetts.

Jean-Francois Hennart, Associate Professor of International Business, Florida International University, Miami, Florida.

George E. Johnson, Department of Economics, University of Michigan, Ann Arbor, Michigan

Bernard Lentz, Department of Economics, Ursinus College, Collegeville, Pennsylvania.

Donald L. Martin, Senior Consultant, Glassman-Oliver Economic Consultants, Inc., Washington, D.C.

George R. Neumann, Department of Economics, Northwestern University, Evanston, Illinois.

John Pencavel, Department of Economics, Stanford University; National Bureau of Economic Research.

Melvin W. Reder, Isidore Brown and Gladys J. Brown Professor of Urban and Labor Economics, The University of Chicago, Chicago, Illinois.

Jean-Jacques Rosa, Fondation Nationale d'Economie Politique, Paris, France.

Neil Sheflin, Bureau of Economic Research, Rutgers, The State University of New Jersey, New Brunswick, New Jersey.

Göran Skogh, Department of Economics, University of Lund, Lund, Sweden.

Leo Troy, Bureau of Economic Research, Rutgers, The State University of New Jersey, New Brunswick, New Jersey.

Gordon Tullock, Center for Public Choice, George Mason University, Fairfax, Virginia.